THE REIGN OF HENRY VIII

The Reign of Henry VIII

Politics, Policy and Piety

EDITED BY

DIARMAID MacCULLOCH

St. Martin's Press   New York

THE REIGN OF HENRY VIII

Introduction and Chapter 7 © Diarmaid MacCulloch; Chapter 1 © E. W.
Ives; Chapter 2 © J. A. Guy; Chapter 3 © N. Samman; Chapter 4 © R.
W. Hoyle; Chapter 5 © D. L. Potter; Chapter 6 © V. Murphy; Chapter 8
© S. House; Chapter 9 © R. Whiting 1995

St. Martin's Press, Scholarly and Reference Division,
175 Fifth Avenue, New York, N.Y. 10010

First published in the United States of America in 1995

Printed in Malaysia

ISBN 0–312–12892–4 (cloth)
ISBN 0–312–12900–9 (pbk.)

Library of Congress Cataloging-in-Publication Data
The reign of Henry VIII : politics, policy and piety / edited by
Diarmaid MacCulloch.
p.   cm.
Includes bibliographical references (p.   ) and index.
ISBN 0–312–12892–4. – ISBN 0–312–12900–9 (pbk.)
1. Great Britain—Politics and government—1509–1547.   2. Great
Britain—Church history—16th century.   I. MacCulloch, Diarmaid.
DA332.R45   1996
942.05'2—dc20   95–19514
                                                           CIP

Contents

CONTENTS

Preface

Collaborative enterprises are always fraught with possibilities for shipwreck, and I am thankful that the help of a large number of people has ensured that this volume did not founder under the gaze of its sponsor as did the *Mary Rose* in 1545. All the contributors deserve thanks for their individual components and for their suggestions made to me for improvements to the whole volume, and they will have their own debts of gratitude to support systems of which I am only partly aware. For myself, I am particularly grateful to the late Professor Sir Geoffrey Elton for his helpful and constructive comments on my own chapter, and to Steven Gunn for his advice which helped to relaunch in its present form his earlier proposal for a similar collection. Equally, I have to thank staff at Macmillan for support and encouragement: Pauline Underwood, latterly Simon Winder, and especially Vanessa Graham, who at a crucial stage of the volume's planning, got the contributors in a good mood by organising an excellent lunch. A summer school group at University College London in 1994 helped me organise my thoughts on the reign of Henry VIII more than they knew. I hope that for them and for many other students, these essays will prove illuminating and enjoyable.

Totterdown, Bristol   DIARMAID MACCULLOCH

Introduction

DIARMAID MacCULLOCH

Historians, particularly early modernists, have developed a weakness for alliterative book titles. However, the subtitle of this collection of essays, 'Politics, policy and piety', does have a practical purpose: it expresses the structure of the collection. The first three essayists deal with the way politics worked in the England of Henry VIII, the second three discuss the way in which politics was applied in the making of policy, and the third trio deals with one vital aspect of Henrician policy, the transformation in the kingdom's practice of the Christian religion. Naturally, the distinction of topics is not rigid; throughout the book these themes will appear in different guises, and the essayists will discuss the same events and phenomena from different points of view.

The aim is to guide the reader from the king's private apartments, the heart of politics and policy, through the realm of England and out to the corners of the kingdom, seeking to gauge the power of the most self-consciously powerful of English monarchs over the minds and souls of his subjects. On the way we meet the king's ministers as they sought to do their master's will, we survey their attempts to improve the institutions of government in order to do so, and we see the court on the move, taking the king to meet his subjects. We look at the detail of the king's most far-reaching intervention in policy, his tangled attempt to divorce his first wife; we see him trying to assert his place among wealthier and better-armed European monarchs, and we meet evangelical reformers trying to reconcile their own agenda of destruction and rebuilding with the frequently mysterious religious agenda of the king himself.

Straight away one should point out that this collection concerns itself with the politics and religion of only one of Henry's realms, England. It touches on the full integration of Wales into the English kingdom, but it says nothing about Henry's other dominion in Ireland. Henry transformed the future of England by

1

his break with Rome, but he made an equally important change of direction in Ireland. This took place in the decade after 1534, when a relationship between the English monarchy and the Fitzgerald dynasty which had been the dominant feature of Anglo-Irish politics for more than half a century broke down irretrievably. Formally, the change was signified when in 1541–2, Henry replaced the complex web of relationships and traditions represented by his title of Lord of Ireland with the proclamation of a kingdom: the troubles of twentieth-century Ireland are directly related to this decision. The reign of Henry VIII represents a turning-point in Irish history too important to be dismissed in an essay appended to a collection on England, and we are thankful not to double the size of this volume by an adequate treatment of the subject.

We begin at the English court: a great machine for exploiting the personality of the monarch to the best advantage. The civil wars of the fifteenth century had been about personality and personal ambitions rather than ideological issues. Some of the more reflective participants in those troubles, such as Sir John Fortescue, may have talked about and tried to analyse the principles on which England was governed, but there was really little disagreement about these principles. Those who start their historical studies in the viciously polarised ideological atmosphere of the sixteenth-century Reformation are likely to find it difficult to get oriented in fifteenth-century English politics, where genealogy and descent are the main issues, and ambition is rarely cloaked by any abstract principle more complex than the good governance of the realm. Like its predecessors through a century of troubled government, the Tudor dynasty hacked its way to power without any more elevated public political programme than securing good governance. However, when safely on the throne, Henry VII claimed the most elevated principle of all: the unique and personal favour of Almighty God, as demonstrated by his victory in battle. Whether or not that complex and private man sincerely believed this, there can be no doubt that it became the guiding principle for his son.

The personal quality of politics remains central to understanding the reign of Henry VIII: something which is particularly stressed in the analyses by Ives, Guy and Samman. Notoriously, and to the delight of recent generations of students, it mattered a great deal in the political world who held the king's chamber-pot, the close-stool, when he got up in the morning. It mattered to find out where the king was, and how to get in touch with him direct; and considering that the court was a fearsomely complex political machine based on an intricately structured world of social difference, it was remarkable that even quite humble people might bring their requests to the king face to face. Elsewhere I have told the story of a gaggle of ordinary villagers from a remote corner of Suffolk who despite all their ineptitude in bribing and wheedling their way through the world of the royal court, eventually found themselves face to face with the king in his Greenwich tiltyard to tell him of their grievance.[1] If they could do it, so could others.

Eric Ives shows how this court political world operated, and discusses the two styles of government by which Henry VIII sought to keep his hands on power while avoiding the tedious side of government. For some periods of his reign, Henry ruled through a group of advisers, many of whom were leading aristocrats and therefore felt themselves born to advise their king. At two other periods, he singled out in succession two individuals, Thomas Wolsey and Thomas Cromwell, whose only justification for exercising power was that the king himself had recognised their outstanding talents. These great ministers were constantly vulnerable to the resentment of those who felt excluded by their power, and when Henry's confidence in them faltered, their enemies were only too ready to take advantage of his suspension of belief, and provide the means to strike them down for ever. Ives discusses how we should understand the operation of faction at court. Too often, beginners in the study of Tudor politics are inclined to treat factions as if they had the definition of a football team emerging on to the touch-line, while equally, critics of the concept of faction have caricatured it in an attempt to ridicule it out of use. Later in the volume, David Potter emphasises just how universal the factional mechanism was in the royal courts of early modern Europe, but he also takes a sceptical view about the influence of English court faction on the conduct of royal foreign policy. There is one notable exception to this, as Potter allows: Henry's approaches to the German Lutheran princes of the Schmalkaldic League during the 1530s were specifically associated with the evangelical grouping around Thomas Cromwell and Thomas Cranmer, and opposition to this policy was the concern of religious conservatives such as bishops Stephen Gardiner and Cuthbert Tunstall.[2] In Henrician domestic politics, we would be foolish if we did not take account of faction, because it was an

essentially personal mechanism in a world where personality was
of especial significance.

John Guy concentrates on the work of the two great ministers,
putting them into context in two different ways. First, he com-
pares their achievement and the changes which they brought
about with developments in France, a comparison which Henry
VIII himself was always making; the king was very jealous of his all-
too-similar contemporary, King Francis I. Second, Guy points out
the political perils which Wolsey and Cromwell both faced, and
which severely limited their freedom of action. Wolsey exercised
more untrammelled power than Cromwell ever did, until his first
big mistake in not securing Henry yet more money from the hard-
pressed taxpayers by the ill-fated Amicable Grant of 1525: this was
the first time that Wolsey had failed to deliver the goods for the
king, and although in the short term he recovered most of his
power, his next failure from 1527 to break the deadlock which
Henry had created by rejecting Catherine of Aragon, made his
position impossible. Cromwell, an appalled spectator of the way in
which his master the Cardinal had eventually fallen from power,
was only too aware that his own good fortune in the 1530s could
end in the same way. Cromwell's own sincere aims of promoting
religious change were constantly curtailed by this consideration,
even after his remarkable reconstruction of Wolsey's power in the
church as vicegerent after 1536, and his other attempts at recon-
structing government suffered in the same way. This means that
we must reassess his relationship to that vexed question, the creation of a new instrument of government known as the privy
council. Later, Richard Hoyle will discuss how successful
Cromwell was in his aim of transforming the financial position of
the English monarchy.

Guy also considers one of the undoubted success stories of early
Tudor government in England: the steady tying-in of the further-
flung parts of the realm to Westminster government. The Tudor
monarchy extended patterns of local government which had previously operated mainly in the heartland of royal authority in the
south-east lowlands, and in particular Wolsey and Cromwell continued to exploit the possibilities of creating a royal affinity: a
typical example of the Tudor penchant for putting medieval institutions to new uses. The problem of how to make the best contacts between centre and locality also lies behind Neil Samman's
examination of the use which Henry made of royal progresses in
the first half of his reign, which included the years of Wolsey's

ascendancy. There has been much study of Elizabeth's progresses, but this is comparatively new territory for study.

As Eric Ives points out, Henry owned more royal houses than any English monarch before or since; however, not only did it take him more than a decade to provide himself with a habitable palace in London or Westminster, but on progress he still needed hospitality from others when he moved far from his home base in the south-east. Samman shows how his choice of hosts was often a carefully calculated sign of political favour. Moreover, the conduct of progresses reveals how Wolsey maintained his political position by his own care in keeping close to the king during his summer itineraries. Those who are familiar with Henry's daughter Elizabeth's brilliant exploitation of the mechanism of progress may be surprised by the limits of Henry's exploration of his realm: he was very timid about venturing outside the home counties. If he had not postponed visiting the north of England until 1541 he might have avoided the most serious rebellions of his reign in 1536. It is arguable that one of the reasons that the conservative west of England did not rise in rebellion in 1536, unlike the conservative north, was that Henry had stirred himself to a rare burst of energy in visiting the west on extended progress in summer 1535.

Richard Hoyle concentrates on the aspect of policy which was one of Henry's chief concerns: the conduct of war, and the way in which it proved the ruin of efforts by Henry's great ministers to revolutionise the finance of English government. The traditional theory of government finance was that it was based on a division between ordinary revenues (largely royal estates and the income from customs) and extraordinary revenues (largely taxation for war); when there was no war, ordinary revenues should suffice. Both Wolsey and Cromwell did their best to put the extraordinary revenues on a new footing, as John Guy outlines in chapter 2: Wolsey by inventing the new flexibly assessed tax, the subsidy, and Cromwell by what Guy styles his 'landmark' attempt from 1534 to make peace as much as war a justification for asking parliament for money. However, even Wolsey's remarkable achievements in levying the subsidy were not enough: witness his desperate and unsuccessful effort to extend the boundaries of government finance with the 1525 Amicable Grant. The 1534 precedent was never exploited to the full; later Tudor governments, lacking Henry VIII's self-confidence, presumably recognised their subjects' lack of enthusiasm for the theory. Richard Hoyle challenges

Guy's viewpoint on the 1534 precedent in chapter 4, and he promises a further exploration of this issue at length in another setting.[3]

If Cromwell's achievement in changing the basis of parliamentary taxation (the extraordinary revenue of the crown) may seem dubious, there is an even greater air of failure about his effort to give a new basis to the other division of crown income, the ordinary revenues. In the short term this was a spectacular success, at the expense largely of the church, so that Hoyle can speculate that in his middle years, Henry had exceeded his father's achievement of comfortable solvency. Yet from 1538 to the end of the reign, with huge expenditure on both defensive and offensive military preparations, the Cromwellian achievement was squandered for good. The sad truth is that no minister of Henry VIII ever invented a way of providing him with enough money for his inflated overseas ambitions; England could not properly sustain continued war without appalling financial strain. Hoyle's figures reveal the disparity between income and expenditure for the decade of warfare between 1542 and 1551; even more alarmingly, they show how government in these years used capital as income, and thus mortgaged the future with a recklessness worthy of Ronald Reagan in the 1980s.

After Cromwell's inspired extension of crown revenues in combination with religious reform, his successors as royal ministers found entirely different pseudo-solutions to royal debt: permanently dispersing the bulk of the crown estate, they also debased one of the most respected coinages in Europe, bringing commercial disruption and misery to the people of England. They would single-handedly have engineered a mid-Tudor crisis even if fate had not stepped in with epidemics and wretched harvests in the Edwardian and Marian years. Since Henry VIII was fond of taking credit for his successes, posterity should equally award him the responsibility for this crime against his people. Nor did his successors, either Tudor or Stuart, find a solution to the hand-to-mouth inadequacy of government finance until the drastic answers forged in two decades of civil wars in the mid-seventeenth century.

David Potter's wide-ranging survey of England's foreign relations puts Henry's wars into the European context of a country which, in the sixteenth as in the late twentieth century, boxed above its weight, or at least tried to. England was a second-rank player in Europe, yet Henry's conception of his personal monarchy compelled him to strut the stage as an equal with the Holy

Roman Emperor and the king of France, while at the same time he constantly worried about what would happen if the two greater powers combined against him. Potter questions whether one should dignify Henry's erratic diplomacy by calling it foreign policy: there is little sense of grand strategy discernible. Even traditional royal claims on foreign kingdoms of Scotland and France which might have been thought to give rise to such strategies were rarely what they seemed.

Historians have made much of the Burgundian alliance in the calculations of England abroad in the fifteenth and sixteenth centuries: that long-standing alignment between England and whoever ruled its main trading partner, the Low Countries – in the sixteenth century, this meant the Habsburgs. Yet Potter suggests that the most constant factor in Henry's calculations was the financial relationship with France created by French debts and agreements to pay England pensions; this was almost as well established as the Burgundian link, taking its origins in the reign of Edward IV. One reason for the confusing hesitations in Henry's relations with France, apparent particularly in the 1520s and the early 1540s, was this question of the money owed by the French. How best could Henry get his due? Ally with France and get the money the easy way? Or invade, and squeeze the money out of the French, for instance by seizing French fortresses such as Boulogne? In view of the importance of the French pension as a factor in diplomacy, it is ironic that one of the main causes of the disastrous state of royal finances at the end of Henry's reign was the accumulated effect of his wars with France.

Virginia Murphy's case-study of royal policy deals with the conduct of Henry's first quest for marriage annulment: a policy which more than any other of his reign was shaped by the king himself, and which therefore sheds invaluable light on the enigma at the heart of this apparent extrovert. The most striking feature of the fearsomely technical case which the king built for himself is the simplicity of the idea at its centre: the king seems to have felt passionately that God was angry with him, and that anyone who suggested that God was not angry with him was the enemy both of God and of himself. Hence he turned viciously on one of the most respected figures of his childhood, bishop John Fisher, and on one of his closest friends, Thomas More, when they dared to contradict him. Equally, he came to trust and promote those who helped him and God by constructing his case, notably the man whom he made archbishop of Canterbury and whom he never betrayed, Thomas Cranmer. We underestimate Henry if we regard his 'great matter' as an irrational lust for a new sexual partner. He saw it as his great confrontation with his maker, as fundamental a conflict as drove Martin Luther to his refuge in the consciousness of being saved by faith through grace alone.

The result of the insoluble confrontation with the pope created by Henry's unique relationship with God was a break with Rome which made the king by accident into the founder of the Church of England. Henry's peculiarly personal Reformation caused the seventeenth-century Anglican historian the Rev. John Strype a good deal of heart-searching as he wrote the history of his chief hero Cranmer:

> We find, indeed, many popish errors here mixed with evangeli-cal truths, which must either be attributed to the defectiveness of our prelate's knowledge as yet in true religion, or being the principles and opinions of the king, or both. Let not any be offended herewith, but let him rather take notice what a great deal of Gospel doctrine here came to light; and not only so, but was owned and propounded by authority to be believed and practised. The sun of truth was now but rising, and breaking through the thick mists of that idolatry, superstition, and igno-rance, that had so long prevailed in this nation, and the rest of the world, and was not yet advanced to its meridian brightness.[4]

Strype was an unimaginative man, not often roused to heights of eloquence in the course of his monumental cut-and-paste histor-ies of the English Reformation; however, his prose briefly sparked into life when he contemplated the painful theological ambigui-ties in Henry VIII's church experienced and tolerated by Cranmer. He was not alone in feeling worry about Henry VIII. At least Cranmer later proved his evangelical credentials (if only at the fifty-ninth minute of the eleventh hour), but King Henry was a difficult figure for the victors of the English Reformation to cele-brate. Rosemary O'Day has pointed out that there was no posthu-mous Protestant cult of King Henry as a kingly hero of Old Testament stature, in contrast to the long-lived devotion to his daughter Elizabeth, the Deborah of England.[5]

My own chapter explores what we can say of Henry's religion, and of how it interacted with the religious agendas of prominent lay politicians and churchmen. Readers may note that for reasons which I explain in the essay, I have chosen to label the reformers of the reign of Henry VIII as 'evangelicals' rather than use the

more usual description 'Protestant', although I have not presumed to impose this discipline on my fellow-essayists. Seymour
House takes another perspective on the question of religious politics, to investigate the way in which they were reflected in drama
and literature, which both shaped and were shaped by religious
changes. Here Thomas Cromwell emerges as innovator, with his
creative perception of how a government might launch out into
opinion-forming to secure consent and approval for a religious
revolution. The Tudors, like many late medieval monarchs, were
already fully alive to the possibilities of using drama and ceremonial to their own advantage, but Cromwell's achievements were to
extend the range of propaganda to the printed word, and also to
use drama as a weapon on a wider public stage away from court as
well as in direct association with it.

Both in House's essay and in Robert Whiting's, the emphasis is
on the dynamism of the Henrician religious revolution, against
much recent 'revisionist' emphasis on slowness and hesitancy in
religious change. The impact of Cromwellian and Henrician
policy was immediate, even if much of that impact was in the first
instance destructive: creating hatred of the past, and hatred of the
bishop of Rome who had betrayed England's king by his resistance to the royal divorce, and thus revealed the treachery of traditional authority in the church. Yet House also hints at the
positive excitement among ordinary people at the discovery of
new faith, even after the death of the vicegerent, its chief patron;
in Henry's last years a ferment of new popular drama continued
alongside the traditional theatre created by the old church; this
hammered home the message of a religion which offered a direct
encounter with God's word in the Bible, despite the temporary
embarrassment of Henry's effort to keep the Bible out of the
hands of ordinary folk.

Robert Whiting provides a framework of statistics which help us
to chart the waning of old institutions. Particularly important are
his indices of decay in aspects of traditional religion which were
perfectly legal, like the extension and beautifying of churches or
the construction of roodlofts; yet what also emerges from his work
is the extreme regional variation in the impact of positive religious
change, as opposed to more-or-less sullen compliance with what
the government wanted. The south-east of England could be
described either as setting the pace or keeping out of step with
the rest of the realm; however, it was the area which Henry himself
knew best, and which knew him best. Henrician government was

well aware of regional differences, and pursued religious change with reference to them: for instance, when in the 1540s the secular colleges of clergy began to be closed in the second phase of dissolutions, virtually none were destroyed in the north of England before Henry's death, a clear acknowledgement that this had proved itself a difficult area in the Pilgrimage of Grace.[6]

The modern flowering of local historical studies has taught us much about Tudor England's religion, but there is still much to do: the more we know, the more complex the picture will become. It goes without saying that individuals will always stand out against general trends, but we must also be sensitive to the fact that adjacent geographical areas might behave in different ways. For instance, both here and in his earlier work, Whiting has shown how conservative south-west England was in the early Reformation, yet one notes in his discussion of the decline of provision for intercessory prayers in wills (p. 215 below) that the trend away from intercessory bequests was particularly precocious in Somerset. A sermon in stone is to be found amid Somerset's wealth of medieval churches, at Montacute; in the chancel of the parish church there, one can still see the emptied image-niches and the provision of carved English scriptural texts, an evangelical programme which was defiantly undertaken in a year of supposed religious reaction, 1543. Such local variations cry out for explanations which lie beyond the capacity of these essays.

The format of the *Problems in Focus* series means that the reader will miss one essential dimension of Henrician politics: its visual impact. All the Tudors had a sensitivity to the visual image: as Seymour House reminds us, one of their most talented servants, Richard Morison, pointed out to Thomas Cromwell that the common people used their eyes before their ears.[7] Henry VIII was exceptionally to find a painter of genius, Hans Holbein the younger, to create a lasting image for himself; we are equally lucky that Holbein extended his work to portray very many of the people whom Henry knew most intimately. Eric Ives ends his essay by drawing our attention to the great mural in the Whitehall privy chamber which was the definitive version of the Holbein image of Henry, and which despite its destruction by fire in 1698, substantially survives in the giant cartoon which the artist made for it. A meditation on the reign and power of Henry VIII would do worse than to begin with this extraordinary survival in the National Portrait Gallery. To look on that picture for any length of time is to realise that Holbein's portrayal of Henry VIII is anatomically impossible; its arms and legs could not connect with its trunk. Even the bloated carcase which Henry became in his last years was not thus distorted out of the proportions of the human frame. Yet this portrayal was high artifice and not incompetence on the part of one of Europe's greatest artists; awe and fear are the first emotions which the picture aims to inspire at the sight of that grimly bulky figure. Certainly that was the effect which the mural had on spectators while it still existed.

The Holbein cartoon may serve as a metaphor for the king and for the 45 years of his reign. One begins with the impact of his power, his ego, his cruelty, his charm: then as the detail fits into place, the picture shifts, and the careful artifice, the frequent shams and bluster, even sadness and loneliness, become apparent. The man at the centre is diminished, absurd. Yet around him, the busy machine of the Tudor commonwealth fills the canvas. And one cannot deny that it is King Henry who has commissioned the craftsmen whose ingenuity has put it together, and King Henry who has made the decision to set it in motion.

1. Henry VIII: the Political Perspective

ERIC IVES

Fifteen years after the death of Henry VIII, Sir Thomas Smith spelled out the theory of the English constitution: 'The prince is the life, the head and the authority of all things that be done in the realm of England'.[1] Thomas Starkey had said much the same 30 years earlier and the formulation would remain a commonplace for many years.[2] Smith, of course, did not mean that the prince exercised all power in person. He distributed 'his authority and power to the rest of the members for the government of his realm, and the common wealth of the politic body of England'.[3] A Tudor monarch, the lawyers said, had two bodies – 'a body natural' and 'a body politic' that 'cannot be seen or handled, consisting of Policy and Government, and constituted for the Direction of the People and the Management of the public-weal'.[4]

However, like much constitutional theory, the monarch as a Siamese twin did not entirely accord with reality. The 'politic' and the 'natural' coincided in one particular 'body' which could most certainly be seen and handled. There was little to encourage Tudor rulers to differentiate the two and definitely not Henry VIII, a powerful, complex and contradictory personality who never doubted for a moment that *l'état c'est moi*.

Government had, of course, long since expanded beyond the possibility of detailed management by any one individual. Throughout his reign Henry had an institutional council to advise him and to act in an executive capacity. It is also true that he depended heavily on individual ministers and for nearly two-thirds of his 38 years on a principal minister. Yet the sovereign was no figurehead and it would be quite wrong to underestimate his direct responsibility – and not only for war and diplomacy which contemporaries saw as the special concern of a king.

Personal monarchy in Henrician England meant direct involvement in government. For example, Thomas Cromwell's list of nearly fifty 'special remembrances to be done with the King's Highness' at a meeting probably on or about 1 November 1533 included diplomatic items as various as policy toward the duke of Bavaria and the payment of ambassadorial allowances, consideration of an offer by the executors of Lord Dacre of a settlement to forestall a crown prosecution, the issue of what to do about fraudulent cloth manufacture in the north, signing various grants (including Cromwell's own expenses) and items concerning the Nun of Kent and other opponents of Henry's divorce.[5] Discussion was in detail and at an executive level, even to deciding on how much money and how many horses should be provided for Richard Pate for his embassy to Charles V.[6]

Another direct responsibility of the monarch was making appointments. The importance of choosing counsellors and ministers is obvious but there was far more to it than filling this handful of posts. Running the royal estate called for an army of officers nationwide – stewards, farmers, bailiffs, receivers, keepers, constables, parkers. Meeting the need for justice required justices and sheriffs in the localities, and court officials, judges and legal counsel for the royal courts at Westminster and elsewhere. Central government had to be staffed; the largest department, the royal household, had a complement of 1500.[7] Some posts were in the gift of particular officials (especially in the common-law courts) and short leases of crown land could be granted without bothering the king, but the bulk of appointments required his personal approval, increasingly, indeed, his actual signature to a 'bill' which instructed chancery to issue the required documents. In 1444 the use of such 'signed bills' had been prohibited because they allowed a feeble Henry VI to sign away crown assets to the importunate.[8] Thereafter first applicants were supposed to be checked and then the formal instructions issued through the king's secretary (and sealed with the royal signet) before passing via the privy-seal office to the great seal, monitored throughout by a chancery master. The restriction had, however, been increasingly ignored by Edward IV and Henry VII and so too by Henry VIII. By the mid-1530s nearly 50 per cent of royal grants were being signed in person.[9] Nor was this merely an administrative chore. Given the limited political resource at the disposal of the Tudor kings, the power to reward was a major political asset and had to be exploited with considerable care. Without it, satisfying one client could easily mean leaving several more with grievances.

A chance survival of evidence allows us to follow the process in the 1520s in some detail.[10] An applicant's first step was to secure a promise of the desired post from the king or someone whose promise the king might be expected to honour such as the queen, Princess Mary or Cardinal Wolsey. This promise was no more than provisional – an indication that appointment was a possibility – and had to be followed by negotiation over terms. The outcome was an agreed text for the grant which was turned into a 'bill' by prefixing it with a petition:

> To the king our sovereign lord. Please it your Highness of your abundant grace to grant your gracious letters patent under your great seal of this realm of England in due form to be made after the tenor ensuing.[11]

This was presented to the king and if he signed – and examples of 'unsigned' bills show things could go wrong even at this late stage – then the grant would be processed by the chancery. Thus the king had to pass a grant twice, once verbally (by himself or a proxy) and a second time by signing in person.

To the weight of paper produced by this competition for grants we must add a miscellany of other documents which were put to the king in person. All in all, by the end of the reign, his signature was being required three or four times a day. Some non-patronage items came up regularly such as the annual appointment of sheriffs each November, but the bulk were casual to a degree. For example, the items other than grants which Henry VIII signed in April 1534 were seven pardons – three for murder, one for housebreaking, two for theft and robbery and one to a fence – passports for the outgoing and incoming French ambassadors, three documents concerned with filling the vacancy at Ely (a few months later Henry would face another, licensing the new bishop to keep a crossbow), a *congé d'élire* for the bishopric of Bangor, a licence to import wine, an exemption from a statute as compensation for flood damage, and an order to restore temporalities to a newly appointed abbot. Finally, Henry signed a warrant to cover the treasurer of the chamber for all payments to date and to give an entry in his books the force of an interim discharge until the king countersigned – which points to another major area where Henry's personal involvement was looked for.[12]

,iven the importance of the personal role of Henry VIII in gov-
_ ,ıment, how did he operate? As we shall see, this varied over
time according to circumstances, to movement within the personnel of his servants and ministers (natural and violent) and not
least to shifts in the king's personality and in his priorities. Some
determinants, however, were constant, in particular the constraint
of place. With the king the focus of Tudor government and politics, it follows that government and politics focused on where the
king was, in other words the royal household. It was the failure to
realise this which led historians of the earlier part of this century
to leave court affairs to Hollywood and the historical novel. But
however important the development of parliament and the
administration in London, Westminster and elsewhere and
however significant the contribution of ministers, England was, in
the ultimate, governed from the court.

Over the last 30 years research has revolutionised understanding of what this implies.[13] Characteristically the court of a
medieval English king was divided into a supply department nom-
inally directed by the lord steward ('the household below stairs'),
and a consumption department or 'chamber' ('the household
above stairs'), charged with looking after the king and his
entourage and ruled by the lord chamberlain. From the later
fifteenth century, however, the household above stairs was transformed as English kings learned from continental example the
value of 'distance' in public life, in other words that the impact
produced by the public appearances of any prominent individual
varies according to their infrequency and the less accessible an
individual is, the more valued access becomes.

The first result was a revolution in the architectural plan of
English palaces. The chamber and its associated apartments
became split between state rooms and private lodgings, or as the
sixteenth century knew them, between the 'watching (guard)
chamber' and the 'presence chamber' with their adjuncts on the
one side, and on the other the 'privy chamber' with its associated
suite of 'privy lodgings'. The king's appearances in the outer
chambers were carefully calculated, and admission to the privy
chamber was restricted to those employed in it or personally sanctioned by the king. Not that conscious withdrawing ended even
there. By the end of Henry's reign an area had been identified or
added within the suite as the 'secret lodgings' where only the
king's chief body servant, the groom of the (close) stool, had the
right of access. This was the embryo of the 'Bedchamber' which

documents which had been stamped. Henry was even happy to have his own will authenticated in this way.

In discussing privy chamber development an impression sometimes given is that the only concern was greater 'distance'. There was, however, a positive dimension. The creation of a privy chamber elite immediately and intimately associated with the king created servants who were uniquely his own and uniquely obedient. Thus, in 1530, when it was decided to send the pope a menacing appeal to grant the annulment Henry wanted, it was William Brereton who led the team which obtained the signatures of the country's peers and other notables.[22] Privy chamber staff were especially important where total confidentiality was required. When Henry had yielded to pressure and dismissed Wolsey, he kept his links with the cardinal alive by sending secret messages (and cash) by gentlemen of the privy chamber.[23] A privy chamber officer embodied the authority of the king. When, a year after Wolsey's loss of office, the earl of Northumberland arrived to arrest him for high treason, the cardinal challenged the earl's commission but yielded at once when Walter Walsh of the privy chamber appeared, saying, 'you are a sufficient commission yourself in as much as ye be one of the king's privy chamber, for the worst person there is a sufficient warrant to arrest the greatest peer of this realm by the king's only commandment, without any commission'.[24] Nor was this a status recognised only within England. For Henry VIII to send one of his privy chamber staff abroad as his ambassador was a gesture of special friendship, and carried the added advantage that the envoy could expect to receive reciprocal status in the court to which he was attached. The privy chamber became, in consequence, a reservoir of enormous diplomatic experience. For example, eight of the twelve noblemen and gentlemen of the privy chamber listed in 1532/3 had served abroad, several more than once.[25] Another way privy chamber status was exploited was in military command. All the admirals and vice-admirals of England for the latter part of the reign were from the privy chamber bar one, and he was already in the more senior post of treasurer of the royal household.[26]

The most influential of the privy chamber staff was the senior chief gentleman who held the post of groom of the stool, followed by the second chief gentleman who stood in as groom in his absence. As literally the royal sanitary attendant, the groom stood closer to the king than any man alive; the regulations for what was a 24 hour responsibility state:

It is the king's pleasure that Mr Norris shall be in the room of
Sir William Compton, not only giving his attendance as groom
of the stool but also in his bedchamber and other privy places
as shall stand with his pleasure. And the king's express
command is that none other of the said six gentlemen [of the
privy chamber] presume to enter or follow his Grace into the
said bedchamber, or any other secret place, unless he shall be
called and admitted thereunto by his said grace.[27]

This closeness alone made it likely that the groom would become
the king's confidant, but the effect was accentuated because the
intimacy was supportable only if the king found the groom personally sympathetic – and vice versa. His first two grooms, William
Compton and Henry Norris, were or became personal friends.
Not that friendship was always an asset. Henry evidently enjoyed
the company of his occasionally impudent gentleman of the privy
chamber, Sir Francis Bryan, but when Bryan became the groom's
alternate, the king threw him out in less than three years.[28] The
groom of the stool was, of course, the obvious person to obtain the
royal signature to documents. He was also the first man the king
turned to when he wanted something done, especially if
confidential – it was Norris whom Henry sent to the fallen Wolsey.
The groom also had considerable influence over who was admitted to see the king. And there were other duties. He kept the privy
purse which as well as meeting the not-insignificant sums Henry
spent in person, could be expanded to allow him to direct a sizeable fraction of government expenditure in person, should he so
wish.[29] The groom was also a key figure in the somewhat mysterious business of the king's coffers – secret treasuries at a number of
palaces where Henry kept large reserves of ready cash.[30]

Within the court, therefore, Henry VIII's rule was located in the
privy chamber, privy lodgings and secret lodgings, with all that this
implied. What of the court itself? When he died Henry possessed
over 50 houses, more than any monarch before or since.[31] They
fell into two groups. The first consisted of large properties which
were capable of taking the full court for weeks at a time. The list
changed over the years – most importantly with the advent of
Hampton Court c. 1525 and the development from 1529 of York
Place as the principal royal residence – but at the end of the
reign the standing houses in use comprised Whitehall, Greenwich,
Hampton Court and Woodstock.[32] Between these properties
the royal household moved from roughly October/November to

June, as considerations of sanitation and supplies indicated and the royal wish dictated. Not that mobility was unbroken. Over the winter of 1526–7 Henry was at Greenwich for five months.[33]

The properties in the second group were the smaller 'houses of abode'. These could accommodate the king and a reduced entourage and were almost all associated with Henry's favourite sport – hunting.[34] Some of them were linked with one of the standing houses, allowing the court to remain put but the king to exploit a wider area for sport. The remainder were further afield and came into their own in the summer and autumn when the king went on progress. Before the court settled for its long stay at Greenwich in October 1526, it had been on the move for at least sixteen weeks, and had visited 30 locations and more, over ten counties. Nor was that all there was to royal mobility. During a progress the smaller court, 'the riding household', could subdivide again for the king to go off for the day or even several days with a handful of attendants.[35]

The political implications of this mobility paralleled the implications of the changes in the structure of the household. It probably did not matter that day-on-day contact with government departments was impossible except when the king was at Whitehall, even though his absences could be lengthy. In 1543 Henry was away from Westminster for the whole of the time between 3 June and the last days of December, apart from one week. It is unlikely, either, that communications presented much of a problem, at least during most of the year. All of the standing houses were easily reached from the capital – most lay in the Thames Valley and were on or accessible from the river, and none was more than a day's ride on horseback.[36] What was important, however, was the need for some special provision to allow a peripatetic king to make his vital input into government, a requirement which was infinitely more difficult to meet when progress time arrived and the retreat to more distant houses. During the reign a number of different solutions were tried, but what could never be avoided were the burden of extra correspondence and the difficult and potentially highly dangerous schizoid existence imposed on the royal council and on individual ministers. Indeed, we can say that this physical separation between the proponents and executants of policy and the king who adjudicated on both created an enduring tension in Tudor rule.

This tension was exacerbated by Henry VIII's working habits. Had the new sovereign in 1509 been a man like his father, these

intrinsic difficulties would have been once more contained by a
man who was fascinated with business and qualified and ready to
act as chief executive of the English state. Henry VII had been the
lynch-pin of a government in which at choice he could take personal charge of any issue (using whatever assistants he chose),
remit both individual items and categories of business to individual councillors and deploy his council in any format and number
and with any terms of reference he chose and at any location –
some to attend him at court and others to spend term time at
Westminster. Henry VIII, by contrast, was not ready to act in this
role. This was not because of lack of ability though he was probably less long-headed than his father, but because he would not
put in the hours. Except when his personal interest was engaged
he could exhibit an alarmingly low threshold of boredom. It did
not follow, however, that he was willing to hand over to others
total responsibility for matters he found tedious, and not only
because, as we have seen, Tudor government made that impossib-
ible. Henry's retention of the right to intervene as and when he
chose was essential to his understanding of monarchy. If that presented problems, these were for others to solve – staff who strug-
gled to get decisions in the course of the morning mass, which
Henry thought an appropriate time to allocate to the regular discharge of business, or who waited for him to return from a long
day's hunting in the hope of securing his attention after supper to
letters which had arrived during the day.[37] That Henry was well
aware that the system waited on him and was happy to let it wait is
obvious from the different priority he gave to parliament. He was
in London or Westminster for 19 of the 27 sessions held in his
reign and for part of six more, and in no case further away than
Richmond or Greenwich. Quite clearly he felt his presence vital
during sittings, but not otherwise. Frequently, indeed, he left
Westminster on the very day of the dissolution.

For councillors and advisers trying to serve a king who would
neither set the agenda firmly nor allow others to do so consistently, life was never dull and potentially was dangerous. A story
from 1546 is instructive.[38] The English were occupying Boulogne
under the treaty which had just ended war with France, only to
find the French continuing to raise the fort of Chatillon opposite
the town. The council advised that counter-action would void the
treaty and Sir Thomas Palmer was sent to Lord Grey of Wilton,
the English commander, with a letter signed by Henry prohibit-
ing hostile moves. By the same messenger, however, Henry sent

verbal instructions for Grey to act and when Grey did so the king
greeted the news with enormous self-congratulation at his own
cleverness in undermining his own written orders. What would
have happened to Palmer had the attack failed is not hard to
imagine.

This, however, was no way to run government, day in, day out.
How could a king at often a physical and frequently at a mental
distance be kept informed on current issues? How he could initiate when separated from the organs of government? How could
he be served by sufficient – and sufficiently senior – councillors
when the council was required during term time to sit at
Westminster to discharge its public and general administrative
functions? Or again, how could individual councillors, lacking the
managerial direction of a Henry VII, be freely available for royal
deployment and at the same time carry out regular administrative
duties? During the reign answers to these questions fluctuated
between two options. The first was that the royal council should
take responsibility, the second that a minister should take on the
role of chief executive, leaving the king to be overall director.
Not, of course, that the decision was ever crudely polarised as 'the
council' or 'a minister'. At no time was the council insignificant,
neither was it a static institution; Henry's two famous 'chief executives', Wolsey and Cromwell, were neither of them 'prime ministers' nor was the particular position and relationships of the one
identical with those of the other. Nevertheless, from the objectiv-
ity of several centuries we can perceive a continuing and productive dialogue between the two alternatives, productive both in the
sense that it created political issues and in that these issues provided the impetus for significant governmental change. Participants
at the time were less dispassionate.

The opening of the reign saw the conciliar option in place –
not surprisingly since the new king was not yet eighteen. He 'was
young and lusty, disposed all to mirth and pleasure and to follow
his desire and appetite, nothing minding to travail in the busy
affairs of this realm'.[39] Henry VII's methods were retained, a combination of officials who had responsibility for specific areas of
activity and an inner ring of the intimate councillors who had run
things under the old king.[40] Evidence is sparse but as these councillors began to countersign royal bills it appears that they saw
themselves responsible for policy as well as administration. There
are even indications that they were ready to encourage Henry's
passion for 'pastime with good company' and to allow conciliar

attendance at court to decline – not realising the danger this posed as the young men he revelled with became more and more entrenched in the privy chamber.[41] As for setting the agenda and liaising with the king as need be, this was possibly done by Richard Fox, bishop of Winchester and lord privy seal.

This apparent continuity, however, masked a revolution. Noble councillors seized on their new freedom to assert themselves against those who had led in the council of the dead king.[42] The news was kept a close secret for nearly 48 hours, only being announced late in the evening of 23 April and within the court, and this was followed early the next morning by the arrest of Richard Empson and Edmund Dudley, the most prominent of the lawyers Henry VII had used to execute the severe fiscal policies of his last years. Two days later general pardon was proclaimed for every offence imaginable, including those which the old king's agents had pursued so rigorously.[43] A token sample of the bonds which Henry VII had used to entangle the great and many of the not-so-great in a web of potential – and actual – indebtedness to the crown were cancelled, and the 'by-courts' were abolished – that is the conciliar groups through which the first Tudor had exploited the law to achieve financial efficiency in government.

Conciliar leadership, nonetheless, could not last: for three reasons. First it clashed with the young king's insistence on freedom of action and his dislike of opposition. The precipitating issue here was his desire to lock horns with France, a bellicosity strongly opposed by those councillors inherited from Henry VII who insisted on the benefits of maintaining coexistence with England's traditional enemy.[44] The new king appears to have been supported by those nobles who saw opportunities in a more forward foreign policy, but the diplomatic situation did not immediately favour English aggression. Nevertheless, after two years or so the king got his way and in November 1511 committed himself to invade France. The second threat to conciliar leadership we have already noted – the advent of a new generation, indeed a new breed of courtiers, and the emergence of the privy chamber as a potential influence upon government. The third factor which spelled the end of council initiative was Henry VIII's increasing confidence in the man he had appointed as royal almoner, Thomas Wolsey. Taking advantage of the intimacy that the post gave – effectively he acted as Henry's personal assistant – Wolsey rapidly demonstrated that he was enormously able and that 'he was most earnest and readiest among all the council to advance the king's only will and pleasure without any respect to the case.'[45] If the king wanted a war he should have a war. Wolsey became quarter-master general of the campaign – and Henry VIII had found a chief executive.

This story of the opening years of the reign has introduced us to the ingredients of Henrician politics – a king intent on the dignity of his position but eclectic in exercising responsibility, a council capable of becoming pro-active, a court which mattered, royal favour as the basis of the power of any individual or group, and the consequence that any chief minister – indeed any minister close to power – had to straddle both court and administration. Each subsequent episode of the reign – the ministerial leadership of Wolsey, conciliar predominance from 1529 to 1532, Cromwell's time as chief executive and the final six years of reliance on a privy council – mixes these ingredients to a different recipe.

Under Wolsey we find a minister secure in royal favour for all but the final months. As chief executive he was the channel between the king and the rest of the councillors. He could effectively propose policy but he was always careful to ensure that Henry 'owned' it. George Cavendish observed the cardinal's methods at first hand:

> All his endeavour was only to satisfy the king's mind, knowing right well that it was the very vein and right course to bring him to high promotion. ... [He] took upon him to disburden the king of so weighty a charge and troublesome business, putting the king in comfort that he shall not need to spare any time of his pleasure for any business that should necessary happen in the council as long as he being there, having the king's authority and commandment doubted not to see all things sufficiently furnished and perfected, the which would first make the king privy of all such matters (as should pass through their hands) before he would proceed to the finishing and determination of the same, whose mind and pleasure he would fulfil and follow to the uttermost wherewith the king was wonderfully pleased.[46]

The other counsellors resented this but were reduced to advising when Henry and Wolsey wished and to discharging the judicial work of the council, while individual councillors carried on being used to manage particular activities.[47] As for the problem of the physical separation of monarch and minister, this was lessened by the king's trust in Wolsey and by the minister visiting court on any

Sunday he could.[48] He also took care to communicate regularly through Henry's secretary and to keep at court a small council attendant of men he could trust, changing secretary and councillors from time to time to avoid them becoming too independent.[49]

From this solution to the problem of managing the role of the king in government the politics of the Wolsey years grew. A minister in his position had to be alert to challenge from two directions, from councillors who resented his pre-eminence and courtiers who wished to make the most of any intimacy they enjoyed with the king. In the years before the divorce crisis broke in 1527 there was political tension from one or other source in at least 1516, 1517, 1519, and 1525.[50] In 1519, for example, the issue was the increasing influence of the privy chamber.[51] In 1525 the failure of the Amicable Grant gave occasion to the grumbles of noble councillors that they should have been consulted more and these found an echo in the king's periodic complaints that he was left without adequate attendance.[52] Wolsey's response both to councillors and to courtiers was creative and astute. In 1519 he had achieved a purge of the privy chamber which proved only temporary, but by the Eltham Ordinance of 1526 he was able to reduce its staff considerably and replace the courtiers he feared most with men he felt he could trust.[53] As for the counsellors, he 'busied giddy minds' not in 'foreign troubles' but in the expanding judicial role of the council and in so doing he brought to completion the evolution of the court of star chamber.[54] Wolsey also manipulated the Ordinances to emasculate conciliar (and royal) criticisms by creating a substantial council to attend the king but then diverting its members by means of the 'small print' to duties elsewhere, leaving Henry once more to his secretaries.

Wolsey lost office in 1529 after two years of increasing difficulty, in essence because the problem of Henry VIII's annulment brought the king into the active management of affairs and led him to consult more widely. In effect Henry VII's system was revived, thus undermining the chief executive. But it was not for long. The newly empowered inner ring of councillors led by the duke of Norfolk could offer no better a conventional solution to the king's difficulty than the cardinal and could not come to terms with radical alternatives based on ideas then being put forward by another royal almoner, Edward Foxe, and his 'think-tank'.[55] As for Henry, though assiduous on business concerned with his 'great matter', he was not ready to take on Wolsey's day-to-day load. By late 1531, therefore, we see Thomas Cromwell coming forward as the man who could cover the work and, more important, had the political skills required to break the logjam.

Cromwell, however, was not Wolsey in lay garb, and not merely because of his lower profile and refusal to play Solon in the star chamber. First, the shift of power back to the court, the immediacy of the king's matrimonial problem and its knock-on effects on foreign policy and finance meant that Henry, willy-nilly, was much nearer to decisions on detail than he had been. Second, the 1530s required a minister who would be pro-active, not reactive. Thirdly, Cromwell was in a different league from the cardinal when it came to political originality. He needed to be. He did not have the advantages of age, European recognition and 'magnificence' which helped Wolsey to impress the king for so long. What is more, the greater involvement of the king meant that Cromwell's arrival did not marginalise the council attendant in the way Wolsey's had done. It was not enough, therefore, to mediate joint royal and ministerial directions to a team of councillors; Cromwell had also to manage an inner ring whose members saw the king more regularly than he did. Nor did Cromwell escape inheriting the problem of the courtiers.

Once again the tensions in the system engendered politics. The threat from the court was the root cause of the minister's stance in the crises of 1536, first the destruction of Anne Boleyn and her associates and then the rejection of Princess Mary and her supporters.[56] In 1540, Cromwell was himself destroyed as his own mishandling of the king gave opportunity to the councillors at court once again to undermine Henry's confidence in a minister.[57] Institutional change, however, was precipitated by an external political crisis – the Pilgrimage of Grace.[58] The loss of control late in 1536 over the northern third of the country was too serious to be met by king and minister with approval for policy coming from the senior councillors at one remove. The political support of these men became critical and soon we find instructions being issued on corporate authority. At the same time royal pronouncements indicate that this emergency council was no longer an inner ring of a larger body of councillors. It had a finite membership and Henry emphasised that it represented the nobility and the great office-holders, a propaganda ploy to counter the Pilgrims' complaints of his listening to 'upstarts' instead of his 'natural councillors'. The result was a small, advisory and executive 'privy council' of senior politicians – in effect 'the privy council', because a continuous history can be traced from this

point to the privy council which met after Cromwell's execution
to initiate a clerk and a council register.

For historians, Cromwell's death has often signified an end to
the importance of Henry VIII's reign. Not so in politics. The
period after 1540 continues to exhibit the tensions of the earlier
years. Royal favour and politics at court mattered if anything more
than ever as the king increasingly used his privy chamber in government, and as he became if anything more unpredictable in his
initiatives – something we have seen over Boulogne in 1546.[59] The
council's triumph over Henry's second chief executive had finally
established its centrality in government, but it became in consequence the cockpit for political struggle. Tension in court and in
council reached its climax at the end of 1546, when repudiation
of the Howards and Stephen Gardiner and the finalising of the
king's will determined who would manage the transition to his
son's reign.[60] As for institutional progress, with Cromwell
removed the problem of the monarch's mobility once more
became pressing. It was no more a practicality for the post-1540
privy council to operate from the court than for its antecedents to
have done so.[61] Soon we find the council dividing between those
in London and those with the king, recreating all the old
difficulties. And the answer? Once again a personal assistant for
Henry, this time not a chief executive with wide responsibility but
the king's secretary, in particular William Paget who from 1543
effectively mediated royal grace and the royal will to the councillors at court and in London, even though when he was present in
either place he stood as their executive at the end of the council
table. For Paget read William Cecil, and we have arrived at the
political system of Elizabeth I.[62]

It remains to ask how individuals at the time responded to the
flow of politics, day on day. First the councillors and the courtiers.
For some historians their posture is self-evident. Since everything
depended upon the king, councillors and courtiers must necessarily have lived in an attitude of anticipation, waiting for the
royal word. As the magnet moved, the iron filings jostled to
respond. The problem with this reductionist view is that the lines
of force in the Tudor state were not exclusively generated by the
monarch – and under Henry VIII, those that were, were active
intermittently. Family, friendship, locality, connection and previous obligation also exerted powerful influences. Competition to
secure honours, jobs and grants led clients to seek patrons who
had an entrée to the king, and patrons to vie one with another to

exploit royal favour. Desire for political influence with the honour and status that it brought set councillor against councillor, courtier against courtier. What is more, with the repudiation of Rome and the challenge to traditional religion, this rivalry easily and frequently began both to produce and to reflect differences in ideology. As G.R. Elton put it: 'You could no more follow Cromwell if you were a convinced papist than you could attach yourself to Norfolk and Gardiner if you thought that there had been no true religion before Luther.'[63] Nor were these forces confined to the court and central government. The ramifications of the Tudor power network were countrywide. There was political power to be exercised and prizes on offer in the localities as well as nationally and the pull of family, friendship, connection and all the rest was as powerful in the one as the other.

Explaining Tudor politics only in terms of councillors and courtiers responding individually and collectively to the king ignores this whole dimension. These other factors engendered groupings through which individuals collaborated to secure the objectives they sought, either power, or prestige, or profit or some combination of the three, or alternatively protection against competitors. The focus of it all was necessarily the king, 'the life, the head and the authority of all things.' In other words, we must put Henry's personal monarchy in the context of faction. This was not a term which contemporaries would have accepted because of its pejorative connotations; Thomas Wriothesley boasted: 'Rather than I would have consented in my heart to any party, tumult or faction in the realm, if I had a thousand lives I would have lost them all, one after another.'[64] The euphemism which was acceptable was 'friends' and the importance of 'friends' *was* axiomatic at every level in the search for royal favour, from the simple competition for grants, offices or privileges, to the grand political coalitions which united against Wolsey in 1529, or polarised the elite in 1536 between support for Anne Boleyn and support for Princess Mary.[65]

This is not to say that personal monarchy and faction are all that mattered in the reign of the second Tudor. A binary model of Henrician politics does not give all the answers. Nor must the phenomenon of faction be exaggerated. Henrician factions were 'soft' rather than 'hard'. Responses to circumstances, they necessarily changed with circumstances. The only substantial example to last beyond a decade is sometimes labelled the 'Aragonese' faction, from its later identification with the cause of Katherine and Mary, but it can be traced from the last years of Henry VII to the attainders of 1538–9.[66] Furthermore, in a faction, individual adherence too is a response to circumstances and, consequently, also 'soft'. There is no surprise in Thomas Wriothesley spending the summer of 1546 in desperate attempts to blacken as heretics the wives of Edward Seymour and of his allies, only to throw in his lot with that faction in the autumn when he saw that it would win.[67] However, 'soft' though the phenomenon may be, what has to be recognised is how constant the element of faction is in politics throughout the reign, from the opening assault on Empson and Dudley, through the challenges Wolsey faced and the bloody conflicts of the 1530s, to the bickering of the final years and the provisions for the accession of Edward VI, fought out around his father's bedside.

Faction, of course, is a generic form of social and political expression, not a peculiarity of Tudor England. Competition to secure the ear of the ruler has characterised personal monarchies from ancient times to twentieth-century dictatorships and even the 'courts' around the leaders of democratic parties. What distinguishes 'party' and 'faction' is that a faction does not overtly exist to promote ideas, certainly not in Tudor England. To say this is not to retreat from the proposition that when the king's 'great matter' became an issue, ideology began to affect factional alignments. It is, rather, to recognise that while ideology may colour the membership and the attitudes of a Henrician faction, the possibility of overt ideological debate was minimal. Policy was what the king had decreed; loyalty had to accept, not argue. Rebellion was the only alternative.[68] For example, historians often write of 'conservative' and 'reforming' factions in the 1540s, but so long as on the one hand the anti-papal statutes and on the other the Act of Six Articles remained in force, expression of ideological commitment could be little more than a preference for tradition or for change. The use by historians of expressions such as 'factional politics based on ideology' is incautious, to say the least.

To discover where ideas and ideology can exist within a factional system we need to turn to what is the distinguishing mark of faction: that goals are expressed primarily in personal terms. This should not be misunderstood to mean that nothing matters but self-interest. The point is that in faction, issues present as individuals. The suitor secures a new favour because of the favour he can mobilise. Policies in this respect are no different from patronage. The politician sells his policy when he sells himself. The king embraces the policy along with the politician. Ideology is part of the portfolio in the competition for favour. When in the 1530s the country moves towards religious reform it means that Henry is trusting Cromwell and Cranmer; when the government becomes anxious about anabaptist heresy it means that Henry is listening to the duke of Norfolk and the conservative bishops. In fact, what triggered the king's rejection of Thomas Cromwell was precisely an identification of the minister with alleged heretical clients.[69]

Finally, what of the role of the king in politics and of Henry VIII himself? That he had ultimate authority and that he could not be taken for granted are both beyond question. It is also clear that the role of his servants and advisers was to implement his expressed will, an expectation which, as Thomas More and many others found, raised the old conflict between the duty to obey the king and the duty to be honest.[70] John Skip's Lenten sermon at court in 1536 probably hit the target: 'a king's council nowadays will move him no otherwise unto any things but as they see him disposed and inclined to the same'.[71] The problem with Henry VIII, however, was to discover how he was 'disposed and inclined', for his readiness to take responsibility for decision was by no means predictable. Something, of course, depended on the topic. Issues of foreign policy and war, matrimonial problems and the succession always had priority with him, not least because they were inspired by self-concern. Something also depended on mood. There are occasions – and more important ones than the Chatillon raid – when the king energetically took the lead or when he bore down contrary advice, insisting that he would be obeyed; he was also not above using an agent to put up a project which he wanted to promote. At the other extreme, however, Henry would sometimes tolerate important decisions being made for him even though he had serious reservations about them. Between the two was the tolerant norm – allowance of the initiatives of others provided that they fell either within the very broadest of agreed principles or in an area where Henry had little interest, and provided that royal advantage was always the first consideration.

Much also was influenced by the king's character. In 1540 Charles de Marillac, the French ambassador, wrote that Henry was plagued by three vices.[72] The first was avarice 'so that all the riches in the world would not satisfy him'. The second was a suspicious nature, so that he 'would fain keep in favour with everybody but does not trust a single man'. The third plague was 'lightness and inconstancy', a preference for opportunism rather than principle. It is an assessment which has much truth in it. Henry had points of extreme sensitivity. Regal dignity obsessed him and anything which appeared to trench upon it could produce a savage reaction, as Princess Mary discovered.[73] He was moved by enthusiasms – often short-lived – and by emotion. He successively worshipped and repudiated Catherine of Aragon, Anne Boleyn and Catherine Howard and the warmth which brought Thomas More to the Woolsack also brought him to the block. Opportunist and devious he certainly was, priding himself in his 'politic practices'. Money undoubtedly motivated him – it is always a good index of the real level of his commitment – and he had a wholly selfish eye for other people's property, as more than one of his subjects found to his cost. As for suspicion, by the end this had come to dominate the man. Herbert of Chirbury put it this way in his biography of the king: 'impressions privately given him by any court-whisperer were hardly or never to be effaced.'[74] Sixty years later, Elizabethan and Jacobean dramatists could still count on an audience recognising Henry's notorious aversion to whispering.[75]

In personal monarchy, interest, mood and character are crucial in determining whether the ruler will dominate the royal entourage and take advantage of its divisions, or whether he or she will be more or less influenced by it. The particular mix which was Henry VIII meant first of all that he was substantially dependent on those around him. This was not only so in discharging the routines of government. In, for example, solving the problem of the Aragon marriage Henry's own intensive study got nowhere. The proposition that under God he was – and always had been – supreme head of the church in England was developed by the Edward Foxe think-tank. Exploiting these ideas through the medium of parliament so as to subdue the church and break with the pope required the political skills of Thomas Cromwell. As for courage, Henry got this from Anne Boleyn.[76] Along with dependence went a second trait – he could be vulnerable. The factions and interest groups of the day focused on a king who was amenable to pressure. Of course we have again to be careful of overstatement. Henry was not the puppet of faction; he remained dominant; he could hold decided opinions; when he did decide it was final. However, the question is, 'Who had helped form those opinions?' "Who had he listened to as he made that decision?' In other words, government policy and initiative did not arise from the monarch's exclusive will; they emerged from the shifting political and individual context around him. The more contentious the issue, the more the full battery of tactics might be tried: restricting access to the king, the claque, the innuendo, the bribe, the diversion. These brought Wolsey down, Anne Boleyn down, Cromwell down and the Howards and Gardiner. Factions did not always get their way, especially where Henry's own emotions and interests were not involved, but on the right issues and in the right circumstances he was vulnerable and men calculated accordingly.

Not all scholars, it is true, agree with this view. Some would argue that Henry was a powerful personality to whom faction was a source of strength, allowing him to play one group against another, keep them in suspense and get the best service from both; episodes, notably in the 1540s, can certainly be read in this way.[77] Others see factions following where the king led, not leading him; undoubtedly this did occur from time to time.[78] But neither is an adequate perspective overall. A full portrait must reveal a monarch who could dismiss Wolsey and then complain 'everyday I miss the Cardinal of York more and more', who was prepared to execute his closest friend when he would not admit adultery with his wife, who had Thomas Cromwell beheaded, only to say that he had been persuaded 'on light pretexts' to destroy the best servant he ever had, who told Cranmer that he would not be able to save him once he was arrested, a king who from time to time could successfully be 'bounced' into decision, be it over the assault on the independence of the church, the decision to cohabit with Anne Boleyn, or the coup against her.[79] To paint Henry VIII in the garb of either 'the universal spider' or 'the Pied Piper' of the Tudor establishment hardly carries conviction.

The image of the king which in actuality did dominate the political scene was painted on the wall of the privy chamber of Whitehall Palace by Hans Holbein the younger.[80] With his father behind him, the figure of Henry VIII stood beside a monumental inscription:

If you rejoice to see the likeness of glorious heroes, look on these, for no painting ever boasted greater. How difficult the debate, the issue, the question whether father or son be the superior. Each of them has triumphed. The first got the better of his enemies, bore up his so-often ruined land and gave lasting peace to his people. The son, born to still greater things, turned away from the altars of that unworthy man and brings in men of integrity. The presumptuousness of popes has yielded to unerring virtue, and with Henry VIII bearing the sceptre in his hand, religion has been restored, and with him on the throne the truths of God have begun to be held in due reverence.[81]

The king's pose was heroic and his eyes engaged directly with the viewer. This was how Henry saw himself, how he wanted to be seen. As his ministers and courtiers passed by, making the obligatory obeisance to the throne of estate, they may well have reflected that art does not always coincide with reality.

2. Thomas Wolsey, Thomas Cromwell and the Reform of Henrician Government

JOHN GUY

Aside from the controversy over the progress of Protestantism in the sixteenth century, no other debate has generally ranked so high on the agenda of Tudor historians as that upon Henry VIII's chief ministers and their role in government.[1] It has conventionally been assumed: (1) that evaluations of the relative 'success' or 'failure' of the careers of Thomas Wolsey and Thomas Cromwell should be indexed largely in relation to their advocacy while in office of blueprints for the reform of institutions; and (2) that fundamental administrative reform in the shape of national bureaucratic government under the management of an elite executive privy council was the distinctive and indeed 'revolutionary' achievement of Thomas Cromwell in the 1530s.

In this chapter I will first explain why these assumptions are likely to be flawed or incomplete. I will argue that a reassessment of the role of Henry VIII's ministers cannot usefully be undertaken without reference to wider issues of context. These comprise: (1) the agenda of Renaissance monarchy which evolved largely independently of the initiatives of individual ministers and their schemes for administrative reform; and (2) what it actually *meant* to be a 'minister' in the reign of Henry VIII. Thereafter, I shall investigate more specifically the role of Wolsey and Cromwell in Henrician government and reassess critically their contributions to the reconstruction of (1) crown finance; (2) the privy council; and (3) the government of the localities.

The agenda of Renaissance monarchy

The attributes of Renaissance monarchy were that it was personal and patrimonial.[2] It was personal because power centred on the ruler and his court. It was patrimonial because court and government were financed ordinarily by income received from the crown estates. The political objectives of the Renaissance monarchs were remarkably consistent.[3] They centred on dynastic security, territorial centralisation, increased revenues to finance the costs of warfare and building projects, the subordination to the crown of the nobility and higher clergy, control of local 'franchises' and feudal privileges, and the augmentation of regal power. This agenda dictated as much the conditions under which Wolsey and Cromwell served Henry VIII as those under which Antoine Duprat served Francis I and Mercurino di Gattinara the Emperor Charles V.

A summary comparison of the French and English monarchies in the early sixteenth century yields some striking correspondences:

(1) The territorial policy of Charles VIII, Louis XII and Francis I, in particular the acquisition and annexation of Brittany between 1491 and 1532 and the emphasis in royal ordinances on a unified legal system and the use of French as a common language, parallels the measures adopted by Henry VII and Henry VIII to reduce the borderlands, Wales and Ireland to the authority of the English crown.

(2) Like Henry VIII, Francis I aimed to create a service nobility. Charles, duke of Bourbon, constable of France, was condemned and his fiefs incorporated into the royal domain following disputes with the king and his mother, Louise of Savoy, which drove him to revolt in 1523. Edward Stafford, duke of Buckingham, who claimed unsuccessfully the office of high constable of England by hereditary right in 1510, found unacceptable the contradiction which he perceived between his ducal status and a royal policy calculated to secure the subordination of 'feudal anachronisms'. He was executed for treason after a show trial in 1521.

(3) Francis I did not break with Rome, but he vigorously asserted his sovereignty as an 'emperor' in his kingdom. Since the beginning of the fourteenth century the civil lawyers in France had maintained that the king was 'emperor' in his realm (*rex in regno suo est imperator*), that he recognised no

superior save God in 'temporal' matters, that the clergy's jurisdiction was confined to purely 'spiritual' affairs, and that the king might tax his clergy. The scholars variously employed by Henry VIII and the Boleyns to prepare the *Collectanea satis copiosa* and defend the royal supremacy in the 1530s knew intimately these French sources which they cited repeatedly. Both Henry VIII and Francis I claimed *imperium* after the manner of Justinian and the later Roman emperors. The theory of Charles Du Moulin, the most systematic defender of royal supremacy in France whose *Commentaries on the Customs of Paris* began to appear in 1539, that the king was 'the source of all justice, holding all jurisdictions and enjoying full *imperium*' and that secular and ecclesiastical lords were equally subject to his authority 'for the exercise of their jurisdictions and lordships' was generically close to the theory which underpinned the Henrician Act of Appeals of 1533. It was not for nothing that one of the earliest decisions of Henry VIII's propagandists was to publish Latin and English editions of the *Disputation between a Clerk and a Knight*, originally written in the 1290s by French civil lawyers to repudiate papal jurisdiction during the clash between Boniface VIII and Philip the Fair.[4]

(4) Francis I subordinated the governors of the provinces to himself. The leading local elite were titled *conseillers* and provided some 50 working members of the *conseil du roi*. Many were invited to court and found places in the king's service, a strategy which also included bishops and the presidents and officers of the parlement of Paris and provincial parlements.[5] These were methods strikingly similar to those adopted by Henry VII and Henry VIII when they bridged the gap between court and country by constructing a crown affinity. All 38 English shires were represented, along with South Wales, North Wales, Calais, Ireland and Jersey. The key was service at court. Leading landowners and JPs were sworn in as carvers, cupbearers, knights, esquires, sewers and gentlemen-ushers of the king's chamber. As many as 600 were on the roll, the majority unsalaried.

(5) The financial reforms of Francis I replaced an outdated system of decentralised debit finance with a new system based on cash payments and disbursements within a central department of finance under the *trésorier de*

l'Epargne (1523, 1532). The royal coffers were finally settled
at the Louvre and provided cash flow for those projects
which the king deemed as being of immediate importance,
a system remarkably similar to that developed by Henry VII
and Henry VIII which centred in turn on the chamber and
privy coffers.[6]

(6)   As soon as Francis I returned from captivity in Madrid
(1526), the King's Council was reconstructed. The *Grand
Conseil* was restricted to legal cases, while in the *conseil du
roi* power was concentrated in a select council within the
larger body called the *conseil étroit* or *conseil des affaires*. This
select council operated as a cabinet council of five or six
members and functioned in the manner of the *consilium* of
the later Roman emperors. State business was conducted at
the will of the king within the royal household. The
Henrician Court of Star Chamber was in some respects
comparable to the *Grand Conseil*, but the reconstructed
privy council of Henry VIII was unlike the *conseil étroit* in so
far as the latter body operated as a collection of individuals
and not as a corporate board. The late-Henrician privy
council was a settled institution which met formally several
times a week. It was provided with a permanent clerk and
kept registers of its proceedings. Yet it met like the *conseil
étroit* in the privy apartments at court, and both bodies
served as executive agencies dealing with political,
financial and diplomatic business in response to royal
requirements and immediate needs.[7]

This comparison of France and England should not be over-
drawn. Some fundamental differences remained. For example,
Francis I did little to revise the system of taxation and continued
to rely principally on the *taille* and the *gabelle*. The French monarchy was wealthier than that of England, but it was weaker politically. The nobility were exempted from taxation – the exact opposite
of the protocol of Henry VIII and Wolsey – and Francis I was
increasingly obliged to allow offices to become hereditary.
Furthermore, by the reign of Henry VIII no useful comparison
can be made between the nature and functions of the parlement
of Paris and the parliament of England.

If, however, it is unwise to draw schematic inferences from my
comparison, it *is* possible to discern trends directly linked to the
aims of the Renaissance monarchies, trends which manifested

themselves in programmes of territorial consolidation and reconstruction and reform in areas such as finance, conciliar organisation and provincial government. Such trends were energised in
the Renaissance by the ambition and mutual rivalry of kings. They
were rarely driven autonomously by the reforming instincts of
humanists and bureaucrats. This is not to deny the influence of
humanism on both Wolsey and Cromwell. Nor is it to deny that
Henry VIII's ministers devised blueprints for the reform of government institutions. It *is* to say that it must be deemed highly
unlikely that such blueprints should be regarded as purely administrative initiatives easily detached from urgent political contexts.
Above all, if claims for the fundamental reconstruction of
Henrician government by Thomas Cromwell on national bureaucratic lines under the management of an elite executive privy
council are to be sustained, then it must be documented con-
cretely that this was indeed Cromwell's intention. The attribution
of this motive cannot be accomplished on the basis of purely cir-
cumstantial evidence.

The nature of 'ministerial' status

For much of the twentieth century it has been claimed that
Wolsey and Cromwell each enjoyed 'prime-ministerial' ascendancy during Henry VIII's reign, but this paradigm is borrowed
from an understanding of Victorian politics. In Tudor terms it is
anachronistic and misleading. Henry's ministers advised the king
and controlled the implementation of crown policy once a strategy had been conceived. But, since the king might intervene or
change his mind at will, policy might waver, collapse or undergo
revision at any moment in the interests of European diplomacy or
domestic expediency. It is scarcely surprising that under so
volatile a system, Wolsey and Cromwell became the victims less of
their own mistakes than of their master's egoism.

Wolsey enjoyed greater latitude than his successor, Cromwell,
but this was because the young Henry VIII intervened less in politics before 1527 (possibly 1525) than afterwards. The turning
point was the king's first divorce campaign, which began in
earnest in the summer of 1527 when Henry personally seized the
initiative from an absent Wolsey in soliciting support and orchestrating the debate.[8]

It is pivotal to remember that in Tudor colloquial speech the term 'minister' did not mean what it means today. To be a 'minster' in the reign of Henry VIII was to be the personal servant of the king and not the public servant of the state. In so far as Wolsey and Cromwell combined these functions, it was because they served the crown at a time when no adequate conceptual distinction between the 'state' and royal government had been established. The notion of the 'state' in the modern sense was hazy and undeveloped before the 1590s, the doctrine of 'ministerial accountability' lay more than a century ahead, and parliament was still an exclusively royal institution which the king summoned and dissolved at will.[9]

It is misleading to assume that Wolsey and Cromwell were appointed to be Henry VIII's chief ministers. Both acquired ascendant positions by a process of accretion and in incremental stages. In any case, the office of 'chief minister' or even 'minister' – understood in a high political sense – did not exist in Tudor England: the term is used loosely by historians to identify the councillor who most conspicuously enjoyed the king's trust and confidence and upon whom he relied to direct the implementation of crown policy. Admittedly less graphic, it would be technically more correct to say that Wolsey and Cromwell were successively Henry VIII's pre-eminent servants and privy councillors. Wolsey's official appointments were those of lord chancellor, cardinal-archbishop of York, and papal legate *a latere*. Cromwell was successively master of the jewels, chancellor of the exchequer, principal secretary, lord privy seal, vicegerent in spirituals (that is, Henry VIII's lay deputy as supreme head of the church), and finally lord great chamberlain.

It *is* true that Wolsey enjoyed exceptional favour and for a while his position was different. Between 1515 and 1525 it can be argued that Henry VIII treated him more as a partner than as a servant.[10] Wolsey enjoyed a uniquely privileged access to the king. They walked arm-in-arm together and were intimate confidantes to the exclusion of others.[11] Only Thomas More enjoyed comparable favour: but this was steadily eroded when he declined to support the king's first divorce campaign.

For a decade Henry and Wolsey governed as a team. The king required a minister to accomplish his 'will and pleasure', and Wolsey triumphantly succeeded. That does not imply that Henry knew or approved of everything Wolsey did, nor did it oblige Henry to stand by his minister when things went wrong. When

Wolsey tamed factionalism in Star Chamber, when he punished enclosing landlords, or when he seemingly achieved 'universal peace' in Europe by a miracle of diplomacy, Henry was the first to claim the credit.[12] But by 1525 Wolsey had overreached himself in foreign policy and finance. His 'Amicable Grant' led to a tax revolt, whereupon Henry denied responsibility for the plan. Wolsey was obliged to perform a humiliating *volte-face*, switching from an alliance with Charles V *against* France to an alliance *with* France against the emperor. Moreover, the French *entente* was risky. It was criticised by leading nobles, it jeopardised England's trade with the Low Countries, and it put Henry VIII on the wrong side of Italian politics when his suit for annulment of his marriage to Catherine of Aragon opened at Rome two years later.

Wolsey was admitted to the council in 1510, and between 1512 and 1514 was the man who alone saw that the way to royal favour was to perform the council's functions strictly in accordance with Henry's wishes. The breakthrough came in 1513, when he successfully procured the equipment and supplies needed for Henry's invasion of France. According to his contemporary biographer, George Cavendish, Wolsey was always 'the most earnest and readiest among all the Council to advance the King's only will and pleasure without any respect to the case. The King therefore perceived him to be a meet instrument for the accomplishment of his devised will and pleasure.' By the end of 1514 Henry VIII valued Wolsey's services so highly 'that his estimation and favour put all other ancient counsellors out of their accustomed favour'.[13] He was promoted bishop of Lincoln. He then negotiated a treaty with France, whereupon Henry VIII lobbied the pope to make him a cardinal. When the archbishopric of York fell vacant, Wolsey exchanged it for Lincoln (September 1514). A year later he was elected a cardinal, and on Christmas Eve 1515 was sworn in as lord chancellor.

Cromwell's rise was slow by comparison. He entered Wolsey's household in 1516 and was his 'counsellor' by 1519. When Wolsey pleaded guilty to the charge of *praemunire* in October 1529, his property was forfeit to the crown. Only Cromwell, as his former solicitor, knew where Wolsey's assets had been conveyed. Cromwell resolved to 'make or mar' his career, and used his interviews with Henry about Wolsey's property as opportunities to play the courtier. He entered royal service in the spring of 1530, and was sworn of the council at the end of that year. His enemies claimed that he offered to make Henry 'the richest prince in

Christendom', a rumour relished by opponents of the
Reformation. It was most likely a smear; but firm proof is lacking
either way.[14]

Within another year Cromwell was Henry VIII's parliamentary
manager. But he was not yet pre-eminent as a policy-maker.
Cromwell never became the king's partner, nor did he ever enjoy
the degree of influence over Henry previously achieved by
Wolsey. He contributed to policy-making at all levels, but never
wholly succeeded in dominating the king's counsels. He was more
subtle, more emollient, less secure politically than Wolsey. Of
course, the political context had changed: Cromwell served the
mature Henry VIII – a ruler who (in Thomas More's phrase)
'knew his own strength'.[15]

Far more than Wolsey, Cromwell had to work obliquely.
Publicly he cast himself as the administrative genius whose flair
was his ability to transform abstract ideas into practical measures.
His organisational powers were unmatched. Like Wolsey, he presented an affable disposition to the world. But the inner man was
ruthless and single-minded. Whereas Wolsey had been envied
rather than feared, Cromwell was feared rather than envied.
Moreover, he was feared increasingly on account of his partisan
politics and covert support for Protestantism.

Not only did Cromwell rise to power by accretion, he also
reached the summit of his career only after Anne Boleyn's fall
(May 1536). For it was not Cromwell but the circle of advisers led
by Edward Foxe and Thomas Cranmer who prepared the
Collectanea satis copiosa and constructed the theory for the break
with Rome and Henry VIII's ecclesiastical supremacy.[16]
Cromwell's role at that stage was largely to implement their ideas
by drafting the necessary legislation, steering it through parliament and stifling opposition in the country. His influence should
not be underestimated. He played the leading part in subordi-
nating the clergy to the crown; he orchestrated the press campaign in defence of the break with Rome.[17] Above all, he
enforced the royal supremacy by means of oaths of allegiance
and extensions to the treason law.[18] When Henry repudiated
Anne Boleyn in the spring of 1536, Cromwell was deft enough to
obtain the evidence needed to destroy Anne and her court allies
in order that Henry might marry Jane Seymour. But he also took
his opportunity to drive his own political opponents from court
on the grounds that they had plotted to restore Princess Mary to
the succession.[19]

The *putsch* of mid-1536 gave Cromwell the pre-eminent ascendancy he had hitherto lacked. His power was real, but it was less secure than Wolsey's for two reasons. First, it had been won, and was increasingly sustained, by factional politics rather than the king's unrestricted licence. The mature Henry VIII did not need a partner; Cromwell remained firmly 'the king's servant'. Attempts to topple him began almost at once. As early as October 1536 the leaders of the Pilgrimage of Grace demanded that Cromwell and his clients be expelled from court as ministerial 'upstarts' and 'heretics'.[20]

Secondly, Cromwell's new authority rested on a controversial extension of his powers as vicegerent in spirituals which Henry approved after Anne Boleyn's fall. Cromwell's original powers had licensed him merely to investigate the wealth and condition of the monasteries. The new powers were comprehensive and were modelled *almost word for word* on those previously enjoyed by Wolsey as papal legate *a latere*.[21] Without delay Cromwell issued injunctions ordering the clergy to defend the royal supremacy in sermons; to teach children the Lord's Prayer, Ten Commandments and articles of faith out of Scripture; and to abandon pilgrimages. Two years later he authorised iconoclasm for images which were superstitiously abused, naming his own agents as commissioners to determine *which* specific images were idolatrous.[22] He restricted the burning of candles for saints and the dead, and (no less controversially) ordered an English translation of the Bible to be placed in every parish church. There will always be a debate about Cromwell's religion, but it was not for nothing that the official explanation of his fall (June 1540) accused him of 'secretly and indirectly advancing the one of the extremes [i.e. Lutheranism], and leaving the mean indifferent true and virtuous way, which His Majesty sought and so entirely desired'.[23]

The reconstruction of crown finance

The ability to tax efficiently is a valid index of the strength of an early modern regime. Henrician government was so successful in this respect that it created 'a system of taxation, which, for its sophistication and attention to the principles of distributive justice, was several centuries ahead of its time'.[24] To this achievement Wolsey made the greatest contribution. Henry VII's experiments in raising new taxes to supplement fifteenths and tenths had been imperfect. Wolsey therefore seized the opportunity as the administrator of Henry VIII's early wars to devise the directly assessed subsidy. This was perfected over the course of a decade with the assistance of John Hales, reader in Gray's Inn in 1514, and baron of the Exchequer from 1522 until his death in 1539, who drafted the necessary legislation.[25]

The trick was to abandon static rates of tax and stereotyped assessments of taxpayers' wealth in favour of a flexible approach designed to maximise receipts. Wolsey rejected the fixed rates and diminishing yields associated with fifteenths and tenths in favour of a system that combined flexible rates of tax with accurate valuations of taxpayers' true wealth. He laid down important principles, beginning in 1513. Taxpayers were to be assessed individually on oath by local officials under the supervision of centrally appointed commissioners, who had power to examine and revise assessments. The commissioners then calculated the tax due from each individual, and in cases where taxpayers were liable to be assessed in more than one category – for example, in respect of the net value of annual incomes, or the capital value of their movable possessions – they were charged in one category only, but that was to be the one which yielded the largest amount of tax. When parliament granted a subsidy, every adult in the country (except married women whose legal personalities were incorporated in those of their husbands) had to be assessed. But only those whose incomes were above prescribed exemption limits had to pay tax. These limits varied from subsidy to subsidy, but a far from negligible proportion of the population was exempt from taxation. This proportion ranged from between 10 per cent to 77 per cent depending on circumstances.[26] In the 1520s and in 1544–7, moreover, graduated rates of tax were in force which increased considerably the proportion of the subsidy which fell upon the shoulders of the rich.[27] Unlike the French *taille* and *gabelle* or the poll tax and fifteenths and tenths which the subsidy increasingly superseded, Wolsey's system of taxation was progressive as well as efficient.

There were teething troubles, but Wolsey learned by experience. He raised £325,000 in parliamentary subsidies between 1513 and his fall, while separate clerical taxation yielded £240,000.[28] This contrasts with receipts from fifteenths and tenths in the same period amounting to £118,000 and 'loans' which totalled a quarter of a million. For the first time since 1334 the crown was levying taxation which accurately reflected the true wealth of taxpayers. But Wolsey became overconfident. In the parliament of 1523 he demanded taxation of £800,000 on top of the 'loans' he had collected in 1522–3. He announced rates of 4s. in the £ on goods and lands, but in the end was forced to settle for less than half this amount to be paid in annual instalments.[29]

He then attempted to 'anticipate' payment of the first instalment of this subsidy on the basis of rigorous assessments. He named commissioners to 'practise' with taxpayers owning £40 and above in lands or goods, who were to pay their first instalment of tax immediately, and not at the date specified in the subsidy act. Only 5 per cent of this 'anticipation' had been paid by the due date, although 74 per cent would be realised within another month. The subsidy of 1523 was eventually levied on the basis of fresh and, possibly for richer taxpayers, somewhat lower valuations, yet it provoked dismay. When the second instalment of tax fell due in February 1525, late payments by the vast majority of all taxpayers signalled burgeoning resistance to Wolsey's fiscal ambitions.[30]

The crunch came after the battle of Pavia when Henry VIII wished to invade France: the war chest was empty. So Wolsey sent out commissioners in March and April 1525 to demand a non-parliamentary tax called an 'Amicable Grant'. The clergy were to pay at the rate of one-third of their yearly revenues or the value of their goods above £10, or one-quarter of their revenues or goods below £10. The laity were assessed according to a sliding scale: those worth above £50 per annum were to contribute 3s. 4d. in the £, those worth between £20 and £50 were to offer 2s. 8d. in the £, and those worth below £20, 1s. in the £.[31]

Wolsey's demand fired a tax rebellion. The 'loans' of 1522–3 had not been repaid and the subsidy of 1523 was still being collected. By the end of April, Wolsey was modifying his demands and was attempting to settle for payment of a benevolence; he was told that, if mandatory, benevolences were illegal by Richard III's statute of 1484, and he finally had to accept voluntary contributions. Discontent reached dangerous levels throughout England. In Essex, Kent, Norfolk, Warwickshire and Huntingdonshire, the Amicable Grant provoked reactions ranging from reluctance to outright refusal, and full-scale revolt erupted in Suffolk that spread to the borders of Essex and Cambridgeshire. The dukes of Norfolk and Suffolk mustered the East Anglian gentry; they successfully negotiated the surrender of the militants. But 10,000 men had converged on Lavenham – the most serious rebellion since 1497.[32]

By May 1525 efforts to collect the Amicable Grant had been confounded by Wolsey's resort to voluntary contributions in London. It was politically impossible to levy additional taxation in the 1520s, and Henry and Wolsey dropped the Amicable Grant in a stage-managed display of 'clemency'. No further taxation was attempted by Wolsey, and in 1529 the immediate needs of the crown were satisfied when the first session of the Reformation parliament cancelled the king's debts (i.e. the 'loans' of 1522–3)[33] and Francis I agreed by the treaty of Cambrai to pay the arrears of Edward IV's pension and to redeem some of Charles V's debts to Henry VIII. As a result Henry VIII received payments ranging from £20,000 to £50,000 a year from France until 1532.[34]

Cromwell's contribution to the development of the subsidy was less in the field of revenue collection than of taxation philosophy. The Subsidy Act of 1534 was a landmark because it justified taxation not on grounds of war but of peace. Henry VIII had so capably ruled the realm 'to the high pleasure of Almighty God' for 25 years that loyal subjects felt obliged to offer peacetime taxation – so the argument ran.[35] Parliamentary subsidies yielded £45,000 in 1535–7 and fifteenths and tenths £36,000. Clerical taxation (including first fruits and tenths) yielded £406,000 between 1535 and 1540.[36]

Yet the lion's share of revenue came from the Dissolution, which yielded £1.3 million between August 1536 and the death of Henry VIII. A distinction must be made between the rents of confiscated lands, which were recurring revenues, and cash derived from land sales, which was the alienation of capital. The gross receipts of land sales totalled £800,000. Gold and silver plate and jewels seized from shrines and elsewhere raised £79,500. Land sales yielded an average of £82,000 per annum after 1539 with sales at their height in 1544 and 1545. Sales of goods and other movables reached their peak in 1541–3 (£14,000). Rents reached their maximum in 1542–3, but thereafter quickly fell. By the death of Henry VIII they totalled £48,000 per annum, less than half the original monastic income despite rent revaluations.[37]

The striking fact is that, in respect of the ex-monastic lands, Cromwell was not the author of a policy of sales. Sales were initially a crisis measure precipitated by the invasion scare that followed the *rapprochement* between Francis I and Charles V at Aigues-Mortes (July 1538). Expenditure of £376,000 was suddenly required to finance the construction of a national network of fortifications.[38] Land sales provided the 'quick fix'. Thereafter, the massive sales discussed below by Richard Hoyle (chapter 4) which funded the king's invasion of Scotland in 1542 and his Boulogne campaign of 1544 were undertaken after Cromwell's fall and execution. True, Cromwell was required to supervise the initial sales and transfer the proceeds to the king's coffers at Whitehall and elsewhere. But it had never been his intention to squander the proceeds of the Dissolution. The entire thrust of his fiscal policy hitherto had been to maximise the crown's long-term income.

In fact, it can be argued that there was a fundamental disjunction between Henry VIII's fiscal objectives and Cromwell's in the 1530s. As in the case of Francis I when the *Epargne* was created first at Blois and then at the Louvre, the king's aim was to accumulate a war chest in the king's coffers.[39] Cromwell's aim by contrast was that the proceeds of the Dissolution should be used to create a permanent landed endowment for the 'imperial' crown. His policy was directed towards the re-endowment of the monarchy so that stability could be assured, the royal household and institutions of government maintained, patronage dispensed, and foreign policy conducted without resort to 'exquisite means' like the Amicable Grant – the type of emergency expedients that provoked domestic political friction.

In other words, the critical element of Cromwell's efforts to reconstruct crown finance was not, as has conventionally been assumed, the establishment of bureaucratic institutions such as the Court of Augmentations or First Fruits and Tenths for the collection of increased crown revenue, or arguably even the extension of the parliamentary subsidy to provide for regular peace time taxation, but rather the recreation of patrimonial kingship in the wake of the Dissolution by means of the wholesale re-endowment of the monarchy as called for *inter alia* in the reigns of Henry VI and Edward IV by Sir John Fortescue.[40] The essence of crown finance under Edward IV and Henry VII was that land revenues were the key to political and financial stability.[41] As Fortescue had argued, the dilapidation of the king's estate had gone too far; the need was for 'a new foundation of his crown'. It was this doctrine that had underpinned the 'land revenue' experiments of the Yorkists and early Tudors, and the same theory underlay the assertion by Henry VIII in 1533 that he would reunite to the crown the lands which the clergy of his dominions held thereof, 'which lands and property his predecessors on the throne could not alienate to his prejudice'.[42] This statement rationalised but was unquestionably underpinned by the *Collectanea satis copiosa*. It was also consistent with the draft in the autumn of 1534 of a scheme for the wholesale resumption by the crown of all ecclesiastical endowments above parish level, to be followed by the provision of fixed incomes for the clergy. The plan was headed: 'Things to be moved for the king's highness for an increase and augmentation to be had for maintenance of his most royal estate, and for the defence of the realm.'[43] In particular, the draft provided that the king should have, 'for the maintenance of his royal estate' the lands and possessions of redundant monasteries. Cromwell was arrested in June 1540 and in July he was dead. His end stemmed from politics, his pro-Lutheran diplomacy, and his support of radical reformers. It may also be the case that his and Henry VIII's financial objectives had all along conflicted.

The reconstruction of the privy council

More complex and controversial is Cromwell's role as author of the reconstruction of the privy council. An initial point should therefore be stressed. The reorganised privy council between 1540 and 1603 did increasingly assume corporate responsibility for national administration under the crown, especially financial and legal administration and local government. The Elizabethan privy council under Lord Burghley did create a buffer between the crown and the provinces, and formed the nexus of a 'national' system of administration.

If, however, the privy council rose to prominence in Tudor administration and enjoyed a clear institutional identity by the reign of Elizabeth I, the fact remains that from the mid-1540s onwards it was largely subsumed physically within the court. Between 1540 and 1544, when Henry VIII embarked for France, the council was often divided between the Star Chamber at Westminster and the king's person.[44] During Henry's absence on the Boulogne campaign members of the privy council were named to attend upon the queen, who was appointed regent.[45] But after the king's return the privy council almost invariably met at court; it met in the privy apartments and kept its records there; and its leading members were courtiers as much as privy councillors. Conversely, members of the royal household continued to play essential roles in government and administration throughout the early modern period.[46]

The Tudor system of government was typical of the Renaissance. The shape of national administration was defined by the political system which underpinned it. Royal requirements and immediate needs were vital. Henrician politics increasingly focused on the court after Wolsey's fall, therefore the council lived and moved there. Elizabeth I ruled from court, therefore the privy council met there. Cromwell was successful as a minister between 1532 and 1538–9 because he attuned his reflexes to the king's commands. Personal and kinship relationships, in any case, so deeply permeated Tudor society that the modern notion of 'efficient bureaucratic' government was neither feasible nor desirable. Cromwell himself repeatedly invoked personal methods of administration, making decisions on the basis of informal conversations and short-circuiting official machinery on innumerable occasions. Indeed, if Cromwell had been the architect of a bureaucratic 'revolution' in government in the 1530s, it could only have been on the basis of bureaucracy for everyone except himself!

The crux of the 'revolution' controversy is the debate on the privy council. How, when, and in what circumstances in the reign of Henry VIII did the reorganised privy council of nineteen or so members replace the large and amorphous council that had advised Edward IV and Henry VII and worked under Wolsey's direction in Star Chamber? Certainly the corporate body of office-holders that existed by the end of 1536 permitted greater efficiency, security, and confidentiality in central government; it comprised only working councillors; and it left Star Chamber free to limit itself to specialist legal work. Precedents existed for the creation of 'privy' conciliar boards emancipated from immediate household tasks. Wolsey created an executive privy council for Ireland in 1520 which operated independently of the king's deputy in Dublin.[47] By the Eltham Ordinance of 1526 he planned (at least in theory) to reduce the size of the English council to twenty executives, of whom those present at court were to meet daily at 10 a.m. and 2 p.m. in the king's dining chamber.[48] Again, the Calais Act of 1536 created an executive council for the government of the town and Calais Pale. Its membership was fixed at eleven named office-holders sitting in order of precedence from the deputy down to the under-marshal.[49]

A 'creationist' view of the privy council was the centrepiece of G.R. Elton's *The Tudor Revolution in Government*. It lies at the heart of any assessment of Cromwell. But although superficially attractive, the balance of evidence is against it. In saying that, I must make one thing clear. Cromwell certainly did contemplate reform, because in June 1534 he scribbled on the back of a letter, 'To remember the king for the establishment of the Council'.[50] What this meant in practice is elusive,[51] but Cromwell had been responsible for implementing council decisions since May 1533 when he first jotted down 'Remembrances to be put into my book for things done in the council'.[52] He had a vested interest in defining the council's working practices, and he doubtless had a blueprint in mind.[53]

But his plans were overtaken by events. The political milieu was turbulent: first Wolsey's fall and More's refusal as lord chancellor to support Henry VIII's divorce campaign, then the Submission of the Clergy and Acts of Appeals and Supremacy. In 1534 Kildare's revolt shattered Ireland. The following year *Valor ecclesiasticus* was compiled. In 1536 came in quick succession the fall of Anne Boleyn, the dissolution of the smaller monasteries, Cromwell's first injunctions, and finally the Pilgrimage of Grace. These events, but chiefly the Pilgrimage, were political upheavals of immense magnitude. They animated structural change by themselves. Henry's most trusted councillors quickly retreated to the sanctum of the 'privy' apartments at court. Not since Bosworth had the need for radical decisions and confidentiality in the council been so pronounced. Moreover, during the fifteenth century, the term 'privy' councillor had been used to distinguish such 'close' or 'continual' advisers at court from members of the great council or council in Star Chamber. Thus Cromwell was styled a 'privy councillor' as early as 1533.[54]

Yet despite the adjective 'privy', Henry VIII's 'court' councillors were not the institutional privy council in 1533. An intrinsic structural difference existed between a collection of 'privy' councillors acting as individuals as in the French *conseil étroit* and the organised institution which functioned as a corporate board in and after the autumn of 1536 and which was assigned a permanent clerk and official registers on 10 August 1540, two weeks after Cromwell's execution.[55]

The council was reconstructed by the spring of 1537. A list (admittedly incomplete) compiled then suggests that thirteen leading office-holders plus Viscount Beauchamp, Jane Seymour's brother (the future Protector Somerset) were included. By contrast second-rank councillors were demoted, enjoying thereafter honorific status during their lifetimes as 'ordinary councillors' or councillors 'at large'. Also excluded were the judges, king's

serjeants, and lord mayors of London, although the senior judges
retained positions in the court of Star Chamber as expert
assessors.[56]

Between the fall of Anne Boleyn and the spring of 1537 a
reconstruction of the council had taken place.[57] Yet Cromwell's
correspondence is silent on the matter. Indeed it has never been
explained how he accomplished 'fundamental reform' in a year
which saw his *putsch* against the Boleyns in the spring and the
Pilgrimage in the autumn. Not only was his career under direct
attack during the Pilgrimage – it was these same opponents who
vilified him as a traitor and heretic in 1540 – but also Henry VIII
was directly challenged to expel Cromwell, his assistant Thomas
Audley, and Cranmer from the council and replace them with
noblemen. Far from the politics of 1536 smoothing a path for
administrative reform by Cromwell, the exact opposite is more
likely. The 'select' group of councillors operating since 1530 had
sparked intense resentment. By 1536 the issue of council membership was explosive, and had Cromwell attempted 'fundamental
reform' before the outbreak of the revolt, the details could not
have failed to reach the Pilgrims' agenda.[58]

It is also astonishing that half the members of the reorganised
privy council were religious conservatives opposed to Cromwell.
By 1539–40 their party was in the ascendant. Cromwell's fall was
precipitated in considerable degree because he was outnumbered
at the council board. It is unthinkable that so shrewd a politician
could have stacked the cards against himself by 'creating' an executive board replete with his opponents. His original intention
when he spoke of 'the establishment of the council' in June 1534
was evidently frustrated.[59]

Finally, the date of the council's reconstruction can be pinned
down to October 1536 when Cromwell's career was on the line. As
soon as the Lincolnshire revolt erupted, Henry's 'select' councillors closed ranks. Cromwell and Audley retired to the sidelines,
though their eclipse was largely tactical – a pretence for propaganda purposes.[60] But from 14 October onwards, the privy council
issued instructions *as a corporate board* to the captains who took the
field against the rebels. No longer did Cromwell write letters as
the king's chief minister on the council's behalf; they were prepared *for group signature at the board*.[61] This distinction is crucial.
The chief generic difference between the amorphous council of
the period between 1514 and 1536, and the later institutional
privy council, was that the amorphous council's letters were issued

on its behalf by the minister of the day, whereas the privy council's letters were written in the name of the council and signed collectively at the board.[62] It is striking that between October 1536 and April 1537, when the revolts in the north were at their height, and again after Cromwell's execution in July 1540, the council's letters were written in the name of the council *and signed collectively*. Furthermore, this pattern is mirrored by the council's in-letters. Before October 1536 correspondents overwhelmingly addressed themselves to the king's chief minister and council conjointly, or even to the minister as an individual. Yet, during the winter of 1536–7, and once again after 1540, they overwhelmingly addressed the privy council *as a board*.[63]

My argument is thus that evidence of political action or executive intervention by a privy council acting as a corporate board is the key to an understanding of the council's reconstruction in the 1530s. In particular, the evidence of letters signed collectively at the board by councillors ordering things to be done is crucial, since letters signed in this way were regarded by their recipients as legal instruments of government without the need for further validation by the privy seal or king's stamp. There is a mass of linguistic evidence concerning the term 'privy council', but it is ambiguous. In September 1536, for instance, Henry VIII talked of summoning his 'Prevy Counsaile',[64] but it is clear from the context that the phrase was no more than a turn of speech. A memorandum written on or about 7 October 1536 was headed 'Personages appointed to attend upon the queen's grace'.[65] It was a list of those ordered to attend on the queen in London. Sixteen individuals were named, and ten were marked with a 'P' for privy councillor. Seven of these did not belong to the 'close' or 'continual' council which attended on the king, and it has recently been argued that this negates my interpretation that the privy council was restructured during the Pilgrimage.[66] This criticism is unconvincing. The memorandum was compiled *a week before* the privy council began to write letters as a corporate board, and I had never cited it as proof of the reconstruction of the privy council. As the original manuscript explains, the term 'P' in this document refers to councillors authorised 'to brake up (i.e. open) the king's letters and to write their opinions'.[67]

By contrast after 14 October, there is proof of the activity in government of a select group of privy councillors working corporately at the board. Cromwell thus witnessed the birth of the elite executive board which by Elizabeth I's reign had assumed responsibility for Tudor government under the crown, but the reconstruction was driven politically. Following the defeat of the Pilgrims the privy council's membership was revised and remained fluid until Cromwell's fall. Yet, far from giving the privy council an organised bureaucratic routine after April 1537, Cromwell on the contrary reasserted his 'ministerial' control over its business, and thereby prevented the council from exercising its authority fully until after his fall. (This was hardly surprising when his enemies were so powerfully represented at the board!) Only after Cromwell's execution was it resolved to give the privy council its own official registers and a professional secretariat, the hallmarks of 'bureaucratic' as opposed to personal government.

The government of the localities

Henry VIII's government remained stable despite war, taxation, and the steep rise of population; the break with Rome, factional politics, and the Pilgrimage of Grace in the 1530s; and the distress wreaked by currency debasements, inflation, and unemployment in the 1540s. If a single reason must be adduced, it is that Henry VIII – whom his subjects regarded as a 'patriot king' – understood the need to win the backing of local magistrates. The methods used to consolidate royal power in the localities were thoroughly medieval and owed nothing to bureaucracy. Wolsey and Cromwell built bridges between court and country by constructing a crown affinity in the provinces. This was a well-established policy begun when Richard II had attempted to split noble and gentry affinities and to replace them with networks of royal power. Some 300 to 400 knights and esquires had been invited to court as supernumeraries. They were not given salaried appointments, but often received annuities and robes.[68] Thereafter, rulers down to Henry VII had courted landowners and JPs in order to widen their power-base in the localities. Edward IV structured his household appointments specifically so as to create a nexus of territorial lordship centred on the court and the Yorkist dynasty. It was said that 'the names and circumstances of almost all men, scattered over the counties of the kingdom, were known to him just as if they were daily within his sight'.[69]

In Henry VIII's reign the focus was on the king's chamber, the main ceremonial department of the royal household. Between his accession and the fall of Thomas Cromwell, Henry VIII appointed

493 chamber officials at court, including 120 knights and esquires of the body.[70] Since the knights and esquires of the body had already surrendered their duties as intimate royal body servants to the gentlemen of the privy chamber, this appears astonishing until one realises that the majority of these posts were not salaried but supernumerary. The exact proportions of salaried and supernumerary appointments cannot be calculated especially at the lower levels, but roughly 70 to 85 per cent of chamber posts were supernumerary. An obvious fiction was in play; supernumeraries did not receive 'bouge of Court',[71] therefore their attendance at court was likely to have been occasional. Yet this structure provided the crown with an extensive network of clientage in the localities. Conversely, supernumeraries gained opportunities to seek crown patronage and potentially to make a career in crown service. In fact, approximately 5 per cent of supernumeraries subsequently advanced to salaried positions at court, a few even to membership of the privy chamber or the council.

Despite the privy chamber's rise as the main focus of court politics, Wolsey and Cromwell continued to recruit supernumeraries from the counties. Their aim was to 'swear-in' landowners and local 'men of worship' as the 'king's servants' and register their names, thereby assuring their allegiance to the crown. Wolsey in 1519 urged Henry 'to put himself in strength with his most trusty servants in every shire for the surety of his royal person and succession' – Edward IV's policy by another name.[72] A special book was begun which recorded the names 'of the king's servants in all the shires of England sworn to the king', listing knights, esquires, carvers, cupbearers, sewers and gentlemen-ushers in order of their counties.[73] Although severely damaged by water, the names of 184 knights, 148 esquires, 5 carvers, 13 cupbearers, 107 sewers and 138 gentlemen-ushers can still be read.[74] This was the roll-call of Henry's local men, and like Edward IV he must have known their names 'as if they were daily within his sight'. By the middle of the 1520s in excess of 200 county landowners or their sons were listed as unsalaried supernumeraries.[75] By 1535 the number had risen to 263, the list being headed by 182 knights and esquires of the body.[76]

The crown's approach to the provinces was bilateral. Not only were local landowners and JPs sworn as the 'king's servants', but conversely courtiers and trusted members of the king's affinity were 'placed' strategically in the commissions of the peace. By 1500 the expanded role of JPs as the crown's unsalaried agents in the provinces had been cemented. Their judicial and administrative duties had been defined by innumerable statutes and proclamations as well as by the commissions themselves. It was axiomatic that the roll-call of the 'king's servants' should be consulted when appointments to the commissions were pending. One might surmise that membership of the king's affinity and of the commissions might ideally coincide. One might perhaps expect a majority of JPs to be listed on the roll-call of the affinity, but this is vastly to overestimate the crown's territorial power.

The greatest correlation between membership of the affinity and the commissions was at the highest social level. A majority of peers and knights who were members of the affinity also served as JPs in their counties. Otherwise the correspondence was less. In Suffolk, Surrey and Kent, half the members of the affinity were JPs under Wolsey; in Norfolk it was one-third. Counties where one-fifth or fewer of the affinity were named JPs included Somerset, Buckinghamshire and Oxfordshire. In the north the correspondence between the affinity and commissions was almost negligible. In Yorkshire under Wolsey (all Ridings) only 8 out of 52 sworn 'king's servants' were appointed JPs; in Northumberland the number was 3 out of 10; and in Cumberland none.[77]

If, however, the relationship between the affinity and the commissions was complex, and varied in individual counties, the traffic flow is clear where correlation of membership exists. Henry VIII augmented the ranks of his affinity by recruiting established 'men of worship' from the localities, and not vice versa. Periodically but infrequently, the crown also chose to reconstruct the commissions of the peace. Wolsey made several attempts to reconstruct certain county benches, for instance those of Kent and Gloucestershire, where the proportion as well as the number of resident JPs was reduced in favour of strategically selected 'outsiders'.[78] He deployed his power most obviously in the north, appointing JPs who were prepared to implement crown policy at the expense of local vested interests.[79]

Again, Cromwell orchestrated a significant turnover in the commissions during the 1530s, notably after the Pilgrimage of Grace. Out of a total of 547 JPs appointed in the commissions issued between 1536 and 1539, 172 (31 per cent) were completely new appointments, and it can be argued that up to 10 per cent of these new appointments can be linked specifically in some way to Cromwell's intervention.[80]

In his letters and instructions to assize judges, sheriffs, and JPs, Cromwell sought to cultivate the ethos of a crown-controlled magistracy. He issued a barrage of circulars in 1535–9 ordering the detention of dissidents, the defence of the royal supremacy, the erasure of the pope's name from mass books, the proscription of St Thomas Becket, the placing of the English Bible in parish churches, among other measures. His use of psychology was crucial. He told magistrates that they were 'specially elected and chosen' for their tasks. Letters were individually handwritten; and Cromwell invoked a two-tier method to reinforce the impact of his instructions: letters under the king's stamp were immediately followed by letters from the minister.[81]

Henry VIII's ministers placed their own 'servants' and dependants on the county benches. Among Wolsey's servants named to the commissions of the peace were Sir William Gascoigne of Cardington, Bedfordshire (treasurer of Wolsey's household 1523–9), Richard Page, Thomas Heneage, Ralph Pexsall (clerk of the Crown in chancery from 1522), Sir Thomas Tempest (comptroller of the duke of Richmond's household), Sir Christopher Conyers (Lord Conyers), Sir Thomas Denys, and William Drury.[82] Private servants nominated by Cromwell to the commissions included John Babington, John Hercy, George Lascelles, John Mering, William Godolphin, jun., John Godolphin, Richard Pollard, John Horsey, John Wadham, Nicholas Fitzjames, Thomas Horner, John Sydenham, Thomas Clerk, and William Vowell (see Appendix 1 for the full list of nominations).[83]

Lastly, Cromwell was attuned to the military potential of the king's affinity. More specifically than Wolsey he aimed to recruit to the king's affinity territorial leaders whose own servants and dependants could be transformed into the nucleus of a battle army. These objectives overlapped with the crown's use of its salaried patronage. In Tudor speech the vassals or dependants whom a landowner had the right to muster in time of war were called the 'manred', and their service lay at the heart of the quasi-feudal military 'system' of Henry VIII's reign.[84] In 1539 Cromwell drafted 'Articles for the ordering of the manred of this the king's realm and for the good advancement of justice, preservation, and maintenance of the common weal of the same'.[85] He planned three things: first, to make all paid royal officials in the counties responsible for the mustering of specified numbers of troops for the king's army as well as for the performance of their normal duties; second, to 'swear' all the important landowners in every county to be members of the king's affinity so that they would be available on demand for musters; and thirdly to select five or six 'head commissioners' in every county who were to direct both police and military functions in their localities under the crown.

This scheme was too ambitious to be implemented. The success of Henrician government in the localities should not be exaggerated. Wolsey and Cromwell aimed at centralised administration and a crown-controlled magistracy. Similar aims characterised the regimes of Charles I, James II, and William III and in each case the crown encountered stubborn resistance. In court–country relations it can be argued that the balance of power remained with local landowners until 1832. A plethora of local networks bisected central ones, and the limited extent to which Wolsey or Cromwell might purge the commissions of the peace exemplified this fact. In and after the 1520s the numbers appointed to the commissions began to swell in almost every county. The root cause of this expansion was that new appointments could not be offset by the removal of inefficient or unworthy JPs. Local power remained in the hands of the resident gentry and it was difficult to purge even serious offenders from the commissions. Cromwell recognised this problem in the 1530s, when only active opponents of the regime were purged from the benches. Passive opponents were left alone, and critics of the divorce continued to be recruited as supernumeraries at court. Despite the treason trials and *causes célèbres* of the 1530s, it was a policy of 'live and let live'. On the one hand, local magistrates feared that rebellion and social turmoil would spring from active opposition to the crown. On the other, the leaders of Henrician government recognised that good relations between court and country depended on mutual tolerance.

3. The Progresses of Henry VIII, 1509–1529

NEIL SAMMAN

The progress is recognised as an important instrument of Tudor government. By visiting the localities a monarch reinforced his authority and was presented to his subjects against a background of ceremony and ritualised splendour: the progress left a lasting impression upon contemporaries and was of great political significance. Henry VI failed to use the progress to impress his subjects and the Great Chronicle described Henry VI's progress of 1470 as 'more like a play than the showing of a Prince to win men's hearts'.[1] It is well known that Henry VII's success in consolidating the country after his victory at Bosworth was in large part due to his exhaustive round of progresses; as the king grew older and the country more stable, Henry VII travelled less far afield.[2] The peripatetic court was a feature of medieval life and the 'saddle kings' of the early medieval period, in particular, had continued their relentless journeys throughout the kingdom. The gradual trend towards a more settled court was already under way by the reign of Henry VI and it has been calculated that the king went on progress for an average of ninety days a year 'beyond his normal residences'.[3]

The development of larger and more splendid palaces in and around the capital reflected the growth of the court as an institution. Larger royal palaces were symbolic of the strength of the monarchy and further encouraged a more settled way of life. Edward IV, for example, enlarged the palace of Eltham and the great hall 'set a standard of architectural magnificence that was not easily to be surpassed' whilst Henry VII's palace of Richmond symbolised the permanence of the Tudor dynasty.[4] The same process is very much in evidence during the reign of Henry VIII, the greatest royal builder of all time, and the development of Whitehall as a power base in the 1530s encouraged the further development of the court. Thus as Eric Ives has already stressed (above, chapter 1) in many senses the link between architecture and politics is fundamental to a complete understanding of the Henrician court.[5]

As the court became more settled the progress was increasingly limited to the summer months. Although the young Prince Henry ascended to a stable and peaceful throne in 1509, the council still acknowledged the expediency of the progress and the new king embarked on several long tours during the early years of his reign. In 1510 the court travelled through Hampshire and Dorset to Corfe Castle, Southampton and Salisbury. The king stayed with several courtiers: with William Sandys at The Vyne, with Robert Knollys, a gentleman usher, at Rotherfield Grey and with Mr Fowler at Malshanger. The king's progress concluded at the end of September with jousts and tourneys at Woking.[6] In the best of medieval traditions, the Henrician progress still provided an opportunity for the redress of grievances. *The Great Chronicle* suggests that the complaints received by the king while on progress in 1510 directly resulted in the execution of Empson and Dudley. During this summer,

> the King rode in his disport into certain countries of this land, where before him and some of this council many of the commons showed grievous bills and complaints against Dudley and Empson.[7]

The following year, 1511, witnessed a very impressive progress. The year began with the birth of a male heir on the 1st January. In the event the prince only survived for seven weeks but as soon as the baby had been born Henry set out on a pilgrimage to Walsingham to give thanks for his son. In July the king and queen embarked on a splendid progress to the midlands with visits to Northampton, Leicester, Coventry and Warwick. At Nottingham the royal couple stayed at the castle, whereas at Leicester they lodged at the abbey. After this ambitious start the king's progresses, though extensive, took the court less far afield. During Wolsey's ascendancy they were confined in most years to the home counties and the south-east of England. The progress represented no homogeneous continuum but reflected the individual political and social circumstances of each year.

The most spectacular progresses were organised for diplomatic occasions: most notably the Field of Cloth of Gold, when the entire English court travelled to Guisnes, just inside the English pale, to spend two weeks in sporting competition with the French court. The Field of Cloth of Gold has been discussed extensively elsewhere and the details do not need to be rehearsed here. The joint progress with Charles V through southern England in 1522 was an extremely elaborate affair. After Charles V's entry into London the two monarchs travelled to Windsor, having stayed at Hampton Court, amidst a round of banquets, hunting expeditions and other celebrations. Henry accompanied the emperor back to Winchester before the imperial retinue boarded their ships again at Southampton.[8]

In the summer of 1519 the king embarked on a very elaborate progress designed to entertain and impress the four French 'hostages'. These four men were staying at the English court to guarantee that the French king would pay 600,000 crowns for the city of Tournai as agreed in the Treaty of London in 1518. During the progress the court stayed with Sir John Ernley, Sir Richard Corbet, Lord Bergavenny and the duke of Norfolk, and was lavishly entertained by the duke of Buckingham at Penshurst in Kent. It has been estimated that the duke spent £1500 on the king's visit to Penshurst; other calculations, however, suggest that this is somewhat exaggerated. Nevertheless the visit imposed a very heavy financial strain on Buckingham.[9] The king was content for nobles, both secular and lay, to be a part of this ostentation, only to surpass their efforts with his own entertainment. In this way the monarch's glory was both reflected and buttressed by his court. The king's authority was not undermined, provided of course that he always did one better! The queen was also involved in the festivities; she invited Henry and the hostages to her manor of Havering-atte-Bower in Essex where the progress continued, 'and for their welcoming she purveyed all things in the most liberallest manner'.[10] This included a 'sumptuous banquet' whilst the king entertained his French guests in a daily round of hunting and shooting. The climax of the progress came at Henry's manor of Newhall or Beaulieu where the king put on an impressive mask costing over £207. In these years the progress was a deliberate vehicle for conspicuous ostentation, which the king combined with other forms of spectacle to gain the maximum effect.

The period before 1530 witnessed an uneven series of progresses ranging from the grand sweep of 1526 to the almost non-existent 'progress' of 1521 when the king alternated throughout the summer between Windsor, Woking and Guildford. This raises the problem of definition; what exactly was the royal progress? The term itself has been used very loosely for the sixteenth century. At one end of the spectrum the progress describes the

elevated festivities of the Elizabethan age, whilst under the early
Tudors it has been less clearly defined. Eric Ives has already introduced us (above, pp. 20–1) to the king's extensive range of principal houses and lesser 'houses of abode'; Henry's travels round
these can be described as the movements of the itinerant court.
Where did the king's progress finish and the itinerant court
begin? Under Henry VIII the two can be easily confused and some
writers have made no real distinction.[11] Whether the king's court
was itinerant or on progress depended not only upon where the
king stayed but also on the time of year and its overall political
significance. Henry's frequent visits to Newhall were usually part
of the itinerant court, but his stay there with the French hostages
in 1519 was part of a grander progress calculated to impress.
Contemporaries used the word progress to denote the king's
movements during the summer months or 'grass season'; this was
the period between August and October when the hay was cut
and provided the best time of year for hunting, and the survival of
certain 'giests' in Henry VIII's reign make the differentiation
between the court on progress and the itinerant court clearer.

Each June the King's route for the summer was published at
court. These 'giests' (the derivation of the word seems uncertain),
detailed the king's precise location for each day and the exact
number of miles between each resting-place. They were the result
of considerable thought and calculation and the same procedure
can be traced through to Elizabeth's reign. Few such giests actually survive for the early Henrician period and the giests of 1528
reveal something of the process which established the king's
route.[12] The distance which the court intended to travel each day
varied from five to seventeen miles, the average for this progress
being nine miles. The designated amount of time for each stay
varied from one night to fifteen days. On the day of the longest
travelling distance the court was due 'to dine by the way at a place
convenient'. The giests were only prepared for the king's outward
journey and ended at Ampthill, where the court was to remain
'during the Kings pleasure'. It was very much up to Henry where
he went and how long he stayed; but he was also subject to the
petitions of those courtiers around him. When the king's plans
were finalised the actual logistical detail was based upon local
knowledge. The route was largely confined by the need for substantial accommodation for the rest of the court and surveys were
conducted in this respect. A report on Hertford Castle, for
example, listed the repairs needed before a royal visit but con-

cluded that there was convenient lodging 'against the time that the King's pleasure shall be to lodge there for any season'.[13]

The precision and detail which constituted the king's giests suggests that the Henrician progress was perhaps more developed than has hitherto been suggested. The giests were eagerly awaited and their contents quickly disseminated to the localities. Nobles unconnected with the intended progress were still appraised of the king's intentions. In June 1527, for example, Sir Arthur Darcy informed his father of the king's progress for that year; the court was due to travel through Hampshire to the bishop of Winchester's palace including a stay at The Vyne, home of Lord Sandys.[14]

Despite owning more property than any previous or subsequent monarch, Henry still enjoyed lodging with courtiers or noblemen and visits to religious houses – that is, before he dissolved the monasteries; he subsequently commandeered several favourite monasteries for use as palaces. The evidence of where the court lodged during the summer progress is not always clear. The privy seal did not always follow the king and an itinerary constructed from grants gives a misleading impression; in March 1523 the king travelled down to Portsmouth, but the privy seal was left behind at Richmond.[15] The cofferer's and comptroller's accounts, however, are an unused source and present a very detailed and accurate itinerary for the years in which they survive. The amount of time which the king spent with noblemen, courtiers, bishops and at monasteries fluctuated widely and is detailed in Table 3.1.

Table 3.1   Number of nights spent by the king outside royal palaces

	No. of nights	% of the year
1510	68	19
1511	68	19
1515	24	7
1518	58	16
1519	56	15
1520	51	14
1521	14	4
1522	100	27
1523	14	4
1525	77	21
1526	113	31
1529	35	10

The lowest figures for the years of Wolsey's ascendancy relate to 1521 and 1523, just fourteen days out of the year (or 4 per cent). This also provides some indication as to the amount of time which the court spent on progress. 1526 was the highest with a total of 113 days (or 31 per cent) followed closely by 1522 with 100 days (27 per cent). The average was 15 per cent of the year. Accurate figures can really only be obtained for the years covered by the cofferer's or comptroller's accounts and the remaining years are, at best, estimates based on the available material. These figures also include journeys by the king outside of the summer progress, but they make up a small percentage of the whole.

The most detailed description of an Henrician progress before 1530 is provided for the summer of 1526 and suggests some clue as to the nature and importance of the early Tudor progress. During this summer the king's journey encompassed seven counties, beginning in Surrey and travelling through Sussex into Hampshire and then north into Wiltshire, Berkshire, Buckinghamshire and Bedfordshire. Throughout the progress the emphasis was upon meeting the prominent men of the locality, staying with noblemen on the way and generally 'making good cheer'. When the king entered the county of Sussex in July 1526 he was met by a delegation including the earl of Arundel, Lord De La Warr, Lord Dacre of the South and Sir David Owen who escorted the king to Petworth.[16] Sir David Owen was sheriff and a prominent courtier, although then in his seventies. He had just retired as chief carver to the king after the reorganisation of the chamber in the Eltham Ordinances.[17] Thomas West, Lord De La Warr since 1525, was also close to the king; he was one of the king's sworn servants and had been deputed in December 1521 to wait on Henry in his privy chamber or wherever the king might eat.[18] The court initially resided at Petworth, a manor owned by the earl of Northumberland which nine years later was to become royal property when the tenth earl sold it to the king.[19] The earl himself was absent and the king was entertained by Northumberland's officers. Upon the King's arrival the traditional exchange of gifts was observed and the officers presented Henry with six oxen and four wethers.

The progress was organised around the hunt and it was through this medium that the king was entertained and met the prominent men of the county, liberally rewarding them with the spoils of the day's kill. Henry VIII has been criticised for his love of hunting. It is well known that he preferred the pleasures of the chase to the tedium of government, but the king's prowess did fulfil an important political role. A report by William Fitzwilliam, treasurer of the royal household, to Cardinal Wolsey in August 1526 illustrates this process and deserves to be quoted in full:

> In likewise hath resorted and come to his [the king's] said presence, sundry gentlemen of the county whom his grace hath also in such familiar and loving manner entertained and rewarded, so as I suppose verily that there is not one gentleman which hath so repaired unto his grace's presence but that hath had of this Highness as well a good word of his own mouth spoken, as venison of his gift, to their singular comfort.[20]

It was a great honour for those who were invited to share in the king's hunt and these men of the shires temporarily became the king's boon companions. The enthusiasm with which Francis I led his own hunting expeditions is testament to the importance of this royal pastime throughout Europe.[21] Henry's success is clearly illustrated by Fitzwilliam's report. The ritual of the hunt was Henry's own way of communicating with his subjects, in a form which was pleasant to both. The progress allowed a wider group of men to take part in the king's sports and as such is comparable with jousting and the king's other pastimes. Whereas jousting was open to a smaller clique based at court, a larger segment of the political nation could participate in the ritual of the hunt. As Fitzwilliam makes clear, the liberal distribution of venison at the end of the day was an honourable reward and one which played an important role in the wider system of patronage.

Wherever the king was expected, considerable sums of money were spent on preparing his accommodation, whether it was a royal residence or that of a courtier. In July 1511, for example, Henry Smith was paid for setting up a new house in Sunninghill Park before the king's arrival on his summer progress.[22] Royal manors might not be visited by the court for a considerable time and invariably they were spruced up before a royal visit. Likewise noblemen spent very large sums before the king's arrival. There was also the problem of space and the need to accommodate not only one's own household but also the king's entourage. In 1539, on a subsequent visit to Wolfhall, Seymour solved this problem by moving his servants to a refurbished barn while the king took over the house.[23]

Competition among noblemen was no less intense while the court was on progress; what might have been recreation for the king was a deadly serious business for his subjects. Courtiers vied with one another to put on the most lavish entertainment for their royal guest and whilst at Arundel in August 1526, Lord De La Warr declared that he was determined to make the king 'right greater cheer'. The king stayed with him at Halnaker, near Chichester, where De La Warr had imparked 300 acres in 1517.[24] The court moved on to Downley, another residence of the earl of Arundel, and subsequently to Warblington, home of the countess of Salisbury. The king's progress continued successfully at Winchester where he continued to have 'right great cheer' with the earl of Arundel, Lord De La Warr, Lord Lisle and the bishop of Winchester.[25] This is important since it shows that after Arundel and De La Warr had done their best to entertain the king they still continued to move with the royal progress.

The latter part of this progress is less well documented, but it is clear that the king stayed with the bishop of Salisbury at Ramsbury, Thomas Lisle at Thruxton, Sir Henry Norris at Compton, Sir Edward Seymour at Wolfhall, Sir William Compton at Compton Wynyates, Sir Edmund Bray at Edgecote and Thomas Empson at Easton Neston in September 1526.[26] The progress effectively ended at the king's manor at Ampthill where Henry resided for sixteen days before making his way back to Greenwich via the priory of Dunstable.

What was the political significance of the king's visit? Was it a sign of favour or an indication that a nobleman/courtier possessed an impressive house or that it provided a convenient resting place? In essence, all three factors at some point played a role.

The splendour and size of a courtier's house was one of the foremost considerations which determined the king's giests; the close proximity of good hunting grounds was also a crucial factor. Household officials were sent into the county of the intended progress to find suitable accommodation. The king visited Elsings, the palatial Middlesex home of Sir Thomas Lovell, more frequently than any other residence belonging to a lay subject. Foreign visitors were invariably housed at Sir Thomas Lovell's mansion. In August 1521 the French hostages were sent to Elsings, ostensibly to avoid the plague, and Queen Margaret of Scotland was entertained there in 1516.[27] As treasurer of the household, Lovell played an important role in Wolsey's administration but perhaps it was the splendour of Elsings coupled with its convenient location which most attracted the king. The inventory of 1524, produced after Lovell's death in May, is proof of the size of the mansion and indicates that a special suite of six rooms was reserved for the king and queen; an interesting anticipation of the 'prodigy houses' of the Elizabethan period. These included the queen's privy chamber and the king's withdrawing chamber.[28] This facility made a royal visit less awkward and less disruptive for the Lovell household. After Lovell's death in 1524, Henry continued to pay visits to the mansion and its new owner, Lord Ros, who was granted an earldom by the king in June 1525.

A visit by the king was also clearly a reflection of Henry's favour. From 1509 to 1530 the court stayed with 16 noblemen and with 32 courtiers. The majority of these men were royal favourites, and there was a significant overlap between those who jousted with the king and those who entertained the court during the progress: at least 12 men fit into this category. The privy chamber played an important role in court politics, but there were a number of men outside the privy chamber who were very close to the king. Of the 32 courtiers whom the king stayed with in the first 20 years of his reign, two were members of the privy chamber, Sir Nicholas Carew and Henry Norris, the rest were members of the chamber or did not hold formal positions at court. Sir Giles Capel of Berwick, in Abbess Roding, Essex, for example entertained the court in 1515, 1519 and 1527. He started giving New Year's gifts to the king in 1516 and was a regular jouster until 1520. Giles Capel was not a member of the privy chamber, nor did he hold any paid position in the chamber. He was, however, clearly in the inner circle at court and well favoured by the king.[29]

Some progresses, like that of 1526, were dominated by visits to noblemen, whilst the progress after the Field of Cloth of Gold was associated with those in the inner court circle. Hunting dominated the proceedings to the extent 'that the King turned the sport of hunting into a martyrdom'.[30] Richard Pace, writing from the court, could find little other news worthy of Wolsey's attention, but it is useful to examine in detail those who played host to the king. By 1520 Sir Edward Darrell was 54 with a long career of loyal service to the king and queen; he had served as a knight of the body to the king early in the reign and since 1517 had held the office of vice-chamberlain to the queen. Henry Norris of Yattendon was close to the king, a gentleman of the privy chamber, and was to achieve prominence later in the decade as groom of the stool. Less information survives for Sir Edmund Tame, who had built a 'fair mansion' at Fairford and was sworn to the king's service as knight of the body.[31] The King's visit to Wolfhall in 1520 was hosted by Sir John Seymour, also a knight of the body. John Seymour did not die until 1536 but his son, Edward, was advancing rapidly in Henry's favour throughout the 1520s. Edward was sworn to the household by 1524 and was one of the rising young gentlemen of the inner court circle who had featured prominently in the jousts of December 1524. In 1525 he became master of the horse to the duke of Richmond and was to achieve prominence later in the reign as the earl of Hertford.[32] These men all owned impressive houses and it is no coincidence that they all came from the inner court circle. This also reflected the nature of this particular progress; it was a relaxed affair which the king used to unwind after the negotiations and effort of the Field of Cloth of Gold.

It was considered a great honour for a courtier or nobleman to be visited by the king and to entertain him at his house. Some men whom the king stayed with were courtiers such as Nicholas Carew, whilst others held important positions in government. The duke of Norfolk was the lord treasurer, Sir John Ernley was the attorney-general and Sir Thomas Lovell had enjoyed a notable career under the Tudors; he was treasurer of the household under both Henry VII and Henry VIII. Sir Henry Marney was chancellor of the duchy of Lancaster and at court was both vice-chamberlain and captain of the guard. In 1523 he was promoted to lord privy seal and created Baron Marney six weeks before his death. Sir John Cutte, of Horham Hall in Essex, was the under-treasurer of England. The noblemen who were honoured by the king's presence were all participants in court ceremonial and most had strong connections with the court. Lord Sandys, who was visited by the king at The Vyne in 1526, had been made lord chamberlain earlier in the same year. Thomas Manners, Lord Ros and earl of Rutland in 1525, was appointed to act as a cupbearer at court in December 1521 and jousted with the king on several occasions during the 1520s.[33] Henry visited Lord Bergavenny in Kent at Birling twice in 1513 and 1515 and at Mereworth in 1519.[34] This reflected the king's favour in the 1510s. Bergavenny received lodging and daily liveries at the court in 1519, an honour reserved only for those closest to the king. At the same time Birling was obviously one of the king's favoured manors and during Bergavenny's period of disgrace in the early 1520s, he was forced to sell the manor to Henry. Henry continued to visit the manor while under royal control, as in September 1527.[35] Bergavenny was allowed to buy back the manor in 1530.[36]

Henry rarely stayed for more than a few days with a courtier or a nobleman; five days was usually the uppermost limit, and the main reason was the lack of space. The king and his court resided for longer periods at ecclesiastical palaces and other religious houses. Monasteries featured prominently on the king's progress. They were expected to provide hospitality and during the medieval period religious institutions were the only dwellings of sufficient size and prestige to accommodate the king and his court. It has been said of Henry VII that his itinerary was 'determined by the monastic geography of England'.[37] The financial crisis of 1433–4 had forced the court of Henry VI to spend over four months at the monastery of Bury St Edmunds.[38] On occasions Henry VIII was likewise driven to take refuge at monasteries but the reason was usually Henry's fear of the plague. In 1518, for example, the court was forced to spend more than three weeks at the abbey of Abingdon during the Easter festivities.

In more auspicious times the king's stay was more enjoyable and he frequently returned to some of his favourite monasteries. The Benedictine abbey of Reading was held high in the king's regard and in 1518, Pace reported to Wolsey that the abbot 'hath made to the [king's] grace and all his servants good cheer'.[39] There was also a certain personal element and several abbots participated in court ceremony. The abbot of Reading, for example, possessed a house in London and exchanged New Year's gifts with the king.[40] The court did not stay at the abbey of St Albans until Wolsey became abbot in 1521, and thereafter became a frequent visitor. During the king's progresses further afield he was often entertained at monasteries. The best example of this was in 1510 when the court stayed at ten monasteries during the course of the progress. Certain monasteries were favoured by the king and he paid frequent return visits, for example, to Woburn Abbey and the priory of Dunstable.

The king often stayed at episcopal residences. Bishops owned a number of impressive palaces and manors. By the late 1520s the archbishop of Canterbury owned 21 houses and it is only in recent years that the splendour of his greatest palace at Otford has been appreciated by architectural historians.[41] The king stayed at episcopal palaces because they were large and could accommodate the court. When the king travelled to Dover in 1520 and 1522 he stayed at the episcopal palaces of Otford, Charing, Canterbury and Rochester. Bishops Waltham, owned by Richard Fox, bishop of Winchester, was one of the king's favourite residences and he stayed there whenever he travelled down to Winchester. The king stayed with Wolsey, or at one of his residences, every year from 1515 to 1529, with the exception of 1519.

Between 1513 and 1522 the king stayed at Lambeth Palace, the London home of the archbishop of Canterbury, whenever business necessitated a visit to the capital. During these years Henry was without a suitable London residence; a large part of the palace of Westminster had been destroyed by fire in 1512 and the palace of Bridewell was not completed until 1522. Lambeth Palace was ideally situated just across the Thames from the palace of Westminster. In 1514 the court spent approximately 34 days at Lambeth from 28 January until 3 March. This proved, however, to be an exceptional year and during the parliament of 1515 the court remained at Greenwich. When Henry made his two appearances in Star Chamber in October 1519 he lodged at Lambeth Palace and paid a further two visits in November and December of that year.[42]

The reception of the king and his entourage by the host – whether nobleman, abbot or city corporation – was the occasion for elaborate ceremony and display. Some entries were obviously more spectacular than others, especially if a political point was being made, as in York in 1541, but whenever the king entered a town a grand reception was laid on for the royal party.[43] This elevated the king's journeys to the south coast, in particular to Dover, Southampton and Portsmouth, into grand progresses. All royal entries were based around a common ritual. The king and his entourage were received by the mayor and other civic dignitaries outside the town and the two parties merged to form a procession which culminated at the cathedral or principal church. After making an offering at the church the king was escorted to his lodging and the ritualised exchange of gifts took place. If the entry was of sufficient importance a range of pageants was devised; as in Charles V's entry to London, but pageants were not the exclusive preserve of state occasions. When the court was received by the city of Coventry in 1511 the king and queen were entertained by three pageants

> one at Jordan well, with the 9 orders of Angels. Another at Broadgate with divers beautifull Damsels. Another at the Cross Cheeping with a goodly Stage Play, and so passed forth and were received into the Priory.[44]

The ritualised exchange of gifts was a feature of every progress; not only when visiting courtiers and noblemen, but also when the host was a city corporation. The size of the gift was frequently a reflection of the political situation and during the king's visit to York in 1541, for example, Henry was presented with 20 fat oxen and 100 fat mutton.[45] When Catherine of Aragon first visited Canterbury she was presented with a silver gilt cup and £13 in new gold nobles. Gifts were also presented to other important visitors: Wolsey was given twelve capons during his visit to Canterbury in 1527 and the king's servants likewise were rewarded. In 1513 whilst on the way to France, the lord steward, the lord chamberlain and Thomas Boleyn all received presents while staying at the Checker Inn at Canterbury.[46]

Whenever the king visited a county there was inevitably an element of ceremony and display, as corporation records show, even if this was not the primary objective. Even when on pilgrimage, Henry was met by all the leading gentlemen of the shire. In October 1522, Sir Thomas Le Strange, of Hunstanton Hall in Norfolk, travelled from Castle Acre to Raynham in order to meet the king on his way to the shrine at Walsingham.[47] It is interesting to note that when Henry travelled to Dover for the Field of Cloth of Gold he took a different route on his return, via Sittingbourne, as opposed to Maidstone and Charing on his outward journey. The mere sight of the royal entourage making its way through the countryside was impressive, even if the court was moving from one royal manor to another.

Disease, or rather Henry's fear of disease, was one of the biggest influences upon the court's itinerary and the progress. In most years it was the plague which affected the court, but in 1517 and 1528 the sweating sickness had a very profound effect. During the autumn of 1517 and summer of 1528 the king made every effort to isolate himself from his subjects, contrary to the very spirit of the progress. In both years the king disbanded his household and fled with a few attendants from one refuge to another in search of safety. The giests were completely abandoned and during the most intense periods of the epidemic state business came to a complete halt. In less dramatic years the plague still continued to shape the king's itinerary to a lesser or greater extent and only 1516 and 1519 appear relatively unaffected by the threat of disease. The plague drove the king to Woodstock at Easter 1518, whilst in November 1522 the court was forced to remain at Hertford Castle because the plague was particularly bad at Greenwich, Richmond and the environs of London.[48] The king's giests were refined each year to take account of the presence of the plague or other infectious diseases. During the progress of

1526, the king prolonged his stay at Winchester because of the plague, and new giests were prepared. In any account of the royal progress disease was a prominent feature, and it helps to explain the uneven nature of the progresses from one year to another during the first half of Henry VIII's reign.

During the ascendancy of Cardinal Wolsey, Henry's progresses were modified, in certain years, by the needs of state and the need for the king and his chief minister to remain in close contact. In 1521, whilst Wolsey was away in France, the king stayed close to the capital and as soon as Wolsey returned in December 1521 Henry travelled down to meet him at Bletchingley in Surrey. On occasions the king would interrupt his progress to visit Wolsey if he felt matters were of sufficient importance. After receiving a letter from Wolsey in June 1518, the king decided that it was imperative that he discuss the matter with his chief minister. Accordingly, Richard Pace wrote to Wolsey informing him that Henry would visit Greenwich on the following Friday (2nd July) where they could meet. The king stayed at Greenwich for three days before returning to Woodstock on 5th July.[49]

Although during the progress Henry devoted much of his time to hunting and meeting the prominent men of the shire, Wolsey continued to keep him closely informed of events on the foreign stage. Wolsey continued to visit the court even when Henry was on his progress and king and minister met every summer on a number of occasions.[50] Wolsey's access to the king was even taken into account when the royal giests were being prepared, as in June 1528. Special amendments were made to the king's proposed itinerary so that Wolsey could visit the court at Ampthill (over 40 miles from London) after the law term had finished.[51] In some years Wolsey travelled a considerable distance to see the king. 1516 marked one of Henry's longest progresses during Wolsey's ascendancy, when the court went as far as Corfe Castle, over 100 miles from London. During the two months that the king was away, Wolsey visited the court twice. At the end of July, Wolsey and the bishop of Durham visited the king at Farnham Castle in Surrey and in September Wolsey travelled to the court at Donnington in Berkshire, whilst Henry was being entertained by the duke of Suffolk. The cardinal did not just visit Henry and then return to London, but spent at least a week close to the court. As Chancellor, he sealed grants on the 10th September at Newbury and at Donnington on the 16th.[52] Wolsey stayed close to the court in August 1519 and whilst the king stayed with John

Courthope at Whiligh in Sussex Francis Pawne was paid 3s.4d. by the king for riding '4 miles beyond Mr Sackville's place to my lord cardinal'.[53]

Whilst the king went on progress Wolsey used his palaces of Hampton Court by the Thames and The More in Hertfordshire to cut down the distance between himself and the court. When Henry was on progress south of London Wolsey resided at Hampton Court and conversely he moved to The More when the king travelled north or west of London. In 1523, for example, whilst the king remained south of London during his progress, Wolsey stayed at Hampton Court. When Henry moved to Henley on the 17th September and then on to the Benedictine abbey of Abingdon and his palace at Woodstock, Wolsey travelled north to The More. The cardinal only remained at his manor for a couple of weeks before having to return to Westminster for the start of the law term. The same occurred in 1526. Wolsey stayed at Hampton Court throughout August whilst the king went on his grand progress through Sussex and then he moved to The More in September when the king travelled north to Langley and eventually to Stony Stratford and his manor at Ampthill.[54] This changes our perception of Wolsey's role in politics. The cardinal did not remain aloof from the court, but moved from one residence to another in order to ease the communication between himself and the king.

The progresses of Henry VIII are part of that transitional period between the typical 'medieval' style progress, designed to consolidate the realm, and the pleasure progresses and spectacular entertainments which characterised Elizabeth's reign. One can make a general distinction between progresses to towns earlier in the reign as in 1510, 1511 and 1516, and the greater emphasis on courtiers and noblemen from 1519 onwards; 1526 was the greatest manifestation of this. Whilst Henry VIII's progresses lacked the sophistication and elaborate devices of Elizabeth I, nevertheless the progress performed a similar role under both monarchs. The Tudors are celebrated for strengthening the links between the centre and the localities, a lesson in politics which the Stuarts were to ignore at their peril, and the successful use of the progress was an inherent feature of this. Whilst the court was a 'point of contact' between the monarch and the political nation, the court on progress was a logical extension of this.

4. War and Public Finance

RICHARD HOYLE

The public finance of the reign of Henry VIII has remained a Cinderella subject amongst historians. The ugly sisters, the Tudor Revolution in government and the politics of the Henrician court have been to the ball not once but many times. Public finance awaits not only its prince, but its fairy carriage too.

The historical interest of the way in which the state was funded can never be doubted, but for a connected history of Henrician finance, one must turn to the work of F.C. Dietz, published as long ago as 1921. Whilst much criticised by more recent historians, Dietz's study has yet to be superseded.[1] Much of the preliminary work from which a new account could be written was undertaken by Geoffrey Elton and his students but whilst we have learnt a great deal from them about the institutions of government finance, we have been told much less about revenue and expenditure. In part this reflects documentary losses, especially from the first part of the reign, and this in turn means that Henrician public finance is often without precise figures and sometimes with no figures at all. In this essay only a small range of questions can be posed and preliminary answers offered. What were the king's ordinary revenues? Were they adequate to support the normal purposes of government? How did Henry finance his wars and with what consequences, both for public finance and the larger economic history of state and society?

I

By convention, both contemporary and modern, the king's revenues are divided into his ordinary or regular income and his extraordinary. The ordinary consisted of two major sources of revenue, the crown lands and customs. The profits of wardship ought to be accounted a branch of the landed income, but the problems of identifying wards and selling wardships encouraged the decision to hive off this work either to dedicated officers (the masters of wards) or, after 1540, to the court of Wards and Liveries. The crown also had a range of smaller incomes, which, like the profits of wardship, fluctuated from year to year. These included the profits of the mint and the common law courts, the income of vacant bishoprics, the fee for the restoration of the temporalities of bishoprics and abbacies. A final category of income which we shall have occasion to notice was the pension paid to English kings by successive French monarchs.

Extraordinary revenue was that granted to the king for extraordinary ends. It was therefore irregular in a different fashion to 'irregular' or 'casual' ordinary income. Broadly speaking, it was taxation for war, whether of the laity or the clergy, either granted by parliament or convocation, or demanded under the prerogative. (It has been argued in recent years that taxation came to be used to finance the ordinary functions of government, a matter to which we shall return.[2]) The crown's income and expenditure was therefore liable to rise and fall in accordance with the requirements of foreign policy.[3]

The crown's ordinary income was largely inflexible and if prone to alteration, was more likely to fall than rise. Partly this was a matter of administrative efficiency. Henry VII's success in raising crown revenue is conventionally attributed to his close attention to detail and his reliance on the chamber as a financial centre, but it also reflects fortuitous circumstances outside his control. At the end of his life Henry possessed the largest estate of any medieval monarch: land had become concentrated in his hands through the death of royal relatives and the attainder of subjects. No endowment had been made for Prince Henry. It was in these special circumstances that Henry's landed revenue in his last years amounted to £40,000–42,000.[4]

Land moved out of the royal estate as royal servants were rewarded or lands were hived off for children's endowments or wives' jointures. Likewise land entered the estate especially as the result of attainder. The result was that the land revenue cannot have remained static over long periods but must have been subject to sudden rises and falls. The reversal of Henry VII's attainders and grants of lands, annuities and offices cost Henry VIII around £15,000 from his landed income between his accession and 1515. To this needs to be added the loss of the estates of Elizabeth of York, Henry VII's queen, which were recycled as a jointure for Catherine of Aragon.[5] When the king's bastard son was created duke of Richmond in 1525, he was granted lands worth £4000.[6] Likewise when Anne Boleyn was established as marchioness of Pembroke in 1532 she was granted lands with a rental value of £5000, some of which was simply subtracted from Catherine of Aragon's jointure.[7] There were other occasions when lands flowed into the estate on a large scale: in 1521 on the attainder of the duke of Buckingham, on the fall of Wolsey, after the Pilgrimage of Grace and finally on the attainder of the marquess of Exeter in 1538. No one has ever calculated how much came to the crown in this way, but such windfalls probably did little to increase income in the long term. As on the attainder of the duke of Buckingham in 1521, the advantage was lost quickly as the lands were granted out.[8]

Even in the absence of firm figures, it is most unlikely that Henry VIII's income from his estates exceeded his father's until after 1536. The revenues from customs also tended to decline gently over the first part of the reign. Duties were levied on the export of wool and cloth and on the import of such commodities as wine. There was, over the course of the early sixteenth century, a switch from the export of raw wool to the export of cloth, a change which because of the differential custom rates, was highly disadvantageous to the crown. Income from customs varied substantially from year to year, from more than £50,000 in both 1519 and 1520 to £44,000 in 1521 but only £30,000 in 1522 (a year of disruption in trade caused by war). But the overall trend was downwards, from around £40,000–42,000 in 1500–20 to an average of £35,305 in 1521–9 and £32,000 in 1530–8.[9]

Henry VII's annual income in 1502–5 is conventionally calculated at around £105,000:[10] his son may have had only £80,000–90,000 from his own resources in the 1520s and early 1530s. However, the question is whether these incomes sufficed to support the crown. In the absence of accounts, it is hard to discover whether Henry stretched income by resorting to debt: certainly he never declared himself bankrupt. The most powerful evidence for financial problems comes from the signs of retrenchment on two occasions following on periods of war, 1515 and 1525, and the apparently straitened circumstances of the early 1530s. The act of resumption of 1515 was part of a wider scheme of economies in government expenditure which included savings amongst the garrison at Tournai, the abolition of the king's spears and the collection of debts. The act itself merely cancelled grants of offices, annuities and custom licences (although, inevitably, most of those who lost concessions ultimately regained them). In all, the crown probably gained £5000–10,000.[11] The need for economy was certainly the stimulus for the reforms of the household in 1525 (which resulted in the Eltham Ordinance of January 1526) although the degree to which savings were sought in the other departments of government has never been elucidated.[12]

It is hard to state with confidence whether or not the government was in financial difficulties in the early 1530s. There had been no recent war (although there is a case to be made that government was fearful of a war launched by the emperor to lend support to the diplomacy of the divorce). In this context it is significant that in the negotiations with convocation in January 1531 over the terms of the clerical subsidy, the idea was floated by the crown that the whole tax should become due on the outbreak of any war.[13] In early 1534 the idea was canvassed that in the event of war, half the estates of the church should be confiscate for the duration of hostilities.[14] David Starkey has suggested that money was extremely tight at this time on the slight grounds that the French pension 'was the foundation of royal finance in these years'.[15] As David Potter shows elsewhere in this volume (chapter 5), after 1525 the pension was worth £21,316 annually or perhaps a fifth or sixth of overall income.[16] Certainly the instructions sent to Sir Francis Bryan, then ambassador in France, in June 1531, lend some support to Starkey's suggestion.[17] The French had suggested that Francis I's own needs required him to delay the payment of 100,000 crowns from the sum due the following November.[18] Henry, caught between his need for the money and his fear that the French might unilaterally withhold the sum rather than defer it, instructed his emissaries to explain why the money was so necessary. It was required for the refurbishment of the navy, the repairing of coastal fortifications (perhaps Dover is meant), and the strengthening of fortifications on the Scottish border. Lastly it was needed to maintain 'our estimation and reputation in such men's minds as esteeming us not to be furnished sufficiently and plenteously would percase take the more courage to do us displeasure' suggesting that Henry felt that the lack of money at home was affecting the very image of the monarchy.

There are other clues which may imply a deficit in revenue. John Guy has read the praemunire manoeuvres of 1530–1 (which resulted in the grant by the two convocations of clerical subsidies totalling £118,840 to be paid over five years, and a number of private compositions) as being a convoluted means of securing a grant of taxation, but this has been doubted by G.W. Bernard.[19] There was a concern to compel noblemen to compound for their debts with the crown.[20] And there was an unsuccessful attempt to secure a subsidy in the parliament of 1532 when the need to refortify the northern border and refurbish the harbour at Dover was particularly stressed.[21]

This echoes the justifications which Bryan was told to retail to the French in the previous year. Hence if there was a shortfall in revenue, it is as likely to have come from a heightened (but presently unquantifiable) expenditure on military matters, the navy and fortifications as from any decline in income (although as we saw earlier, income is likely to have gradually declined until after 1536). It tends to be overlooked that 1532–5 did see warfare in two theatres, on the Anglo-Scottish borders in 1532–3 and in Ireland in 1534 and later. As both these wars were sizeable charges on income at a time when the government had lost the French pension (last paid in November 1533), it would not be surprising if 1534 and 1535 saw some financial stringency. This may help to explain why in these years the crown was actively striving to extend its revenue base. In the six or seven years before 1540, the crown's income was greatly increased, partly by tapping new sources (the church) and partly by securing a reaffirmation of its prerogative right of wardship. Whilst it is impossible to apportion responsibility for the design and execution of these projects (for simple lack of evidence), there are hints that the campaigns against the church and for the recovery of feudal rights predate Cromwell's rise.

First and foremost of the augmentations of royal finance was the church. The crown had always drawn some revenue from it, but in a characteristically irregular fashion, from fees for the restoration of temporalities to bishops and abbots, the income of episcopal estates during vacancies and from the clerical subsidy (which was originally a tax on behalf of the pope). Annates, a fee due to the papacy on the provision (appointment) of clergy to a small number of benefices for which its sanction was required, were stopped by statute in 1533. In its place, a statute of 1534 established the principle of taking a fine when any cleric took up a new benefice at a rate of one year's assessed value of the benefice: this was First Fruits. At the same time a continuing clerical tax was instituted charged at the rate of a tenth of the assessed valuation of the benefice ('Tenths') on a new assessment made in 1535 (the *Valor Ecclesiasticus*). Individually the taxes were harsh, together they were oppressive. Clerical protests forced concessions: by an amending statute of 1536, the first fruit paid by a new incumbent was to be the assessed value of the tenement less the tenth due the same year and the fellows of the colleges of Oxford, Cambridge, Eton and Winchester were granted exemption. But whilst this removed one source of complaint, it did little to assuage the general clerical anger seen in the Pilgrimage of Grace. Archbishop Lee of York went so far as to blame the whole rising on opposition to the clerical tenth.[22] Nor did the establishment of an annual tax on the clergy mean that the crown had foregone the clerical subsidy of which there were grants in 1540, 1543 and 1545. It is a telling comment on their political impotence that after 1536 the clerical estate became the most heavily taxed segment of English society.[23]

Of greater financial significance was the dissolution of the monasteries.[24] The dissolution statute of 1536 permitted the suppression of all monastic houses with an income of less than £200 unless licensed to continue. Their lands were to pass to the king: their inmates were either to transfer to larger houses or have faculties to become secular clergy. Only heads of houses were to be pensioned. The act did not touch the larger houses but was dressed in the guise of a reform of the morally corrupt and spiritually disreputable section of monasticism. A few additional houses were confiscated in 1537 for the alleged treason of their members in the Pilgrimage of Grace. But from late 1537, and especially from mid 1538, the crown used roving commissioners to secure 'voluntary' surrenders from the heads and inmates of houses of their lands and goods. The last surrender, of Waltham Abbey, Essex, was taken on 23 March 1540. The legality of such surrenders was open to doubt: a statute of 1539 guaranteed the crown's title.

I have suggested elsewhere that the dissolution has an obscure parliamentary prehistory stretching back to 1529. A proposal to confiscate church lands and annex ecclesiastical jurisdiction to the crown in the name of reform circulated that year and whilst the major elements appear not to have been taken further, some minor proposals formed the basis of the anti-clerical status of that session. The matter then appears to have lain undisturbed until the first parliamentary session of 1534. Amongst proposals drafted for this was one that if war be declared against England at the pope's instigation, the king was to have half the church's temporal lands towards the cost of defence. In advance of the second session of 1534, an elaborate scheme ('Things to be moved for the king's highness for an increase and augmentation to be had for maintenance of his most royal estate and for the defence of the realm, and necessary to be provided for taking away the excess which is the great cause of the abuses in the church') was drafted for legislation.[25] Whether this document was sanctioned by the king cannot be established, but it did originate within government. Whilst a number of its suggestions never passed into legislation, others suggested there, notably the outline of the Statute of First Fruits and Tenths and the lay subsidy, found their consummation in statute. The 'Things to be moved ...' proposed the confiscation of all ecclesiastical estates, episcopal and monastic, out of which the crown was to support the whole clergy with annual salaries ranging from 2000 marks for the archbishop of Canterbury to £5 for monastic novices and nuns. It cannot be conclusively proved that this particular section of 'Things to be moved ...' was put to either house of parliament, but there are hints that it was. It was on the failure of these plans that a new strategy for achieving a dissolution was adopted. Cromwell's visitation of the monasteries as vicegerent in 1535 was certainly intended to effect reforms in both spiritual and personal conduct, but it was the cover under which an enormous quantity of bogus information about monastic immorality and lax living was gathered. When the commons were confronted with this in 1536, it persuaded them to grant a partial dissolution as a monastic reform. But this was not a trick which could be brought off twice. The main phase of the dissolution, 1538–9, was carried through by administrative fiat and only retrospectively (and obliquely) approved by parliament.

If the laity were disappointed that the dissolution produced few public benefits (the loss of monastic hospitality bothered some contemporaries greatly), it nevertheless had the great virtue of filling the royal coffers at little cost to them. The only financial innovation of these years which did fall upon the laity was the extension of wardship.

The right to wardship (which was shared by the crown with many private landowners) was a profitable archaism. If a man who held land by a military tenure, that is by an obligation to undertake military service for his lord, died leaving an heir within age who was therefore deemed incapable of undertaking military service, then the body of the heir and his lands came into the hands of the lord. The lord could keep the lands in his own hands or could sell the wardship back to the family or a third party. The owner of the wardship also controlled the marriage of the ward. Hence the right to wardship could be highly lucrative. It was also (with obvious good reason) evaded by transferring property to feoffees to uses who would hold the land until after the heir inherited or came of age.

Uses clearly cost the crown a great deal of revenue, but so long as their validity was recognised by the law there was little which could be done.[26] As early as 1526 the council decided on the rigorous prosecution of evasions of royal rights. In 1529 an agreement between the crown and a number of peers, which was intended to result in legislation, conceded the legality of the use but gave the crown the right to a third of any ward's land settled on feoffees. The other concessions made show how the crown was willing to trade its acceptance of the use for a modest increase in its rights. Nothing was done about passing this agreement into law until the parliamentary session of 1532 when it met with much opposition in the commons and was quietly dropped.

The king then abandoned legislation by compromise and adopted a new strategy using the will of Lord Dacre of the South as a test case. In January 1534 a Kent jury found that the will had been made with the intent to defraud the king of his rights. When Dacre's feoffees appealed against this verdict in Chancery, a special hearing of the issues by the judges found, after an intervention by the king himself, that the use was illegal and the Dacre will invalid. This left the way open for the crown to reclaim wardship but also brought into question a century or more of land titles. A statute of 1536 (the Statute of Uses) legalised uses whilst preserving the whole range of the crown's feudal rights.

Nonetheless, individual families would only occasionally suffer the misfortune of a wardship (although for those who did, wardship could be a financial disaster). The laity therefore escaped lightly in the reconstruction of Henrician finance, the more so because there was no extension of regular taxation over the laity in the way there was over the clergy. The view of a number of historians that the subsidy statutes of 1534 and 1540 saw the extension of taxation to cover the ordinary costs of the crown is erroneous. It rests on a characterisation of the 1530s as a decade without extraordinary expenditure. An analysis of the financial materials shows that military expenditure was running at a higher level than might at first be supposed. In fact £175,000 was paid for troops and ordnance through the office of First Fruits and Tenths between 1 January 1535 and December 1540.[27] The subsidy of 1534 was intended as a retrospective grant to cover the costs of the Anglo-Scottish war of 1532–3 (which had been concluded before the making of the grant), the repression of Kildare's revolt in Ireland, and the construction of fortifications and the building of a new harbour at Dover. The taxation of the laity remained an extraordinary levy, closely tied to the financing of military expenditure (if not always active war).[28]

Lay taxation was not an augmentation of the regular revenues. The other new areas of royal income probably doubled revenue. Over the six years 1535–40 Sir John Gostwick, treasurer of First Fruits and Tenths, received £90,069 from first fruits and £156,252 from tenths, say £42,000 annually.[29] The rewards of wardship were by comparison paltry, the average for the eight years within the decade 1541–51 for which accounts survive being only £9004.[30] The new income derived from the smaller monastic houses was less impressive than might be expected. On the basis of the figures collected in the *Valor Ecclesiasticus*, the income of all monasteries was in the region of £162,000 gross; after the deduction of expenses, officer's fees and other charges, £136,000.[31] Nothing like this accrued to the crown. In the year ending at Michaelmas 1537, the court of Augmentations had from its receivers £27,732, to which can be added £6987 for the sale of church goods and £5948 for fines for the continuance of monasteries. The following year, 1538–9, receipts from the receivers were slightly smaller at £24,223, and the sale of church goods came to £3214. The conclusion seems to be that the dissolution of the smaller houses was worth about £25,000 in rent net of charges paid out locally. (The receipts for fines on leases were always small.) The dissolution of the larger houses was compromised by the need to honour their grants of cheap leases and annuities and the obligation to pay pensions to the ex-religious. In 1551 monastic pensions still cost £42,877.[32] Hence the full theoretical value of the monasteries could not be realised in the short term as may be seen from the next Augmentations account. This covers four continuous years, Michaelmas 1539–43, the first two of which are those in which monastic revenue was probably at its highest whilst in the last two it was already diminishing. The total receipt for rents and one or two other items over the four years was £177,806, suggesting that at its peak the dissolution might have been worth a little less than £50,000 annually in rent.[33]

This conceals another dimension of royal finance in these years. Henry started offering monastic lands for sale the moment he received them, selling lands with a value at sale of £29,848 in 1537–8 and £80,622 in 1538–9. In the four years 1539–43 he sold lands at an average rate of £66,000 annually.[34] This was not a total loss to the royal revenue. Sales at the time were made with a reserved rent of a tenth of the rent previously due. They were also sold by military tenure making the purchasers liable to wardship in the future. And there was a countervailing influx of purchased lands into the crown estates.[35] Nonetheless, it may be seen how quickly the process began of running down assets to fund present expenditure. This was not simply a case of the royal playboy being flash with his cash. Sizeable sums were delivered to the royal coffers: Augmentations transferred around £150,000 back to the reserves in 1537–43 and Gostwick a further £59,140 (although he also had £130,712 out of reserves).[36] And whilst Henry began to build in an expansive fashion in these years, Augmentations and First Fruits were also funding a considerable volume of military expenditure. We have already seen how Gostwick paid out £175,000 for the transport of soldiers, ordnance and other costs between 1535 and 1540. In 1540 Augmentations spent about £23,000 on broadly military causes, notably fortifications at Calais and along the southern English Coast.[37]

In our present state of knowledge it is hard to be certain exactly how the royal finances worked in these years. But the general conclusion must be that the middle-aged Henry VIII had at his disposal a much greater income than either the young king or his father. This was drawn almost entirely from the church, from clerical taxation and from monastic disendowment. Clerical taxation would continue so long as the statute remained in force but the monasteries could only be dissolved once. Their lands therefore needed conserving, but this was the Age of Plunder. In a mere seven years Henry not only threw away the advantage which the dissolution had given the crown but also undermined the future basis of royal finance.

II

Establishing how Henry VIII financed his wars is none too easy. The problem is that war was funded largely out of central reserves or coffers, money held by the king under his own control in the privy chamber. Surplus balances creamed off the Exchequer and the revenue courts were held there on deposit. We sometimes see the money being salted away and released, but if accounts were kept of the coffers, they do not survive until after 1542.[38] Hence we can never know whether the surviving evidence describes all the deposits and withdrawals out of the king's private treasury. Nor can we discover how much was in the coffers at any given moment. Put in modern terms, we have some paying-in books for a deposit account, some requests for money to be transferred to a current account, but we may not have them all; and we entirely lack bank statements.

An estimate of the cost of war between 1509 and 1515 can be established from the payment books of John Heron, treasurer of the Chamber. In 1512 he paid out a total of £181,468 to military ends, £682,322 and 10,040 crowns in 1513, and £92,000 in 1514, making a little under £960,000 over three years. By contrast, in 1509–11 he had spent only £4515 on military expenditures.[39] Heron's own abstract of disbursements shows that he spent £173,058 between May 1509 and 1 November 1512 on the costs of war.[40] Some sums were drawn from elsewhere: Sir Thomas Wyndham had £16,500 for naval expenses direct from the customs of Southampton.[41] And these calculations may overestimate actual expenditure, for usually we cannot tell whether any unspent balances were returned to the Chamber.[42]

Expenditure on war in 1512–14 came to around a million pounds. There is no satisfactory explanation as to where these enormous sums were found. Around a third was drawn from taxation. Lay taxation between 1512 and 1517 (three fifteenths and four subsidies) raised around £260,000, much of which was only received after the cessation of hostilities.[43] Clerical subsidies granted in 1512 and 1515–16 probably brought in about £74,000, making the total yield from taxation about £334,000.[44] As it happened, £488,894 was paid out by the Chamber in June 1513 alone.[45] Henry was extremely liquid, but where this money came from remains a mystery. One possible explanation would be that it was drawn from reserves accumulated by Henry VII. The late B.P. Wolffe took some trouble to dismiss the Baconian tradition that Henry was supremely rich at the end of his reign, showing that the Chamber contained only small sums after his death.[46] Instead he supposed that the war was funded out of taxation supplemented by forced loans. But, as we have seen, taxation revenue fell far short and there is little evidence for forced loans: certainly none were asked in London. There is evidence that individual peers were approached but no number of forced loans could have bridged the gap between £0.33m and £1m. A solution to this problem comes from David Starkey's discovery that Henry VII kept the major reserves not in the Chamber but in a treasury controlled by the groom of the stool.[47] We have no evidence whatsoever as to what was held there, but in the light of the figures for expenditure after 1512, it seems an inescapable conclusion that very large sums had indeed been accumulated by Henry VII and were frittered away on his son's first war.

The financing and costs of warfare in 1522–3 contains as many if not more puzzles. The problem again is that we have only a part of the evidence. The king certainly had reserves on which he could draw, but the war was apparently funded out of treasuries controlled by Sir Henry Wyatt and Edmund Peckham which were stocked with taxation revenues. We also have to postulate the existence of an additional treasury, controlled by Wyatt, into which the lay subsidy granted in 1523 was paid, but for which no accounts survive.[48]

The political background to the financing of the war is familiar enough. In the spring and summer of 1522 the government launched an unparalleled survey into individual wealth and military capacity, the returns of which are collectively known as the Military Surveys.[49] Armed with this information the crown demanded loans of all those valued at £20 or more in goods or lands at a rate of 10 per cent. Those worth £300 or more paid 13.3 per cent and the very wealthy with £1000 or more at a rate to be negotiated with the commissioners. Then, in a second round of loans during 1523, all those worth £5 or more in goods were required to lend at a rate of 10 per cent of valuation. Altogether the loans taken of the laity were worth about £212,000 (see Table 4.2). Similar loans were also demanded of the clergy which yielded about £62,000.

Here it is necessary to recap on ground already covered by John Guy (above, chapter 2). In the parliament which convened in April 1523, Wolsey sought a grant at a rate of 4s. in the pound (20 per cent) on both goods and lands which, it was calculated, would raise £800,000. It has been argued that this was merely a negotiating ploy and the real objective was to secure a grant of 2s. in the pound, but this need not be so. The king did finally secure his grant of 2s. in the pound, payable in halves in early 1524 and 1525 with two additional subsidies charged on richer taxpayers due in 1526 and 1527. At the same time he also had a grant from Southern Convocation of a clerical subsidy of £120,000 payable over five years on the basis of a new valuation of benefices (the first since 1291). A further attempt to raise money in the spring of 1525 (in the hope of exploiting the French defeat at Pavia) by demanding an Amicable Grant of 4s. in the pound (20 per cent) or more of the 1522 valuation collapsed when the royal will faded in the face of public objections and civil unrest.[50]

The achievements of these years must never be denied: but they were insufficient. The broad balance sheet, so far as it can be ascertained, can be found in Table 4.1. Several cautions must be borne in mind when using this table. There are obvious gaps: there may also be some less easily detected overlaps. It has been assumed that the disbursements in Peckham's summary accounts for 1 June 1521–5 June 1524 are distinct from those contained in the book of Chamber payments which ends on 1 January 1523.[51] It also needs to be remembered that the receipts do not include all receipts of extraordinary income, only those within the period of the account, and that the figures for the subsidy are for payments into the Exchequer. It may therefore be helpful to give estimates of the value of the extraordinary receipts of these years (Table 4.2).

There is a chance that Table 4.1 will be overturned by the discovery of new materials. That danger apart, it may be seen that the war of 1522–3 was almost entirely funded out of extraordinary income. Whilst Wyatt had £49,000 out of the coffers on 7 August and 22 October 1523, he had earlier, on 8 June, paid into them £30,000 of loan money.[52] The implication seems to be that the sums held as a cash reserve were relatively small and nothing on the scale of those expended in 1512–14. And unless fresh evidence is discovered of new disbursements on a considerable scale, it may be seen how little was spent on war. Total expenditure appears not to have exceeded £400,000 (Table 4.3). The account of Sir John Daunce, treasurer of war, for March 1522–November 1527 amounts only to £100,094.[53] Table 4.2 shows that the value of the extraordinary revenues may have reached £550,000, but this is misleading in two important respects. In the first place, the lay and clerical loans ought to have been repaid out of the lay and clerical subsidies. This was a promise made when the loans were sought and reiterated by Wolsey as the subsidy bill passed through the commons.[54] As it was, the failure to secure a grant of 4s. in the pound made this impossible, for a subsidy of that size was required

Table 4.1   Cost of war 1522–1524

		Receipts (£)	Expenditure (£)
John Mucklow, treasurer of the Chamber, and Edmund Peckham, 1 June 1521–1 June 1523[a]		NI	46,999
Disbursements from the Chamber 1 June 1523–1 June 1524[b]		NI	NI
Edmund Peckham's treasury, 1 June 1521–15 June 1524[c]	opening balance	7,849	payments for war expenses 123,325
	clerical loan	65,801	balance at 15 June 1524 7,467
	loan of nobility	43,147	130,792
	clerical subsidy (pt)	13,995	
		130,792	
Sir Henry Wyatt's loan treasury, 29 Sept. 1522–28 Feb. 1525[d]	receipts from loans	161,279	payments for war expenses 193,711
	transfer from king's reserves	49,000	transfer to king's reserves 30,000
	from Peckham	5,800	223,711
		216,079	
Sir Henry Wyatt's subsidy treasury[e]	anticipation of the subsidy	15,943	NI
	balance of the first subsidy	57,850	
	second subsidy	66,464	
	third and fourth subsidies	15,261	
		155,518	

NI = No Information. All figures in Tables 4.1–4.4 have been rounded to the nearest pound.

[a] Calculated from *LP*, III (ii) no. 2750: expenditure is for military activity only.

[b] No accounts survive: postulated on the assumption that the accounts following are not for the Chamber but a separate fund.

[c] *LP* IV (i) no. 417; (iii) app. 37. These are summary accounts which refer to the same fund, but they cannot be reconciled in detail. The transfer to Wyatt in October 1523 of £5800 may be a closing balance as the fund was wound down.

[d] *LP*, IV (i) no. 214.

[e] No accounts survive. For the existence of this treasury see text, note 48. The figures presented are for gross receipts at the Exchequer taken from R.S. Schofield, 'Parliamentary Lay Taxation', Table 40, part b.

Table 4.2   Estimated value of extraordinary income, 1522–1527

	(£)	(£)
Loans from laity:[a]		
First loan paid to Wyatt	104,286	
Second loan paid to Wyatt	59,993	
Noble loans paid to Wyatt	11,160	
Lay loans paid to Peckham	9,657	
Loan of city of London paid to Peckham	20,000	
Loan of staple of Calais paid to Peckham	6,500	
Total		211,596
Loans from clergy (south province):[b]		
Bishops and prelates	38,567	
Clergy	17,683	
Total		56,252
Loans from clergy (north province):[c]		
Paid to abbot of St Mary's York		6,002
Lay subsidy granted 1523:[d]		
Yield of all four subsidies		155,518
Clerical subsidy granted 1523:[e]		
Southern province	120,000	
Northern province		
Total		120,000
Total		549,368

[a] *LP*, IV (i) no. 214; (iii) app. 37.
[b] *LP*, IV (iii) app. 37.
[c] E101/58/7 (badly abstracted in *LP*, IV (i) no. 2216).
[d] Schofield, 'Parliamentary Lay Taxation', Table 40, part b (gross receipts at the Exchequer).
[e] Dietz, *English Public Finance* (1st edn) p. 227: I am unable to find a figure for the northern province.

to repay the loans *and* finance a further season's campaign. In fact the taxation granted in 1523 barely sufficed to satisfy the debts contracted in 1522–3. Secondly, not all this money was available to the crown at a single moment. By late 1523 the crown had only small balances in hand. Money was drawn from the coffers to allow the troops to be paid in November. The subsidy was anticipated (that is richer taxpayers were asked to pay early) but even so the crown had only the promise of £44,500 coming in before the end

Table 4.3   Expenditure on war, 1539–1552

	Expenditure in the reign of Henry VIII (£)	Expenditure in the reign of Edward VI (£)	Total (£)
French wars: siege of Boulogne, fortification of Boulogne and other French towns, 1 January 1544–1 May 1550	1,013,026	329,527	1,342,552
Costs of fortification and garrison at Calais and Guisnes, 30 Sept. 1538–31 July 1552	276,766	94,664	371,430
Cost of war against Scotland, 9 Sept. 1542–1 May 1550	350,243	603,873	954,116
'Sea charges during the wars'	265,024	213,838	478,862
Journey to Landrecies in aid of the emperor, 1544	36,500		36,500
Fortifications in England and wages of garrisons, 1 March 1539–29 Sept. 1552	203,206	87,457	290,663
Repression of rebellions, 1549		27,330	27,330
Total	2,144,765	1,356,688	3,501,453

All figures are rounded to the nearest pound. There are minor discrepancies between the totals presented here and those in the printed text.

Source: SP10/15 no. 11, printed in abstract in C.S. Knighton (ed.), Calendar of State Papers, Domestic Series, of the reign of Edward VI, 1547–1553 (1992), no. 721.

of November. There was therefore a serious problem in funding the expeditionary force through the winter.[55] No campaign was launched in 1524 as much because of the problem of arranging alliances as a shortage of ready money. As most of the subsidy was received after the cessation of war and not devoted to paying off the loans, there is a genuine question as to what happened to it: [56] but even if all subsidy receipts were held as ready cash, they fell far short of what was required to launch a continental campaign in 1525. This is the background to the Amicable Grant.

These years were a high watermark in the development of the crown's money-raising techniques. Even so, the broad lesson of 1522–4 was that it was not possible to launch a protracted military campaign out of taxation revenue. The figures allow no other conclusion. A costing for the 1522 campaign came to £372,405, roughly the total raised by lay loans and subsidies in the five years 1522–7.[57] Whilst the use of prerogative loans could bring in money fairly quickly, even heavy loans failed to engender sufficient income, and loans were loans; there was the expectation that they would be repaid. The subsidy simply could not bring in money fast enough, and it is questionable whether enough domestic credit could ever have been raised to release immediate cash on the promise of repayment out of the subsidy.

How, then, was it possible for Henry VIII and his son to maintain continuous war, for long periods on two fronts, for most of the decade between 1542 and 1551?[58] It is possible to quantify the expenditure with some confidence for in the financial stocktaking of the early 1550s an elaborate digest of military expenditure before and after the king's death was compiled.[59] This is summarised in Table 4.3.

The declaration places costs in Henry VIII's lifetime at a little over £2.1m and a little under £1.4m for his son. If a narrower definition of military expenditure is adopted, which excludes the costs of fortifications and garrisons, then the costs of war 1542–7 fall to around £1.6m, say four times the cost of the campaigns of 1522–4.

It was possible to fund war on this scale only because of the most breathtaking acts of will by the king and by the subordination of every aspect of government finance to the imperative of war.[60] As the character of the war changed, there were enormous cost overruns. When in early 1544 the plan was for both Charles V and Henry to advance on Paris, Wriothesley costed a three-month campaign in France at £250,000. Of this he could only see assured receipts of £134,000, including £50,000 borrowed abroad and £40,000 from the sale of lands.[61] The balance was to be raised piecemeal where it could, including an additional £50,000 from land sales and £30,000 from the sale of monastic lead. In fact the actual costs far exceeded this if only because the war turned into one of occupation after the siege and fall of Boulogne. In November 1544 Paget estimated the charge of the first six months of 1545 at £90,000, most of which was to be spent on garrisons, but in the year following Michaelmas 1544, £560,000 was spent on war.[62] Even when there was no money, there was a refusal to acknowledge the impediment. As Wriothesley wrote to the privy council in September 1545:

> As to money, I trust you will consider what is done already. This year and last the king has spent about £1,300,000, his subsidy and benevolence ministering scant £300,000 and the lands consumed and the plate of the realm melted and coined. I lament the danger of the time to come. There is to be repaid in Flanders as much and more than all the rest … though the king might have a greater grant than the realm could bear, it would do little to the continuance of the charges this winter, most of the subsidy being paid, the revenues received before hand and more borrowed from the mint than will be repaid these four or five months … and yet you write me still, pay, pay, prepare for this and that.[63]

Wriothesley mentions the chief sources of income in his letter. Lay taxation (Table 4.4) was worth give or take £0.9m between 1542 and 1552. In the beginning there were similarities with the pattern of taxation in the 1520s; a loan in 1542 (retrospectively converted into a grant) followed by a subsidy in 1543 (to be paid in the early months of 1544, 1545 and 1546). And as in 1525, there was a demand for an emergency grant, except that in 1545 it was called a Benevolence and not an Amicable Grant. This was, in effect, a subsidy without parliamentary sanction, demanded of all those with lands of £2 or greater or goods of £3 6s. 8d. at a rate of 8d. in the pound or, if their lands or goods were worth more than £20, then at 1s. in the pound. Then the parliament of 1545 granted another subsidy over two years and two fifteenths. But this was not all: in the summer of 1546 selected richer taxpayers (with lands worth £2 or more and goods of £15 or more) were to pay a contribution at 4d. in the pound on lands or 2d. on goods, *monthly* for five months. This mixture of parliamentary and prerogative

Table 4.4   Estimated yields of taxation, 1543–1552

	(£)	(£)
Lay Subsidies:[a]		
1543 (i)	78,703	
1543 (ii)	59,181	
1543 (iii)	56,423	
1545 (i)	114,050	
1545 (ii)	100,285	
Total		408,642
Fifteenths:		
Two fifteenths granted 1545, say		59,000
Reliefs:[b]		
1549	52,278	
1550	48,337	
1551	45,887	
1552	44,550	
Total		191,052
Loan, 1542[c]		112,229
Loan, 1544[d]		12,930
Benevolence, 1545[e]		119,581
Contribution, 1546[f]		
Arrears of Henrician taxes received by Edward VI[g]		8,420
Clerical subsidies granted 1543, 1545, 1548, estimated		126,000
Total		1,037,854

[a] Gross figures drawn from Schofield, 'Parliamentary Lay Taxation', Table 40, part b.
[b] Alsop, 'Exchequer of Receipt', pp. 227–8.
[c] Dietz, *English Public Finance*, p. 165.
[d] Ibid., p. 164.
[e] Ibid., p. 165.
[f] Apparently no complete accounts survive.
[g] Alsop, 'Exchequer of Receipt', p. 225.

taxation was probably the heaviest that England had experienced since the fourteenth century. Somerset's protectorate was more modest in its taxation demands. The four reliefs (subsidies in all but name) collected in 1549–52 were worth only £191,052 and no recourse was made to prerogative taxation or loans.[64]

The clergy did not escape taxation either. Grants of clerical subsidies were made in 1543, 1545 and 1548, all of them at a rate of 6s. in the pound (the first and third payable over three years, the second over two). The total yield may be estimated at no more than £126,000.[65] The clergy also contributed to the Benevolence of 1545 and the Contribution in 1546.

Taxation, lay and clerical, contributed a little more than a quarter of the costs of war.[66] Not significantly more was found by the sale of land. It is impossible to offer an exact figure for receipts from land sold, but the sales which passed through the Court of Augmentations in the ten years ending at Michaelmas 1551 totalled £817,324. The actual figures, when allowance is made for the sale of land belonging to General Surveyors, is probably nearer £900,000.[67] This was doubtless a disappointment. In 1545 the crown amended the terms on which it sold land to stimulate demand.[68] It tried to encourage sales by enlarging the range of land available by persuading parliament to confiscate the chantries. The preamble to the chantries statute of 1545 stressed the fiscal imperative: the 1547 statute was so 'that they [the commons] might thereby be relieved of the continual charge of taxes, contributions, loans, subsidies, the which by reason of wars they were constrained in the late king['s] ... reign to abide'.[69]

But more important as a contribution to the cost of war than either taxation or land sales was debasement. Debasement was simply the reminting of the coinage with a lower precious metal content. Coin brought to the mint was replaced by coin with an equal nominal value but which contained less precious metal and more alloy. The balance of the precious metal, itself made into coin, was a profit to the crown. Debasement started in May 1544 and continued until July 1551. The precious metal content of both gold and silver coins was reduced in 1544, 1545 and 1546 and silver again in 1551. The gold content of the sovereign dropped from 23 carats 3 grains (there being 4 grains to the carat) to 20 carats, silver from 4 oz fine to 3 oz fine. The technical dimensions of debasement do not concern us here, merely its profit. The best modern estimate of the surplus of the various mints between 1544 and 1551 is £1,270,000.[70]

These estimates of the income drawn from taxation, land sales and debasement amount to about £3.2m of the £3.5m listed in Table 4.3. If the yield of the lay subsidy and fifteenths granted in 1540 is included on the grounds that they funded the erection of the domestic fortifications included in that table, then there remains an unexplained balance of around £150,000. This is a smaller sum than the actual debts carried by the government in 1552, for which we have various estimates, all of which agree on a figure in the range of £220,000–250,000 divided between money borrowed abroad and debts contracted at home.[71]

III

It would be unduly negative to say that there is little common pattern in the funding of Henry VIII's wars. The broad conclusion is surely that taxation, even heavy taxation, could not sustain war over more than one or two years. Prerogative taxation appears to be more effective than parliamentary taxation. The loans of 1522–3 and 1542 and the benevolence of 1545 generated more income in a shorter space of time than any subsidy (with the exception of the first of the pair granted in 1545).

Long periods of war therefore required the sustenance of an alternative source of income. In 1512–15 there appears to have been a substantial sum released from the royal coffers. In the 1540s the continuance of war was made possible by the king's willingness to manipulate the currency for profit and to sell the very foundations of the new solvency in crown finance achieved during the 1530s. Henry VIII's legacy to his successors as monarch lay not in the small inroads he made into French territory around Boulogne,[72] but in the damage he did to their financial interests.

Debasement destroyed the financial basis of not only the crown but all landowners. Prices set in the market place, of foodstuffs, manufactured goods and labour, quickly found a new level. Comparing prices before and after the period of monetary inflation, we find the price of foodstuffs rose by 85 per cent and labour by 50 per cent.[73] Landed income, rents and fines, remained static. Indeed, in the longer perspective debasement merely added to the late medieval problem of falling rents. Landowners were generally not successful in reversing this tendency in the early sixteenth century: but debasement then more than halved the real value of their income in the space of five years. Yet, as consumers, they were paying more in money terms for whatever they bought which, as neither the crown nor other landowners still farmed demesnes, was most staple consumables. Whether landowners recognised their dilemma is far from clear. Increases in rent took place only in the longer term due to the inflexibility of tenures and the resistance of tenants. Indeed, many landowners, including the crown, never made good their losses. Likewise debasement undermined the value of taxation revenue. The fifteenth was levied at a fixed rate whilst the individual assessments for the subsidy ceased to be real and came to be fixed according to a nominal scale of values pertaining to the pre-debasement era. Only in the customs was the government able to overcome the effects of inflation by increasing the customs rates, which it did in 1557. Strangely there was never any attempt to produce a new valuation of ecclesiastical benefices.

Inflation therefore diminished the purchasing power of the crown's landed income whilst the income itself was substantially reduced by sale. Lands to the value of £40,000–45,000 were sold between 1542 and 1552. (This figure includes the sale of chantry lands which were not a part of the royal estate in 1542.) As the remaining crown lands in 1551 were worth a little under £150,000, sales in the previous decade amounted to about a fifth of the estate as it existed after the dissolution. In the short term the crown could both sell land and see its income rise as the burden of monastic pensions diminished.[74] Happy though this might seem, it is still true that 'income from her [Elizabeth's] estates was in real terms actually lower ... than it had been for the two decades immediately before Henry VIII began his raids on the wealth of the church'.[75]

The confiscation of the monastic lands and the extension of taxation over the church promised royal affluence and fiscal independence. In the 1540s much of that promise was lost. As a consequence, what matters in English history is not the financial revolution of the 1530s (whether this is seen in terms of institutional reorganisation or the enlargement of revenue) but the dissipation of the revenue base in the 1540s. It was that decade which saw the pattern of English monarchy established for the future: relatively poor in its own resources, necessarily frugal (or prone to run into debt quickly), unable to fight foreign wars without taxation (which never covered their costs) and obliged to balance its books by sales of crown lands. This pattern was maintained until the 1620s: it was then a further decade of war, this time civil war, which led to the reconstruction of state finance after 1660.

It necessarily follows that the sale of assets and debasement in the 1540s came about through the inadequacy of taxation income. Are we therefore to suppose that the essential problem of funding war was that taxation could not effectively tap the wealth of the nation?

On the contrary, it must be recognised that war taxation in the early sixteenth century was (albeit for short periods) extremely burdensome. The government had three means of raising money by direct taxation. Each area contributed a fixed quota to the fifteenth. Contemporaries thought that it was a regressive tax which bore especially heavily on the poor. The subsidy was charged on a different section of society and at a different rate from subsidy to subsidy. The subsidy of 1543 was near universal; all those with £1 or more in goods contributed whilst that of 1545 looked for contributions from those with £5 or more in goods. Prerogative taxes and loans excluded the poor if only for ease of collection. The loans of 1522–3 were levied on those with £5 or more in goods, the benevolence of 1545 on those with £3 6s. 8d. or more. Taxpayers contributed on the valuation of either their lands or their goods but never both: they paid on whatever category brought the greater sum to the crown. By lands was meant income, the rental value of lands or fees or annuities. But goods assessments were made not on the profits of those goods but on their capital value. Modern direct taxation is based on income, but the equivalent to a sixteenth-century tax on goods would be a tax on the value of a taxpayer's house and furnishings, his family's clothes, car, money in the bank and investments and, if they owned a business, the value of the stock in shop and factory.

There are clues to suggest that the government was tender towards poorer taxpayers. In a memorandum of late 1544, it was noticed as an advantage of a benevolence that it would 'not grieve the common people'.[76] Administratively this made good sense for the majority of the subsidy was paid by a small minority of taxpayers. And there may have been a fear that persistent taxation would stir rebellion.[77] But the richest taxpayers were caught by every levy. And the demands made upon them were very harsh. In 1522–3 taxpayers assessed at £20 were expected to find 10 per cent of that in late 1522, 5 per cent in early 1524 and again in early 1525. If the Amicable Grant had been successfully implemented, they would have paid at a rate of one-eighth of their *1522* assessment. If we treat the loan as a tax, then a taxpayer with £20 in the Military Survey would have been worth only about £17 after the second subsidy, from which the Amicable Grant asked him to find £2 10s. more.

The experience of the richer taxpayers in the 1540s can be summarised in similar terms. Worth £50 in 1543, the taxpayer paid 5 per cent (£2 10s. 0d.) of his valuation in the first year of the subsidy, then $2\frac{1}{2}$ per cent in each of the following years, reducing his assessment to £45. He may also have contributed to one or more loans. In 1545 he paid 5 per cent of his assessment to the benevolence leaving him with £43. With rounding, he was then worth £40. In the summer of 1546 he may have been sufficiently unlucky to pay the contribution at 1s. 8d. in the pound (8.3 per cent), reducing his assessment to £36 17s. 0d. During the following year he also paid 1s. 4d (6.7 per cent) in the pound in each year towards the subsidy. His valuation was only about then about £32 or, with rounding, £30. Hence, in the space of five years, subsidy taxation and the benevolence had reduced the value of his goods by two-fifths. To this needs to be added the payment of loans, the fifteenth and the locally carried costs of furnishing troops or personal war service.

Sudden demands on this scale produced an immediate crisis of liquidity. Coin must always have been in relatively short supply. Challis has estimated the size of the circulating medium in 1542 at only £1.23m, or only about £1 per adult.[78] Taxpayers held little of their assets in the form of coin and so were obliged to sell assets in order to raise money. Confronted by Wolsey's demand in 1523 for a subsidy of 4s. in the pound,

> it was proved that there was not so much money, out of the king's hands, in all the realm, for the fifth part of every man's goods is not in money nor plate. For although five men were well moneyed, five thousand were not so. The gentleman of lands hath not the fifth part of their value in coin. The merchant that is rich of silk, wool, tin, cloth and such merchandise hath not the fifth part in money. The husbandman is rich in corn and cattle, yet he lacketh the same. Likewise victuallers and all other artificers be rich in household stuff and not in money.[79]

In September 1522 Tunstall reported that few clergy could find their loan until after Michaelmas when they had received and threshed their tithe corn. As the loan touched every man, none would lend. There were reports in spring of 1525 from Cambridgeshire that there was no money available: in May, in Kent, men were bringing produce to sell at market but could only sell if they accepted at half their produce's value.[80]

The markets were doubtless flooded with produce at the moment when others hoarded their coin. The result was a collapse of trade and a sharp deflation. Merchants, most of whose taxation assessment was held as circulating capital, were especially badly affected. In 1525 the duke of Suffolk persuaded the Suffolk clothiers to pay a sixth of their valuations in the Military Survey towards the Amicable Grant. The clothiers were then forced to go to their workmen and artificers and tell them that as their 'goods be taken from us', they were now unable to give them work.[81]

Such a pattern must have been repeated throughout England. Taxpayers had to sell assets to pay tax: diminished capital obliged them to cut back on their activities. The result must have been unemployment. Add to this the inevitable contraction in the home market and the dislocation in international trade which war brought and it may be seen how taxation produced an immediate depression. But one may also generalise beyond this by arguing that the diminution of mercantile capital brought about by taxation was not easily repaired. Short periods of heavy taxation, compounded by the other costs of war and trade depression, ate into capital accumulated over many years, if not decades. Add to this inflation in the 1540s, the availability of crown lands for purchase (which provided a safe haven from taxation and debasement) and it is all too easy to postulate that by the 1550s there was a severe shortage of merchant capital in England. The view of one recent historian, who exculpates government by claiming that 'the social and agrarian problems which certainly existed had nothing to do with the particular circumstances of mid-century ...'[82] could never be accepted by an economic historian who, even without knowledge of the 'mid-Tudor crisis', would expect the consequences of government policy to be dislocation, depression and unemployment.[83] War in the 1540s, prosecuted for the vainglory of monarchy, not only destroyed the future fortunes of that monarchy but rent the very fabric of society. Such are the consequences of the sport of kings.

5. Foreign Policy

DAVID POTTER

I

For the sixteenth-century, as for the medieval, sovereign, the making of foreign policy was unquestionably part of the royal prerogative. It was not susceptible to routine political controls or to popular participation. The relations between states were, strictly speaking, the relations between dynastic rulers. On the other hand, like other domains of governance, it was subject to the loose convention that the ruler act by taking the good counsel of his advisers, although a ruler with sense was able to recognise the difference between the possible and the desirable. The conduct of diplomacy and the waging of war were inseparable, the risks taken in foreign relations high and the cost of war was a fact bound to involve interests wider than those of the court and the aristocracy. These basic propositions generate most of the debate that has developed about the nature of Henry VIII's conduct of his relations with foreign powers, notably over the extent of the king's actual control of his own policy. No ruler in Henry's position could possibly manage his foreign relations alone; he was bound to take advice and it is in the nature of that advice and the extent to which the king could be manipulated that some of the main problems lie. Henry was particularly preoccupied by foreign policy and, judging by the periods of well-documented exchanges with ministers, took more interest in war and diplomacy than in most other areas. Yet in foreign relations above all, it is in the strategies and expedients devised to carry out basic objectives that the skill lies and here the evidence of the king's abilities is much more debatable.[1] From around 1512 to 1513, English diplomacy was increasingly dominated by Thomas Wolsey, who remained pre-eminent in the conduct, if not the determination, of policy until his ejection from office in 1529. Thereafter, the same problems remained but the circles within which the king sought advice were more changeable and included longer periods of intense personal involvement by the monarch.

How effectively were Henry and his main advisers informed about foreign affairs? The king's participation in diplomacy varied sharply in intensity during the reign. In the 1520s, he was kept informed largely by Wolsey. In 1528 cardinal du Bellay, the French ambassador, had at least 40 audiences with Wolsey and only one with the king. From Christmas 1535 to September 1536, Eustace Chapuys saw the king nine times and Cromwell at least twelve. Of course, decisions also depended on the quality of information received from English envoys abroad. Wolsey testily remarked that only two out of twenty items of news were likely to prove accurate. Correspondence with residents abroad was designed partly to give reasons for audience and therefore access to the foreign court. Ambassadors could then practise the arts of fine-tuned observation of demeanour and dissection of responses. Otherwise, as Jean du Bellay pointed out in 1529, they were left somewhat in the dark, especially at times of secret manoeuvres. The only other recourse was to rely on secretaries and informal agents to report tittle-tattle, comings and goings, and then sift the evidence.[2] In conducting audiences, Henry could be disconcerting and seems to have used unpredictability as a weapon; taken by Cromwell to see him at Easter 1537, Chapuys was treated to an unexpectedly vehement denunciation of the emperor, much to Cromwell's mortification. A little later, in pontificating ignorantly to Chapuys about the state of French succession law, he admitted 'that most of what he said was more for debate and to be the better informed'. The French envoy Castillon confirms that 'his language is not at all open, but ever mixing in some complaints, as is his manner of negotiating'.[3]

It is important to know something about Henry's ambassadors as a group. England had no career 'diplomatic service' at this time, though the corps of people the king employed abroad was beginning to take on some characteristics of one. It was, of course, smaller than those of the French or imperial governments. The overall numbers tell an obvious story. Of 268 distinct missions carried out by 114 individuals during Henry's reign, 75 were directed to France, 55 to Charles V as king of Castile or emperor, 42 to the ruler or regents of the Low Countries and 22 to Rome. Scotland received only 23 formal missions and there was no resident there until late in the reign, probably because of the role of the king's sister, Queen Margaret. Spain, Germany, the

Swiss, the Hanse, Scandinavia, eastern Europe and Venice received between them only 50 missions.[4] In comparison, Francis I despatched 614 separate missions confided to 315 individuals during his reign. Germany received 105 and England followed with 96, there were 88 missions to Switzerland, 56 to Charles V, 18 to Turkey, 12 to Denmark, 6 to Hungary, 5 to Poland. While Henry VIII sent 28 missions to Italy, Francis I sent 153.[5]

The embassies exchanged between England and France in the period 1475–1520, analysed in depth, may be compared to those during the reign of Henry VIII. Some interesting contrasts emerge between the French and English diplomatic staff: the proportion of clerics employed in England was higher (27.78 per cent rather than 16.36 per cent). In France, it was the middle ranking nobility who plainly dominated this and most other realms of government employment. The number of commoners was higher in England as was that of the titled nobility. In France, the latter were poorly represented.[6]

If we look at the 114 envoys despatched during Henry VIII's reign, most were ambassadors with commissions to negotiate (the true definition of ambassadors), though a number were plain envoys sent to convey messages.[7] Many were employed only once or twice. If we count those who were commissioned more than three times (57) and add the 17 others who, though only employed once or twice, clearly occupied important posts like that of resident ambassador, we have a total of 74 who may be said to constitute the core of Henry's diplomatic service. Of these, 44 were certainly laymen, 25 clerics and another 5 possibly so. When we count only those who at some stage occupied the post of resident ambassador, the proportion is much the same: 17 clerics and 28 laymen. However, when we count the most frequently employed envoys, those who carried out between 7 and 18 missions during the reign, the numbers are balanced and reflect the continuing necessity for the inclusion of civil and canon lawyers in sensitive and complex embassies. There were seven laymen in this group: Thomas Boleyn, Francis Bryan, Richard Wingfield, Richard Pace, William Paget, Edward Poynings and the German Christoff Mont – and seven clerics: William Knight (the leader, with 18 missions), Stephen Gardiner, Cuthbert Tunstall, Edmund Bonner, John Clerk, Richard Sampson and Nicholas Wotton.

The proportion of clerics employed therefore increased under Henry VIII in comparison with the earlier period, clearly so in the first half of the reign when there were Wolsey protégés who replaced some of the envoys left over from Henry VII. By the end of the 1530s attitudes were changing among those involved in diplomacy. Norfolk called for the revocation of Bonner from France in 1540, since he was the second bishop to have proved personally obnoxious to Francis I. Wallop at the same time was testy about the sending of 'these bishops' to replace Wyatt as envoys to the emperor.[8] However, in comparison with the resident envoys sent by Francis I, the number of clerics remained substantial. The equivalent key group of envoys despatched more than three times or holding resident posts yields 114 names, of whom only 21 were clerics (18.4 per cent). The French sent churchmen in substantial numbers only to Italy. Of the 25 resident embassies in England over 1515–47, only three were carried out by clerics. The French memoirist, Brantôme, could therefore find it odd that a bishop should be sent as ambassador to the court of Elizabeth.[9]

Of the 44 laymen, 16 may be considered essentially as high politicians and courtiers, drawn from the peerage and gentry, including the dukes of Norfolk and Suffolk, Thomas and George Boleyn and essentially privy chamber men such as Anthony Browne, Francis Bryan, Thomas Cheyney, Henry Knyvett and Thomas Wyatt. The advent of such men as highly trusted ambassadors is linked to the higher profile generally of gentlemen of the king's privy chamber in politics. Bonner, on being sent to France as resident in 1538, requested the sending of a gentleman of the privy chamber, Anthony Browne in the event, to be presented with him.[10] Others were essentially military men such as Edward Poynings, John Wallop and Richard Jerningham. The role of the soldier diplomat is an interesting one. Brantôme bemoaned the fact that, at a certain crucial point, France had 'no gallant man of the sword' as envoy in Rome since he might have exploited the revolt in Naples.[11] The succession of French soldier diplomats in Scotland from the 1540s is an example of this.

It has been thought that diplomacy in the early sixteenth century did not in any real sense constitute a career or part of a legally defined *corps*; envoys were chosen for specific missions according to royal favour and did not 'progress' from post to post. By the 1540s, however, it is clear that some royal councillors were specialists in diplomacy and rose in the king's estimation by their performance as envoys abroad. There were councillors who started their careers in diplomacy and went on to powerful positions at home, such as Stephen Gardiner, William Paget and

Thomas Wriothesley. Their equivalents were the du Bellay brothers in France and the Granvelles in the emperor's service. In the
court and council there was usually a small number of men who
carried out the vital secretarial work in the administration of
foreign policy. Some of them, like Richard Pace and William
Paget, had extensive experience as diplomats. Others, like Brian
Tuke, Thomas Wriothesley and William Petre, had only very
limited foreign experience. Wriothesley was trained in the service
by Cromwell and drafted many of his foreign despatches.
Cromwell, as king's secretary, is an interesting case of a leading
minister with no direct experience of diplomacy.[12]

The post of ambassador was highly honourable. The 'caressing'
of an ambassador enabled him to give useful testimony to the
magnificence of his host prince.[13] The poor treatment of an envoy
was a direct snub to 'that high and most honourable estate ...
being our ambassador there, and representing in manner our
person'.[14] Most of these envoys were in a position to shape their
reports in order to influence royal policy, but there were limits.
Most of them were primarily concerned to carry out their commissions to the letter and not to exceed instructions. Resident
ambassadors, often cut off for some time from instructions, had
the widest room for manoeuvre but sometimes did not have the
political clout of the chamber diplomats and nobles sent out on
special embassy.[15] Except for major figures such as Norfolk,
Gardiner and Paget, it is unlikely that most of them had a clear
overall picture of English diplomatic objectives. To judge by
Gardiner's memorandum to Bonner in 1538, it seems that ambassadors briefed their successors on the main issues but confined
themselves mainly to bilateral relations. Paget in fact lamented
late in the reign that, whereas the envoys of other princes routinely corresponded with each other to exchange news, English
envoys were seldom 'put in the picture' of overall strategy and
kings 'use not to communicate to their Ambassador any other
things than of the place where they serve'. Thomas Wyatt's mere
sending of a despatch for the king unsealed via Gardiner in 1538
brought a sharp reprimand from Cromwell 'for albeit his grace
doth not mistrust him, yet he noteth some folly in you to do it
without his express commandment'.[16]

It has been suggested that there was a tendency for most 'career
diplomats' in Henry VIII's reign to be rather simplistically pro-
imperial.[17] Pace, Tunstall, Gardiner and Paget are obvious examples. The reasons, in view of the evidently unsatisfactory

performance of Charles V as an ally, are difficult to plumb. In some cases it was no doubt the result of inherited prejudice in favour of the house of Burgundy, in others the result of personal experience and judgement. Gardiner's attitude was summed up in 1547: 'of France it must be taken for a rule, they be so wanton they cannot do well longer then they see how they may be scourged if they do not.'[18] All this was only partly offset by the fact that the part-time diplomats of the Chamber and the court were more likely to display a degree of francophilia.

As for the preconceptions that underlay policy, the history of English foreign policy in the sixteenth century has been bedevilled by attempts to fit it into convenient patterns and to ascribe to rulers 'grand strategies' which, while nebulous even for nineteenth-century statesmen, were out of the question for those of the Tudor period.[19] Henry VIII has been honoured as the originator of the modern navy and his reign seen as a turning point towards what under Elizabeth would be an 'oceanic strategy', the idea that, as it withdrew from a dominant military role on the European mainland, England was 'seeking a new role' in the world.[20] It will be one of the arguments here that Henry VIII and his advisers were categorically unable to formulate grand strategies like the balance of power, the formation of a 'British policy' or of an 'oceanic role' because of the fundamental uncertainties of the international system. These uncertainties dictated that, for a small country of medium power like England, the priority was to survive in the exceptionally changeable and unpredictable waters of European diplomacy in the age of the Habsburg–Valois wars.

Henry has also been seen, in the second half of his reign particularly, as envisaging a dominion of the whole British Isles by a long-term policy to subordinate Scotland. This requires some attention. War with Scotland, it was once argued, preceded that with France both in terms of chronology and of priority.[21] However, that policy was neither consistent nor sustainable. There is, of course, no doubt that Henry VIII at moments in his reign promulgated an extremely aggressive policy towards Scotland. R.G. Eaves, in his analysis of Henry's early Scottish policy, argued that, with his sister installed there and his nephew king of Scots, Henry thought it was only a matter of time until he might annex the country.[22] This seems an unrealistic proposition given the fact that Scotland still had its own monarch and was patently enmeshed in its traditional alliance with France. Pollard, followed by Wernham, saw the evolution of English policy towards Scotland in the light of strategies to dominate the whole British Isles, gradually adumbrated during the 1530s and culminating in the assumption of the crown of Ireland and the imperious moves against the Scots in 1541–2. Yet Cromwell's schemes for the ordering of the realm should not be extended into the area of foreign policy towards the Scots.

It is certainly true that, from 1542, Henry made some determined moves to control Scotland and that, after the death of James V, he began to take his supposed title to Scotland more seriously. Printed propaganda began to make the case. In reality, policy towards Scotland always seems to have shadowed the development of policy towards France. When Anglo-French relations were close, as in the late 1520s and early 1530s, a series of Anglo-Scottish treaties followed.[23] The beginning of war with France in 1543, however, drew Henry's attention elsewhere and his later Scottish policy of military intimidation lacked direction. One historian has characterised Henry's policy towards the Scots in the 1540s as a mixture of imperiousness and treachery, employing espionage and the stirring up of border trouble.[24] Another has more recently argued that Scotland remained subordinate to Henry's European policy throughout his reign. The claims to Scotland were essentially part of Henry's arsenal to render the Scots more tractable. War there was meant to head off trouble and free Henry's hand.[25] Recent research tends to confirm this. On the eve of his expedition to York to confront his nephew James V, in April 1541, Henry declared openly to the French ambassador that 'the Scots are accustomed to dance to the French tune'.[26] Even before he came to York, he had been warned that James had promised Cardinal Beaton he would not turn up. Yet Henry exposed himself to a rebuff while not even militarily prepared for more than a reconnaissance in force. The general aim seems to have been to provoke the Scots in order to derail French plans, while Henry moved steadily towards an understanding with the emperor. French policy at this time envisaged a grand alliance with Scotland, Denmark and German princes such as the duke of Cleves.[27] All the provocation imaginable, though, failed in this objective until Henry was obliged to declare war himself in November 1542, eight months before the beginning of war with France.[28]

Scotland should be seen as only one important variable in the calculation of English policy that because of its historic links with France clearly became more of a problem during Henry's reign.

Some English envoys in 1524 made the point explicitly that Scotland was for Henry the same kind of strategic problem as Italy for the emperor and France: 'For if it be so that the Emperor's Majesty hath much desire to the affairs of Italy, for his purpose the King our master hath no less cause but much more to employ his treasure and puissance in the matters of Scotland.'[29] However, Elizabeth Bonner has argued that the very nature of the Anglo-French-Scottish relationship precluded any successful English imperialism towards Scotland. Sir Thomas More had seen this clearly in 1516 when he satirised calculation of policy in the French council on what to do about the English: conclude a meaningless treaty and meanwhile keep the Scots standing by 'ready to start an invasion at a moment's notice'.[30] Henry himself could not have failed to be aware of these implications but his determination to turn his attention towards war with France in 1543–4 ruined any attempt to exploit his victory over the Scots at Solway Moss. By 1543, he was more interested in a dynastic union through his son's marriage to Mary Stuart, by the precarious policy of creating a pro-English party in Scotland.[31] Despite the great victory of 1542, Henry's later Scottish policy cannot be seen as other than an abject failure.

Henry's claim to the kingdom of France was a feature of his diplomacy that was present both at the start and the end of his reign. As Charles V, who had enough hereditary claims of his own in France and Italy, is supposed to have told Wolsey: 'The law of God bindeth every man to claim and ask his right'.[32] The negotiation of alliances directed at third parties was usually done with the ostensible purpose of bringing the enemy 'to reason' over such claims. Yet it is obvious that the claims to France were invoked and allowed to sleep as convenience dictated. As Steven Gunn has pointed out, Henry was decidedly flexible about them and treated them much as a litigious landowner might treat his rights in a lawsuit; he could assert them or not at his convenience.[33] The king's claims to France, especially in the first half of his reign, were used as often as not as negotiating devices. Henry invaded France in 1522 with no special mention of the claim but brought it forward more prominently in the campaign of 1523. He was prepared, in the discussions with the emperor to exploit Pavia in 1525, to accept Picardy and the renewal of his pension from France as his condition for peace. The two Anglo-French treaties of 1527 that created the treaty of 'Perpetual Peace' with France – significantly the first permanent Anglo-French treaty since the twelfth century – specifically ruled out any further military prosecution of English claims to the French crown.[34] While the French, for their part, affected to believe that Henry had given up his claim by the treaty of Perpetual Peace, Henry continued to glory in it, but circumstances dictated a new attitude. In 1536 Eustace Chapuys reported an exchange with Henry in which the English king had cast doubts on the emperor's claims to Burgundy on the argument that females could not inherit French duchies. The ambassador felt bound to point out that this undermined Henry's own claims in France and the king had to make a lame reply. Chapuys concluded that Henry was not prepared to spend money to conquer a kingdom that would cost even more to hold.[35]

What were the wider attitudes to Henry's claim to France? While careful to pay due respect to the king's 'just' grievances against the French in 1523, the author of the parliament speech attributed to Cromwell certainly argued against the drain of revenue in campaigns there, when the French would render a march on Paris strategically impossible – 'the winning of Thérouanne which cost his highness more than 20 such ungracious dogholes could be worth'. Yet his argument in favour of subduing Scotland: 'who that intendeth France to win with Scotland let him begin', cannot be viewed as an expression of state policy, though it certainly made some sense.[36] George Bernard has pointed out that the evidence for popular opinion on Henry's declared aim to recover his kingdom of France is contradictory. Hall, of course, chronicled a degree of enthusiastic support in the years of opportunity, 1523–4. In Kent, there were at least grumbles in 1525 that the objective of conquering France was a waste of money.[37] However, discontent was as great when, in 1528, Henry declared war on the emperor and it is amply recounted by Edward Hall. Jean du Bellay had no illusions about the popularity of Wolsey's policies, remarking that 'it is a great thing to go against nature' in trying to make the English love the king of France.[38]

Claims to France should be discussed in the context of diplomatic rhetoric generally. More's scepticism about 'treaties of universal peace' was to be shared by the poet Skelton in his *Speke, Parott* of 1521, even though Skelton was not on the 'inside' of policy-making.[39] This raises the question of how widely foreign policy was thought about and discussed in an informed way. Hall's chronicle indicates that at least the ceremonial events of diplomacy were widely known and commented on. When conferences took place and treaties were concluded, they might be kept secret or declared openly. In the former case, they might never have become public knowledge or only in general terms when they were followed at an interval by consequences such as war. This was the case in the agreements made with Charles V in 1520–1. Richard Pace wrote to Wolsey in 1521 during the Calais conference that 'the commonalty of this realm, of every sort, had no knowledge of such secret matters, as Your Grace hath treated and concluded with the Emperor'. Hall's narrative certainly confirms a simplistic general understanding.[40] Treaties were often presented as grand alliances for the defence of Christendom against the Turkish menace. This was certainly the case in 1518–21 and again in the treaties with France of 1527 and 1532 and with the emperor in 1543. Henry's ploy in that year to extract voluntary contributions for his new ally's war against the Turk was, though, predictably cold-shouldered by his subjects, who evinced little interest in the Balkan threat. For Scarisbrick, the option of a Crusade of all Christian rulers could hardly have been taken seriously.[41] Skelton, though, appealing to some extent to city opinion, seems to have taken the propaganda at its face value, while Hall wrote that Wolsey had been sent to Calais to treat for general peace 'considering the murder & effusion of Christian blood, and the trouble that might ensue to all princes of Christendom, by invasion of the great Turk'.[42]

In a sense, the problem of long-term strategies applies to the makers of policy in any age. What renders the subject historiographically difficult is precisely the personal and dynastic nature of thinking on foreign affairs. For states since the eighteenth century, a conception of long-term 'interests', however artificial or arbitrary, provided a sheet-anchor in the inevitably unpredictable problems of international negotiations. In the world of dynastic politics, such a guide was unavailable. The problem is compounded in diplomatic relations by the inevitably broad chasm between what rulers, statesmen and officials said or did and what they actually meant, since it is axiomatic that the conduct of foreign policy was riddled with deliberate deception as a tactical imperative. However, the conduct of 'permanent' diplomacy, with resident ambassadors the norm in the major states from the first quarter of the sixteenth century, generated a greater amount of information and appropriate techniques of deception.

The very fact that Henry VIII's reign lasted for nearly 40 years should introduce caution when considering any long-term pol-

icies. The basic diplomatic and military conditions which he
inherited in 1509 were profoundly different from those of the
1540s and required different responses, while the emergence of
the divorce was a major diversion of foreign policy from paths it
might otherwise have followed. Henry became king at the end of
a period when his father had dealt with a number of powers
which were being consolidated in western Europe: France, Spain,
the Netherlands and the lands of the emperor Maximilian I. His
launching of war with France in 1512 should be seen as the continuation of a long tradition in this framework. Lesser powers like
the Sforzas in Milan or the kings of Naples played their part in
this. At the end of the fifteenth century, it was the power of
France which seemed likely to establish an hegemonic position –
a 'monarchy' in the usage of the period – in western Europe,
principally as a result of French attempts at predominance in
Italy. The alliances forged opportunistically by Henry VII in 1489
with Burgundy and Ferdinand of Aragon, initially designed to
defend the independence of Brittany, formed part of an alignment that was intended to limit this French power but which, by
the unpredictable deaths of heirs, created the 'empire' of Charles
V that was to take shape between his accession in Spain in 1516
and election as emperor in 1519. This posed the possibility of a
'monarchy' of a different sort. The late fifteenth-century struggles
in Italy had also made of the Spanish kingdoms a major player on
the European scene for the first time.[43]

The first decade of Henry VIII's reign therefore saw a major
transformation of the international system which created essentially a bipolar power structure in Europe. It is important to
remember this when we consider the part played by England in
what looks simplistically like a triangular relationship but was a
decidedly irregular one. When the Anglo-imperial alliance was
falling into a state of advanced distrust in 1524, Charles V's diplomats were advising him to make peace with France rather than let
Henry VIII betray him. De Praet, an extremely hostile ambassador
in England, argued that, should the emperor not be able to hold
all his acquisitions and should God not allow him to rule
Christendom alone, the next best was to share it with France.[44]

England, though peripheral geographically and of modest
resources, was the most important of the lesser kingdoms (it
should be remembered that English diplomats always insisted in
precedence over other *reges simplices* after France).[45] However,
with a population of 2.5 million it could not for obvious reasons

carry the same weight as France with at least 16 million or the emperor's Spanish dominions with 7.5 million, not to speak of all his other resources. Henry's revenues, based mainly on his father's reinvigoration of the domain, stood at around £110,000 in the 1520s. In 1523, Francis I's ordinary revenues were 3.2 million *lt.* (around £350,000) but could be doubled in that year by extraordinary means. Charles V had revenues of around 2.25m ducats (£560,000) in the 1540s. Neither sum was adequate to defray their war expenditure.[46] Henry's revenues were limited but so were his commitments. Those of Francis I and Charles V, on the other hand, were virtually open-ended. England could not be ignored economically and the influence of London as a trading centre was growing. This meant that it could not easily stand aside from struggles for power on the European mainland and practise a policy of 'splendid isolation' *avant la lettre*. Standing aside exposed England to the conclusion of treaties between foreign powers that either neglected its interests or were dangerous.

Most western European monarchies of the sixteenth century were, in Perry Anderson's memorable phrase, 'machines built for the battlefield'. Henry VIII was no less interested than contemporary sovereigns in martial glory and he presided over some minor victories during his reign but could not compete with the other powers militarily in any way that was analogous to the power of his predecessors from the mid-fourteenth to the mid-fifteenth centuries. This is not to say that English military capabilities were negligible. English archers retained a reputation on European battlefields long after military technology had outstripped them. But Henry's celebrated early victories and gains in 1513 were 'soft' targets. In capturing Thérouanne and Tournai, Henry gained honour but only picked off isolated French outposts in Habsburg territory, easier targets that did not seriously damage French defences. Ferdinand of Aragon had already asked sardonically whether English troops would be able to compete on the European mainland and doubted whether Henry would be able to buy enough mercenaries. The French commander La Trémoïlle in 1523 was contemptuous of his English adversaries. Even within England, there was a widespread conviction by the 1530s that depopulation and decline of archery and warlike valour had left the realm dangerously exposed.[47]

The uncertainty and weakness of English military resources were addressed by the General Proscription of 1522, though this did not lead to major change. In fact, the army of invasion of 1523 was shipped to France efficiently and rapidly and, though it was unsuccessful, this was as much to do with the lateness of the season and a decline in the possibility of wars of rapid movement. The war with the Low Countries in 1528 was a non-starter because of the determinants of English economic interests in the Low Countries. However, the campaign of 1544 shows signs of new developments. Henry had wanted to attack Boulogne since the start of his reign but had been advised against it by Wolsey and others and had not found the opportunity. In 1544, he was determined to take it. His success, and even more so his ability to hold on to it precariously against French counter-attack, is a testimony both to French problems and to the improvement and modernisation of English military organisation in fortification work.[48]

The English had a rather contemptous opinion of French peasants as soldiers, a view shared by many French commentators.[49] France had a significant problem in recruiting a national infantry in the sixteenth century, notably in the failure of the Legions of 1534. It sought a solution by extensive recourse to the mercenary market. The English problem was different in that the 'quasi-feudal' method of recruitment through commissions to leading landowners that worked tolerably well into the early Tudor period was inadequate by the 1540s, partly because the crown could no longer be sure of their resources and partly because of changes in the structure of gentry households and rising costs of military equipment. Attempts at using a shire militia in 1544 were unsatisfactory.[50] Interestingly, the 1540s also saw England in the market for German mercenaries on a significant scale for the first time, though Henry's success in this was chequered and to some extent he was outwitted by the French.[51]

England, then, was not in a position to influence the main European struggles directly. The fact that Italy constituted the main theatre for military competition and 'wars of magnificence' meant that England could have only a peripheral effect, either by diversionary wars or the subsidy of campaigns fought by other powers (as in 1516 and 1527–8). In their report of January 1524, Sampson and Jerningham, in stressing the divergence of Henry's interests from those of the emperor, added that, while Italy was of no interest to Henry, the emperor 'is led and reduced to have none other thing in his mind than the affairs of Italy'.[52] At no time was this more starkly apparent than during the campaign leading up to the imperial victory at Pavia and the problem was to recur in the joint Anglo-imperial invasion of France in 1544.[53]

Ambitions in France could be prosecuted only with the active support of the Habsburgs and, preferably, some support in France itself. The problem was that neither was to be relied on, while a victory in alliance with the emperor always risked aggrandising the latter too much. Henry had learned early on the lesson that a foray into France on his part could be used by his allies for their own benefit and with little long-term advantage to himself. His envoy in the Low Countries, William Knight, reminded Wolsey of this in 1524: 'they here hath other imaginings in their minds, as the late king of Aragon by colour of helping of the king unto his right in Gascony and Guyenne, did get at the kings's charge the kingdom of Navarre.'[54]

In 1523, Henry's preference was for an attack on Boulogne but Wolsey saw no great advantage in this, persuading his master to mount a deeper thrust into French territory in order 'to annoy the common enemy ... whereby he may be driven to offer and come unto reasonable and honourable conditions'.[55] This was what the emperor and the constable of Bourbon wanted as well, for their own reasons. Lack of adequate Habsburg cooperation and sheer logistical problems in the event rendered a spectacular campaign fruitless, as the king had perceptively foreseen in a long analysis of the plan beforehand.[56] The English envoys with the emperor told him that Henry had made great sacrifices in 1523, giving up on the Boulogne project 'the winning whereof should have been inestimable commodity both for the surety and advancing of the king's pale by land, as also by the sea for the haven'.[57] By the end of 1524, the imperial ambassador was reporting the deep disillusionment of the English.[58] The limits of large-scale international military cooperation were revealed again when Henry next mounted a substantial expedition, this time to capture Boulogne and Montreuil in 1544. Despite improvements in English supply administration since the 1520s, even this plan (much more to the king's taste) revealed English dependence on imperial policies which had little to do with English interests.[59]

The elaborate diplomacy launched by Wolsey between 1518 and 1521 – the treaty of London, the Field of the Cloth of Gold and the Conferences at Calais and Bruges – was the diplomatic response to the basic problem of involvement in European affairs. Peter Gwyn has argued that for both Henry VIII and Wolsey in the 1520s, there was a predilection for some form of involvement in Europe either in peace or war. The treaty of 1518 terminated a period of two years in which England had gradually become more isolated as its partners in the League for the Defence of the Church (October 1516) fell away and came to terms with France. The treaty also restored Tournai to France in return for compensation and has been regarded as a triumph of Wolsey's diplomacy, making Henry the arbiter of Europe. Future wars between the participants were to be arbitrated by a third party such as England.

J.J.Scarisbrick has, indeed taken very seriously this period of Wolsey's mediation policy (called *vermittlungspolitik* by the German historian, Busch) as an international conflict-settling mechanism.[60] That this all gave Henry and Wolsey the balance of power in Europe presupposes that the powers took their rhetoric seriously and that English policy could be shifted altruistically. This all seems dubious but there is no doubt that it magnified the image of English policy in those years.[61] 'Conspicuous display' could take the form of elaborate diplomacy or war. The resort to war between 1522 and 1525 was another means to the same end. In this, Scarisbrick argued, the king and his cardinal were more or less agreed though they differed significantly over the details of tactics. Recent historians have tended to minimise the extent to which the 'pacific' Wolsey was constantly trying to restrain a warlike monarch. In 1523, it was Henry who was sceptical, in 1525 it was Wolsey.

From the late 1520s, English policy was to some extent hamstrung by the determination of Henry VIII to get an annulment of his marriage, the result of which was to limit his freedom of manoeuvre between Francis I and Charles V. As Jean du Bellay shrewdly observed, the divorce could only favour French interests 'and will be in the future a means to bring the King of England to his knees'. In fact, France went far to accommodate Henry's needs over the divorce in 1530–3 but naturally French interests ultimately prevailed.[62] To some extent, no amount of fancy diplomatic footwork could solve the problem since Henry VIII's matrimonial impasse was not susceptible to solution by an ally such as France.

II

Given this basic framework, how could English policy be formulated? Henry VIII and his advisers had three options: (1) total disengagement; (2) the mediation of peace between Francis I and

Charles V; (3) the choice of military alliance between Francis I and Charles V. In the 1520s, English policy swung uneasily between the last two. From the 1530s it hovered between (1) and (3), though the option of total disengagement was never an entirely serious one. As Eustace Chapuys, the imperial ambassador, put it in 1542, for England 'neutrality was neither sure nor profitable'.[63] Indeed, it is erroneous to suppose that Henry VIII was a neutral onlooker of the European scene in the 1530s. The pressures for these choices were largely outside English control. The path of peace mediation was obviously an attractive one in the 1520s. Gilbert Jacqueton argued long ago that the 'idea of mediation ... constitutes one of the plans pursued with the greatest consistency by English policy in this period'.[64] It served the purpose of increasing Henry's prestige at relatively low cost. The conferences held by Wolsey at Calais and Bruges served the purpose both of exercising influence and of enabling England to discharge its obligations honourably under the terms of the peace treaties of 1518. As he told the king, 'by your wisdom and counsel ... the greatest part of Christendom shall be ruled and governed'. It was the kind of rhetoric likely to appeal to Henry, as Chapuys must have known in 1542, when he suggested that an Anglo-imperial alliance would 'pacify' Christendom and that 'without your Majesty there can be nothing stable'. Henry would deserve to be called 'the Father of Christendom' and 'it lieth now in the King's Highness' hands to make the world new again'. For Stephen Gardiner in 1538, the aim of such negotiations was to free England from dependence on the promises of king or emperor: 'Me thinketh it were possible they should depend of us and then the King's Highness, as he is Emperor indeed in his realm, so he should in deed *imperare* through and over all and himself no further to care what other men do but all they care what he doth. In that me think were greatness.'[65]

In the course of the 1521 talks, Wolsey was able to maintain the freedom of manoeuvre that enabled Henry to opt for a Habsburg alliance in 1522. Similarly, at the end of the 1520s, with Francis I and the emperor on the road to concluding a peace treaty that paid little attention to English interests, Wolsey again had recourse to the idea of intervening as a mediator of peace. English intervention in the war against Charles V in 1528 was at best half-hearted, and a negotiated settlement under Wolsey's aegis, as in 1518, seemed an attractive proposition, though one which was overtaken by events. Offers made to the French ambassador in 1528 testify to the desperation of Wolsey that no peace be concluded without England as a 'principal contrahent'. Wolsey had hoped to be present himself at the Cambrai negotiations but was prevented by the Blackfriars court. In fact, in 1528–9, England seems to have been substantially out-manoeuvred by France, which moved towards reconciliation with the emperor, with Wolsey and Henry virtually unaware until a late stage. Offers of mediation then made were useless.[66]

The tactic of offering mediation seems to have been a consistent response of Henry and his advisers to a failure of diplomacy by other means. When Henry found his policy in northern Europe in a mess by 1534, having supported Lubeck against Christian III of Denmark and vastly overestimated the power of the Hanseatic cities, he fell back on offering arbitration between the various Protestant powers in the form of high profile embassies headed by Foxe and Bonner.[67] Faced by the menace of the Franco-imperial rapprochement of 1537–8 that led to the truce of Nice, it was instinctive for Henry, vainly in the event, to offer his mediation in order to exclude the pope from the negotiations.[68] As ever rapidly informed of the course of events by his envoy with the emperor, Thomas Wyatt, Henry responded energetically. The talks, which led from the Franco-Netherlandish truce of Bomy (16 June 1537) to the agreement of the French and the emperor at Monzon in October to hold peace talks, posed the danger that England would be excluded from the process and isolated.[69] Henry therefore sent John Dudley to join Wyatt at Barcelona, ostensibly to inform the emperor of the birth of Prince Edward but in reality to offer his mediation. Wyatt took the lead in suggesting that matters had gone so far by bilateral talks handled by French and Spanish negotiators 'that the king should be delivered of the travail of a mediator in that'. This was to draw out the emperor, who had been secretive about the talks until then. In reality, he was uncertain about the outcome of the talks that were scheduled in December near Leucate on the frontier and wanted to keep his options open.[70] He gave enough of a response for Henry to continue to pose as mediator when the Leucate conference failed. In February 1538, he was able to instruct Gardiner to go to the French king and offer 'an indifferent and friendly mediation', saying that the emperor had agreed to it. At all costs he was to dissuade Francis from allowing the pope to interfere, acutely raising the point that the pope, with his family claims to Parma and Piacenza, was in no position to gratify

Francis over Milan 'long the thing which our good brother most coveteth and wherein we would earnestly travail to satisfy his desire'.[71]

III

During his reign, Henry swung around his alliances by the treaties with Louis XII in 1514, with Charles V in 1520–2, those of 1525–7 with France, elaborated in the 'Pommeraye' treaty of June 1532, and in 1543 by the treaty of Mutual Aid with the emperor. In fact, none of these alliances should be regarded as long-term commitments. The fact that Henry was in an active alliance with the emperor or the king of France did not preclude extensive preparations for its abandonment if necessary. Examination of the documents on war and diplomacy very rapidly leads to the conclusion that opportunism was all in these affairs and that, given the uncertainty of events, the primary objective was to keep options open as long as possible.[72] In the case of 1522, the decision to opt for an alliance with the emperor was the result of a calculation over the previous two years of the likely advantage to England. The treaty of 1518 had formally committed England to an arbiter's role. In reality, even before the Field of the Cloth of Gold, at Dover in May 1520 Henry and Wolsey had concluded a secret agreement with Charles V. There seems no reason to doubt the deceptive strategy engaged in by England in 1520 but this does not necessarily imply that policy had been fixed and that the main objective was to deceive the French. It seems more satisfactory to conclude from the range of commissions drawn up for Wolsey during the 1521 Calais conferences that the aim was to keep options open for as long as possible in order to obtain the best terms.[73] The 1525 treaty of The More was preceded by months of secret negotiations between England and France, even before the battle of Pavia raised the new problem of excessive imperial power in Europe. For Wolsey, these talks had the merit of keeping options open while the outcome of the struggle for the control of Lombardy remained in doubt. For France, they were almost certainly a device to prevent any serious consideration of an English campaign to help the duke of Bourbon in Provence.[74] Henry's envoys with the emperor in Spain and with the regent in the Low Countries tended to argue, in what looks like a concerted campaign, that Charles, while personally a man of good will, was plagued by conflicting advice and interests, was concerned mainly for his own profit, had no interest in prosecuting Henry's interests and would abandon him when necessary. De Praet, Charles's ambassador in England, was in his turn vitriolic about what he saw as Henry's double-dealing with the French.[75]

It was certainly natural for outsiders to think that England had changed sides because of the fear of the emperor's preponderance after Pavia. A treatise on English policy drawn up in the mid-1530s certainly argues that Henry 'although not long before he was for his life Imperial' was both moved by his French brother's plight and, 'fearing the Emperor would grow too great', had decided to offer the support that enabled Francis to stand up to the emperor's pressure in Spain. In the 1530s, Henry was wont to raise the prospect of the emperor's pretensions to a 'monarchy' with the imperial ambassador.[76] The conclusion of the treaty of Perpetual Peace with France by Wolsey at Amiens in 1527, though battered by the Franco-imperial treaty of Cambrai in 1529, remained the sheet-anchor of English policy down to the mid-1530s and was technically in force until 1543. One fundamental problem with it, as Wolsey discovered in 1528, however, was that the idea of switching alliances could not operate smoothly since war with the Netherlands was not a practical proposition. As Steven Gunn has made clear, Wolsey attempted to use the threat of war to the Anglo-Netherlands cloth trade in order to bring Charles V to a settlement. Henry VII had done something similar in the 1490s but by 1528 the Antwerp market was not so vulnerable to English embargo, while the English cloth merchants were more dependent on it than ever.[77]

Only from the mid-1530s can England be said to have practised a policy of precarious neutrality for a while. Though W.C. Richardson argued that Henry personally supervised a policy of 'determined neutrality' distracted by Cromwell's unwise predilections for German and Baltic allies,[78] it was a situation that was clearly highly uncomfortable to the king. Henry had tried to draw Francis I into his cause but the failure of the French king to effect a settlement with the pope in Henry's interests in 1532–3 and his effective rejection of Henry's invitation to join him in breaking with Rome in 1534 brought an end to Anglo-French understanding.[79] By 1535, both Henry and Anne Boleyn were profoundly disillusioned by the French alliance. While keeping open talks with the French for an anti-imperial alliance, late in 1535 Henry instructed John Wallop in France to contact Hannart, the imperial envoy there, to propose a renewal of the old alliances with the emperor. Eustace Chapuys in England pointed out, however, that Henry, though disillusioned with the French alliance, was reluctant to abandon its certainty.[80] He told Hannart that Henry's pose of offering his alliance to the highest bidder would not work. It was notorious, he said, that Henry was in no condition to wage war against any power. Chapuys, and to a much greater degree Hannart, were hostile to the idea of dealing with a schismatic ruler. The death of Catherine in January 1536 was seized on immediately by Wallop, who argued that the main cause of friction had been removed. The English position was weak. Charles V referred Hannart to the judgement of Chapuys, whose main concern was the safety of Princess Mary.[81]

The death of Catherine did indeed open the way for more even-handed handling of the Franco-imperial struggle and early in April 1536 Chapuys made approaches to Cromwell for a renewal of the old alliance between Henry and the emperor.[82] The years between 1537 and 1542 provide a useful case-study of the predicament of English diplomacy in this unequal triangle. In the summer of 1536, entertaining the blandishments of the French and the Habsburgs, Henry was reported as having remarked in his chamber that he would stay out of the conflict as neither side had done anything for him. Subsequent events showed how uncomfortable this neutrality was. The truce of Nice was viewed by some, including Thomas Cromwell, as posing a massive threat to England. The search for allies in Germany was part of Cromwell's response, though it proved disastrous in his relations with his master.[83] The cold treatment of English envoys at the French and imperial courts throughout the next eighteen months was reported in minute detail for the scrutiny of the king and his advisers. Sir Thomas Wyatt at the imperial court could talk about Henry VIII being put 'last out at the cart's arse' by Francis I and Charles V. Yet the danger was relatively brief, as Henry may well have realised, since it depended on a Franco-imperial rapprochement that was at best fragile. By December 1539 and the emperor's visit to Paris, Wyatt first covered his options by advising 'we had rather your Majesty did yet doubt the worst, that is to say their conclusion, than to conceive uncertain hope of their disagreement'. But he concluded that 'we see not for all these entries, for all these joining of arms, knitting of crowns and such ceremonies, that they should determine to part the world between them'.[84] That England would eventually opt for war with France was not, however, inevitable but rather dependent on the exploitation of the growing rift between France and the emperor and the extraction of the best terms available from the emperor.[85]

It was essential to undermine any Franco-imperial agreement not to deal with England.[86] The despatch of the duke of Norfolk to France in February 1540 was designed precisely to explore this possibility. He was instructed to offer an alliance that would force the emperor to give up Milan and the remittance of half the French pension. Norfolk made a number of crucial reports on this mission. Firstly, he sought to confirm the view that a Franco-imperial alliance against England was unlikely: 'I am the most abused man living if these men intend any war to England for surely if the French King be not the most false man living, he loveth no prince living so much as the King's Highness.' Secondly, he decided to cover himself by saying that Francis and the emperor might be able to agree and reported that the pension offer was a non-starter. Thirdly, he made the interesting report that the French court was deeply divided about the emperor.[87] At the imperial court, the ambassador, Wyatt, went through some sharp encounters with his host over the winter of 1539–40. Wyatt had used undiplomatic language in taxing the emperor with 'ingratitude' and the emperor had been similarly heavy-handed in replying that a superior could not be ungrateful to an inferior. In February 1540, he thought the emperor might even be trying to engineer a break with England.[88] From Wyatt, Henry also learned that someone in France had disclosed a plan, first discussed at the Boulogne meeting in 1532, for England and France to carve up the Netherlands between them by military action. It took little speculation to conclude that the culprit was the French king's chief minister, Montmorency, and when Norfolk put this to Francis I he was visibly shaken. Norfolk also used the opportunity to describe Charles V's contemptuous words to the English ambassador, with the suggestion, always welcome in France, that Charles was aiming at a universal 'monarchy'.[89]

By the summer of 1540, the way was open for England to exploit the split between France and the emperor. How would it do this? The decision on war with France took shape slowly during 1541 and 1542 in response to the opportunities provided and did not constitute a clearly worked out long-term plan. Throughout 1540, John Wallop, ambassador in France, was under instructions to detach France from the emperor and work closely with Marguerite of Navarre. There was even a project raised for a new meeting of Henry and Francis at Calais.[90] Wallop, like Cromwell, continued uncertain about Franco-imperial intentions, reporting in November that 'I think the French dangerous to meddle with and little to be trusted' but the turning-point probably came with the failure of the emperor to agree an agenda for the handing over of Milan in April 1540.[91] Cromwell's fall was ostensibly welcomed both by the emperor and by France but, by the summer, it was widely rumoured that the English and the emperor would get together. The English ambassador to the emperor, Pate, wished it were true; 'it maketh them all as I am informed to tremble.'[92]

After an interval, Henry sent Stephen Gardiner to accompany the emperor on his journey from the Netherlands to the Imperial Diet over the winter of 1540–1. It was in effect Gardiner and Eustace Chapuys who established the basis for Henry's new alliance with the emperor in the spring of 1541, though no final treaty was signed until 1543. At Regensburg Gardiner began talks with the emperor's minister, Granvelle, about the possibility of an Anglo-imperial alliance. Granvelle's very tentative offers were nearly derailed by the issue of the papacy and rescued only by Gardiner's determination.[93] The English side of these talks was relatively poorly documented until the modern rediscovery of Henry's dispatch of 17 June 1541 to Gardiner and Knyvett in Germany. From this, we learn that Chapuys had brought serious proposals from Mary of Hungary for ways round the difficult problem of the pope. In private conference, Henry had declared himself ready to be the emperor's friend and to refrain from dealing with any other prince for ten months.[94] This was a serious business, since Henry was clearly laying himself open to double-dealing by the emperor, who could always use his negotiations with England to put pressure on the French. However, Henry was himself quite capable of double-dealing and he proceeded to entertain proposals from France during the following year for a closer alliance based on the marriage of his daughter Mary and the duke of Orleans.[95]

There is no clearer case of Henry keeping his options open and negotiating for the best bargain than during 1541 and 1542. In fact, the months between the summer of 1541 and the summer of 1542 saw a furious battle between the two great powers for his alliance that completely reversed the isolation of 1538–9. As Edmund Bonner put it to Granvelle, 'the king our master is as much and more solicited'. The French hoped as late as the summer of 1542 to clinch a deal including a marriage alliance, though their refusal to agree to a deal over the English pension and the dowry undermined their case. In May 1542, terms were still not agreed with the emperor. Bonner was sent to the emperor's court, now in Spain, to resume the talks started by Gardiner since the ten months were up. In England at the same time, Chapuys entered serious talks with Gardiner.[96] It took, however, until the end of the year to hammer out an acceptable treaty, to be drawn up as the Treaty of Mutual Aid of February 1543, signed in London but kept secret until Henry's decision to break openly with France in July 1543.

This was a real reversal of alliances, since it overturned the Anglo-French treaty of Perpetual Peace of 1527 and brought to an end a period of 18 years in which Henry had, by warm or cool alliance with France, kept out of major European conflicts. The process by which it was effected illustrates the fact that such changes were not the result of long-term strategic calculation but of the perception of an opportunity and the very muddled and long-winded exploitation of it.

It was not, of course, apparent to all why England should have needed to go to war in 1543. Some foreign observers thought it strange that England should embark on war with its neighbours locked in conflict. Henry, as might be expected, put forward his honour as the later justification.[97] Probably, it was the experience of being left out of the peace negotiations in 1538 and the prospect of gain that weighed most. Henry by 1541–2 had more freedom of action than he had enjoyed since 1527. In addition, his ostensible triumph against the Scots freed him from fear of invasion in that direction. That he opted for war was as much a calculation of profit and loss as anything else.

IV

Given all these short-term problems, how far did the pursuit of honour and prestige underlie the shaping of English policy? It has been the custom more recently to ascribe greater prominence to the ruler's personal pursuit of 'glory', 'honour' and 'reputation'; it seems reasonable to suppose that such categories correspond closely to the way in which the king viewed the world.[98] This approach has much to commend it and is indeed commonplace among the public declarations made by rulers of the sixteenth century.[99] It is a view very much represented in the London-based and broadly 'official' chronicle of Edward Hall, in whose eyes Henry VIII shaped his policy in defence of his honour against the slights and betrayals of other princes. There is no doubt that there was much reference to the maintenance of the king's 'honour' at every stage of diplomatic negotiation. Wolsey's staging of the Calais conferences of 1521 has been interpreted precisely in the light of the cardinal's need to maintain royal honour during a diplomatic volte-face. Walker has argued cogently that the maintenance of the king's honour was one of the motivating principles of the king's life.[100] It would, however, be artificial to make too much of this. 'Honour' was part of the normal rhetoric of exchanges between dynastic rulers. Henry's agents were urging the French on to battle in Italy in 1536 by arguing that not to do so was 'dishonourable', though of course England had an interest in stirring up trouble between Francis and Charles, as much as the French did in avoiding a pitched battle if possible.[101] While the declarations of governments in defence of their policy tell us much about propaganda, they are ultimately difficult to accommodate in a process of historical development and should not obscure the fact that war and diplomacy were dangerous and serious matters involving deceptions, gambles, great expenditure and high risk.

Just as prominent in the talk of diplomats were the ideas of 'profit', 'utility' or 'commodity'. The reality of diplomacy involved bargaining, as Peter Gwyn has pointed out.[102] At the very start of Henry's reign, his envoy to Spain reported that Ferdinand of Aragon advised keeping the peace with Louis XII as long as it 'standeth (with) the honours and profits of your highnesses'. With other rulers, there was no 'reasonable cause' to break the peace. Wolsey advanced 'le bien et prouffit de son maistre' as well as 'utilité' to Jean du Bellay in 1528.[103] Stephen Gardiner was quite clear in his diplomatic advice of 1538 that 'the chief hinderance consisteth ever in the opinion of profit, or disprofit which the French King or his council shall conceive'.[104] Edmund Bonner, no lover of the French, in 1539: 'Crafty people they are, and for their own profit and commodity desirous to have all the glory and honour too, another man bearing the charge.'[105] The maintenance of honour did not exclude a careful calculation of profit and loss in any policy. When Stephen Gardiner was negotiating the terms of the Anglo-imperial alliance in 1542, for instance, his argument that it would be costly to England in military expenditure – 'I told him he spake of much honour but it was costly' – was discounted by the imperial envoy Chapuys with the argument that the alliance would either force Francis I to back down without war or would ensure that Henry 'should not spend much more than his Majesty now spendeth in fortifications'. A war would also enable Henry to acquire honour and vast sums in the arrears of pensions that, in the English view, were owed to the king by France. Finally, 'how can worldly honour, quod he, be increased but with cost?'[106]

The role of the French pension in the calculation of Henry VIII's foreign policy was, in fact, one of the few constants and reflects the leading role played in Henry's view by Anglo-French relations. Insistence upon it was part a question of honour, part a matter of finance. Henry was never prepared to forgo it completely and it created an unusual relationship between the two powers, at once a guarantee and convenient *casus belli* should the need arise. Ostensibly a dishonourable relationship, it was made palatable for the English king by regarding it as a tribute paid for the – temporary – possession of the crown of France. Henry VIII even justified his war with the emperor to some envoys in March 1528 by arguing that he was bound to defend France 'which is our true inheritance and for which our brother and ally the French King, payeth us yearly a great pension and tribute, wherefore we of justice and equity, must maintain that land, out of which we have so fair a rent and such a profit.'[107] From the French point of view, it was part of a useful financial network that included the Swiss and a number of German princes.[108] It was also something more. President Charles Guillart, in defending the conclusion by France of the treaty of The More with England in August 1525, which reestablished the pensions, did so by arguing that they induced Henry, confronted by rebellion and factions at home, to make peace with France and force the emperor to release Francis from captivity. Certainly, Edward Hall believed that the alliance with France in 1527 was the result of 'the great pension and profit that the king of England had out of France ... and not for mere love'. For French diplomats in England, Henry was 'an old wolf'; Castillon in 1538 called him a ruler 'who loves gold and silver more than any prince I know' and 'one of the most avaricious princes in the world'.[109]

The pension from France was made up essentially of financial debts accumulated since Louis XI took on an obligation to pay

Edward IV at the rate of 50,000 *écus d'or*, or about £10,000 p.a., by the treaty of Picquigny in 1475. It was augmented by the treaty of Etaples in 1492, when Charles VIII added to it the obligations contracted by his wife, Anne of Brittany, to Henry VII under the alliance of 1489. Louis XII continued paying this until the war of 1512, by which time the debt was nearly paid off, but by the treaty of 1514 he took on new obligations, increasing the principal owed to 1 million *écus d'or sol.* The treaties of 1518 and 1525 added further sums until from 1527 Henry VIII was supposed to receive 94,736 *écus sol.* a year, worth £21,316 p.a.[110] In addition, provision was now made for a perpetual pension to be paid from Henry's death onwards, though the French refused later to accept it. The treaty of Cambrai (1529), though in some ways a serious reverse for Wolsey's diplomacy, provided for Francis I to take on Charles V's debts to England to be paid at nearly 100,000 *écus sol.* a year. Such sums were obviously a significant drain on French resources.

The French pension was an important supplement to the income of Henry VIII, especially after its augmentation in 1525. From 1475 to 1509 France had paid 1,231,250 *lt.* to England (the *livre tournois* fluctuated at around 8 to the £ sterling). From 1509 to 1547, it paid 3,651,893 (less 540,000 remitted as Henry's contribution to the common war effort in 1527–9). Henry therefore received two and a half times the amounts received by his predecessors over a comparable period. Well might Wolsey dwell in his speech on the treaty of Amiens on the treasure likely to be had from France.[111] Of course, not all this money came in gold to England; there were exchange costs and some was detached at Calais to pay for works and the garrison. However, the sums that did flow into Henry's coffers were enough to cause difficulties when the flow was cut off. What we might call the financial nexus between England and France was at its most significant between 1527 and 1533, the years of close alignment between the two powers. Payments stopped after November 1533. Henry remitted that of May 1534 to help his ally. The November 1534 term remained unpaid and it was reported that it had been reallocated to the German princes to stir up trouble for the emperor there.[112]

When talks resumed in January 1535 over the proposed marriage of Princess Elizabeth and the duke of Angoulême, and implicitly a renewal of the Anglo-French alliance, Henry's stock had dropped to the point that the French admiral Chabot could demand an end to the pensions and England's claim to France.

Henry exploded in anger and, though he hinted he would be willing to forgo the perpetual 50,000 *écus* pension, the council squashed even that in further talks. Subsequent talks at Calais in May broke down on that and similar problems.[113]

It would be a mistake to suppose that the pension ceased to be of significance for English policy, since its cessation became a major grievance. In 1538, Henry declared that he had regarded the cessation of the pension as part of his response to French demands for aid in a renewal of war with the emperor, 'a friendly abstinence of payment whereby he had liberty to use ours as his own' as long as it was not regarded as a war contribution. This was evidently a version of the acrimonious exchange between the king and the French envoy d'Inteville in September 1535, when he had come to demand a substantial contribution towards any possible French war costs and Henry had been prepared only to offer remission of the pension arrears.[114] By 1536, the treaty of Perpetual Peace had been narrowed down to mutual aid in case of invasion and this clearly did not cover the French war of aggression launched in 1536. The French for their part claimed that Henry had been asked for aid under the treaty in 1536 and had failed to give it. Henry claimed that Francis had defaulted on his obligations under both the treaty of Perpetual Peace and the treaty negotiated by the French envoy Pommeraye in 1532 for mutual aid in case of seaborne invasion. Francis had made a treaty with his enemy the pope and concluded marriage alliances with the pope's family and the king of Scots.

The issue was very much the dominant one between England and France when Gardiner drew up a memorandum on the subject in 1538. In the talks between Gardiner and Chapuys of 1542 already mentioned, the imperial ambassador claimed that the unpaid pension was cause enough for a war in which Boulogne, Ardres, Montreuil and Thérouanne could be seized as security for it.[115] The privy council drew up a case on the pension in 1542 to be put forward in France and computed the arrears alone at 880,256 *écus*, or £205,393.[116]

The negotiation of Henry VIII's last peace with France in June 1546 was as concerned with the pensions as with the possession of Boulogne and English power in Scotland. The French king refused to countenance the payment of arrears but was brought to accept the resumption of payments of virtually the entire sums as owed in 1529, to be repaid in twice yearly instalments until the discharge of the debt in 1554. Only then was Boulogne to be handed back. In fact, this was followed by the full reactivation of the pension: on 1 November 52,368 *écus sol.* were paid at Calais by Antoine Bonacorsi for a full half-term of the pensions. However, despite an expression of intention, no attempt was made to re-institute the pensions paid to prominent English courtiers that had been such a feature of the earlier part of Henry's reign.[117] That, however, was the last of such sums ever paid. The death of Henry VIII in the following January nullified some small part of the obligations and Henry II of France, who succeeded in March, was not prepared to countenance continuation of the payments. The issue remained a live one until the Anglo-French treaty of March 1550 reduced the obligations to a minimum and made provision for rapid payment of the remainder in return for the restoration of Boulogne.[118]

Henry's foreign policy had not only to be 'honourable'; it needed to show a profit. Perhaps this was what Thomas More meant when he wished for an 'honourable and profitable peace' in 1522.[119] The sums extracted from France were greater than those obtained by Edward IV and Henry VII, though much more subject to the vagaries of war. In the late 1520s, the pension was a useful way of indirectly subsidising French policy, in effect of making war on the cheap. Until 1532–3, it helped the creation of a close relationship between England and France, with pensions actually paid on both sides.

V

In addition to the large sums transferred directly to the English crown, the tradition of French payments to English councillors had begun with the pension itself in 1475. M. Giry-Deloison has analysed in detail the profile of those paid in this way.[120] Wolsey's pension had reached 7500 *lt.* before 1521, in part as compensation for the bishopric of Tournai. The payment of arrears brought this to 25,000 (12,500 *écus*) in 1525 (though, like the king's pension, much of it was remitted between 1527 and 1529). From 1527, Norfolk was raised from 875 *écus* to 3000 and Suffolk from 875 to 1500 *écus* (3000 *lt.*). In 1540, Norfolk, then on mission to France, wrote to ask whether he could expect his pension to be restored, since he could not maintain his household expenditure 'unless the pension of France shall continue'.[121] There came a point at which Henry found this all too unequal and at the Boulogne meeting of 1532 he proposed to pay pensions to the French ministers. They refused and Henry spoke to Francis saying he could no longer tolerate the pensions unless they were reciprocal. Francis, anxious to maintain the amity, agreed. The French chancellor, *grand maître* de Montmorency and admiral Chabot were each receiving 1000 *écus* as pensions from Henry VIII in that period.[122]

How far was it expected that 'pensioners' would influence English policy in French favour? Francis I openly declared that payments were made 'so that they should set their hand to maintaining the amity'.[123] Most money from France went to the king, of course, but the sums paid to individual courtiers and councillors were not negligible. Steven Gunn has shown, for instance, that Suffolk's pension constituted 17 per cent of his revenues.[124] When Wolsey made his declaration on the war with France in the Star Chamber, 13 February 1528, there were those who said 'that the French crowns, made him speak evil of the Emperor' but this was a natural cynicism.[125] Pensions were not enough to make Wolsey and courtiers like Suffolk and Norfolk automatic advocates of pro-French policies. The fact that the pensions were paid openly meant that Henry knew who was in receipt of them and could take account of this where necessary.

Factions of a 'pro-French' or 'pro-imperial' kind at Henry's court are unlikely to have been created by such payments. Charles V certainly thought they were and made similar offers. He had talked himself of compensating Wolsey for his loss of pension in the period of 1522–5 but by the 1530s he was not in a position to pay anything.[126] Thomas Cromwell, having risen to prominence after the heyday of the French pensions, did not receive one but his foreign policy attitudes were hardly shaped by this. He was tentatively offered one in 1536 though the French ambassador was anxious that he might be further offended. However, the practice of pensions had ceased two years before and no payment to him is recorded.[127] Pensions to individuals, as M. Giry-Deloison had perceptively pointed out, were the consequences not the causes of treaties.[128]

On the other hand, there is no doubt that individuals had reputations for 'pro-French' or 'pro-imperial' leanings. John Russell was described as a 'man more for our purposes than any man here' by du Bellay in 1528 while John Wallop was viewed as the reverse. Thomas More was 'a very wise man and fairly well disposed to us'. Francis Bryan's reputation was as the person who 'if his heart were opened a fleur de lys would be found therein'; 'by nature somewhat haughty, as it is thought here but you can be sure that he is a very bad Spaniard'.[129] 'Factions', when they existed, were shaped by a melange of personal affinity and interest, financial connections and religious views. Stephen Gardiner's widely known hostility to France seems to have begun as a result of the dressing-down he received from Francis I at Marseilles in November 1533. Even in the case of religion, predilections for a 'conservative' or 'radical' stance on reform did not automatically determine views on foreign policy. The duke of Norfolk was regarded as 'pro-French' by 1540 but shared the conservative views of the strikingly 'imperial' Stephen Gardiner.[130] In any case, factions had few consistent policies other than to serve the king. Suffolk spoke out against the French alliance in September 1533 while receiving his pension of 3000 *lt.* (£318) and in any case can hardly be viewed as a 'faction leader'.[131] Norfolk, known as a pro-imperialist in the 1520s, though not necessarily as a result of hostility to Wolsey's policy, emerged as pro-French by the late 1530s, possibly out of antipathy to Cromwell. The emperor was certainly convinced he had been seduced by French payments.[132] However, both Norfolk and Suffolk waged war energetically against the French when called on to do so. Anne Boleyn and her friends may have advocated a French alliance in the late 1520s and early 1530s but became disillusioned with it by 1535.

Such considerations lead to the question of how far Henry's policy was shaped by the vagaries of court faction and conspiracy. It has become customary to regard the Henrician court as more faction-ridden than those of the Valois and Habsburg. While the atmosphere of insecurity and menace was undoubtedly greater in England, as a result of the problems of succession, divorce and schism, the play of interest was not really very different from that in any other major court. One recent historian has characterised the court of Francis I as having a 'unity of outlook', in contrast to the faction-ridden English court.[133] Yet the tensions between the major courtiers in the supposedly tranquil court of France, admiral Chabot and *grand maître* de Montmorency, were often expressed in foreign policy terms, with Montmorency enjoying an unequivocally pro-imperial reputation. Chabot swung uneasily between hostility to the emperor and an erratic policy of peace with England. English envoys to Charles V in the 1520s reported the tensions between chancellor Gattinara and the Spanish grandees while the imperial court was in Spain but Charles's multiple commitments meant that he could escape any permanent faction battles.

To some extent, the historian's notion of factions in English foreign policy formation goes back to Henry's reign itself. As Eric Ives has pointed out, both Englishmen and foreigners to some extent took it for granted. The speech by president Guillart at Paris in 1525 certainly seems to convey the idea that Henry in 1512 'being led by the chiefs of the said factions, particularly the young men, he broke the alliance with France'.[134] The idea of a 'peace' and 'war' party struggling for Henry's favour in the early years has been widely canvassed. Yet it is vital to remember that much of the evidence for this comes from the reports of foreign envoys who were not always well informed but who often assumed that power lay in the hands of the English 'seigneurs'.[135] Much of what we know about Wolsey's attitudes to his rivals in the late 1520s stems from comments by the cardinal, made to the French ambassadors Jean and Guillaume du Bellay, that had ulterior motives. He constantly gave the impression that he was beleaguered and virtually the only friend France had in England. The motive was obviously to head off demands for more aid by the French.[136] Nor does the picture of Henry and Wolsey often at odds over policy any longer look convincing. Wolsey was a convenient cover for the king; he continued to ascribe the war declaration of 1528 to the cardinal until he admitted to Chapuys in 1536 that it had been his own work. Talk of dissension among Henry's advisers over foreign policy is common at most periods of the reign, certainly during the periods of close relations with France, 1518–20 and 1525–32, but again much of what we know of them is filtered through foreign ambassadors.[137] Curiously, the major overthrows of the reign, of Wolsey in 1530 and Cromwell in 1540, were extensively justified abroad as though the reactions of foreign rulers were of urgent significance in internal politics. Francis I affected to express great pleasure at the destruction of both ministers. Henry showed a certain anxiety to ensure that a respectable and credible explanation was digested.[138]

There is no doubt that most of the king's advisers had their preferences but there seems little evidence that foreign policy was ultimately made as a result of pressure on the king by factions. The major factional crises of the reign (1518, the later 1520s, 1536) do not seem significantly to have altered foreign policy. Indeed, recent studies that have emphasised the king's ultimate

control of policy and the importance of consensus among his
advisers should caution against the assumption that Henry VIII
was in some ways a uniquely manipulable ruler.[139] Only with the
fall of Cromwell in 1540 do we see a factional struggle that, in its
outcome, did affect the thrust of English policy and even then this
was not immediately apparent. Ultimately Henry, like his fellow
sovereigns, laid down the broad outlines in the light of the opportunities that existed and the dangers to be avoided.

VI

Henry's last years were spent trying to grapple with the consequences of his determination to hold on to Boulogne, the prize
that had beckoned since the early years of his reign and which he
had so narrowly managed to take in September 1544. The pro-
longation of war with France until June 1546 brought out all the
problems we have seen generated by the uncertainty of dealing
with two major powers who were likely to isolate England.
Between the Franco-imperial peace of Crépy in September 1544
and the autumn of 1545, a real Franco-imperial rapprochement
seemed possible. The attempted mediation of an Anglo-French
peace by the representatives of the Schmalkaldic League failed
largely because of this. Gardiner, still hostile to France and
favourable to the emperor, saw no way to escape the 'thraldom'
of dependence on German troops but to make peace.
Significantly for the doctrine of Henry's 'honour', he claimed it
had been satisfied by holding on to Boulogne without an ally. In
May 1546, William Paget argued for peace with France by pointing out, of the Germans, 'there is little trust to be given there,
not much to the Emperor and none to any other friend that I
can see'. Paget, no natural friend of France, consistently argued
against military adventurism in the 1540s. Rebuked by Henry for
talking too much of peace, he told his colleagues that continuing
the war was so impractical 'as my heart bleedeth in my body,
when I think of it'. He proved instrumental in pushing the
council to persuade Henry to a peace which left the king in
possession of Boulogne while recognising ultimate French rights
to it, and with a financial deal over the pension that satisfied
the French.[140]

The devices and stratagems employed by Henry, or more properly his advisers and diplomats, show some continuity with the past. However, the growth of continuous diplomacy and the emergence of the bipolar European power system, far from being a source of security for England, was a constant threat. Added to the highly unstable state of English politics internally from the 1520s onwards, foreign policy became a matter of day-to-day tactics rather than of long-term planning.

6. The Literature and Propaganda of Henry VIII's First Divorce

VIRGINIA MURPHY

By the summer of 1527 Henry VIII had decided to divorce his wife of eighteen years and to marry Anne Boleyn.[1] All had not been well in the king's marriage to Catherine of Aragon for some time while his relationship with Anne, which had begun in early 1526, was becoming increasingly serious.[2] In the spring of 1527 the king revealed that he had developed doubts – his famous 'scruple of conscience' – about the validity of his marriage to Catherine.

Rumours that the king intended to obtain an annulment were circulating by July 1527 but the precise origins of the divorce remain obscure. The first clear evidence of the direction the king's mind was moving comes from the preceding April. The aged bishop of Winchester, Richard Fox, was then quietly interviewed about the circumstances surrounding the marriage. Indications that Henry meant to act on his doubts appeared in May when Cardinal Wolsey secretly convened a court at Westminster to inquire into the validity of the royal union.

Wolsey's response to the king's announcement was to secure the opinions and support of leading scholars on the divorce. Adjourning the Westminster trial in late May, he declared that skilled canon lawyers and theologians would be consulted about the king's 'great matter'. Among those named was John Fisher, bishop of Rochester, with whom Wolsey was soon in discussion. By early June Fisher had twice written to Wolsey in general terms about the king's situation. At the beginning of July, Wolsey first broached the subject openly to Fisher, putting the king's case to the bishop and sounding out Fisher's own position. He further told Fisher how at the king's command he had commissioned certain individuals learned in the law to write their opinions;

Wolsey's and the king's efforts in this direction were so successful that the cardinal could speak of the books 'growing into vast volumes'.[3] In this way a vigorous and wide-ranging pamphlet debate on the divorce was inaugurated.

This chapter will chart the evolution of this polemical campaign from its beginnings in 1527 to the mid-1530s, when the direction of the debate was overtaken by the pressing need to justify the break with Rome. In particular, it will focus on the writings of John Fisher, the queen's leading advocate, and on a succession of king's books. Appearing from 1527 onwards, these treatises were produced on Henry's behalf and were ostensibly written by him. Most importantly, they allow us to follow the development of the king's thinking through the entire course of the controversy.

A number of central themes will be pursued here. It will be argued that from the outset the king followed a coherent policy: in contrast to the traditional interpretation, it will be shown that the king consistently attacked his marriage on grounds which disputed the pope's authority to dispense, asserting that his union contravened divine law and could in no circumstances be dispensed from. This was, moreover, a policy personally directed by the king. Henry actively commissioned treatises, supervised their preparation and contributed to their composition. In all this he was crucially supported by a term of scholars who were responsible for researching and producing the series of king's books. Finally, this chapter will consider how the treatises were actually prepared and written by this scholarly circle.

Henry's doubts were related to Catherine's previous marriage to his elder brother, Arthur. Catherine, daughter of Ferdinand and Isabella of Spain, and Arthur, heir to Henry VII, had wed in November 1501. Within five months, however, Arthur, aged only fifteen, had died. In order to maintain relations between England and Spain, Catherine was next betrothed to Arthur's younger brother, Henry. Her first marriage, however, presented difficulties for the projected union with Henry, for marriage to a brother's wife was expressly forbidden by scripture.

The biblical basis for all the church's prohibitions concerning marriage is the book of Leviticus in the Old Testament. There, not one but two passages specifically forbade marriage with a brother's wife. Leviticus 18:16 stated 'You shall not uncover the nakedness of your brother's wife; she is your brother's nakedness'. Leviticus 20:21, repeating the prohibition, added the penalty for those who transgressed the law: 'they shall be childless'. In apparent contradiction to Leviticus, however, was another passage in scripture. Deuteronomy 25:5 commanded marriage with a brother's wife when, precisely as in Henry's case, the first brother had died without children.

If her previous marriage had been consummated, it meant that Henry and Catherine were related in the first degree of affinity and a papal dispensation would be required before they could marry. (Affinity is the relationship that exists between a person and the relatives of their spouse. It is created by sexual intercourse and therefore by a marriage which has been consummated.) Although Catherine always maintained that she and Arthur had never had intercourse, the English and Spanish elected to proceed cautiously. In 1503 they requested a papal dispensation from the impediment of affinity from Pope Julius II who duly granted it. Although long delayed for diplomatic reasons, the marriage between Henry and Catherine finally took place in June 1509, shortly after his accession to the throne.

The union, however, produced only one surviving child, a daughter Mary, in 1516. All Catherine's other pregnancies had tragically ended in stillbirth or the death of the infant shortly after birth, the queen last conceiving in 1518. The king did have one son, Henry Fitzroy, born in 1519, but he was illegitimate, the issue of Henry's affair with Elizabeth Blount.

In attacking the validity of his marriage, there were two avenues the king could pursue. The first and more moderate centred on Julius's dispensation, alleging that any of a number of technical faults in the bull had rendered it invalid. This approach thus tacitly acknowledged the pope's power to dispense while maintaining that he had acted improperly when doing so. In focusing on the scriptural prohibition in Leviticus against marriage with a brother's wife, the second and potentially more radical line of attack called into question the exercise of papal authority. It charged that the king's marriage contravened a divine law which was indispensable.

Following Henry's disclosure of his doubts, in July 1527 Wolsey left England on an embassy to France, returning only in late September. In his absence the king continued their efforts to obtain learned and influential support for his position. Although Henry and Wolsey were apparently at first working together to achieve the divorce, at this time the king assumed – and never again relinquished – control of his great matter.

Historians have long debated whether Henry or his chief minister was the dominant partner, ultimately responsible for formulating policy. In contrast to the conventional image of a king who left even the management of the divorce to his minister, this chapter argues that Henry took a direct part in orchestrating the polemical campaign from the summer of 1527 when he initiated the earliest known exchange of the controversy.[4] This first encounter featured two of the most outstanding and distinguished participants in the entire debate. Ranged on the king's side was Robert Wakefield, the noted humanist and university lecturer in Hebrew at Cambridge. Against him stood his patron, John Fisher, bishop of Rochester, who would soon emerge as the queen's principal defender. A theologian of international reputation, Fisher was the single most prolific contributor to the pamphlet debate, writing seven or eight books on the divorce before his imprisonment in 1534 – so many, in fact, that he himself could not be certain of the number. Their engagement is considered in some detail because it set the agenda for much of the ensuing controversy.

The exchange consisted of a treatise by Fisher to which Robert Wakefield replied on behalf of the king. Although neither work has survived in its entirety, the general direction of their arguments can be reconstructed from extant sources.[5]

Wakefield's treatise was initially composed in the first person plural, 'in the name of the king himself' and was only later carefully altered to the anonymous third person.[6] At least initially then the work was to be seen as emanating from the king's own pen. This may not have even been the first such king's book, for Henry refers in a letter to an earlier work he called 'our book'.[7] It may actually have been this work, rather than Fisher's, which opened the exchange between him and Wakefield. These were among the first in a long succession of king's books which appeared throughout the debate in Henry's defence. Like Wakefield's, many were written in the first person plural, as if composed by the king himself. The king's books typically began with an address justifying Henry's decision to seek a divorce. This often focused on the succession and the personal and political problems raised by the absence of a male heir.

As well as lending his name to this work, Henry also contributed to its composition. The treatise was prefaced by an address from Henry to Fisher, for which the king had written the draft.[8] The address thus provides particular insight into the king's thinking at the very outset of the divorce. The tone of the address was hostile. It began by criticising Fisher for encouraging the king to remain in such an abominable and wicked marriage. In his own defence, Henry maintained that he had acted out of ignorance; at the time he had married, for example, he had not been as skilled in languages nor as familiar with scripture as he now was. Fisher was more deserving of punishment than Henry for he urged the king to persist in his fault. Henry had carefully considered the matter and closely examined sacred scripture. Mindful of his own salvation, the peace of his conscience and the security of his realm, he had decided to refer his cause to the judgement of very learned men and weighty fathers. From their councils and decrees, he would determine whether or not he should remain in his marriage.

Much of the address dwelt upon the failure of the king's marriage to have produced a son. It was essential for Henry to be lawfully married since all depended on his having a male heir. The king sought a divorce only with the greatest sorrow but was aware of the dangers if he should die without a legitimate male successor. The death of his children clearly showed that Henry's marriage was displeasing to God and was both illicit and abominable. To support this claim, the address compared the Latin and Hebrew translations. It focused on the final phrase of Leviticus 20:21, which specified the penalty for those who broke the law. In the Latin text of the Vulgate, this concluded 'he will be without children'. According to the address, however, the original (and more authoritative) Hebrew version differed significantly. The king had heard from learned men that the Hebrew instead read 'sons'. Clearly the king had no sons (or at least not any legitimate ones).

By substituting the Hebrew for the Latin, Leviticus was thus cleverly made to fit Henry's situation exactly: he had married in contravention of Leviticus and as a result had incurred the punishment threatened there, as the loss of all his sons proved. This narrow understanding of Leviticus is important for it allowed Henry to reconcile Leviticus with his own circumstances. How deeply Henry believed the views expressed in the address, especially the rewording of Leviticus, is impossible to say, although it is probable that they reflected a genuine and strongly held conviction.[9] Certainly the connection between the king's failure to have produced a surviving son and Leviticus would become a central theme of the treatises produced in his name.

As he related in the address, Henry was persuaded that his marriage was contrary to divine moral law from which neither the pope nor an angel could dispense. Both Leviticus 18:16 and 20:21 (where the injunction was repeated for greater emphasis) forbade marriage with a brother's wife. The words of John the Baptist in the New Testament confirmed the prohibition. Finally, the decrees both of popes and of general councils prohibited Christians from marrying their brother's wives. The address also considered Deuteronomy 25:5, the one exception usually allowed to Leviticus. Deuteronomy was clearly awkward for the king, and his supporters would spend considerable energy attempting to gloss it away. According to the address, Deuteronomy was no longer binding upon Christians and did not in any case apply to the same persons as did Leviticus.

The stance which Fisher took was consistent with that adopted in his discussions with Wolsey in the summer. At that time the bishop had admitted that the authorities were divided as to whether marriage with a brother's wife was prohibited by divine law. He himself believed that it was not so forbidden. The pope, moreover, could interpret ambiguous passages in scripture; that popes had on more than one occasion dispensed in such a case proved that the dispensation was within their power.

Fisher now divided divine law into four categories: papal (canon) law, which, ratified by divine authority, emanated from the popes, apostles and general councils; the law of the Gospel promulgated by Christ (the law of the New Testament); divine positive law (part of the law of Moses in the Old Testament) which lasted only until the promulgation of the Gospel; and divine moral law, which derives its force from natural law and is eternally binding. Neither the Gospel nor divine moral law prohibited union with a brother's wife. Such marriage was forbidden only by divine positive law. God would never have commanded marriage in Deuteronomy if it had been against the law of nature. The prohibition against marriage with a brother's wife was binding only to the extent that it had been renewed by the church. The pope might thus dispense in this case and once properly dispensed such a marriage could not be dissolved.[10]

Wakefield chiefly directed his treatise to a question which Fisher had posed: 'whether marriage in which the pope dispensed a man to marry his brother's wife was firm and indissoluble?'[11] Wakefield's response repeated many of the arguments made in the opening address. He challenged Fisher's four-fold division of divine law, arguing that the law of nature and the law of God in both the Old and New Testament prohibited the king's marriage to his brother's wife. The decrees of popes and general councils further confirmed Leviticus. The exception in Deuteronomy, on the other hand, was only temporarily permitted by Moses to the Jews and did not pertain to Christians. Only God, not the pope, could dispense from divine law. The pope's dispensation had no force in this matter and it was clear that the king's matrimony was invalid and should be dissolved.[12]

Significantly, then, Wakefield does not base his case on any alleged insufficiency of the original dispensation. Rather, he relies solely on the argument that the king's marriage to his brother's wife contravened both divine and natural law, and that it was beyond the power of the pope to dispense in this case. This challenges the conventional interpretation that Henry was initially reluctant to employ the Levitical argument because of the implied threat to papal power. Historians have instead thought that at the outset the king preferred to rely on the more limited arguments assailing the bull. According to this view, Henry began to talk of an indispensable impediment only when he had failed to obtain his divorce by other means. Thus, the argument continues, while the issue of the divine law may have fleetingly surfaced in 1527 and again in 1528, it did not come to dominate the debate until after the adjournment of the second trial over the marriage at Blackfriars in mid-1529; indeed, it may not have emerged until as late as 1530 when it was raised during the consultation of the English and continental universities.[13] In contrast, the examination of Wakefield's treatise has shown that as early as 1527 the king had come to the conclusion that his marriage contravened a divine law from which the pope could not dispense.

The story of how Wakefield became involved in the king's great matter is particularly well documented and provides insight into the recruitment of scholars in the divorce controversy. It shows Henry taking an active and independent role in enlisting support and organising the debate. In the summer of 1527, Wakefield was drawn into the controversy by Richard Pace, diplomat and humanist, whom he was then tutoring in Hebrew at Syon near London. Wakefield had initially supported the queen, helping Pace to compose a book in her defence which Pace presented to the king. Although Pace reassured him that Henry was only interested in the truth, whether it advanced his cause or not, Wakefield was reluctant to become further involved without the king's express permission. Pace recommended Wakefield to Henry and urged him to make clear his position so that he could benefit from Wakefield's learning.

The king must have been persuaded by Pace for it was around this time that he met Wakefield at Richmond, near Syon. In the course of their interview, Henry gave Wakefield a copy of a book by Fisher and commanded him to reply. Promising to write an 'immense volume', Wakefield rashly assured the king that he would respond to Fisher in such a manner that he 'shall be ashamed to wade or meddle any further in the matter'.[14]

Fisher may also have become involved in the debate as a result of personal intervention by the king. The bishop had originally promised Wolsey that he would not act or speak about the divorce without the king's express approval but then Henry summoned Fisher to an interview at Westminster. The king related how his conscience was troubled and how he had consulted his confessor (John Longland, bishop of Lincoln) and other learned men. Still dissatisfied, he now turned to Fisher for advice, urging him to declare his mind freely. This may be the occasion when Fisher, as he later recalled, received a direct command from the king to inquire into the matter of the divorce.

Edward Foxe, the Cambridge theologian, had also been involved in enlisting Wakefield's support. At the king's request, Foxe, accompanied by John Bell, had visited Wakefield at Syon. They commanded him to establish three conclusions (which they outlined) concerning the Levitical prohibitions. Wakefield complied, but Foxe, reportedly envious of him, told the king that the work was not Wakefield's but John Stokesley's. Wakefield was long acquainted with Stokesley, whom he had taught Hebrew, once describing him as an 'excellent theologian and proficient in the three main languages'.[15] Wakefield spent several nights at Stokesley's house discussing the matter with him while he proved Foxe's three conclusions. When subsequently questioned by the king, Stokesley admitted honestly that the book was not his but Wakefield's alone.

The involvement of Stokesley and Foxe may mark the beginnings of a group of scholars around the king. These individuals were responsible for composing treatises in support of the divorce, but their role in promoting the king's cause also extended beyond the pamphlet debate. At their centre stood Foxe. As early as 1527, he was sufficiently close to the king for Pace to describe him to Henry as 'he in whom you put the most trust'.

Perhaps as recognition of Foxe's growing occupation in the divorce, Pace sent a Hebrew alphabet to him by way of the king. Pace believed that within a month Foxe would be sufficiently knowledgeable to compare the Hebrew, Greek and Latin translations of the Bible to advertise Henry of the truth to the king's 'great advantage'.[16] As Pace may have anticipated, Foxe would shortly assume a prominent role in the debate.

During the autumn of 1527 Henry continued to take a leading part in the divorce. In October he approached Thomas More. Walking with him in the gallery at Hampton Court, the king suddenly began to speak of his great matter. In the summer of 1527, More had heard certain charges moved against the bull of dispensation which concerned Leviticus and Deuteronomy. They were intended to prove that the prohibition against the king's marriage was from divine law. More himself believed that the argument that certain faults in the bull rendered it insufficient held out a greater possibility of success. His conversation with Henry now revealed how the king's thinking had developed over the summer. For the first time More learned from Henry that the king's marriage allegedly contravened the law of nature. The king told More how 'it was now perceived that his marriage was not only against the positive laws of the church and the written law of God but also in such wise against the law of nature that it could in no wise by the church be dispensable'. Henry next read to More the biblical passages which had influenced him and asked More's own opinion. Benignly accepting his response, the king referred him to Edward Foxe. More was to read with Foxe a certain book that was 'then in the making for that matter'.[17] The work still in preparation was another of the king's books. Although this treatise has not yet been located, it is possible to trace much of its later history.[18]

After his talk with More, in November 1527 the king convened a group of bishops and others skilled in divine and civil laws. This assembly may also have included members of Oxford and Cambridge universities. The king presented a book to this gathering 'containing the reasons and causes moving the mind of his Majesty'.[19] The bishops met first at Hampton Court where they agreed on the form the book should take. It was later read at York Place before a meeting of bishops and many learned men.

Several contemporary sources suggested that the idea for the meeting had been Wolsey's; it may be significant that the meetings took place at two of his residences, Hampton Court and York

Place. During the cardinal's ascendancy, these had acquired pre-eminence over the king's court. If it is the case that Wolsey provided the inspiration for the meeting, then this is a rare instance of the cardinal's involvement, however limited, in the pamphlet debate.

The king sought the advice of the bishops and other scholars so that he might free his conscience from his scruple and obtain tranquillity for himself, his succession and his kingdom. This was the same justification which the king had offered in the address of Wakefield's treatise. By the mature deliberation of the bishops, all the arguments which could be adduced for or against the king's marriage were collected into one volume. That the book contained arguments for both sides may be because, as several contemporary accounts suggest, the government encountered an unexpected degree of opposition from the bishops. In any event, the bishops and other learned men also assembled did agree that the king had good reason to be troubled and that the matter should be submitted to the pope.

The king accordingly sent Stephen Gardiner and Edward Foxe, who had earlier shown the unfinished version to More, as ambassadors to the papal court with the book. In March 1528, Foxe and Gardiner presented the book to Pope Clement and one of his advisors, Cardinal Lorenzo Pucci. Another copy of the book was given to Cardinal Campeggio who would shortly be appointed Wolsey's fellow judge to hear the king's case in England. The ambassadors were to relate how the king's scruple had developed and in particular how he came to regard the sudden death of his male children as divine punishment. If the question of whether a divine law prohibited the king's marriage was raised, they should refer to his book, which explained how Deuteronomy and Leviticus could be reconciled.

The volume was known as the king's book and was said to be 'by the king's labour and study written'.[20] It began with an epistle from the king to Wolsey and other prelates which may have been delivered before one or both of the assemblies. This epistle directed a question to the cardinal and other clerics, presumably asking their opinion on the validity of the king's marriage. To the king's case Wolsey had then appended a collection of scholarly opinions which dealt with matters of law.

The king appears to have adopted a more moderate position than he had earlier done in Wakefield's tract. This new book discussed whether the pope could dispense from the impediment of the first degree of affinity. Opinions of learned men could be found for both sides. The king himself adhered to the view of those who maintained that the pope could so dispense. A difficulty remained, however, if certain causes rendered the dispensation surreptitious (that is, if it suppressed relevant facts) or obreptitious (if it actually misstated them). In this case, if such causes existed which would make the dispensation void, there is no doubt that the matrimony which had preceded from it would be null.

The emphasis on the insufficiency of the bull and the admission that the pope might dispense may be due to Wolsey's participation in the preparation of the book. The cardinal is generally believed to have preferred the more cautious approach centring on the dispensation. A year later the French ambassador reported that Wolsey would rather 'declare the dispensation ill-founded' than deny that the pope could dispense and thus 'subvert his power which is infinite'.[21] This view is supported by both Henry's and Wolsey's modern biographers. J.J. Scarisbrick has observed that Wolsey 'never cared for the Levitical argument with its awful implied challenge to papal authority ... and instead staked Henry's case on the inadequacies of the particular bull of Julius II', while Peter Gwyn believes that the cardinal pursued a policy which concentrated on the technical faults in the dispensation.[22]

The precedent for the affair of the king's book of November 1527 may have been Henry's involvement in the campaign against Martin Luther at the beginning of the 1520s. In July 1521 the king had published the *Assertio Septem Sacramentorum*, a response to Luther's *De Captivate Babylonica*. The *Assertio* was a considerable triumph for the king. As a reward for it, the pope conferred the title of Defender of the Faith on Henry and the book itself proved to be a popular bestseller both in England and on the Continent. It opened with an epistle directed to the pope, followed by a preface to the reader. Like the king's book of November 1527, it was despatched to Rome, and was formally presented to the pope in October by John Clerk.

Wolsey was also involved in the preparation of this book. As was the case in 1527, the idea for the *Assertio* was apparently his. In May 1521 he exhibited an unfinished version of it at a public burning of Luther's books in London. It was Wolsey who gave instructions to Clerk about the book's presentation to the pope and who even chose the dedicatory verse to be appended in the king's hand at the end of the work.

Although Henry certainly worked personally on the *Assertio*, it is now widely accepted that the book was a collaborative effort and that, as in his later contributions to the debate on the divorce, he received help from others in compiling it. Thomas More, for example, referred to the 'makers' of the *Assertio*, describing himself only as a 'sorter out and placer of the principal matters therein contained'.[23] Henry was very probably also assisted in his work by a commission of Oxford and Cambridge theologians who met in May 1521. And like the assembly of bishops in November 1527, which may also have included members from Oxford and Cambridge, this meeting was convened by Wolsey. Thus, in the preparation of the king's book of November 1527 and in its presentation to the pope, Henry and Wolsey may have drawn upon their earlier and fruitful experience in attacking Luther.

Throughout 1528 the king and his team of writers continued to work actively on the propaganda campaign, producing a whole succession of king's books. Their efforts would eventually culminate in the work presented in the king's own name to the legatine trial over his marriage in 1529. The series of king's books which lay behind the legatine work survives in a complex body of related and often fragmentary manuscript drafts.[24] The earliest of these drafts which can be dated comes from the beginning of 1528, composed a few months after the assembly of bishops the preceding November. Like the 1527 king's books, these drafts were written in the first person plural and most commonly began with a preface purportedly by the king. They focused on the Levitical prohibitions, declaring that they were moral laws and still in force. They make no mention of any defects in Julius's dispensation. The drafts of the king's book thus show Henry and his supporters continuing to advance exclusively the Levitical argument in 1528 and early 1529.

An examination of the drafts also sheds light on how treatises in the debate were actually composed. The king's books borrow extensively from one another, quoting many of the same authorities and reproducing many passages. As the circumstances of the debate altered, treatises were revised and updated, sometimes over the course of years.

In producing this series of tracts, the king's writers probably drew upon a collection of authorities which had been compiled in the course of their research for this purpose. Graham Nicholson has established that such a document, the *Collectanea satis copiosa*, was assembled in 1530–1 by the king's propagandists to provide material supporting his claims of independence from Rome.[25] The existence of a comparable document for the divorce would explain why the same authorities and arguments, often in the same order, recur so consistently throughout the king's books.

This source collection probably resembled the king's books which were based upon it: there, references from similar sources were usually grouped together and then arranged hierarchically, with the most authoritative cited first: scripture (the Old Testament before the New), followed by popes, general councils, patristic and scholastic writers. Such source collections may have been modelled on the commonplace-books in universal use throughout Europe in the sixteenth century. Commonplace-books consisted of extracts from texts, usually Latin ones, which were considered authoritative. These excerpts, collected by the compiler in the course of his reading, were then systematically organised under headings. Commonplace-books were effectively storehouses which supplied an abundance of materials on a theme for written composition. Although compiled privately by individuals (or sometimes by groups), commonplace-books were public documents, their contents intended for public recycling in writing and speaking. All this is generally consistent with what we know about the surviving compilation, the *Collectanea*, and what we can surmise about the missing source collection for the divorce.[26]

Presided over by two legates, cardinals Wolsey and Campeggio, the second trial over the king's marriage lasted from May to July 1529 when, like the first two years earlier, it was adjourned before sentence was given. At least fourteen 'little books' were exhibited to the legatine court, eight on behalf of the king and six in defence of the queen. Pre-eminent among these must be the work submitted in the king's own name and known from its opening words as 'Henricus octavus'.[27] It represented the first formal and public statement in England of the king's position. The bound copy of the manuscript, from the shop appropriately known as King Henry's binder, was produced with great care and at evident expense, reflecting the importance attached to it.

John Stokesley later revealed the authorship of 'Henricus octavus'. In 1535 he referred to the king's book which had been made before his 'going over the seas in embassy' in October 1529, not long after the adjournment of the legatine trial. Its writers were 'Mr Almoner' (the king's almoner, Edward Foxe),

'Mr Dr Nicholas' (Nicholas de Burgo, an Italian Franciscan based in Oxford) and Stokesley.[28] Both Foxe and Stokesley had figured in the propaganda campaign from its earliest days, while to the king's team of writers can now be added the name of de Burgo. By 1531, de Burgo had become 'so secret in the king's great matter' that Cromwell was advised that he should be denied licence to return to Italy.[29]

Henry himself may have had a hand in the composition of 'Henricus octavus' for he was working on at least one book in 1528 when its first drafts were being prepared. He wrote to Anne Boleyn of 'my book' which 'makes substantially for my matter, in writing whereof I have spent above four hours this day'.[30] In June he was also engaged in writing a book. Brian Tuke related how late one night Henry visited him and 'for the most part going and coming turns in for devising with me upon his book and other things current'.[31]

'Henricus octavus' was revised especially for presentation to Wolsey and Campeggio during the trial, with an address to the legates added at the beginning. This probably contains the full text of the speech Henry delivered before the court on 21 June. The king promised to explain why he had changed his opinion and now considered his marriage suspect, which he had contracted in good faith as a young man. The address dwelt upon Henry's troubled conscience and his growing belief that his marriage was invalid. After lengthy meditation on divine matters and with the inspiration of the heavenly spirit, Henry had realised that his nuptials were not true and legitimate. At issue was the succession which affected both the king personally and the realm generally, 'whose certain well-being ... depended on this matter'.[32] Henry had unlawfully entered into marriage to his own great unhappiness and that of the kingdom. The awareness of this had disturbed his soul for several years.

The address also constituted an appeal to Wolsey and Campeggio. The king's soul had been greatly burdened. With his conscience settled, however, he would at last obtain a real tranquillity and the seedbeds of war and dissent, which in the future could damage the public quiet of the kingdom, would be utterly removed. Unless the judges intervened, he could not secure the peace he sought and he appealed to them to settle the controversy by the authority granted to them by the pope. He made plain what outcome he desired, asking them to decide that his marriage could not continue without violating divine law and should be abrogated.

In the next part of the address, Henry set out to explain the reasons which had led him to contemplate dissolving his marriage. The king's marriage, which both divine and human law opposed, did not meet the requirements for a genuine and legitimate union. Among these conditions was that children should be procreated, as God himself had instituted. Yet those who married their brother's wives were denied sons as a divine punishment for their offence. The king had read in Leviticus about the prohibitions relating to marriage. These had emanated from God and were not of human institution. Henry had considered the reasons for their establishing, namely, to encourage the cultivation of many virtues. God had both urged Jews and converts to exhibit such virtues and had severely punished those who married within the prohibited degrees. As proof the king cited the words of God in both chapters 18 and 20 of Leviticus, employing the same version of Leviticus 20:21 as had Wakefield's treatise nearly two years earlier. Silently substituting 'sons' for the all-inclusive 'children', the paraphrase of Leviticus served to reinforce the point that the king had suffered the very penalty prescribed there: he who has married his brother's wife 'will be without sons'.

The relevance to the king's own situation was soon made explicit. Henry lamented that he was publicly thought to have esteemed his welfare and that of his kingdom and descendants less than his own private feelings. Moreover, he had experienced the penalty which God threatened to those who marry their sisters-in-law; he had lost all his male children either to miscarriage or death.

Only in its closing pages did 'Henricus octavus' raise the subject of the bull of dispensation.[33] In comparison to the Levitical arguments, however, this received only summary treatment. The king derived no consolation from having a bull witnessing that the church had sanctioned his marriage. Rather he felt his conscience becoming more and more entangled when he learned the opinions of all the best and most accepted doctors of the church (although, in contrast to the earlier discussion of Leviticus, none of these doctors are quoted or even identified). Some, it was alleged, thought that the laws of matrimony which are regulated by divine law were not susceptible to human dispensation; others believed that the pope could dispense with them but only for the most urgent and clearest cause of public necessity and of human affairs. There could be no liberty or compensation for rendering null the mandate of God. Even if the king conceded that the pope could mitigate the severity of the law, having consulted all the most learned (and again unnamed) men in law in the kingdom, he considered that the dispensation suffered from so many and such obvious faults that they utterly invalidated it. The nature of these faults, however, is also left unspecified.

Some had so little faith in the efficacy of the bull that they had recourse to a 'new dispensation from long ago'. This apparently paradoxical reference was to the so-called Spanish brief. Issued in 1504 to console Catherine's mother, Isabella, on her deathbed, it had surfaced again in Spain only in the autumn of 1528. It differed from the bull in certain significant ways which were detrimental to the king's case. It could be easily shown, 'Henricus octavus' claimed, that the brief had been cunningly fabricated and was plainly surreptitious. Henry, in whose interest most of all it was to know of it, had never heard of it, nor was it of the sort which Henry VII and Ferdinand had pledged to seek. In short, the brief was dismissed as a forgery.

Those papal documents, which Henry knew had no force, could offer no comfort for his stricken conscience. This was especially true since Henry had long been convinced by far weightier and more powerful reasons that his marriage was entirely illegitimate, even if those papal rescripts had retained their force and had been validly and legally issued by the pope. In other words, even if the pope could dispense and even if he had done so properly (which he had not), the king did not believe that his marriage was valid. 'Henricus octavus' thus returns full circle to Leviticus and the nature of the impediment to the king's marriage.

On the queen's side the most significant treatise exhibited to the legatine court came from the bishop of Rochester. Accepting the king's earlier invitation to the judges and others to throw what light they could on his matter, Fisher submitted a treatise to the court on 28 June.[34] In a dramatic speech, Fisher affirmed his willingness to reveal his opinion on the king's marriage after two years of diligent study. He believed the marriage could not be dissolved by any power, human or divine. Speaking on the eve of the nativity of John the Baptist, he announced that he was prepared to die for his belief as had the Baptist before him. This was a reference to Herod's execution of the Baptist, who had condemned Herod for marrying his brother's wife. Fisher's treatise argued his case in six axioms, but he attached the greatest importance to the first two, concerned respectively with the theological and the legal issues. The first stated that there was no impediment between Henry and Catherine which the pope could not remove, because only human, not divine, law prohibited marriage with a brother's wife. The second argued that the pope had removed any obstacle to the marriage in assenting to it in his dispensation. It countered specific charges which could be levelled against Julius's bull.

Although the king had already submitted 'Henricus octavus' in his own name to the court, he was sufficiently concerned by Fisher's unexpected intervention to arrange for a reply to be drawn up. This answer was in two parts, which appear separately on the list of tracts exhibited to the court, and correspond to Fisher's first and second axioms. Both were composed by Stephen Gardiner who had been involved in the divorce from its beginnings. In 1528, for example, he had helped Foxe convey the king's book to the pope. By the legatine trial, he was probably already part of the king's circle of scholars since one of the drafts of 'Henricus octavus' is very likely in his hand. Although Gardiner has long been recognised as the author of both parts of the reply to Fisher, the two sections differ significantly in their contents, tone and ostensible authorship. The marked differences between the two parts very probably reflect Henry's influence on the section which purports to be his.[35]

In the legatine list of tracts, only one section is openly attributed to Gardiner. In a heading on the manuscript, it is described as having been composed 'on behalf of the king'.[36] It is written in the third person, with the king referred to throughout as 'Royal Majesty' or the young Henry as 'prince'. The other section appears anonymously in the legatine list but is presented as the king's own work, composed 'as it seems by the King himself'.[37] Unlike Gardiner's, this section is written in the first person plural, in the voice of the king. Like his other legatine submission, 'Henricus octavus', it commences with an address from Henry to the judges.

The difference between the two sections extends to the attitude each takes towards the bishop of Rochester. Throughout Gardiner's section, Fisher is respectfully addressed as 'Reverend Father'. The tone is moderate and restrained. In contrast, the king's section is an embittered personal attack on Fisher for publicly opposing the divorce, revealing Henry's furious reaction to the bishop's speech and treatise. Such strength of expression was not uncharacteristic of the king; his *Assertio*, for example, had been noted for the virulence of its assault on Luther while, as we have seen, Wakefield's treatise was signally offensive to Fisher.

Expecting the support of all his best councillors, Henry expressed his surprise at finding Fisher in opposition. He was particularly aggrieved at the bishop's alleged change of heart. According to the king, Fisher had earlier approved the reasons which had convinced Henry that his marriage was incestuous and illegitimate. The bishop had judged these reasons to be so weighty and powerful that he believed Henry's earlier peace of mind could not be restored unless the pope was consulted. Now, however, after so many months and before such a great and distinguished an assembly, Fisher chose to declare his opinion openly. Rather than discussing the matter so publicly, greatly harming the king's conscience, the bishop instead should have advised Henry privately. The king also took especial exception to Fisher's reference to John the Baptist and the implied comparison of Henry to Herod. Disassociating himself from this, the king denied that he was acting the part of Herod and attempting some crime similar to his.

The king's section attacked his marriage on the same grounds as 'Henricus octavus' and the earlier king's books. In response to Fisher, it argued that there was an impediment from divine law to the royal marriage. It challenged the central plank of Fisher's first axiom which had denied that the king's case was included in the Levitical prohibitions forbidding marriage with a brother's wife. Instead it argued that Leviticus and Deuteronomy could be glossed in a number of ways which would resolve the seeming contradiction between them.

Unlike the king's section, Gardiner's did not dispute the pope's power to dispense in Henry's situation. Explicitly excluding the question whether the pope had the authority to remove the impediment, it confined itself to the narrower issue of the validity of Julius's particular dispensation. Gardiner denied that Julius had given his assent properly according to agreed forms. Thus, the king's name was associated only with that section which questioned the pope's authority while the more technical and less contentious discussion of the insufficiency of the bull was left to Gardiner. In both the treatises submitted on his behalf to the court, then, Henry's case rested overwhelmingly on the prohibition of the law of God found in Leviticus.

It is clear that by the time of the legatine trial there was now a discernible group of scholars emerging around the king. This included Gardiner and the authors of 'Henricus octavus', Foxe, Stokesley and de Burgo. In the autumn of 1529, this circle was joined by Thomas Cranmer, following an accidental meeting that August with Foxe and Gardiner at Waltham Abbey. Foxe swiftly recommended Cranmer to the king, who sent for him. They met at Greenwich in October where Henry commissioned him to write his opinion on the divorce. Cranmer was soon employed more generally in promoting the king's cause with other members of his team. In late 1529, Thomas More asked to discuss the king's matter with 'some such of his graces learned counsel as most for his part had laboured and found in the matter'. Henry duly assigned Cranmer, along with de Burgo, Foxe and Edward Lee, with whom More had 'diligent conference'.[38]

A year later this same group is again found acting in concert to advance the king's case. Henry sent Stokesley, Lee and Foxe to Fisher to urge him to retract what he had written in Catherine's favour and to defect to Henry.[39] Lee also contributed directly to the pamphlet debate, after mid-1532 writing a tract on the divorce, and he should be considered one of the king's 'spiritual learned counsel'.

The king's scholars promoted the divorce not only before individuals like Fisher and More but also before larger bodies. In early 1530, for example, they helped secure the opinions of the universities of Oxford and Cambridge against the king's marriage. Edward Foxe and Stephen Gardiner were sent to Cambridge where a copy of a book by Cranmer featured in their discussions with the doctors of the university. Foxe also went to Oxford; amongst the other royal delegates there may have been de Burgo.[40]

A number of this circle – Thomas Cranmer, Stephen Gardiner and Edward Foxe – also eventually moved in the Boleyn camp. This latter group, which also came to include Thomas Cromwell, Thomas Audley, speaker of the House of Commons, and Sir George Boleyn, Anne's brother, was responsible for supplying the king with radical ideas about royal authority. Cranmer's introduction to the Boleyn circle had rapidly followed his interview with Henry and by the end of 1529 Cranmer was part of their team; after their meeting in Greenwich, the king referred him to the Earl of Wiltshire, Anne Boleyn's father. Cranmer stayed at the earl's residence, Durham Place, recently acquired from Wolsey, while he composed his treatise. This may have been the work mentioned during the consultation of Cambridge University a few months later. In January 1530 Cranmer, along with Lee and Stokesley, would also accompany Wiltshire on an embassy to the emperor and pope.

By the spring of 1529, Stephen Gardiner, originally a protégé of Wolsey's, had begun to support Anne; in July he was appointed the king's principal secretary. Edward Foxe had also been a member of Wolsey's household; by late 1529 he had also become close to Anne Boleyn. First granted a benefice in 1529 in the bishopric of Durham (whose revenue had been granted to Anne's father), in 1535 Foxe was rewarded with the bishopric of Hereford for his support of Anne. It was probably under Foxe's direction that the compilation of scriptural, historical and patristic texts, the *Collectanea*, was prepared.[41] Supplying the king's propagandists with a wealth of arguments justifying Henry's personal and England's provincial independence from Rome, the *Collectanea* crucially provided the ideological basis for the Royal Supremacy. Foxe is the obvious link between the *Collectanea* and the earlier research project which resulted in the compilation on the divorce, for which he may also have been responsible.

A third member of the king's team, de Burgo, had also been a client of the cardinal's. Around the time of the legatine trial, he, like Foxe and Gardiner, began to receive advancement. In July 1529, de Burgo, 'one of the king's spiritual learned counsel', received a payment 'by way of reward' from the Treasurer of the Chamber's Account.[42] The following month Henry asked Wolsey to arrange a benefice for him and at the beginning of the next year de Burgo received a further sum at the king's command. Earlier recruited by Wolsey to his Cardinal College in Oxford, in 1532 he was appointed reader in divinity at its successor, King Henry VIII College.

Like de Burgo, the king's earliest writer, Robert Wakefield, survived the loss of his first patron to enjoy royal favour. Wakefield's support of the king caused a permanent rift with his original patron, Fisher, which may have led to the loss of his stipend from St John's College, Cambridge. Around the time his stipend ceased, Wakefield began to receive payments from the Treasurer of the Chamber's Account, the same source from which de Burgo was paid. His career at Oxford also prospered. Around 1529, the king appointed him to the regius praelectorship in Hebrew there. In 1532, at the same time de Burgo was named reader in theology there, Wakefield became a canon of King Henry VIII College. Like Foxe, Gardiner and Cranmer, Wakefield also later came within the sphere of the Boleyns, and specifically under the patronage of Anne's father, Thomas Boleyn. Wakefield was already acquainted with another of the Boleyns for he had earlier taught Anne's uncle, James.

Following the conclusion of the legatine trial, the debate continued with a further confrontation between Fisher and Gardiner.

Probably between mid-1529 and early 1530, Fisher produced another version of his legatine tract which in turn led Gardiner to revise the king's section of his legatine submission. Gardiner's new work was related to the body of manuscript drafts of 'Henricus octavus', further connecting him to the government's pamphlet campaign.

In the spring of 1531 the government decided to put their case to a wider audience and turned for the first time to the printing press. Around April, the king's printer, Thomas Berthelet, who was responsible for producing many officially inspired books in the 1530s, published *Censurae academiarum*. In November this work became even more easily accessible when an English translation appeared as the *Determinations of the universities*.[43] *Censurae* began with the favourable determinations of seven foreign universities, gathered by the king's agents during 1530. The lengthy treatise which followed (which remarkably never mentions the king or his marriage) argued two central propositions: first, both divine and natural law equally prohibited a Christian to marry the widow of a brother who had died childless; secondly, the pope was unable to dispense such marriages whether they were already contracted or yet to be so.

This treatise, however, had not been written specifically to uphold the university decisions. Rather it was a much revised and expanded version of the king's legatine book, 'Henricus octavus'. When he revealed its authorship in 1535, Stokesley had also provided a clue to the subsequent history of 'Henricus octavus' as *Censurae*: it was 'afterward translated into English ... by my lord of Canterbury (Thomas Cranmer)'.[44]

At least three pre-publication copies of *Censurae* survive, but of particular relevance here is the manuscript which has elsewhere been called the presentation copy.[45] A complete fair copy, this was elaborately bound by the same shop responsible for 'Henricus octavus', and was probably destined for the king or at least for a member of court. The presentation copy reveals that even on the eve of publication, the text, particularly the seventh and final chapter, was still being revised.

The presentation copy is the first of the king's books to imply, perhaps as a means of exerting pressure on the pope, that the government was considering taking practical steps in England to achieve the divorce. According to the presentation copy, a Christian should not obey a pope who commanded him, contrary to divine and natural law, to marry or remain wed to a woman already related by blood or marriage. The responsibility of a Christian went beyond passive disobedience, however, for he should also resist the pope with a firm and Christian spirit, even if threatened by a thousand excommunications or other ecclesiastical penalties. The presentation copy next discussed the role bishops should play in cases of incestuous marriages. Following the example of Dunstan, archbishop of Canterbury, bishops should not allow persons to continue in such a marriage but should strongly urge them to separate. Contrary to the pope's command, Dunstan had refused to absolve a certain earl for marrying a relative.

By the time *Censurae* was printed, this notion of resistance had been more fully developed.[46] *Censurae* elaborated upon the example of Dunstan, adding the stories of three other bishops who had defied the pope and risked the penalties of excommunication. In doing so, it tacitly enlarged the circumstances when episcopal resistance was permissible, since one of the additional examples was not, like that of Dunstan, confined to a dispute with the papacy over marriage. This final chapter reads like an exhortation to the English bishops to intervene in the king's case. If the pope should allow incestuous marriages, the duty of a good and devout bishop is not only to withstand him openly; he should also reproach the pope so that persons thus coupled part. If these individuals follow their own desires rather than their bishop's teaching, he should threaten them with excommunication.

As an additional incentive, *Censurae* held out the prospect of divine punishment to those bishops who failed to act. How else, it asked, would they perform their duty as bishops, if, because of the threats and tyranny of popes, they did not call back into the way of truth their lost sheep, for whom they were answerable to God's terrible judgement? How would they avoid that grave punishment which He threatens to those who will not make known to a wicked man his sins?

Censurae moved on to the role of individual Christians in a conflict with the pope. As bishops should not listen to the pope or follow his commands in such circumstances, so ought all other Christians. This applied even to private individuals as long as they, having been instructed by the holy spirit, understood that their marriages were incestuous. This category of persons authorised to act by the holy spirit was, of course, clearly meant to include the king. These Christians could and should not only dissolve their marriages but should also strongly resist the pope, even if he threatened a thousand suspensions or excommunications.

Censurae outlined the duty of a Christian when his private conscience, enlightened by the holy spirit and the knowledge of
sacred scripture, moved him to act. Without fear of punishment,
he could and should divorce a woman forbidden by both divine
and natural law and free himself from the yoke of that presumed
marriage. *Censurae* thus emphasised that all Christians, and especially bishops, had an obligation to resist the improper exercise of
papal authority. This may suggest that Henry was contemplating
acting through the English bishops or even taking matters into
his own hands as an individual Christian and proceeding unilaterally. Both such courses of action were under discussion in the
autumn of 1530.

Following the publication of *Censurae* and the *Determinations*,
the debate began to move in two directions. One continued to
focus narrowly on the divorce, and particularly on *Censurae*. The
queen's supporters, most notably John Fisher and her chaplain,
Thomas Abel, produced responses to *Censurae*. In return, the
king's advocates, including Edward Lee and the authors of
Censurae, composed at least five treatises attacking Fisher or Abel.

At the same time, other treatises appeared which began to
point the way forward to the break with Rome. At the crossroads
of these two great controversies of the 1530s, over the divorce and
the Royal Supremacy, stood the *Glass of the Truth*. Like *Censurae*
and the *Determinations*, the *Glass* came from the press of the royal
printer, Berthelet. It was written between May 1531 and April
1532 since it mentions that the king was in the twenty-third year
of his reign. This dating can be narrowed somewhat further, for
the *Glass* was in circulation by February 1532, when it was read by
a priest in St Albans. It was probably composed after the
Determinations, since it represents an advance on the arguments
found there. It is generally accepted that Henry had a hand in its
preparation although the real work was probably left to others.
Written in the form of a dialogue between a theologian and a
canon lawyer, it was a more readable, popularised account of the
king's side than had previously appeared. Interwoven throughout
was a patriotic appeal to the king's loyal subjects to help secure
the succession of a male heir 'for his honour and quieting of conscience, for our great wealth, and for the prosperity of this his
noble realm'.[47]

The theologian declared the invalidity of the king's marriage
to be beyond dispute. Leviticus forbade Christians to marry their
brother's wife. The pope cannot dispense from the law of God or

the law of nature; as Leviticus was part of divine law, it was there-fore indispensable by the pope. The lawyer considered whether the king's cause should be heard within the realm. While earlier sections of the *Glass* drew upon the divorce compilation, many of the lawyer's arguments were derived from the *Collectanea*. The pronouncements of General Councils, especially the Council of Nicea, showed that his cause must be determined in England, the province where it had originated. In comparison to *Censurae*, the bishops in the *Glass* acquire a greatly expanded role and now play an essential part in resolving Henry's difficulties: to the English bishops, and specifically to the metropolitans, belongs jurisdiction over the king's case. In introducing this notion of provincial inde-pendence, the *Glass* thus announced the new direction of policy, one which would ultimately secure the king his divorce.

After the publication of the *Glass*, the course of the pamphlet debate was soon overtaken by rapidly accelerating events. By the end of 1532 Anne Boleyn was pregnant and in late January 1533 she and Henry were secretly married. In May Cranmer annulled the king's first marriage and ratified his union with Anne. With the king's divorce and remarriage thus secured, defending the coming break with Rome now became the government's chief concern.

From the appearance of Wakefield's treatise in 1527 to the pub-lication of the *Glass* in 1531/2, the king and his supporters had followed a consistent line. This centred not on the bull or brief, but on a prohibition in the law of God to his marriage. This was expressed in Leviticus, manifested in his 'childless' state and, most importantly, was indispensable by the pope. Henry thus favoured a more uncompromising position than has previously been supposed, one which inevitably set him on a course of con-frontation with the papacy.

7. Henry VIII and the Reform of the Church

DIARMAID MacCULLOCH

Two provinces of the western church Catholic happened to co-incide with the frontiers of the medieval kingdom of England: Canterbury and York. There were clear contrasts between them. York was much smaller than Canterbury, with only three dioceses to Canterbury's fourteen; it was remoter from the centre of national affairs, and it was a poorer region overall. Either province had its own clerical parliament, Convocation, but the Convocation of Canterbury met while the national parliament was assembled and had real significance as a lawmaking body; York more or less rubber-stamped decisions from the south. After long and bitter disputes over three centuries from the Norman Conquest, the archbishop of Canterbury had emerged with a subtly-adjusted title of precedence over the archbishop of York: 'Primate of All England', as against York's 'Primate of England'.[1]

This relationship reflected the realities of power in the medieval kingdom of England and Wales, which more than any other major European state, was a unit under centralised direc-tion. In ordinary conditions, power lay in the south-east and around the capital city in the Thames valley; Lambeth Palace near London, the archbishop of Canterbury's headquarters, looked directly across the Thames to the ancient seat of government in the Palace of Westminster. This tradition would be one of Henry VIII's chief assets in his idiosyncratic Reformation: more an act of state than any other major break with the old church in sixteenth-century Europe. This chapter is therefore a study of the Reformation in personal and political terms: it considers a small political and ecclesiastical world and how those in it acted and thought, and it concentrates in particular on the thoughts and actions of Henry VIII himself. Out of his world came a church which puzzled observers at the time, yet which briefly in the 1540s

embraced a wider spectrum of religious opinion than any version
of the church in England since.

Compared with other provinces elsewhere in Europe,
Canterbury and York were in satisfactory condition in 1509. In
Henry VIII's other Tudor territory, Ireland, the church was in a
state of extreme confusion because of the country's political frag-
mentation; on the other hand, from the 1470s it was being swept
by a religious revival led by friars, which had no parallel elsewhere
in the British Isles. The late medieval Scottish church was the
victim of much greater diversions of finances for the benefit of
the nobility than in England: profitable monastic offices were
colonised by non-monastic protégés and members of noble families, and parish revenues were siphoned off for the foundation of
collegiate churches, whose main function was the uphill struggle
to pray for the salvation of Scottish aristocrats.[2] England's church
government was far more orderly than administration in either
Scotland or Ireland, and there were none of the scandals of
central church government in Rome. Looking at the English
church, one could see much that was good, much that was indifferent, but little that was disastrous.

If the church in England had problems in 1509, they were the
problems of complacency born of success. In the late fourteenth
and early fifteenth century, the church had faced a real challenge
from the Lollards, a movement which initially attracted some powerful political backing and some of the best minds in the English
universities. The Lollards had then chosen the wrong side in politics, and they had been rooted out of polite society. They survived
in defensive and occasionally persecuted communities scattered
through lowland England; although we have realised in recent
years that Lollard leaders were slightly higher up the social scale
than we thought, and that Lollardy was at least sustaining itself on
the eve of the Reformation, the movement as a whole was not
showing any dramatic signs of expansion. For all the fears of some
bishops, it was not going to overturn the old order single-handed.

The church had won, and as part of its victory, in 1407 it had
even banned the unlicensed use or independent translation of
the Bible in English, a highly unusual ban in Europe and a deliberate triumphalist reaction to the Lollard stress on Bible-reading.[3]
Every new king in the unstable politics of fifteenth-century
England had hastened to bolster his position by buying the
support of the church, funding lavish building projects and courting leading churchmen, who generally backed whatever regime

had captured the throne. Henry VII put some curbs on the church's legal independence, but these did not greatly change its relationship to the kingdom.[4] The English church remained a pair of independent provinces, with their own parliaments, courts and legal system; working hand in glove with the monarchy, but confident of their own ultimate integrity.

Into this rather stuffy world came Henry VIII: the man who would blow the system apart. Henry's religious policy won few unqualified admirers within the Protestant church of England before the nineteenth century, when the Oxford Movement influenced a new breed of church historian. They wanted to find a suitable ancestry for their view that their church was the true heir of the pre-Reformation western Catholic church, and not the residue of a Protestant revolt against it; they therefore lovingly excavated the Henrician Reformation as being reassuringly Catholic without the pope. One Anglo-Catholic, writing anonymously in 1891, summed up their attitude in extreme form: 'It has been well said that almost the only real reform that remained to be carried out at the death of Henry VIII, was the translation of the new services into English.'[5]

This was a deliberately comprehensive put-down for the Reformation carried out under Edward VI, which as fossilised in Elizabeth I's church settlement of 1559, in reality created the Anglican church's liturgy and official statement of doctrine still in place at the present day. The comment also conveniently ignored some features of the Henrician Reformation which did not fit the Anglo-Catholic bill: Henry had eliminated the monastic life, destroyed all the shrines of England and Wales, and struck a mortal blow at a complex of beliefs about the afterlife centring on purgatory, which had been at the heart of late medieval religion in northern Europe. Other Anglo-Catholics could be as virulent as any Roman Catholic about Henry. At a modern stronghold of Anglo-Catholicism, the Shrine of Our Lady near the site of Walsingham Priory in Norfolk (dissolved by Henry in 1538), Anglican pilgrims process to a twentieth-century hymn containing a swift pen-portrait of the founder of the church of England:

But at last came a king who had greed in his eyes,
And he lusted for treasure with fraud and with lies.[6]

Henry's was a strange sort of Catholicism, even after one has subtracted the pope. Yet as far as the king himself was concerned, his Reformation also proceeded without Luther or Zwingli, let alone

an obscure young French exile called Jean Calvin. Luther and
Henry detested each other, and it was actually the more thor-
oughgoing Reformation of Switzerland which made the first
important Reformation contacts with the king. The first of the
only two major names among the Continental Reformers ever to
meet King Henry face to face was Simon Grynaeus, a south
German humanist academic who became first colleague and then
successor to Johannes Oecolampadius, the radical theologian at
Basel University in Switzerland.[7] Grynaeus visited England from
Basel in spring and early summer 1531; he came over supposedly
to look for Greek manuscripts in English libraries, but in reality to
see whether the evangelical Reformers could mastermind a better
deal than the pope had been prepared to countenance for Henry
to rid himself of Catherine of Aragon.

Grynaeus was enthusiastic for Henry VIII's theological arguments
about his marriage, and for a few months in 1531, he cherished a
vision of England poised on the springboard of a dramatic reformation. However, he was unable to persuade the great names of the
Continental Reform to present a united front on the divorce:
hardly surprisingly, since they had failed to do so on the more basic
issue of what the Christian church believed about the eucharist.
Henry's fleeting encounter with the Swiss Reformation seems to
have left no impression on the king, although it would have great
significance for Thomas Cranmer in the long term. Henry could be
politely appreciative when Continental Reformers later sent him
their works to augment his impressive library, but there is no evidence that their writings directly affected his thinking.[8]

Catholicism without the pope: Reformation without Reformers.
It is easy to mock Henry's religious policies, as the whims of a man
who flattened a village church and churchyard to build his fantasy
palace at Nonsuch, and who redeployed the church windows of
Rewley Abbey outside Oxford to light his bowling alley at
Hampton Court.[9] Yet Henry took his special relationship with
God very seriously. The 1485 Act of Parliament which had recognised the *fait accompli* of his father's accession after the battle of
Bosworth could find no stronger justification for the event than it
was 'to the pleasure of Almighty God', ignoring the somewhat
embarrassing question of hereditary right; the Tudor dynasty
knew that it had been put in place by God's peculiar favour, and
not by much else.[10]

Moreover, Henry took time off from the pleasures of hunting
and war, not only to read theology voraciously, but to write it.

Unlike his great-great-nephew King James I, he put his name to the title-page of only one printed book, the *Assertio Septem Sacramentorum* of 1521, and even then most of the donkey-work was done by a committee of experts. However, Virginia Murphy has demonstrated in chapter 6 that this represents a fraction of the king's output in the 1520s, most of which remained in manuscript. Later, throughout the years of the Reformation, the king was an assiduous corrector of others' theological drafts, and an improver in the margins of others' ideas – a practice not dissimilar to his approach to musical composition. He meditated, for instance, on the Coronation oath which he himself had sworn, and toyed with the idea of making some significant changes for the future to emphasise royal control over ecclesiastical affairs, speaking of 'imperial jurisdiction'.[11] From autumn 1537, now recognised by parliament as enjoying just such imperial rights in all the institutions of his kingdom, he revealed an extraordinary will to rush in where theological professionals feared to tread: when revising his bishops' published statement of doctrine (the *Bishops' Book*), the king made bids to improve on the divinely authored text of the Ten Commandments, attempting for instance to tone down the biblical text's condemnation of image-worship. His editorial work earned him a schoolmasterly rebuke from Archbishop Cranmer: 'all the long sentence before ... is the very words of God in Deuteronomy, which would be recited sincerely without any addition.' Later on in the same notes, a royal effort to tinker with that perennially difficult phrase in the Lord's Prayer, 'lead us not into temptation', was successfully torpedoed by the archbishop: 'we should not alter any word in the scripture ... although it shall appear to us in many places to signify much absurdity.'[12]

The king indeed turned to theological activity for comfort in successive great crises of his life, crises which were associated with his tangled matrimonial affairs. Virginia Murphy has already shown how his efforts to rid himself of the Aragon marriage were fatally complicated from the beginning by his obstinate refusal to see the question as anything else than theological: a confrontation between his own sin and an angry God (above, chapter 6). Likewise in his grief at the loss of Jane Seymour (for whom a natural death in 1537 intervened before royal boredom), Henry turned to revision of the *Bishops' Book*. Humiliated and betrayed by his fifth wife Catherine Howard, he took solace during 1542 in reading and moodily annotating newly delivered devotional manuscripts, and his continued theological musings culminated in a fusillade of ecclesiastical activity during the first half of 1543, including the final published version of a revised doctrinal statement for his church, appropriately named the *King's Book*.[13]

Henry's vision of his relationship with God changed over time. As a young man, he was the conventionally pious son of a king who had imitated the devotion of his medieval predecessors. Henry VII sought an easy passage through purgatory with foundations designed to pour out prayers to God for him from grateful clergy and the poor and sick: the Savoy Hospital in London, and a mammoth chantry to serve his tomb in Westminster Abbey. The tone of the royal household was set by the intense devotional life of Henry VIII's grandmother Lady Margaret Beaufort, a woman whose turbulent political career had left her with much to be grateful for, but also with an intense and frequently tearful consciousness of the changeability of human affairs. More prepared to experiment than her son the king, Lady Margaret had been guided by her close associate bishop John Fisher into financing new ventures in humanist higher education, alongside her investment in the purgatory industry: the intimate weave between the two aspects of her benevolence was symbolised by her foundation of university chairs of theology (with Fisher as first occupant at Cambridge) which were to be funded as part of the new royal chantry foundation at Westminster Abbey.[14]

In the grounds of Henry VIII's principal homes at Richmond and Greenwich were brand-new convents of the reformed order of Observant Friars, whose church buildings would loom over the two palaces' gardens until the beginning of Elizabeth's reign, ruinous and baleful reminders of the past, more than two decades after Henry had destroyed their communities for opposing his wishes.[15] Near Richmond were the Carthusian monks of Sheen, and a mile across the river from the palace stood the unique community of Bridgettine sisters and brothers at Syon Abbey. Syon, with its witness to the mystical intensity of the fourteenth-century St Bridget of Sweden, was an aristocratic convent with wide influence among the elite of London and the English nobility generally: it was 'the virtues[t] house of religion that was in England', said the London chronicler Charles Wriothesley at its suppression in 1539. The royal family, Wolsey and Syon between them accounted for half the dedications of printed books in the first two decades of Henry VIII's reign.[16]

Altogether, this complex of royal monastic foundations built within the previous century was intimidating proof of the continu-

ing liveliness and creativity of the church's devotion. William
Tyndale, with no friendly intent, described the constant tolling of
bells between Syon and Sheen in Richmond's royal enclave
around the river Thames, sounds with which the young king
would have grown up: 'when the friars of Syon ring out, the nuns
begin; and when the nuns ring out of service, the monks on the
other side [at Sheen] begin; and when they ring out, the friars
begin again, and vex themselves night and day, and take pain for
God's sake.'[17] It is noticeable that all these communities were
deeply involved in the resistance to Henry's plans to annul his
first marriage and break with the bishop of Rome. Henry must
have felt a beleaguered man when those indefatigable, all-
encompassing bells turned hostile: one should appreciate the
personal dimension of his later enmity to clerical power, with
these constant reminders of the devotional claustrophobia of his
youth so near to hand.

From his early years, the king showed himself torn in his attitude to the power represented by the bells of Syon and Sheen.
He did the things expected of him with enthusiasm, going on pilgrimage to Walsingham and hearing several masses a day at the
variety of altars available to him in his palaces. He was instinctively
a loyal son of Rome; when in 1512 he entered his first war, against
Louis XII of France, his main declared reason was his horror at
Louis' rebellion against the pope's authority.[18] However, there
was another side to Henry even in the early years. He was already
attacking benefit of clergy and sanctuary, and he was unsympathetic to the church hierarchy's inept attempts at self-assertion in
the controversy over whether a London merchant called Richard
Hunne had died an heretical suicide or an innocent murder
victim of a church official. At the final act of this prolonged
drama at Baynard's Castle in November 1515, Henry was provoked to declare before the assembled notables of the kingdom
that 'by the ordinance and sufferance of God we are king of
England, and the kings of England in time past have never had
any superior but God alone'.[19] Even the result of the first French
war, that supposed crusade for the pope, resulted in a similar declaration. One of the war's meagre gains was the city of Tournai,
which the English occupied for six years up to 1519. A row developed over who would be bishop there: Henry's chief minister
Thomas Wolsey or a French nominee. The French candidate
appealed to Rome, and the subsequent dispute produced a claim
from Henry in late 1516 that he now had 'supreme power and

lord and king in the regality of Tournai without recognition of any superior'; furious at an oblique threat of excommunication from pope Leo, Henry issued dark threats.[20]

In this instance, the conflict led nowhere; Leo chose to defuse the situation with a conciliatory letter to the king, and by February 1517 peace had broken out. Soon Tournai was French again, and in the meantime, a far more serious threat had arisen to trouble the Holy Father: Martin Luther. Henry's rebuke to Luther, the *Assertio Septem Sacramentorum*, was both a vigorous and a remarkably concise and effective defence of traditional religion, which would seem incongruous in later years. Indeed, Sir Thomas More mischievously reminisced in the 1530s that he had vainly tried to persuade the king to tone down passages in the *Assertio* which acclaimed papal supremacy, particularly in its second chapter, 'Of the pope's Authority'.[21] Famously, the work won Henry the papal grant of a title to rank alongside those of the Holy Roman Emperor and the Most Christian King of France: Defender of the Faith. He would obstinately cherish this honour, and hand it down to his successors.

Yet the faith which Henry was defending radically shifted in the crisis of his first marriage. The fiasco of the Blackfriars trial, described by Virginia Murphy (above, chapter 6) propelled Henry away from his fitfully intense acceptance of the church's authority. The king who always had to be right was forced to admit that he had been wrong, that he had been deceived by clergymen: he had been wrong to fight France for the pope in 1512, wrong to write the *Assertio*. He must reconstruct his mental world, with no coherent set of instructions as to how to do this. The results were unpredictable, confused observers at the time, and have gone on confusing. The immediate result in 1529 was to propel Henry away from Thomas Wolsey towards the aristocrats at court who were uninhibited in their suspicion of clerical power. Such magnates as the dukes of Norfolk and Suffolk had no sympathy for the Continental Reformation (although Suffolk's few brain-cells would later suffer successful assault by the evangelical belief of his remarkable fourth wife, Catherine Willoughby).[22] To call their views anticlerical is inaccurate. They were anti-prelatical, suspicious of the pretensions of higher clergy to equality with aristocrats and (worse still) to an independent and superior jurisdiction within the realm: in particular, they saw such prelatical arrogance personified in cardinal Wolsey. Their hostility to higher church authority was paralleled in another anti-prelatical group: leading figures among the

London common lawyers. Christopher St German, a barrister of the Inner Temple who was equally conservative in his general religious outlook, expressed in his writings an intense pride in the English common law, a system unique in Europe which had bred one of the few professional groups independent of the clerical profession. St German consistently argued for common law's superiority within England to the provisions of the church's own canon law.[23] One man who knew this legal circle well, Wolsey's servant Thomas Cromwell, would soon master-mind the moves which decisively and permanently asserted that superiority.

In summer 1529 the aristocratic clique around Suffolk and Norfolk drew up a programme which was not simply intended to complete the personal and political ruin of Cardinal Wolsey, but also proposed an attack on the power of the church hierarchy generally, by giving the king the power to reform abuses in the church, drastically pruning the church's wealth and even considering the dissolution of all English monasteries. King Henry expressed in extreme form the anti-prelatical stance of this group when in October 1529 he said to the imperial ambassador Chapuys that the only power which the clergy had over laymen was absolution from sin.[24] This was a vision of the universal church as little more than a trade union of confessors: if authority was to be provided for such a shapeless body, it would best come from the anointed monarch of the realm. Attacks on the absolute power of the papacy could claim medieval precedents, although they had rarely proved as subversive of papal monarchy in practice as in theory; even Henry's break with Rome might have left him a doctrinal traditionalist in all other respects. What was different from the past was that Henry's assertion of his unique place in the English church (so conducive to his natural arrogance) might now gather to itself some of the flotsam of the theological upheavals taking place at the same time on the Continent.

For Henry said more to Chapuys, in a conversation which must have electrified the ambassador, quickly accustomed though he was becoming to Henry's efforts to shock him. The king now thought that his old enemy Luther had written many truths as well as much heresy in his attacks on the church. Here we can detect another influence on him more radical than that of the aristocratic leadership: Anne Boleyn. Despite recent doubts expressed by George Bernard, there is little reason to dismiss the genuine interest in church reform which Anne was showing by the late 1520s, bringing her to read a wide range of reformist works. Through her, they reached the king. Anne introduced Henry to the writings of William Tyndale, and possibly also to those of the stridently anticlerical common lawyer Simon Fish; these put into words Henry's resentments against clergymen, and reinforced his growing conviction of his own absolute power over cleric and layman alike in the realm.[25]

It is important to decide what label we should give radical reformist opinion around Henry VIII, because the obvious description 'Protestant' presents serious problems for discussion of the Henrician Reformation. It was a label only created in the same year as the Blackfriars marriage hearing, 1529, and it was invented in a foreign country to describe a foreign situation: the crisis in the Imperial Diet at Speyer. In 1530s and 1540s England, therefore, it was an alien and awkward as were 'perestroika' and 'glasnost' in 1980s England, and the first signs of it becoming nat-uralised in English discourse only appear tentatively in the bitter polarisations of Mary's reign, after 1553.[26] 'Lutheran' is nearly as bad, not least because traditionalist Catholics like ambassador Chapuys applied the label without discrimination to anyone whose religious views they disliked. During the 1520s, Luther had a major influence on English enthusiasts for religious change, but I have argued elsewhere that his variety of reformism was already beginning to give ground in England to the more radical theologi-cal influences of Strasbourg and Switzerland in the 1530s. This was probably because of the pre-existing native dissent of Lollardy, which was much closer to the theology of Strasbourg and Switzerland than to that of Luther.[27] There was also the unpredictable effect in the two universities of enthusiasm for Erasmus and other humanists, which could lead to radical scepti-cism about the claims and structures of the old church, and there was the equally unpredictable effect of common law studies on those who practised them. Besides this, the independently devel-oping strand of reformism in France was particularly significant for Anne Boleyn herself, because of her personal links with groups around the French court in which reformism was strong.

All these labels have a tendency to give a premature precision to people's outlooks at a time when new religious identities were only painfully and gradually being created out of a myriad indi-vidual rebellions against and unhappinesses with medieval Catholic theology. The vague label 'evangelical' is perhaps the best solution to the problem of description, precisely because it is vague. What it conveys is a necessary distinction from at least three groups of religious conservatives in politics who like the evangelicals supported the royal campaign for the divorce in the late 1520s and early 1530s: first, the anti-prelatical aristocratic circle at court; second, lawyers like St German, whose prime quarrel with the medieval western church was over jurisdiction; third, humanist academics who did not choose to leave the Catholic fold.

For the evangelicals, the major rallying-point was the need to reconstruct religion out of the scriptural text of the Good News, the *evangelion*: what is so useful about this criterion is that it relates to that major phenomenon in the pre-Reformation English church, its ban on the vernacular Bible. Richard Rex has convincingly shown that on the eve of the break with Rome, orthodox senior English churchmen like John Fisher were openly admitting that it would be a good thing if the Bible were in English; also undeniable, however, is that in the middle of many other worries and struggles, they did nothing about bible translation. Cuthbert Tunstall, bishop of London, indeed rejected the approaches of William Tyndale in the 1520s, and in the 1530s and 1540s non-evangelical bishops of previously impeccable humanist credentials such as John Stokesley and Stephen Gardiner deliberately dragged their heels against initiatives of translation.[28] The Roman Catholic church would have to wait until the 1580s until it acquired an English version of scripture without a health warning attached. By contrast, the evangelicals consistently emphasised the priority of creating direct access to scripture, and the publication of an official version of the Bible would be the lasting positive achievement of the 1530s.

There is plenty of evidence for Anne Boleyn's patronage of bible production and bible reading; likewise Anne also proved to be the earliest significant patron of a group of clergy who were to emerge as the leaders of the movement to disseminate evangelical opinions during the 1530s and later. She showed a marked preference for Cambridge graduates and dons; Cambridge men would take the lead in the early Reformation over Oxford, despite the powerful counter-influence at Cambridge of John Fisher. One can point as a minimum list of Boleyn protégés to William Bettes, Thomas Cranmer, Edward Crome, Nicholas Heath, Hugh and William Latimer, Matthew Parker, Nicholas Shaxton and John Skip: admittedly, not all would remain evangelicals for all their career.[29] Three of these men (Crome, Shaxton and Skip) were from Gonville Hall in Cambridge, where Anne's great-great-uncle had been Master; a Gonville layman who also had close connections with Anne was Dr William Butts, and he would have an important role in promoting the evangelical cause at court after Anne's death because of his continuing closeness to the king. One of Anne's most significant evangelical protégés has been neglected probably thanks to male chauvinism: the royal silk-woman Jane Wilkinson (sister to the civil servant and future peer Edward North) was to be one of the chief financial and moral mainstays of the Protestant Marian exiles two decades later.[30]

Alongside Anne, Thomas Cromwell and Thomas Cranmer emerged as the great patrons of evangelicals when the two men become prominent in the king's counsels during 1531, and they both managed to survive her fall in 1536. The evolution of Cromwell's religious opinions remains mysterious: he may have followed a similar development to Cranmer, who apparently remained a conservative humanist until 1531, but who then rapidly developed sympathy for and understanding of German Lutheran belief – Cranmer indeed sealed his Lutheran allegiance with the extraordinary step of breaking his clerical vows of celibacy, when he married Margarete, the niece of Andreas Osiander, a German Lutheran theologian. Thereafter Cranmer can be adequately defined as Lutheran in his evangelicalism throughout Henry's reign, retaining a belief like Luther in Christ's real and corporal presence in the eucharistic elements of bread and wine; his abandonment of real presence belief some time after 1546 was a useful peg on which his Catholic enemies could later hang charges of inconsistency. Cromwell's belief cannot be so closely examined, and analysis is muddied by the unlikely accusations of sacramentarian heresy (that is, denial of the real presence in the eucharist) with which he was destroyed in 1540. However, it is clear that from the moment of the archbishop's consecration in spring 1533, Cromwell and Cranmer worked closely together to push an evangelical agenda of change on the church; it was Cromwell who was most responsible for achieving that key item on the evangelical agenda, the official authorisation of an English Bible. A topsy-turvy scrap of evidence for their close cooperation is that the stray surviving letter-book of Cranmer's outgoing correspondence for 1533–5 contains almost no copies of his letters to Cromwell; clearly they were preserved in a separate administrative file, a testimony to a special relationship.[31]

Cromwell's partnership with Cranmer was an unequal one, and Cromwell's dominance in it was formalised thanks to Henry's grant to him of a unique status in the church: vicar-general and vicegerent in spirituals. The grant of the vicegerency became necessary because of the humiliating failure of Cranmer's first major excursion into reform: an archiepiscopal visitation of the Province of Canterbury during summer 1534. A trio of conservative bishops, Longland of Lincoln, Stokesley of London and Nix of Norwich, disrupted the proceedings by protesting against Cranmer's exercise of his jurisdiction, Stokesley and Longland using the highly damaging argument that Cranmer's powers to visit were derived from the pope; Corpus Christi College, Oxford, later followed suit, perhaps inspired by hints from the College Visitor, Stephen Gardiner.

It was clear after this that change in the church would have to be engineered in other ways. The passage of the Act of Supremacy in November 1534 specifically confirmed the king in rights of visitation as Supreme Head of the church, and this was followed by the granting of the commission which created Cromwell's vicegerency, probably on 21 January 1535. Henceforth Cromwell's jurisdiction, deputed from that of Henry as Supreme Head, outranked Cranmer's, just as Cardinal Wolsey's authority as legate delegated from the pope had outranked Archbishop Warham's powers as primate.[32] Cranmer, however, showed no sign of resentment at the erosion of the ancient powers of his office. It is clear that he felt out of his depth in politics, and he consistently took his lead from Cromwell. On one occasion it would have been better if Cromwell had listened to him: during 1538 or 1539 Cranmer tentatively advised Cromwell that the widowed king should remarry someone within the realm, since 'it would be very strange to be married with her that he could not talk withal'. Cranmer, with his German wife, spoke from experience! Yet Cromwell, clearly appalled at the thought of the promotion of one family from among his aristocratic rivals, brusquely pushed aside the suggestion, saying that 'there was none meet for [Henry] within this realm'; and the stage was set for the Anne of Cleves debacle which destroyed the vicegerent.[33]

Evangelicals might disagree among themselves about such political matters and about how far they wished to push religious change, yet two external factors forced on them a unity of purpose and outlook. First was their nervousness about religious radicalism beyond the pale, the assorted reassessments of mainstream Christianity which were crudely summed up as Anabaptism. Such radicalism was a Continental phenomenon which only marginally affected Henry's England, mostly as Continental Anabaptists escaped to England to seek a slightly less hostile atmosphere. Only a small minority of English people were influenced by these immigrants, and there are no traceable Anabaptists within the political nation of Henrician England, in contrast with the sympathy which the radicals initially found among aristocrats and civic leaders in the Low Countries. Cranmer, for instance, was involved in the persecution against Anabaptism right from the first English campaign against them in spring 1535; he then personally examined and disputed with some of them, and he would remain at the centre of official efforts to combat their doctrines, including the only two burnings for heresy to take place in the reign of Edward VI.[34]

Perhaps still more significant in uniting the evangelicals was the consistent hostility and danger of attack which they experienced from the various conservative groupings, symbolised by the abusive phase which traditionalist Catholics quickly coined in the 1520s, 'the New Learning'. At the time this term was never applied to humanism, as has misleadingly become common in modern historical writing, but always to those of evangelical outlook; the phrase much annoyed evangelicals, prompting them in turn defensively to accuse traditionalists of being the real innovators. Conservatives may not have known much about theology, but they knew what they disliked.[35]

However, conservatives were divided in politics as evangelicals were not, in ways which proved fatal to any attempt to put up effective resistance to the gradual spread of evangelicalism within the church during the 1530s and 1540s. Fundamental to their divisions was the crisis over Henry VIII's campaign for annulment of his first marriage. This was not a contest between the Old and the New Learning: Luther was as consistent in his hostility to the annulment and in his sympathy for Catherine of Aragon as were the Holy Roman Emperor and the pope. The big fight about the annulment between 1527 and 1529 was among religious conservatives. The chief actors in the drive to get the king what he wanted included John Stokesley, Stephen Gardiner, Richard Croke, Robert Wakefield and the duke of Norfolk, while many others who became sucked into the royal research industry did not enter it as evangelicals: witness Thomas Cranmer. Championing queen Catherine were John Fisher and (much more discreetly) Thomas More, together with the great names in the complex of convents around the royal palaces. The chief researchers in the king's camp had previously been part of the same world of devout, refined humanist Catholicism.[36] This breach among conservatives would never be healed. Moreover, the natural supporters of the old church had been split during the 1520s in a different way, by their attitude to Wolsey: either loyalty to a provider of lavish patronage, or principled detestation, often connected with the cardinal's high-handed attempts to redirect monastic wealth for his own collegiate foundations. Wolsey, for instance, signally humiliated Richard Nix of Norwich, the model of a conscientious traditionalist bishop, and an anonymous chronicler of Butley Priory in Suffolk described the cardinal's monastic dissolutions as being to the shame, scandal, destruction and ruin of all the monks and nuns of England.[37]

A sign of what might have been possible for conservatives against evangelicals is the changing political stance of Thomas, Lord Darcy of Templehurst. Darcy, a veteran royal servant particularly on the northern English border, had actually been the scribe for the radical programme for attacking the power and wealth of the church put forward by the anti-prelatical aristocrats in summer 1529. By 1535, increasingly alarmed at the direction taken by the church with Thomas Cromwell as vicar-general and vicegerent, and in particular at the rapidly developing attack on the monasteries, he was in regular treasonable communication with Eustace Chapuys, discussing rebellion against the king; in 1536 he joined the rebels in the Pilgrimage of Grace, surrendering his charge of Pontefract Castle to them. If other prominent conservatives had followed suit, notably the leader of the expeditionary force against the rebels, Thomas, duke of Norfolk, then the evangelicals would have been doomed. But Darcy remained the most prominent traditionalist nobleman to rally to the Pilgrims' banner. The defenders of traditional religion had hesitated, and their cause was ultimately lost.[38]

Throughout the 1530s the problem for conservatives was to decide when enough was enough, and when to make a stand. This is best exemplified by the dissolution of the monasteries, an operation of remarkable efficiency which within eight years extinguished all monasteries, nunneries and friaries within England and Wales. At no time during this process did the government officially condemn the principle of the monastic life (a fact which would be of use to those Anglicans who revived it by private enterprise in the nineteenth century); indeed on the only occasion that parliament was consulted about an extension of the dissolution, in spring 1536, the plan was presented in the preamble of the Act as an effort to strengthen the greater monasteries, even though the government simultaneously blackened the reputations of the monks as much as it could. Richard Hoyle has elsewhere under-lined the clever strategy of this measure: it contained an escape clause for the preservation of worthy smaller monasteries, which allowed any member of parliament who knew that accusations of depravity did not apply to his own local house, to vote for the measure without too much struggle of conscience. Hoyle inter-prets this as a tacit admission by the government that it could never secure conscious parliamentary assent to a radical strategy of dissolution. Gradualism was the key.[39]

The final parliamentary dissolution legislation of 1539 merely recognised a *fait accompli* without further explanation: what else could it do, after the approving noises about greater monasteries in the 1536 preamble? Richard Hoyle, indeed, argues for a consis-tent strategy of wholesale dissolution from the beginning of the operation. It is possible, however, to look for consistent differ-ences of vision even among those involved in planning the disso-lution. We tend to see the process through the office papers of Thomas Cromwell, since that is the archive which has happened to survive; how would it look if the archives of Framlingham Castle and Kenninghall Palace were intact, and we could hear the conversations around the conservative leader the duke of Norfolk, who was equally intimately involved in the monastic dissolutions? If there was indeed no unified vision of what would happen to the monasteries, then it was all the harder for the conservatives to construct a unified opposition.

In this as in all the major steps of religious change, we need to consider the man at the centre of politics: the king himself. From the mid-1530s, Henry was deliberately presenting a policy of balance, of Janus-like impartiality, in his religious strategy. One can see this in his successive attempts in the 1530s and 1540s to take a leaf out of the Reformers' book and issue statements about what his church actually believed: the subtly adjusted three-way balances between Catholic tradition, Catholic humanist reform and evangelical innovation within the Ten Articles (1536), *Bishops' Book* (1537) and *King's Book* (1543) remain both confus-ing to the novice student and flashpoints for controversy among scholars. Even the Six Articles of 1539, at first sight a savagely uncompromising traditionalist document, made one major con-cession to evangelicals in the Articles' description of auricular confession: they said that this sacrament is merely 'expedient and necessary to be retained and continued ... in the Church of God', a departure from medieval doctrine which infuriated the conservative bishop of Durham, Cuthbert Tunstall. Remarkably and surely significantly, they also opened with a repeated reference to the 'Church and Congregation of England'. '*Congregatio*' was a word which Erasmus had suggested as an alternative translation to 'church' for the Greek '*ekklesia*', but it had become more than a piece of humanist pedantry; it was taken up by such alarming evangelicals as the bible translator William Tyndale. In the Articles, the source was probably the Lutheran Augsburg Confession of 1530, where Philip Melanchthon had defined the church as the '*congregatio sanctorum*'.[40]

The strategy of balance was repeatedly announced by both Henry and his primate of all England, Cranmer; it was clearly something which much impressed Cranmer about the king's religious policy. John Guy has already noted how the official explanation of Thomas Cromwell's fall stressed his 'leaving the mean indifferent true and virtuous way' (above, p. 43). Later, in a major speech to parliament in December 1545, Henry denounced both those who 'be too stiff in their old mumpsimus' and those who were 'too busy and curious in their new sumpsimus', and he reduced himself to tears as he pleaded for unity in his realm.[41] What is interesting about this speech is that it echoes a major public text by Cranmer of five years before, his Preface to the official Great Bible. Henry picked up not only Cranmer's description of the Bible as a 'most precious jewel', but also Cranmer's general Janus-like strategy in his Preface, which was a twofold sermon addressed both to those 'that be too slow, and need the spur', and those who 'seem too quick, and need more of the bridle'.[42] When Cranmer chose six preachers for the reorganised Canterbury Cathedral foundation in 1540, he 'set in Christchurch [Cathedral] ... three of the Old Learning and three of the New ... and said that he had showed the King's Grace what he had done in that matter, and that the King's pleasure was that it should be so.'[43] It was no coincidence that the only major Reformer whom the king made strenuous efforts (ultimately in vain) to tempt into an English visit was that habitual seeker after the middle way and moderator of Luther's angular faith, Philip Melanchthon.

The strategy of balance was not mere empty rhetoric. From time to time we can catch fleeting glimpses of the furious rows and back-room fudges which produced the successive statements of official doctrine: for instance the exasperated remarks by Hugh Latimer (not a man born to compromise) about the painful creation of the *Bishops' Book* in July 1537:

> As for myself, I can nothing else but pray God that when it is done it be well and sufficiently done, so that we shall not need to have any more such doings. For verily, for my part, I had liever be poor parson of poor [West] Kington again, than to continue thus Bishop of Worcester ... forsooth it is a troublous thing to agree upon a doctrine in things of such controversy, with judgements of such diversity, every man (I trust) meaning well, and yet not all meaning one way.[44]

Occasionally also the working papers behind statements survive, vividly illustrating the continual process of compromise forced by the king. One such set consists of a pair of drafts for the 1536 Ten Articles, trying to construct what would become Articles 6, 7 and 8 on images, honouring of saints and praying to saints. The second of the two drafts is consistently evangelical in flavour, giving only a grudging role to images and saints, and only one phrase from it appears in the eventual text of Article 7. More was used from the first of the drafts, and corrections on it reveal an interesting tussle between Cranmer and Cuthbert Tunstall. Tunstall adds to the secretary's text an affirmation that 'we may pray to our blessed Lady and John Baptist, the Apostles or any other saint particularly as our devotion doth serve us, without any superstition'; Cranmer sharply corrects the end phrase to 'so that [i.e. as long as] it be done without any vain superstition'. The combination of the two bishops' alterations arrives in the finished text. Noticeably, the elements of the first draft which were cut out include a long meandering introductory discussion of the limitations of images as poor men's substitutes for books, together with a rather silly list by Cranmer ridiculing the more esoteric calls of devotees on saints' time, including 'St Apollonia for toothache ... St Barbara for thunder and gunshot, and such other'. The final product is a far less discursive, far more focused and dignified piece of prose; above all, it contains something to please both evangelicals and traditionalists, and something to annoy them both.[45]

The royal strategy of balance was not just arbitrary political expediency; it reflected the deep rift within the king's own theological outlook which had opened up fully by the beginning of the 1540s. In many ways, the king jettisoned the past in his last decade. Most importantly, the idea of purgatory, central to the faith of northern Europe for centuries, lost its grip on him. In 1536 he was still prepared to put up a vigorous and rather effect- ive attack on a paper compiled by Hugh Latimer against purgat- ory. For instance, he gleefully knocked down Latimer's unwise use of the argument from silence on the subject in selected early church writings: 'Must the saints take occasion to write where you think place is for them, or where they think it meetest?'[46] However, already in his proposed revisions of the *Bishops' Book*, in late 1537 or early 1538, Henry showed that he was drifting away from any lively belief in purgatory. The *King's Book* which was the eventual fruit in 1543 of this process of revision generally made changes in a conservative direction, but significantly this was not so on purgatory. Even the name was now declared suspect: 'we should therefore abstain from the name of Purgatory and no more dispute or reason thereof.' The *King's Book* still commended masses for the dead, yet not to deliver people from purgatory pain but merely out of charity because the dead are part of the body of Christ, like us. Now purgatory's ancient power over human destiny was reduced to the vaguest of assertions, and as the most recent historian of the chantries' destruction has said, this 'effectively cut the ground from beneath the chantry system'.[47]

There are other signs of Henry's changing ideas. His suspicion of clerical pretension encouraged him in the *King's Book* to down- grade the sacraments of confirmation, extreme unction and to reject the full traditional mystique of priestly ordination.[48] He also changed his mind on the character of individual confession to a priest; in the *Assertio* in 1521 he and his tame academics had put the traditional view that it had been instituted by God himself. By 1539, when the king was in other respects backing an extreme conservative religious reaction, he had changed his mind on con- fession; it was not instituted by God. He got very angry when Bishop Tunstall argued the traditionalist case, and he tore Tunstall off a strip in one of the longest letters he ever wrote: especially remarkable since Henry hated putting pen to paper. As already noted, this was the only significant point which the king allowed the evangelicals to win in the Six Articles.[49] We can also get an insight into Henry's mind from his rather complacent annotations to his personal psalter which date from the 1540s. These reveal that he remained proud of his achievement in destroying shrines and sacred images, which he completed in 1542: he repeatedly noted God's anger against false worship and idols, and singled out a mention of Phineas, an Old Testament judge who rescued Israel from the consequences of idolatry.[50]

Alongside this was the king who remained a conservative to his dying day. He never accepted the central Protestant doctrine of justification by faith, despite all Cranmer's efforts to persuade him, especially in the revision of the *Bishops' Book*; so he had lost his hold on purgatory while not finding his way to a coherent replacement doctrine on salvation.[51] To see this is to make some sense at last of the apparently baffling twists of policy and inconsistencies in the king: he was caught between his lack of full belief in either of two mutually opposed ways of seeing the road to salvation. What did he have instead? A ragbag of emotional preferences. He cherished his beautiful personal rosary, which still exists; he maintained the mass in all its ancient Latin splendour and he left instructions in his will for a generous supply of requiems, in line with his new rationale for them in the *King's Book*.

Henry was at his most reactionary and obstinate on the subject of marriage – understandably, since this had lain at the heart of his recurrent personal crises. He insisted (against the facts of scripture and church history) that marriage was one of the basic scriptural sacraments like baptism and the eucharist, and his bishops obediently pandered to his prejudices when they were compiling the *Bishops' Book*: there marriage managed to pull rank on the sacraments of baptism and the eucharist by having been 'instituted by God and consecrated by his word and dignified by his laws, even from the beginning of the world'. The king liked the bishops' work on marriage so much that it was preserved virtually unaltered in the *King's Book*.[52] Henry also upheld the ancient ban on clerical marriage, additionally refusing to release from their celibate vows the monks and nuns whose lives he had shattered and whose communities he had destroyed. He added a special personal provision to the Act of Six Articles that people who had taken vows of widowhood should be treated as severely as other celibates under the Act if they broke their vows; that exposed them to the threat of execution as felons. Yet even in his obstinate traditionalism on marriage, his anticlericalism asserted itself; he said that married clergy would form dynasties which would be even more of a threat to royal power than the celibates![53]

Henry VIII once described 'the law of every man's conscience' to be 'the highest and supreme court for judgement or justice'.[54] He was afforded the luxury of erecting his private conscience into the guiding religious teaching of an entire kingdom, and it was a luxury which he often abused. His prized theory of balance could turn to murderous paranoia, most notably in the incident in which three prominent evangelical clergy and three prominent papalist Catholics were executed on the same day (30 July 1540), but also all through the 1540s, when more evangelicals and papalists died for not fitting the king's conscience. His last year of life was particularly full of abrupt swings of mood. In January 1546 Cranmer was eagerly presenting him with plans for further liturgical change, acting on signals from the king himself, but nothing came of them; in spring and early summer Henry allowed a murderous campaign against the evangelicals by conservatives, yet by August he was suggesting to the French ambassador the abolition of the mass in both England and France. In December the duke of Norfolk and the house of Howard, aristocratic backbone of traditionalist religion, were brought low because of the dying king's fury and fear when Norfolk's heir the earl of Surrey (ironically himself a favourer of evangelical reform) rashly stressed Howard royal blood; Bishop Gardiner was then also in disgrace, and the future of the realm was in the hands of evangelicals.[55]

Amid these swings of fortune, all through the 1540s, the key people close to the king's person were evangelicals: notably his long-trusted doctor William Butts (d. 1545), Sir Anthony Denny, the chief gentleman of his privy chamber, quiet compliant Archbishop Cranmer and the king's last wife from 1543, Catherine Parr. His son's education, so vital for the future of England's religion, was in the hands of evangelicals from Cambridge, when it would have been perfectly possible to choose orthodox Catholic academics.[56] However much Henry was in his lifetime balancing change, he was stacking the odds after his death in favour of the evangelicals. It is worth noting a reminiscence of Martin Bucer, the reformer of Strasbourg who like Philip Melanchthon always sought consensus and the middle way among evangelicals. Only a year after Henry's death, Bucer claimed that he had recently offered the king a book attacking compulsory clerical celibacy against the writings of Bishop Gardiner of Winchester and others; however Henry replied

> that he had rather I should defer for a season the publishing abroad thereof, for he trusted to come to pass that I should speak of this and other controversies in religion at some time peaceably with Winchester, and other learned of his realm, to the intent a godly concord and unity in religion might be

sought forth, and a further instauration [i.e. renovation] of the churches, which his purpose I might have hindered, if Winchester (whose bitterness in writing he did in no manner wise allow) should have been provoked to write any more openly against us [the evangelical reformers].[57]

Bucer's words add some weight to the possibility that Henry, confident both of his abilities as theological referee and of his own survival on this earth, was planning further to alter his church's balancing act, and move England in an evangelical direction.

What united the diverse strands of Henry's religious policy? Apparently Henry's conviction of his unique relationship with God as his anointed deputy on earth, a conviction strong enough to be shared by his devoted but not uncritical admirer Cranmer. Once or twice Henry half-heartedly entered negotiations which implied some surrender of his Royal Supremacy: first at the Imperial Diet at Regensburg (Ratisbon) in 1541, when in diplomatic isolation he was eagerly courting the emperor's favour, and second in that fevered summer of 1546, in response to a quixotic mission from an ultra-Anglophile papal envoy, Gurone Bertano. It is difficult to believe that Henry would ever seriously have contemplated surrendering the Supremacy. Increasingly in the decoration of his palaces and personal possessions, he identified himself with the Old Testament hero-king David, who in his youth had slain Goliath as Henry had slain the Goliath of the papacy. In his last years, the king turned for comfort to the songs of David in the Psalms and to the thoughts of David's son Solomon in Proverbs; who better, after all, than his fellow-monarchs to speak to the private thoughts of a king? We still have his own copies of both books.[58] Henry's illustrated psalter makes the point straight away. Psalm 1 begins 'Blessed is the man who does not walk in the counsel of the ungodly ... his delight is in the law of the Lord, and on his law he meditates day and night': against this verse, Henry scrawled 'note who is blessed'. Above is the picture of a royal bedroom, with a king meditating day and night on a book: a king who is both the Old Testament king who wrote the psalm, and the Tudor king, dressed in the clothes familiar to us from Holbein portraits. After a career in which he had discovered the full meaning of an English king's supremacy in the church, Henry had no doubts that he was that blessed man of whom his royal predecessor had spoken.

8. Literature, Drama and Politics

SEYMOUR BAKER HOUSE

Writing to Sir William Paget shortly after the death of Henry VIII, Bishop Gardiner of Winchester complained

> Tomorrow the parishioners of this parish and I have agreed to have solemn dirge for our late sovereign lord and master in earnest as becomes us and tomorrow certain players of my lord of Oxford's, as they say, intend on the other side within this borough of Southwark to have a solemn play to try who shall have most resort, they in game or I in earnest.[1]

Gardiner asked for Paget's intervention in the name of the privy council to stop this play since the inhabitants of Southwark obeyed neither the local justice of the peace 'whom the players smally regard' nor the bishop himself: 'his nay is not much regarded and mine less'. This pair of antithetical ceremonies marking the king's death indicates not only the importance popular drama had come to assume during the second half of Henry VIII's reign but the defiance by reformers intent on taking a more radical line than that permitted by the ecclesiastical and secular authorities alike. It also illustrates a general trend to be observed in the relation of literature and drama to politics in the reign; that is, that debate over religious issues involving politics at the highest level had become an occupation as much at street level as it was among the governing classes.

As Bishop Gardiner's plea suggests, efforts to prevent public expressions of dissent and even outright disobedience by players during the late king's reign had not been an unqualified success. Despite numerous royal proclamations, municipal injunctions, episcopal inhibitions and finally imprisonments and executions, plays and playing continued along the trajectory facilitated by Thomas Cromwell in the early years after the break with Rome,

although his fall in 1540 precipitated a sharp decline in patronised drama for the rest of Henry VIII's reign.

The highly charged political atmosphere surrounding such performances meant that all parties – those offended and those
delighted – were potentially at risk. Gardiner's complaint to Paget
is cautious – the ambiguous 'as they say' allows for the possibility,
at least in theory, that the players were claiming the earl's protection without his consent.[2] As an embattled conservative who had
been excluded from the Council of Regency for the young king
by the dying Henry VIII, the bishop could hardly afford to accuse
Oxford, holder of the realm's oldest peerage, of directly sponsor-
ing such inflammatory antics.[3]

By the end of Henry VIII's reign, drama had grown away from
its traditional or seasonal themes such as Robin Hood and May
games, to embrace impromptu performances explicitly treating
contemporary religious and political developments. Reformers
castigated the secular content of earlier days, preferring instead
more godly matters, grounded in scripture, presenting Protestant
doctrine. A similar change had occurred in court performances.
While there had long been itinerant players presenting interludes
for the entertainment of England's political elite in gentry and
noble houses and corporate halls throughout the country, by the
1530s some players were offering far more radical fare than they
had previously, sheltering behind the protection of a patron,
exploiting the uncertainty of the times. In the case of elite drama,
the contrast between the old and the new can easily be seen, for
example, by comparing the entertainment provided in 1528/29
for the Plymouth civic leaders by the duke of Suffolk's servant
'with the dancing bear and the dancing wife' with Thomas, earl of
Wiltshire's production of a farce in 1531 during a dinner with the
new French ambassador which depicted the late Cardinal Wolsey's
descent into hell. He later had it printed, for wider circulation.[4]

Because performers were an integral part of court festivities
and public spectacles, their promoters, whether individual or
civic, had always been ideally positioned to exploit their appearances for personal or political ends. Elite entertainments and
masques commonly illustrated moral and chivalric themes or
demonstrated political affinities, public spectacles intended for
state occasions reinforced traditional concepts of royal authority
and piety, and popular entertainments followed their local religious and seasonal themes. Typical among the entertainments at
court before the king's 'great matter' intruded was Wolsey's lavish

allegorical production in 1522 featuring ladies named Beauty, Honour, Perseverance, Kindness and the like. Held prisoner in a painted castle by exotic women gaolers representing less desirable qualities such as Danger, Disdain, Scorn, and Strangeness, the fairer ladies are eventually rescued by the chivalric knights of Nobleness, Pleasure, Gentleness, and others. The king most likely took part.[5] Later that year at the entry of Charles V into London, the customary pageantry had employed heavily allegorical iconography illustrating royal and chivalric themes and pious conceits. For the benefit of those few who could understand them, learned Latin orations reinforced the imagery. Ironically, the final pageant along the emperor's route from Greenwich to St Paul's was a tableau depicting England's most famous saint, Thomas Becket, whose cult would soon fall prey to England's rush of iconoclasm in 1538.[6]

At times, players dealt directly with the contemporary politics that preoccupied their employers. Controversial political entertainments, such as Wiltshire's anti-Wolsey farce, were explicitly in-house affairs for the benefit of guests whose political views were sympathetic to their host's. In this case, his guests included Wolsey's erstwhile opponent the duke of Norfolk and Claude de la Guiche, the recently appointed French ambassador; among them, pro-French diplomacy, aristocratic pride or simple blood ties combined to cement a common political posture. Less private but still quite restricted were plays such as that satirising the cardinal at Gray's Inn during the 1526–7 Christmas festivities. Although written about 1506 and featuring the personifications of Dissipation, Negligence, Lord Governance, Disdain of Wanton Sovereignty, Inward Grudge, and others, the inherent flexibility of dramatic presentation allowed a reorientation for the purposes of polemic, but still relied on heavily allegorical figures to project its message. Drama still spoke obliquely, and behind closed doors, even if the allegory was a bit too transparent: John Roo cooled his heels in the Fleet for offending the minister, and Simon Fish, who acted Wolsey's part, was forced into temporary exile.[7] Entertainments of this sort required no fundamental reorientation in dramatic strategy, either for the viewers or the promoters. Nor did they present any new development in dramatic content: such displays were simply *ad hominem* attacks on a despised political opponent.

When the Lutheran reforms reached England, the content of elite court festivities began to change. In place of chivalric themes we find a type of entertainment bred not from merriment or *ad hominem* partisan politics but drama concerned with national, even international, religious controversy. In presenting this new subject matter, court drama dispensed with allegory and spoke more directly, if still using fictive representation. In John Heywood's conservative *The Foure PP* (1531?) certain proposed reforms regarding Christian praxis are discussed shortly after they became current in English polemical debate. His characters are not personifications of abstract virtues or vices but rather participants in a debate on the very issues then facing the church. Through comic exaggeration, Heywood defused the Lutheran attack on traditional practices such as pilgrimages and the veneration of relics, ending with a plea for tolerance under the continued guidance of the church. The question then became, how was the church guided?

Because the Protestant reforms were not limited to sacramental theology but rather centred on the issue of Catholic inerrancy, the Lutheran doctrines addressed by *The Foure PP* were quickly subsumed in the more immediate concern of the royal supremacy. After 1529, parliament began to adjudicate in matters previously outside its jurisdiction, threatening the age-old autonomy of the English church. In 1532, the English clergy had capitulated to royal pressure, forfeiting its independent jurisdiction and recognising, in some ill-defined manner, the king's claim to primacy in the affairs of the English church. For Catholics, it was a novel and threatening situation, and drew a response from Heywood that further exploited the strategy he had employed in *The Foure PP*. Speaking directly to the current political situation, his *The Play of the Wether* (performed Lent, 1533?) addresses the debate on ecclesiastical autonomy through the thinnest of fictions. By using innovative staging which recreated a Tudor monarch's 'presence chamber' and its protocol, and by peopling his drama with recognisably English characters drawn from contemporary society, Heywood skilfully eased the audience into drawing aside his fictive veil. The play urges the king to preserve the status quo by taking matters into his own hands away from the self-serving petitioners in parliament. This tacit admission of the royal supremacy was a bitter pill for Catholic conservatives, although it is sweetened by Lucianic humour and the promise of an end to ecclesiastical reforms. Its humorous tone and temperate polemic place *The Play of the Wether* firmly in the early sessions of the Reformation Parliament when the integration of cultured entertainment and political controversy was still possible. But in both Heywood's plays, the absence of rhetorical distancing, the dissolving fictive features, and the innovative techniques all reveal the growing politicisation of the stage. Heywood's career as a dramatist temporarily ended in 1539. His conservative stance led to an indictment and recantation in 1544, but with Cranmer's help his *Foure PP* and *The Play of the Wether*, whose conservative offerings were now more tolerable, were reprinted and a new comedy, *The Parts of Man*, was commissioned.[8]

Heywood's controversial drama notwithstanding, the extreme political uncertainty following Wolsey's fall in 1529/30 and the lack of identifiable policy during the next few years suggests a reason for the drop in patronised performances which continued until a strong anti-papal programme had been hammered out after 1534. During the fraught months of 1534–5, players of only a handful of patrons are known to have made the rounds of various civic and municipal venues: the king and queen, Mary, Lord Lisle, George Boleyn, and the earl of Derby. Those festivities which were put on assumed an increasingly explicit political content, generally in step with current official policy. In the winter of 1533–4, with the campaign to elicit support for the royal supremacy in full swing, the Christmas revels at the Inns of Court were a far cry from traditional farce – directed primarily against the pope and his supporters, the festivities included 'such pastimes as hath not been seen and the pope is not set by [i.e. spared]' and drew comments on their innovation and boldness. Spectacles mocking the pope were seen not only at elite venues: in the very streets of London players derided the pope and his cardinals.[9]

Anti-papal propaganda gained momentum as the need to combat resistance grew. Opposition to the reforms by leading citizens and respected clerics hardened the official attitude on dissent, and as the executions began, spectacles were presented using startlingly macabre verisimilitude. The French ambassador described one outdoor pageant which Henry VIII watched approvingly on 23 June 1535. The scene depicted a chapter from the book of Revelation which featured the decapitation of various ecclesiastics. It was fit entertainment indeed – the day before, Cardinal John Fisher, bishop of Rochester, had been executed and little over a week earlier three other priests had been put to death.[10] The king was said to have openly displayed himself 'in order to laugh at his ease, and encourage the people' and sent an ominous message to Queen Anne to the effect that she should see the pageant repeated on the eve of St Peter, five days later. More executions followed. Public drama and political action were now explicitly wedded.

This politicisation of dramatic spectacle raised problems concerning attendance. When displays were used to advertise a contentious state policy, the difference between private entertainment among like-minded peers and official public spectacle was immediately apparent. Thomas More realised that at such events, the appearance of consent was implied by mere attendance; in 1533 he remained conspicuously absent at Anne Boleyn's coronation. Several years later, the French diplomat Marillac made explicit the connection between attendance and consent. In June 1539 he described a 'game of poor grace' on the Thames designed to demonstrate the king's resolve in the face of an anticipated papal interdict (Henry VIII had been openly excommunicated the previous year) and possible invasion. Earlier that year both Spain and France had recalled their ambassadors from London, and the king was currently engaged in a massive fortification scheme against the threat of combined Catholic action. Some grand demonstration of English defiance and ultimate victory was necessary to boost morale, or, in Marillac's words, 'to show people that this king will entirely confound and abolish the power of the Holy Father'. The king's household, therefore, staged a public performance in which a barge bearing the royal arms overthrew one representing the pope and his cardinals after a lengthy and presumably highly entertaining water battle. In his report Marillac pointed out that he had to rely on eyewitness descriptions, for he himself 'deemed it contrary to duty to be a spectator'.[11] In short, Marillac's absence too assumed the dimensions of a public political gesture.

Resistance to the government's programme continued despite executions and other public spectacles. Uprisings such as the 1536 Pilgrimage of Grace, in which thousands of armed men were led against towns and royal strongholds by disaffected members of the northern aristocracy, posed an especially grave threat and clearly identified the religious reforms as central to the opposition. Such revolts added urgency to the authorities' growing propaganda efforts. For the Londoner or semi-urban gentry, printed literature such as *A Remedy for Sedition* by Cromwell's client Richard Morison, might serve to bolster loyalty to the crown's policies, but an appeal to the non-literate majority of the population was essential. Accordingly, an attempt was made to regulate conventional media such as preaching. The problem became particularly acute during the suppression of the monasteries. Despite periodic complaints about the wealth and indolence of the regulars, popular sentiment was by no means univocal in condemning the longstanding monastic houses vital to the local economy – ballads and poems had circulated supporting them – so a new campaign was begun to discredit them in the eyes of the people. Cromwell's appointment in 1534 as vicegerent in spirituals had given him extraordinary powers of visitation, and he soon orchestrated disclosure of the more notorious examples of monastic depravity and fraud in conjunction with their findings.[12] Other avenues were also explored. Arguing that 'into the common people things sooner enter by the eyes, than by the ears: remembering more better that they see than that they hear', Richard Morison urged Cromwell to replace the content of secular folk drama with more aggressive and topical matters detailing 'the abhomination and wickedness of the bishop of Rome, monks, friars, nuns, and such like', coupled with exhortations for obedience to the king.[13] In the economy of the royal supremacy, anti-monasticism was consistent with anti-papal politics. At the same time, it could be used as a means of criticising not only the sanctity of religious vows, but the panoply of Catholic practices which made up the daily routine of religious life. In short, whether he was convinced by Morison or not, anti-monastic drama would suit Cromwell's needs admirably.

In the religious sphere, drama's suasive potential had long been exploited. The great English cycle plays developed and informed piety while entertaining audiences from all strata of society. By mixing tragedy and comedy, farce and scriptural instruction, practitioners had long realised that dramatic representation was easily the richest medium available to early modern England.[14] This had important consequences for the use of drama as an instrument of public policy during the Henrician Reformation.

It was at this time that Cromwell recruited John Bale, a former East Anglian Carmelite whose reforming plays fitted well with the programme to depict the regulars as both treasonous and fraudulent. From 1537 until his exile in 1540, his troupe toured the country under Cromwell's protection, presenting the reforming message to civic corporations, guilds, monasteries, and even the court itself.[15] Initially shaped for popular audiences in his native Suffolk, Bale's work not surprisingly draws heavily on the traditional conceits and structures of native English cycle and miracle plays. His surviving plays, as well as the titles of lost works and the works of other playwrights active during this time, confirm that clerical playwrights had naturally turned to drama to present the reformed theology they had come to support. Bale's works in particular show a tendency to use scripture as a refracting lens for viewing contemporary events. This lent itself readily to the creation of a biblical typology which was later popularised by John Foxe. For Cromwell, their polemical value lay in the presentation of English history through select biblical narratives that literally give divine sanction to the royal supremacy. In addition, they argued for the abolition of many non-scriptural practices he favoured but was unable to implement unilaterally. These advanced Protestant views required careful handling, since they condemned beliefs the king was known to support.

Perhaps following on the successful symbiosis of Bale's talents and the political instinct of his patron, other Protestant playwrights tendered their services to Cromwell, or were recommended to him by his clients. One such priest, Thomas Wylley, vicar of Yoxford, performed at Cromwell's house in Lent, 1538, with his juvenile scholars. He offered additional plays for Cromwell's promotion, including one called 'Rude Commonalty', perhaps touching on the uprisings of 1536–7, and an unfinished one called 'Woman on the Rock, in the fire of faith affining and a purging in the true purgatory, never to be seen but of your Lordship's eye'. These may have been too radical, for in the end he was not patronised.[16] Significantly, both Bale and Wylley were more fully Protestant than official policy allowed; both had written reforming drama for local consumption well in advance of the government's campaign against the pope or the monasteries and certainly before their association with Cromwell, and perhaps most importantly, both relied upon the protection of a Protestant patron without whom they doubtless would have fallen victim to the Henrician statutes against heresy. As it was, Bale had twice been imprisoned before Cromwell rescued him 'on account of his plays', and Wylley's approach to Cromwell required the facilitation of one of Cromwell's clients to bear fruit. In short, the use of biblical texts in reforming drama did not originate with Cromwell but rather was recognised by him (and other like-minded policy makers) as a valuable political tool.

Although composition dates for his works are sketchy, most of Bale's works were written before his association with Cromwell, which began in January 1537. Many are narrow in focus, like his lost work 'On the King's Two Marriages' which clearly referred to the marriage with Anne Boleyn and could not have been played after May 1536 when proceedings against her had begun. Evidence suggests that he updated his plays following his recruitment. In particular, his *King John* shows signs of augmentation to incorporate fresh revelations stemming from Cromwell's visitation of the monasteries. It is certain that he tailored his productions carefully to suit the political situation, following the dictates of his patron. Cromwell's hand is seen most clearly in the precise matching of venue, audience, and subject matter over which he alone had control.

The most telling use of the new directness in patronised drama lies in Bale's performance before the king and court at Cranmer's house in Canterbury on the evening of 7 September 1538. The timing was crucial, coinciding not only with Cromwell's injunctions to the clergy restricting traditional observances and warning that further reforms of traditional praxis were forthcoming, but with the culmination of the campaign against relics which Cromwell had been energetically pursuing for over a year. The play Bale seems to have performed on this occasion was his lost 'Against the Treasons of Thomas à Becket' at the very time when Cromwell's agents were busy stripping the Becket shrine itself. What the courtiers saw before them on stage was in fact being enacted at Becket's shrine nearby as they watched the performance. In this case, attendance at one implied acquiescence to the other. Continental reaction was predictable. The papal nuncio pressed for revenge for the destruction of Becket's shrine, but Cromwell had anticipated such responses, particularly by the emperor. He had his secretary Thomas Wriothesley, who participated either in the dismantling of the shrine or in the play itself, brief English agents abroad in handling hostile foreign queries concerning the iconoclasm. Writing to Cromwell from Valencia less than a month afterward and well before the official suppression of the cult in November, Thomas Knight mentioned that 'Every man that hearkens for news out of England asks what is become of the saint of Canterbury. But Master Wriothesley *who played a part in that play* had before sufficiently instructed me to answer such questions.'[17] The play itself was meant primarily for domestic consumption, made more compelling by the king's presence. Cromwell's opponent Bishop Gardiner was due back through Canterbury around the time of the performance, and perhaps it is not too pessimistic to see the timing of the play and the simultaneous dismantling of Becket's shrine as Cromwell's way of greeting his political adversary. As it was, Gardiner was delayed, and did not arrive until late September. When told of the destruction, he said 'he misliked not the doing at Canterbury ... saying that if he had been at home he would have given his counsel to the doing therof, and wished that the like were done at Winchester.' He need not have worried on that account – Cromwell sent his shrine-wrecking crew to St Swithin's in Winchester Cathedral after they had finished with Becket.[18]

Later that year, at Christmas, Bale performed again in Canterbury although this time the king did not attend. The play was *King John,* a virulent anti-monastic and anti-papal piece designed to shock as much as to evangelise. Knowing Cromwell's gift for timing, a reasonable guess for the performance would be on the Feast of Becket, 29 December. In any case, the play's message was clear – in the words of a young witness, the play showed that 'it is a pity that the Bishop of Rome should reign any longer, for if he should, the said Bishop would do with our King as he did with King John'.[19]

Cromwell's use of the stage, while nothing new for a courtier, stimulated others to follow suit. In 1537 the number of recorded performances jumped remarkably, and continued to rise yearly until 1540. Although performance dates are notoriously difficult to establish due to the various systems used to reckon the fiscal year, and our records are far from complete, it is clear that in 1539–40 there were nearly four times as many dramatic performances by troupes acting under the auspices of a named patron as there were in 1534–5.[20] New troupes under new patrons continued to emerge as long as he remained in power. What is new is the type of plays courtiers were presenting. Rather than dancing bears and chivalric romances, religious or biblical themes became fashionable. Shortly after her husband, with the king and court, watched the September play at Canterbury denouncing Thomas Becket, Lady Lisle instructed John Husee, her agent in London, to get a scriptural play for the upcoming Christmas season in Calais. Having procured the necessary player's garments, Husee wrote that he would try to find 'some good matter for them. But these new ecclesiastical matters will be hard to come by.' A few days later he reiterated his pledge to try to find some of 'these new Scripture matters' but cautioned 'they be very dear; they asketh above [20 shillings] for an Interlude'. In the meantime, he sent over an interlude called 'Rex Diabole', hoping it would do.[21]

Following Cromwell's execution, patronised performances declined rapidly, and there was a virtual absence of scriptural drama in the vernacular until well into the following reign.[22] But judging from the increasing efforts of officials to control it, street-level drama was flourishing. Popular religious plays were common enough in some villages during the vigorous anti-papal posturing of the late 1530s, due doubtless to the official promotion of a strongly anti-Catholic line. The French ambassador Marillac observed in 1539 that 'As to sports and follies against the Pope made on land; there is not a village feast nor pastime anywhere in which there is not something inserted in derision of the Holy Father.'[23] In 1540, the official religious policy swung back toward a more conservative stance but popular Protestant drama, having originated at the parish level, did not.

The problem for the authorities lay in controlling these impromptu performances, which did not always coincide with official policy. The political instability of the times tempted many to extemporise during public gatherings. In May 1537, a play in Suffolk of how the king 'should rule his realm' featured a character called 'husbandry' who was emboldened to say 'many things against gentlemen more than was in the book of the play'. After a fruitless search, neither the playbook nor the actor was apprehended.[24] Following the cessation of further reform in 1540, players became increasingly critical of the Henrician church and its personnel. In 1541 priests were publicly slandered in an interlude staged in London, and the following year, in March 1542, the convocation of Canterbury asked the king to censor 'public plays and comedies which are acted in London, to the contempt of God's Word'.[25] Public plays were prohibited in London by order of the mayor in April 1542; the injunction had to be repeated a year later in April 1543, and further buttressed in May by the Act for Advancement of True Religion, which resulted in the imprisonment of 20 joiners for playing. Days later, four of the Lord Warden's own troupe were incarcerated, indicating that patrons were not always willing or able to protect their companies. Such censorship failed to extinguish the plays – rather it drove them back underground where they were impossible to police. The privy council tried another tack – in 1544 a royal proclamation banned covert performance of interludes in 'suspicious, dark, and inconvenient places'; instead, plays must be staged in the houses of the nobility, City officials, gentry or 'solid citizens', or openly in common halls or streets.[26] This proclamation was repeated for the

next two years. Four months later, in January 1545, the players of
the earl of Hertford were further restricted – they could play only
in private houses of influential citizens. And in an ironic echo of
Morison's advice to Cromwell in 1535–6, Bishop Gardiner is said
to have ordered the players of London to avoid 'any more plays of
Christ' – instead, he suggested they return to the traditional
themes of 'Robin Hood and Little John'.[27]

The content of these vernacular plays is impossible to recreate,
but it appears many were biblical and most dealt with religious
issues. The alarm they engendered in the authorities – particularly religious conservatives like Gardiner – suggests that these performances offered reformed views far in advance of the official
teaching on the church and its sacraments, thus combining the
twin terrors of the Tudor administration, sedition and heresy.
Looking back from exile, John Bale characterised them as a powerful tool in the progress of the Reformation, much as John Foxe
saw the printing press. Writing of the English ecclesiastical
authorities, Bale noted the extent of the conservative reaction:

> None leave ye unvexed and untroubled – no, not so much as
> the poor minstrels, and players of interludes, but ye are doing
> with them. So long as they played lies, and sang bawdy songs,
> blasphemed God, and corrupted men's consciences, ye never
> blamed them, but were very well contented. But since they per-
> suaded people to worship their Lord God aright, according to
> his holy laws and not yours, and to acknowledge Jesus Christ
> for their only redeemer and saviour, without your lousy
> legerdemains ye never were pleased with them.[28]

Drama at court and in the parishes had experienced a sea-change.
Explicitly political and openly confrontational, the stage had
become a pulpit from which to preach reform as well as to pro-
claim policy. Its content too reflected this change: scripture, at
the heart of the reformers' message, became the core of their dialogue. If Bale's plays are indicative, scripture was virtually enacted
onstage much as it was in mystery plays, but with an interpretation
consistent with the Protestant *sola scriptura*.

The dramatic preoccupation with political content and the
development of strategies consistent with its presentation on the
stage was paralleled by similar phenomena in print, although
here the change was less pronounced since the upper level of
English society had customarily utilised books and tracts in political wrangles and required less tutoring in literary polemic than

they did in dramatic debate. As in the case of drama, the religious controversies which began with the Lutheran heresy were overtaken by the royal supremacy. The establishment of a measure of official orthodoxy around 1540 inhibited further debate at this level, but expressions of dissent beneath it remained active. And as in the case of drama, censorship failed to eradicate the continuation of religious controversies in the popular press.

Beginning in the 1530s, a partisan literature emerged which capitalised on the increase in literacy and appealed to a much broader spectrum than had any previous controversy. Although they never reached the staggering levels of German controversial publications on the Continent, political tracts, translations, ballads, and single-sheet folios were pouring off the presses in record numbers. Each new political development produced its cluster of printed works. Typical of this literature were the flytings surrounding the fall of Cromwell and the corpus of poems which appeared immediately after the execution of Barnes and others in 1540.[29] Unlike open performances which were of necessity public, literary compositions could be produced and consumed privately, and short verse tracts were easily disseminated orally. As the pool of participants widened thanks to financial patrons or the politics of a printer, the proliferation of unofficial pamphlets far exceeded the efforts of the authorities to control it. Works from abroad exacerbated the problem. In 1538 they were banned, ineffectively.[30] England's printers themselves were largely favourable to the Reformation. Many were arrested or placed under recognisances and their inventories were periodically checked. Despite this harassment, a dedicated core gladly adopted the evasions necessary to secure a readership for their often heretical works. Books frequently bore false colophons (or none at all) and carried no attribution of authorship. By the end of Henry VIII's reign, steps were being taken to prohibit the printing of anonymous material at home.[31] Policing the book trade effectively was beyond the capabilities of the early Tudor state.[32]

Before the break with Rome, Tudor literature adhered more neatly to the distinctions between court and popular, learned or rustic owing to the vast gulf which separated the governing from the governed classes. Humanist texts routinely explored political issues and while they established the dialogue as the preferred literary genre for learned debate[33], viewed contemporary issues through an explicitly theoretical lens opaque to those unlettered in Latin. Literary self-promotion, court factionalism, and contemporary

political issues informed this literature, but it is uncertain to what
degree, if any at all, such works penetrated into the predominantly
oral culture available to the majority of English subjects. Printers,
aiming at the highest end of the Tudor social scale, selected for
publication only those texts which had a captive academic or legal
market, or else had been successful in the bespoke trade of manuscript production. Occasionally they produced texts at the request
(and cost) of a particular patron for purposes of his own aggrandis-
ement.[34] Controversy, of course, fuelled the market for select texts,
but the debates of the 1520s were waged on nothing like the scale
of the religious battles a decade later.

In general, the most common books of the early Tudor times
were religious manuals or service books, chronicles, allegorical
romances in translation, or legal compendia. As such, they were
directed to a known and trusted market. The main single category
of printed texts was literature supporting traditional piety.[35]
Gospel harmonies such as Nicholas Love's version of the
Meditations on the Life of Christ redressed the centuries-old ban on
English scripture, while primers and books of hours, although still
in Latin, were traditional best-sellers. Catechetical writing in
English abounded, ranging from works in the *ars moriendi* genre
to the illustrated *Shepherd's Kalendar,* which ran through at least
five editions between 1503 and 1528. There was limited circulation outside London, which housed the overwhelming majority of
England's printers during the early sixteenth century and consumed most of the output from their presses. Literary tastes in the
provinces are harder to assess. Manuscript collections of prose
and verse compiled for the gentry indicate a certain dovetailing
with the literary standards set by the London market. But popular
tastes generally ran to less refined, and certainly less weighty,
genres. A vigorous oral culture flourished – Oxford bookseller
John Dorne was selling upwards of 170 ballads a day in 1520.[36]
These cheap printed texts, selling for a halfpenny or a penny
apiece, constituted a liminal area between oral and literate
culture which was especially ripe for exploitation, since such texts
could easily be performed and transmitted from memory. Later,
when the debates spread outward from London as political and
religious changes were implemented in the parishes, scriptural or
godly poems appropriated the metrical patterns and even the
melodies of popular ballads 'as their route to the people's
heart'.[37] As a result, the censorship of popular verse became one
of the government's priorities.

Although Catholic authors had engaged Luther's reforming works in Latin as soon as they had appeared on the Continent and English authorities had taken judicial action to counteract the spread of heretical beliefs as they surfaced,[38] defence of traditional religious doctrine in England had been confined to the pulpits, courts and colleges. The appearance of Tyndale's New Testament in 1526 ushered in the first generation of reforming English texts. The immediate response was to burn all copies, and repeat the ban on earlier Protestant works, whether in English or Latin. By 1528 it was clear that suppression alone would be inadequate. Citing his literary ability and rhetorical skill, Bishop Tunstall of London authorised Sir Thomas More to read and refute – in English – the heretical literature circulating in England.[39] So long as it dealt with what was still seen as a theological controversy, English religious polemic remained relatively straightforward and Catholic apologists like More could engage reformers primarily on sacramental rather than political grounds. But following the submission of the clergy, the task of refuting heresy became more complex as religious conservatives found their stance against heretical reformers compromised by their monarch's campaign against Roman jurisdiction. More's debate with Christopher St German illustrates this dilemma. St German was not a theologian but a lawyer, whose works dealt with the role of the church in the political nation. Seeing his writings as heresy required a strategic expansion of More's original brief, and a subtle shift in his focus. Nonetheless, polemic at this level, however enmeshed in questions wider than theological reform, remained largely confined to the upper levels of society. It used narrative techniques and rhetorical devices familiar to humanist controversial writing aimed at a learned audience: lengthy, complex, and sprinkled with a wealth of patristic and classical allusions, these works addressed an audience of policy makers whose cultural backgrounds tied them more closely to one another (despite emerging confessional differences) than those over whom they exercised political control.

In 1529, a short and violently anti-monastic popular tract had appeared. Eschewing learned debate, Simon Fish's *Supplication for the Beggars* presented outrageous charges against the regular orders and the sacramental theology surrounding purgatory. Fish's work is remarkable in several ways; first, it was not a product of official policy yet it appealed to the king to correct abuses in the regular clergy unilaterally; second, it offers an historical

reading of the causes of clerical oppression, tracing the origins of
alleged papal hegemony in England back to King John; and
finally, its brevity and satiric tone suggest a readership which
included not only the political elite but the entire English nation.
Henry VIII was reputedly quite favourable – certainly he supported the dissolution of the monasteries and the execution of
those regulars who had resisted his policies. And more importantly, the work's depiction of the regulars as parasites and traitors
easily lent itself to exploitation. Readers who could ill afford to
follow the theological or political debates in more lengthy and
expensive tomes could easily purchase and digest Fish's tract.
More's refutation of it is telling – his *Supplication of Souls* runs to
more than ten times the length of Fish's work. Clearly, the point-
by-point rebuttal typical of learned debate was inappropriate in
the popular vein. Reforming literature, parallel to but independent of official policy, had come of age and introduced not only
new strategies for controversial debate, but new content as well.

From the very beginning of the royal campaign against papal
jurisdiction in England, the government sanctioned the use of the
press for propaganda. Initially the works produced by evangelical
Protestants such as Tyndale and Fish had been useful in supporting the separation from Rome and justifying the dissolution of the
monasteries. Commissioned works were printed. In 1530/31, the
king's printer issued two editions, one Latin and one English, of
the official apology for the schism. The English version, *The determinations of the moste famous and mooste excellent uniuersities* (discussed by Virginia Murphy, chapter 6 above), coincides with
More's controversial English efforts and confirms that debate was
expanding beyond the limitations formerly imposed by the use of
Latin alone. Taken together, these works, one defensive, the
other offensive, both official instruments of a policy at times contradictory and frequently confusing, illustrate the twofold task of
the Henrician Reformation: to effect a jurisdictional break with
the papacy while preserving a modicum of traditional religious
observance. It was not long before an even wider audience was
sought by royal agents. The mobilisation and control of an ever-
increasing number of subjects was essential for the success of the
ongoing reforms, and for this, political literature needed a more
common touch.

Cromwell need not look far for helpful suggestions. In 1534,
John Rastell, a Protestant printer, suggested that he combine anti-
papal printed works with prescribed sermons. Foreign precedents

were drawn to his attention, and the use of prophecies was mooted. In 1536 Chapuys told him how the French had frequently interfered with English policy in the past and were now threatening to take England by force 'as another Dauphin had done in the time of King John; and that on this subject they had invented certain prophecies, which they had got printed, to encourage the said Dauphin ...' Another printer, Thomas Gibson, had also suggested to Cromwell that certain prophecies could be overhauled to give them a pro-Henrician slant. Whether Cromwell needed such prompting to the propagandist trade or not, it is certain that by 1536 he was actively supporting writers and preachers in defence of the political changes he had undertaken.[40]

Parallel with the official campaign against papal jurisdiction ran one informed by more basic theological concerns. Paramount in the works of most reformers was the demand for vernacular scripture. As early as 1516, support for wider access to the Bible had its most eloquent plea with the publication of Erasmus's new Latin translation of the New Testament. He opposed restrictions on the basis of language, and advocated its widest possible distribution, even to those levels of society not normally literate:

> I wish that every woman would read the Gospel and the Epistles of Paul ... I wish these were translated into each and every language ... read and understood not only by Scots and Irishmen, but also by Turks and Saracens ... I hope that the farmer may sing snatches of Scripture at his plough, that the weaver may hum bits ... to the tune of his shuttle, that the traveller may lighten his journey with stories from Scripture.[41]

Miles Coverdale, instrumental in producing the English Bible, echoed Erasmus's concern in the 1530s when he wished that 'women at the rocks, and spinning at the wheels ... should be better occupied than with "hey nonny nonny – hey trolly lolly" and such-like fantasies'.[42] It was doubtful, however, that his proffered substitute, the *Goostly Songs* (1535) which included such works as 'Let Go The Whore Of Babylon', would ever gain popular currency.[43] Once an English Bible was made available, indeed prescribed for all parish churches in 1538, Protestant zealots quickly championed scripture over all other reading material in the same way they championed godly plays over traditional English drama. In 1539, Thomas Derby, clerk of the council, wrote in his 'official' account of the Reformation that

They have now in every church and place, almost every man, the Bible and New Testament in their mother tongue, instead of the old fabulous and fantastical books of the Table Round, Launcelot du Lake ... Bevis of Hampton, Guy of Warwick ... Calisto et Melibee ... and such other whose impure filth and vain fabulosity the light of God hath abolished there utterly.[44]

That same year, Cromwell's propagandist Richard Taverner echoed the condemnation of secular reading while lamenting that

The tales of Robin Hood, of Bevis of Hampton, of Sir Guy of Warwick with such other fables are greedily read and read again. But the holy Bible of God, which treateth of earnest matters, that is to wit, of our belief in Christ, of true repentance ... we set little by.[45]

As the only authority recognised by both reformers and conservatives, the Bible's appeal was immense and under Cromwell's near decade-long management of the press, scriptural material quickly permeated literature of every sort. At times, this reduced rhetorical strategy in controversy to exegetical wrangling. Popular songs too contained scriptural material, although with the exception of Coverdale's collection, few survive from the reign. The Protestant preoccupation with scripture meant that following 1540 when official policy no longer encouraged evangelical reform, censorship began to focus on the English Bible in addition to explicitly heterodox works. Although a royal proclamation of 1541 repeated the earlier command that all parish churches buy a Bible 'of the largest and greatest volume', it insisted that 'no lay subjects reading the same should presume to take upon them any common disputation, argument, or exposition of the mysteries therein contained ...'[46] Two years later, further restrictions were enjoined which effectively shattered the Erasmian ideal of a scripture-chanting ploughman and placed statutory restrictions on publishing and playing: the 1543 Act for the Advancement of True Religion lamented the rise of heretical 'printed books, printed ballads, plays, rimes, songs, and other fantasies' which it prohibited. Non-religious songs and plays were permitted, and traditional English authors such as Chaucer and Gower were acceptable but lay access to the Bible was severely curtailed. Noting that 'the lower sort' of subjects were prone to argumentation and dissension arising from their reading of scripture, the Act stipulated that henceforth 'no women, or artificers, prentices, journeymen, servingmen ... husbandmen nor labourers' might read the Bible. Women of gentle status or above might have access to it if they kept their study to themselves. The magisterium of the established church would be preserved. By 1545, Erasmus's aim of universal access to scripture found an ironic echo in the royal justification for its censorship. Speaking to parliament on Christmas Eve, the king complained that the 'the most precious jewel, the word of God, is disputed, rhymed, sung, and jangled in every alehouse and tavern'.[47]

In addition to introducing scriptural content and exegetical method into wide literary circulation, reformers in the Henrician Reformation, despite their frequent condemnation of late-medieval allegory, turned to the past for confirmation of the justness of their cause. Adopting a typological view of history which saw English events prefigured in scriptural narrative was one expression of this backward glance. Another expression was the resurrection of a popular literary figure for polemical purposes. In c.1536 John Gough had printed an old anti-clerical tract, *Jack Upland*, which he attributed to Chaucer, and in 1542, William Thynne included a similar complaint against the church and its ministers, *The Ploughman's Tale*, in his edition of Chaucer's works. These works, combined with *The praier and complaynte of the plowerman unto Christe* (1531) and *I playne Piers which can not flatter* (published around 1550 but clearly Henrician in composition), polemically inverted earlier catechetical efforts such as *How the Ploughman learned his Paternoster* (1510) in which a learned cleric had patiently instructed an obtuse rustic in the elements of his faith.[48] English narrative tradition had given the reformers a spiritual ancestor whose lineage was tied to both Chaucer and Langland. This tactic was also useful in that it evaded the strictures on heretical works by passing itself off as Chaucerian, thus arousing little suspicion. Once the Henrician strictures against publishing lapsed under Edward VI, a veritable explosion of tracts featuring the ploughman as Protestant hero appeared and the motif retained its efficacy even to the Marprelate controversy in c.1589.[49] But despite the popularity of the ploughman conceit, there were many for whom Piers's polemical catechism was lacking in substance.

The Henrician reforms had left little remaining of the most popular religious instructional texts from the preceding years. From the turn of the century until the dissolution of the monasteries, some of which had become important centres for the translation and composition of religious works for English lay readers, a growing number of editions were published in English, catering to a mushrooming demand for instruction in various aspects of traditional Catholic piety, including meditation.[50] Frequently reprinted manuals or guides such as Richard Whitford's *The Pomander of Prayer* and the various translations of St Bonaventura's *Life of Christ* had run through many editions before 1537; after that, they were simply dropped. The highly saleable and equally uncontroversial *Imitation of Christ,* which saw at least 13 editions between 1503 and 1535, was only once reprinted – in 1545 – until Mary was on the throne. In their place one found the authorised primers, formularies, and collections of official sermons, and an increasing number of exegetical commentaries on individual biblical works, especially the Psalms: 15 English editions of the Psalms alone appeared between 1535 and 1548.[51]

Pious English subjects looking for devotional instruction beyond the official formularies were forced to rely on propagandists like Taverner, whose popularity was great only when translating Erasmus.[52] Following the conservative reaction in 1540, works adopting a reformed posture fell under increasing disfavour. Even writers of a milder stamp were forced to recant or seek exile, or both. The career of Thomas Becon, one of the most prolific Tudor authors of religious works, is instructive. Patronised in 1538 by Thomas, Lord Wentworth, who also set John Bale on his path as a writer for the new regime, Becon's active preaching life was terminated by his arrest and recantation in 1541. Eschewing exile, he adopted the pseudonym of Theodore Basil and 'changed the form of teaching the people from preaching to writing'.[53] Between 1541 and 1543, Becon produced at least nine works aimed at guiding laymen in the basic Protestant approach to worship and duty ranging from the scriptural commentary of *News out of Heaven* (1541?) to a patriotic exhortation against England's Catholic enemies personified by Cardinal Reginald Pole in *The New Policy of War* (1542). His works were so popular that his translation of Bullinger's *The Golden Book of Christian Matrimony* was 'for the more ready sale set forth in my name by the hungry printer with my preface'.[54] But his most typical works under Henry VIII were part of a series of Socratic dialogues which outwardly resembled the popular colloquia of Erasmus – sharing even the names of their interlocutors – but lacked their classical allusions and rhetorical refinement. Beginning with the publication of *A Christmas Banquet* (1542), Becon's dialogues provided a catechetical exploration of the Christian life, anchored in scripture and linked to the church calendar. His ties with the radical book trade in London led to a second recantation in 1543, and his works were banned in 1546. The continued popularity of his works, many of which ran to several editions, attests to the increasing demand for devotional tracts as growing numbers of literate laity sought greater participation in and control of their own spiritual lives.

The Henrician Reformation profoundly changed not only literary and dramatic content but its strategies and techniques as well. The Lutheran reforms, strongly felt on the Continent, were only just beginning to move English subjects when the crisis of the king's 'great matter', more momentous and more urgent, carried both issues to levels of society that had not previously contributed their voices, however discordant, to the political chorus. Acute awareness of the political situation permeated conventional means of expression, encouraging directness and provoking unprecedented efforts at censorship and control. The authoritative presence of English scripture imparted new content and occasioned new narrative strategies as the current struggles were viewed through a biblical lens. Throughout the Tudor period, writers adopted drama as a medium of political debate because of its great potential for oblique discourse. Under Henry VIII, drama, while exhibiting this potential, had offered enhanced opportunities for direct discourse both in the form of official propaganda and in popular alternatives. Literature, with its production and consumption centred in London, lent itself naturally to political use from the start. England's governing class did not hesitate to turn to print – nor did the clerics whose religious convictions were tested by the royal supremacy. The appearance of an English Bible established not only the Word but also an appetite for exegesis among England's growing reading public, and exegesis had political as well as theological dimensions. The proliferation of these hybrid tracts overwhelmed secular and humanist literature and buried English devotional prose for decades. It is a telling observation that the greatest devotional works of the Henrician era – a time of intense lay religious ferment – were written from within either the cloister or the Tower. With the accession of Edward VI, both literature and drama would remain located at the centre of renewed political and religious controversies.

9. Local Responses to the Henrician Reformation

ROBERT WHITING

Issues, interpretations, sources

Until 1529 the traditional religion of the English people retained the approval of the English government. From 1529, however, a complex of political, financial, and personal factors combined to produce a significant modification of official attitude. Increasing hostility to the papacy culminated in the act declaring royal supremacy over the national church in 1534. This was followed in 1536–40 by the suppression of all religious houses. The financial and legal privileges of the clergy were eroded, while their status as the prime provider of religious knowledge was undermined by the legitimisation of the English Bible in 1538. The founding of chantries was restricted in 1529, and the confiscation of their property threatened in 1545. Saints' days were reduced in 1536. Pilgrimage, relic veneration, and offering to images were prohibited by the royal injunctions of 1536–8. Despite the continuing persecution of heretics, particularly after the Six Articles of 1539, these years thus witnessed an unmistakable alteration of official attitude towards vital components of traditional religion.

What remains most controversial about this alteration is its reception by the local communities of Tudor England. According to one view, argued by historians such as Christopher Haigh and J.J. Scarisbrick, the Henrician Reformation attacked a traditional religion that still retained the firm support of the English people. The Reformation therefore met considerable local resistance and only slowly took effect. According to the opposite view, propounded by scholars such as A.G. Dickens, the devotion of the English people to traditional religion was already in substantial decline.

The Reformation therefore encountered general acceptance and rapidly prevailed.

The aim of this chapter is to evaluate the impact of the Henrician Reformation upon each major component of tradition- al religion. To this end it will examine evidence from the increas- ingly wide variety of sources explored by researchers in recent years. These include not only contemporary chronicles and histor- ies but also state papers, chantry certificates, court records, epis- copal registers, churchwardens' accounts, and wills, as well as extant art and architecture. Each source-type inevitably possesses its advantages and limitations. Wills, for example, survive in sufficient number to permit the statistical analysis of their pream- bles, which may indicate religious beliefs, and of their bequests to religious practices and institutions. But wills must be used with care. They were usually written by clerics rather than directly by testators; and they generally represent the propertied rather than the poor, and the older generations rather than the young or middle-aged. On the other hand, attempts to minimise their evi- dential value have not always been convincing. For instance, it has been denied that the decline in bequests to prayers for the dead after about 1530 indicates any waning of belief in the traditional intercessions. It is argued that the testators who omitted such prayers often employed traditional preambles, and must therefore have remained 'essentially Catholic' in their beliefs. In reality, a testator's use of a traditional preamble shows only that he (or his amanuensis) still believed in the saints; it does not necessarily reveal his attitude towards purgatory, intercession, or any other component of traditional religion.[1]

The papacy

Of all religious institutions on the eve of the Reformation, the most remote from English men and women was the papacy. Popes, nev- ertheless, were still depicted in their plays and in church art: at St Neot in Cornwall, glass of 1528 shows the papal blessing of the local saint. In most cases they seem to have dutifully paid their Peter's Pence. Often, as in the south-west in 1530, they continued to purchase papal indulgences. It was commonly believed that 'we have redemption through pardons and bulls of Rome'. Some layfolk, it is true, already 'despised the authority of the bishop of Rome'. John Household, in the diocese of London, denounced the pope as a 'strumpet' and 'common bawd', who 'with his pardons had drowned in blindness all Christian realms, and that for money'. Yet such dissent was apparently limited to small groups, found mainly in the south-east. Traditionalists could still describe papal headship as 'the confession and consent of all the world'.[2]

How did local communities react to the official suppression of this headship in 1534? Resistance was initially restricted to a small minority, largely monks or friars and only occasionally laymen like Sir Thomas More. Even in the risings of 1536, the northern 'pilgrims' sought only to restore the pope's spiritual headship, 'without any first fruits or pension to him to be paid out of this realm', while even this limited demand was absent from the articles of the Lincolnshire rebels. In most regions, in fact, the great majority of people appear to have acquiesced in the removal of Roman authority. Churchwardens' accounts from throughout England show that the payment of Peter's Pence now rapidly ceased. Papal indulgences were no longer purchased, and appeals from consistory courts to papal arbitration were no longer attempted. By about 1537 the government was confident that 'privy maintainers of [the] papistical faction' had been reduced to 'muttering in corners as they dare'. By the end of the reign, even in the south-west, most churchwardens' accounts explicitly acknowledged the ecclesiastical supremacy of the king.[3]

Religious orders

As examples to the living and as intercessors for the dead, monks, nuns, and friars undoubtedly retained the respect of numerous laypeople on the eve of the Reformation. Men and women still resorted to monasteries for charity or in pilgrimage, and to friaries for sermons or for confession. On the other hand, conflict between layman and monk was not infrequent. In 1527 a mob of 300 people violently demolished a weir of Tavistock Abbey and allegedly conspired to attack the abbey itself. According to Christopher St German in 1532, criticism of the religious was now common; certainly it was voiced by a number of contemporaries.[4]

Some statistics appear to confirm that enthusiasm for the religious was now substantially lower than at its medieval peak. The number of new foundations of abbeys, priories, and priory cells had fallen from 13 in 1350–99 to 6 in 1400–49 and nil since 1450. New foundations of friaries had dwindled from 13 in 1350–99 to

1 in 1400–49, 2 in 1450–99, and 1 since 1500. Of analysed wills from the period 1520–30, moreover, the percentage containing bequests to monks ranged from a relatively modest 17–18 in the dioceses of Durham, Exeter, and York, and 11 in the archdeaconry of Lincoln, to 8 in the archdeaconry of Huntingdon, 3 in Suffolk, and nil in the archdeaconry of Buckingham. The percentage containing bequests to friars ranged from 28 in the dioceses of Durham and York, and 22–23 in Exeter diocese and Lincoln archdeaconry, to 16 in Huntingdon archdeaconry and nil in the archdeaconry of Buckingham. Lay wills from Norwich show significant support in 1490–1517 for monasteries and friaries, the latter receiving donations in as many as 47–50 per cent, but also a partial decline in donations to both types of community in 1518–32. Support for the religious thus seems to have survived, especially in the north and west, but to have been less impressive than in earlier generations.[5]

As official hostility to such institutions became increasingly explicit, local investment dwindled and then ceased. In Devon and Cornwall the percentage of testators bequeathing to monks fell from 17 in 1520–9 to 11 in 1530–5 and nil in 1536–9, while the percentage bequeathing to friars dropped from 23 to 21 and 9 before ending altogether. In London the first percentage fell from 17 in 1523–5 to 8 in 1529–30 and nil after 1534, while the second declined from 43 to 33 and nil. Similar slumps occurred in the archdeaconries of Huntingdon and Lincoln and elsewhere.[6]

In 1536 the dissolutions were allegedly resented by 'all the whole [north] country'. The rebellious northern 'pilgrims' certainly demanded the restoration of suppressed abbeys, and attempted to reconstitute recently dissolved communities at York, Sawley, and elsewhere. In most regions, however, resistance to the suppression was rarely more than small-scale, as at Exeter's St Nicholas' priory in 1536. Many laypeople indeed proved willing or even eager to assist. In 1539 the abbot of Glastonbury was condemned by a jury of local men, bills against him being presented by his tenants and others. Confiscated property was bought and not infrequently desecrated by the wealthy. In c.1540 John Leland discovered that at Barrow Gurney in Somerset, a nunnery was 'now made a fair dwelling place by Drewe of Bristol', while at Melwood in Lincolnshire the monastery had become 'a goodly manor place'. Malmesbury Abbey was used for weaving by a local clothier. At Gloucester the Franciscan and Dominican friaries had been converted into a brew-house and a draping-house.[7]

The plunder of dissolved houses by their lay neighbours was by no means uncommon. In 1538 it was reported from Warwickshire that 'the poor people, thoroughly in every place, be so greedy upon these houses when they be suppressed that by night and day, not only of the towns but also of the country, they do continually resort as long as any door, window, iron or glass or loose lead remaineth in any of them'. Even in Yorkshire, the buildings of Roche Abbey (including its church) were rapidly stripped by gentlemen, yeomen, and other local people. Windows, lead, and timber were seized, and service books 'laid upon their wain cops to piece the same'. 'All things of price' were 'either spoiled, carped away, or defaced to the uttermost'. Against only limited resistance, and with extensive acquiescence or cooperation, a second component of traditional religion had been effectively destroyed.[8]

Secular clergy

As mediators between the laity and God, and in particular as performers of the sacraments of baptism, absolution, and mass, secular clerics had played an indispensable role in the popular religion of medieval England. That the priesthood retained the respect of many laymen on the eve of the Reformation is suggested by its levels of recruitment, particularly in the Midlands and the north. In the diocese of Lincoln the average annual number of ordinations reached 172 in 1515–20 and 141 in 1522–7. Bequests to the secular clergy, as gifts, as tithe- or mortuary-payments, or as fees for intercession, still featured in 66 per cent of wills from the dioceses of Durham and York in 1520–33, and in 70 per cent from the diocese of Exeter in 1520–9. In 1526, for example, the Yorkshireman Nicholas Fitzwilliam not only bequeathed his 'best beast' as a mortuary, 'after the laudable custom of Holy Church', but also donated 6d. 'for tithes forgotten', 6s. 8d. to his vicar, 'to pray for me', and more money and a doublet to another priest. In the period 1520–30, moreover, bequests to the secular cathedrals at Wells and Lincoln were specified by as many as 84–98 per cent of testators in their respective dioceses.[9]

Other evidence nevertheless modifies this optimistic picture. The number of new foundations of secular colleges – communities of secular priests or chantry chaplains – declined from 43 in 1350–99 to 29 in 1400–49, 17 in 1450–99, and only 5 after 1500.

By the early sixteenth century, moreover, levels of recruitment to the secular clergy appear to have been proportionately less impressive in the south, and particularly in London. And there is evidence – most frequently, again, from the south-east – of hostility to priests. 'In this time also', lamented John Colet in 1511, 'we [clerics] perceive contradiction of the lay people.' 'Now of late', claimed St German in 1532, 'the great multitude of all the lay people have found default as well at priests as religious.' 'Antichrists' and 'whore-mongers' were among the words used of the clergy by dissidents in the diocese of London, and similar disrespect was displayed by poets and pamphleteers like John Skelton and Simon Fish. And in some areas, including Sussex and especially London, lay–clerical disputes over tithes and other dues were by no means infrequent. The most notorious, in 1514, was the case of Richard Hunne.[10]

Sir Thomas More, on the other hand, admitted laymen's 'grudge' against clerics but thought it less extensive than claimed by St German. In most regions, certainly, the number of tithe-disputes remained relatively low: only 10 were reported from the 1148 parishes of Norwich diocese in 1524. Similarly uncommon were verbal or physical assaults upon clerics and disobedience to church courts. The courts may indeed have been valued by many layfolk, whose disputes they resolved without excessive cost or delay. In general it seems probable that the relationship between priest and people was less frequently characterised by discord than by harmony.[11]

In the 1530s, however, it is possible to discern the beginnings of a marked decline in lay respect for priests. Its signs included an apparently rising number of verbal and sometimes physical attacks, a phenomenon observable even in remote areas like Cornwall, Devon, and Lancashire. In 1545 Henry VIII himself lamented the tendency of laymen to 'speak slanderously of priests'. There seems simultaneously to have been a proliferation of individual or communal resistance to clerical dues. Mortuary suits in the archdeaconry of Chester rose from 8 in 1500–29 to 13 in 1530 alone. At Down St Mary in Devon, in c.1533, the parishioners refused as a body to pay their parson his tithes, mortuaries, and other customary dues. The priest concluded that his entire parish contained 'not above five or six honest men and women'.[12]

The governmental attacks of 1529–34 seem also to have triggered a waning respect for ecclesiastical privilege and jurisdiction. Although the northern rebels demanded the restoration of sanctuary, benefit of clergy, and ecclesiastical liberties, laymen in most regions exhibited little inclination to defend such rights. On the contrary, an Act of 1536 complained that many people had 'attempted in late time past to disobey, condemn and despise the process, laws and decrees of the ecclesiastical courts of this realm, in more temerous and large manner than before this time hath been seen'. In the diocese of Chichester, for example, respect for spiritual sanctions such as excommunication and suspension appears to have entered a significant decline.[13]

Recruitment to the priesthood was also beginning to plunge. In Lincoln diocese the average annual number of ordinations slumped from 141 in 1522–7 to 80 in 1527–35 and only 22 in 1536–46. The figure for Durham fell from 27 in 1531–5 to nil in 1536–41 and 3 in 1542–7, and similar declines occurred in the dioceses of Hereford, Lichfield, London, and York. The percentage of testators bequeathing to secular cathedrals fell only slightly in the diocese of Wells, but by 1545 had slumped to 74, 56, and 54 in the archdeaconries of Lincoln, Buckingham, and Huntingdon. In Durham and York dioceses the percentage bequeathing to secular clerics fell from 66 in 1520–33 to 55 in 1534–46. In Exeter diocese the decline was from 70 in 1520–9 to 56 in 1530–9 and 36 in 1540–6. In London the percentage in 1534–46 was only 23. Support for the secular clergy was by no means destroyed, but seemed now to have entered a substantial decline.[14]

Parish churches and chapels

The primary centres of popular devotion in medieval England had been the churches and chapels of parochial communities. On the eve of the official Reformation these continued in most areas to be built and furnished in impressive number and at considerable expense. A survey of wills, inscriptions, and other sources from eight counties – Cheshire, Devon, Kent, Lancashire, Middlesex, Norfolk, Suffolk and Yorkshire – has identified some 250 parish churches and chapels with firmly datable evidence of major construction in 1490–1569. Of these, no fewer than 132 experienced such construction in 1490–1509, and 129 in 1510–29. The largest sums were usually donated by local gentlemen – like the Tames of Fairford in Gloucestershire, who financed its 'fair new church'. But substantial benefactions came also from merchants, such as John Greenway at Tiverton in Devon, while yeomen, husbandmen, and the lower ranks made smaller contributions. Three windows at St Neot, dated 1523, 1528, and 1529, were donated by the local wives, young men, and young women.[15]

Though such investment earned status for individuals and communities, its primary impulses appear to have been religious. Sometimes it was intended to honour a specific saint. When, in c.1500, the Cornish church of St Mabyn was 'new builded', a hymn was sung in praise of Mabyn herself. In most cases, however, it was evidently designed for the welfare of the donor's soul. An inscription of 1517 at Tiverton reminded spectators that the south chapel had been erected by the Greenways, for whom (together with their family and their friends) it requested prayer. The early-Tudor glass at St Neot contains depictions of the donors, invocations of the saints shown above them, and exhortations to pray for their souls. Viewers are urged, for example, to 'pray for the souls of Katherine Borlase, Nicholas Borlase and John Vyvyan, who had this window made'.[16]

Fabrics and furnishings were maintained by income from an often extensive variety of sources. Among the most lucrative were gifts, bequests, rents from donated properties, contributions from religious guilds, and the traditional church ales. Lesser sources included the sale of candles, the hire of seats or funeral crosses, and fees for burials or commemorative obits. A particularly impressive index of support for parish churches is the percentage of testators still bequeathing to them. In the period 1520–30, this ranged from 95–97 in Norwich and Suffolk, and 76–92 in the diocese of Lincoln, to 61–65 in Somerset and 49–53 in the dioceses of Durham, York, and Exeter. Such statistics do not mean that the neglect or even robbery of churches was by any means unknown. Some 71 cases of disrepair were reported from the archdeaconry of Chichester in 1520, while the reconstruction of Probus church in Cornwall in 1523 was deliberately obstructed by a local gentleman named Nicholas Carminow. The evidence nevertheless suggests that support for parish churches in general remained high.[17]

This support was not eradicated by the Henrician Reformation, but does appear to have begun to wane. In the eight counties sampled, the number of churches and chapels with evidence of construction dropped from 129 in 1510–29 to only 65 in 1530–49. Building previously planned seems sometimes now to have been abandoned. The percentage of testators bequeathing to parish churches was also beginning to fall. By the last years of the reign it had fallen to 75 in Suffolk, 70 in Lincoln archdeaconry, 62–64 in Huntingdon and Buckingham archdeaconries, 49 in Durham and York dioceses, and 43–46 in Exeter diocese, Somerset, and London.[18]

Churchwardens' accounts similarly suggest the beginnings of a deterioration in the financial health of parish churches. An analysis of 32 south-western parishes with extant accounts reveals that the average annual income per church in 1535–41 was £12 in rural areas and £20 in towns. In 1541–7, when the purchasing power of money was beginning to decline, the average in rural areas remained at £12, while that in towns fell to £18. Among the reasons for this decline was a reduction of contributions from religious guilds. There were also possible indications of a waning respect for the sacred buildings and their furnishings. These included examples of expropriation and theft – as at Long Melford, where the church was 'despoiled' in 1532 – as well as of neglect or deliberate destruction. By c.1540, at Barnstaple in Devon, a chapel dedicated to the recently vilified Thomas Becket was 'now profaned'. At King's Sutton in Northamptonshire, where a chapel of St Rumwold had stood 'of late', the once-hallowed edifice was now 'defaced and taken down'.[19]

Religious guilds

After churches and chapels, the institutions most vital to popular piety in later medieval England were frequently the parish-based religious guilds. In several areas on the eve of the Reformation these appear to have remained not only numerous but also active, prosperous, and locally supported. Their membership was mainly lay, and sometimes was drawn from a specific age- or status-group such as the young men or the married women. They were supervised by their own elected wardens, who included women as well as men: at Ashburton in 1525–6, the wives' guild was overseen by Leve Dolbeare. Often they were dedicated to a saint, and maintained an appropriate image. In most cases they organised prayers or masses on behalf of their deceased. In the south-western parishes with extant accounts, the average number of such guilds in 1535–41 was 5 in towns and 6 in rural communities. In Cornwall and Devon, moreover, the percentage of testators making bequests to religious guilds in 1520–9 stood as high as 57. The wills nevertheless suggest that in other regions – and particularly in the south-east – support for such institutions was less enthusiastic. The comparable percentage in 1520–30 stood at 24 in Somerset, and 14–15 in Durham and York dioceses and Lincoln archdeaconry, but only 10 in Huntingdon archdeaconry, 5 in Suffolk, and 2 in the archdeaconry of Buckingham.[20]

What was the impact of the Henrician Reformation upon such groups? The evidence, though sometimes obscure, suggests that the late-Henrician years not infrequently witnessed their local dissolution. The south-western accounts show that in 1541–7, the average number of religious guilds began to fall – in urban parishes from 5 to 3, and in rural parishes from 6 to 5. In most areas, moreover, bequests were beginning to decline. By the last years of the reign, the percentage of wills with bequests to such fraternities had fallen to 28 in Exeter diocese, 13 in Somerset, 10 in Lincoln archdeaconry, 8 in Durham and York dioceses, 4 in London, 3 in Suffolk, 2 in Huntingdon archdeaconry, and nil in the archdeaconry of Buckingham. Though not yet destroyed, another significant component of traditional religion had suffered substantial damage in the years of official reformation.[21]

Sacraments and rituals

Clerically performed rituals, and in particular the sacraments, continued on the eve of the Reformation to play crucial roles in the religion of the English people. 'Without baptism no soul may be saved', proclaims an inscription of c.1522 on the font at Goodmanham in Yorkshire. Esteem for mass is indicated not only by the apparently high levels of attendance at its performance – on week-days as well as Sundays, according to an Italian visitor in c.1500 – but also by the frequent and often substantial expenditure of individuals, groups, and parochial communities upon the requisite ritual apparatus. The Italian visitor was impressed by the crucifixes, candlesticks, censers, patens, cups and other treasures to be found in parish churches. By 1529 the apparatus at Long Melford in Suffolk included over 152 items of cloth, such as altar cloths, sepulchre cloths, and banners, as well as 44 copes and vestments; 50 items of metal, such as paxes, pyxes, and crosses, together with 13 chalices; and 46 mass books and other liturgical literature. A wide range of associated rituals retained their popularity. On Palm Sundays, for instance, the parishioners of Long Melford would solemnly parade the consecrated host around their churchyard, with bell-ringing and singing, and would kneel to adore it.[22]

Traditional views of the sacraments were sometimes vehemently challenged – by John Household, Robert Rascall, and Elizabeth Stamford, for example, in the diocese of London in 1517, or by the Londoner Nicholas Field in 1530. Field not only denied transubstantiation but also attacked the festivals and fast days enjoined by the church. The records nevertheless suggest that overt opposition was still relatively limited in extent, and was largely concentrated (once more) in the south-east.[23]

After about 1530, particularly in the south-east but also in some distant areas such as Yorkshire, it appears to have increased. In Colchester, by 1540–2, more than half of the adults reportedly absented themselves from church on Sundays and holy days. More significant, however, is the evidence of declining expenditure upon ritual apparatus, and of its increasingly frequent sale or theft. At Long Melford, by 1541, cloth items had diminished in number to some 84; copes and vestments to 42; metal items to 35; chalices to 9; and service books to 40. At Halberton in Devon, 'of their devilish minds against God and Our Blessed Lady', John Warren and Christopher Sampford stole vestments, chalices, ornaments and service books from the parish church in 1545. Local support for the traditional sacraments and rituals was by no means eradicated by the Henrician Reformation, which did not directly target them. It nevertheless appears probable that the overall level of such support was now entering the first stages of an extended and eventually devastating decline.[24]

Intercession

Prayers and masses for the dead, hastening their passage through the pains of Purgatory and into the eternal joys of Heaven, unquestionably continued to attract substantial support from the English people on the eve of the official Reformation. Sepulchral inscriptions still commonly urged the living to intercede for the departed. 'Pray for the soul of Joan Burton ...', pleads her brass of c.1524 at Carshalton in Surrey; 'on whose soul, Jesu have mercy.' Chantries were still founded to provide prayers and masses 'for the souls of the founders and all Christian souls' – as in 1526, when a chantry of Our Lady was established by Brian Palmes, Katherine Ursewick, John Courtney, and Agnes Rockchurch in the Yorkshire church of Badsworth. In three counties of the north and west, namely Lincolnshire, Wiltshire, and Yorkshire, new chantry foundations had totalled 97 in 1350–99. They fell to 60 in 1400–49, but then recovered to 75 in 1450–99 and 81 in 1500–48.[25]

In three counties of the south-east and Midlands, however, namely Essex, Kent, and Warwickshire, the total in 1350–99 was a modest 32; and thereafter it declined continuously, to 23 in 1400–49, 18 in 1450–99, and only 10 in 1500–48. With some exceptions, the regional variation suggested by these statistics appears to be indicated also by the wills. The percentage of testators arranging intercessions in 1520–30 ranged from 79 in Lancashire, and 70–72 in the dioceses of Durham, Exeter, and York, to 60–62 in Huntingdon archdeaconry and Suffolk, 44–49 in Somerset, and only 22–26 in the archdeaconries of Lincoln and Buckingham. In London, between 1479–86 and 1529–30, the percentage bequeathing to anniversaries for souls remained at a modest 21, while that bequeathing to chantries fell from 43 to 20. It was also in the south-east that denunciations of intercession were apparently most common. In Buckinghamshire in 1530, for example, William Wingrave denied the very existence of Purgatory, and ridiculed the idea that masses could deliver souls.[26]

After about 1530 such denials appear to have increased. Between 1535–41 and 1541–7, moreover, the percentage of south-western parishes recording expenditure on intercessions fell from 94 to 85, while the percentage recording expenditure on the public reading of bede rolls – to facilitate prayer for deceased benefactors of the church – now dropped from 81 to 55. But a more significant trend of this period was the marked decline of chantry foundation. In three analysed counties, the number of new foundations dwindled from 28 in 1520–9 to 8 in 1530–9 and only 1 in 1540–8. The cessation was faster in Essex, where none were founded in 1530–48, than in Yorkshire, where 7 were founded in 1530–9 and 1 in 1540–8. The late-Henrician years saw also a significant increase in the private suppression of intercessory institutions. The trend is again evident even in the south-west and the north. At Halifax, for example, a chantry founded by Alice Frith in 1515, 'to the intent to pray for the soul of the founder and to do divine service in the said church', was terminated in c.1539, when Sir Edmund Ackroyd appropriated its lands to his own use. A chantry at Badsworth ceased to operate in c.1543; land that had maintained its priest was diverted to church repairs.[27]

The testimony of wills is once more suggestive. In Lancashire the percentage with bequests to intercession rose to 90 in 1530–9 but fell to 60 in the following decade. In Durham and York dioceses it fell to 51 in 1534–46, while in Exeter diocese it slumped to 51 in 1530–9 and 33 in 1540–6. In Suffolk the decline was to 48 in 1534–46; in Huntingdon archdeaconry, to 42 in 1535 and 18 in 1545; in Somerset, to 26 in 1530–4, 28 in 1535–9, and 11 in 1540–4. In Buckingham and Lincoln archdeaconries the percentage rose, but only to a modest 32 and 28 in 1545. The comparable figure for East Sussex in 1530–46 was 54, while for London in 1534–46 it was only 20. The evidence thus indicates that although overall support for intercessions had in general remained substantial until about 1530, it thereafter entered an unmistakable and sometimes drastic decline.[28]

Saint veneration

A practice similarly retaining much of its traditional appeal on the eve of the Reformation was the veneration of saints. They remained the primary focus of most church art, like the glass erected at St Neot in 1523–9. The cult of the sacred figure might be international, as with the Virgin Mary; national, as with Thomas Becket; or merely local, as with St Neot himself. In c.1500 the Italian visitor noted Englishwomen's habit of carrying rosaries, for prayer to Our Lady as well as to God, while memorial inscriptions often asked spectators to say an Ave as well as a Pater Noster. 'O Blessed Lady of Pity', pleads a Carshalton brass of c.1524, 'pray for me, that my soul saved may be.' Testators similarly continued to commend their souls not only to God or Christ but also to the Virgin Mary or the saints. On the eve of the Reformation such commendations were found (for example) in approximately 98 per cent of wills from the city of York, 93 per cent from the dioceses of Durham and York, and 88 per cent from Suffolk.[29]

Dissident voices were sometimes heard – as in the diocese of London in 1517, when two men and a woman spoke 'against praying to saints'. They seem to have become more frequent after about 1530: Thomas Bennett, for example, declared bluntly that 'We ought to worship God only, and no saints'. But more significant than such outbursts was the declining proportion of testators who chose to commend their souls to Mary or the saints.

In York this percentage fell only slightly, from 98 in 1501–37 to 96 in 1538–46. In the dioceses of Durham and York, however, the decline was from 93 in 1520–33 to 80 in 1534–46. The diocese of Canterbury saw a fall from 95 in 1532–4 to 80 in 1535–40 and 63 in 1541–6; London, from 85 in 1530–9 to 67 in 1539–47; Suffolk, from 88 in 1520–33 to 55 in 1534–46. Once more, and particularly in the south-east, it appears that a formerly important feature of traditional piety was now beginning to decline.[30]

Images

Until the 1530s, three-dimensional representations of God or the saints continued to be widely utilised as aids to prayer: they were still honoured by lights, by offerings, and by pilgrimage. In 1526 the Yorkshireman Nicholas FitzWilliam donated 5lb of wax to the sacred figures in Arksey church, and asked to be buried 'afore St John Baptist'. In the same year, at Canterbury, a critically ill woman was reportedly healed by an image of Our Lady; 'by reason of the which miracle, there is established a great pilgrimage'. Substantial expenditure was still devoted to the construction and ornamentation of such figures, and to the erection of often elaborate rood-lofts for their display. In 1525–6 alone, the parishioners of Ashburton in Devon paid 1s. 2d. for repairing images on St John's altar, 2s. for St Julian's light, 3s. 8d. for erecting St George, £8 for painting the image-housing of St John, and no less than £21 1s. 6 ½d. in part-payment for their new rood-loft. Long Melford church boasted more than 17 figures, including a Holy Trinity in the chancel and a Jesus and Mary in the Martin aisle. In 1529, moreover, its Lady chapel contained some 46 'jewels' – principally coats and girdles for an image of Our Lady, and offerings to it in the form of beads, silver, and gold.[31]

'Pilgrimages and worshipping of images' were already sometimes decried. Thus Alice Cooper, in London diocese, refused to seek healing for her injured child from a figure of St Lawrence, and protested that 'none ought to go on pilgrimage to any image ... but only to Almighty God'. Pilgrimages, she thought, were 'nothing worth, saving to make the priests rich'. It again seems probable that such denunciations increased after 1530. In 1539, to cite but one example, at Chelmsford in Essex, William Maldon bluntly told his traditionalist mother that kneeling before the crucifix was 'plain idolatry'. More important than such verbal outbursts, however, was the apparent willingness of most local communities to acquiesce in – or even to cooperate with – the Henrician assault upon the 'superstitious' image.[32]

A survey of churchwardens' accounts from throughout England shows that after the injunctions of 1538, lights before saint-images were virtually everywhere extinguished. Offerings were also removed. At Long Melford, for instance, the treasures accumulated by the image of Our Lady up to 1529 had disappeared totally from the church's inventories by 1541. Many and probably most of the once-venerated figures were themselves deposed. Even the relatively remote diocese of Exeter saw the execution, 'throughout this diocese', of royal orders 'for defacing and pulling down of all such idols and images as whereunto any offerings and pilgrimages had been made'. Among those destroyed by the commissioner Dr Heynes was 'an image called St Saviour' at St Maur-in-the-Sand. The impact of such campaigns was sometimes recorded by Leland in c.1540. At Brougham, in distant Westmorland, he noted the apparent continuance of 'a great pilgrimage to Our Lady'. At Cleeve in Somerset, on the other hand, he found a chapel where offerings to Our Lady had apparently ceased, and an inn which had 'a-late' been used by pilgrims. In Cheshire he noted an apparently suppressed 'pilgrimage of Our Lady of Hilbre', while at Liskeard in Cornwall he saw a chapel of Our Lady 'where was wont to be great pilgrimage'.[33]

According to John Hooker, the perpetrators of this iconoclasm were sometimes 'marvellous hated and maligned at'; yet it seems rarely to have encountered effective resistance. A minor exception occurred at Exeter in 1536, when workmen destroying the saint-figures in St Nicholas' priory were attacked by several women. These were arrested by the mayor and the destruction was duly completed. More often the local response to the official campaign was either acquiescence or cooperation. At Rewe in Devon, numerous mantles, coins, rings, girdles, beads, and other treasures – all formerly 'offered there to certain images' – were removed from the church by four of its parishioners in 1538. These later explained that they had acted in accordance with the royal injunctions recently 'sent into all shires', and had redirected the offerings to the maintenance of the church, 'as lawful was for them to do'. Support for the destruction was generally strongest in the south-east. 'The Azotic Dagon falls down everywhere in this country', rejoiced a clergyman of Kent in 1538. The Boxley rood, 'a wooden god of the Kentish folk ... begirded with many an offering', was exposed to the mockery of the Maidstone townspeople, 'some laughing heartily, some almost as madly as Ajax'. It was then transported to St Paul's in London, where, after a sermon against it by the bishop of Rochester, it was hurled into the congregation, torn to pieces, and finally committed to the flames.[34]

Images untainted by offering or pilgrimage remained legal throughout the reign; yet even these were losing their appeal. In the dioceses of Durham and York, the percentage of testators making bequests to images fell from 23 in 1520–33 to only 1 in 1534–46. In addition, the entire sample of churchwardens' accounts from throughout England records the erection of no more than one new image between 1538 and 1547. The 32 south-western accounts tell a similar tale. The percentage recording investment in rood-figures (which remained legal) rose from 6 in 1535–41 to 20 in 1541–7; but the comparable figure for other images declined from 31 to 10, while that for rood-lofts fell from 19 to 10. Another important element of traditional religion had experienced manifest decline.[35]

Sites and relics

One final component of medieval religion that remained import-ant to many English people on the eve of the Reformation was the veneration of sacred sites and of physical or material relics. Holy wells, usually associated with local saints, continued to be visited for healing in Cornwall and elsewhere. Thus St Cadoc's well was sought for the expulsion of diseases, and St Nun's for the cure of the insane. The relics of innumerable holy individuals were still revered in local chapels and parish churches. The parishioners of Perranzabuloe, Crantock, Cubert and St Newlyn in Cornwall preserved the crosses and relics of their patron saints, and assembled at St Newlyn in Rogation Week for their display. Parish churches occasionally boasted a more exalted souvenir, like the 'relic of the pillar that Our Saviour Christ was bound to' at Long Melford in 1529. The bodies of nationally famous saints, like Canterbury's Becket, Durham's Cuthbert, or Lincoln's Hugh, were usually to be found in their cathedral or monastic churches. At Durham the ornate shrine of St Cuthbert contained accommo-dation for his devotees, who made offerings and prayed for 'his miraculous relief and succour'.[36]

Gifts to St Hugh at Lincoln usually totalled £36–39 per annum until 1532. On the other hand, the average annual offerings to Becket's and other shrines at Canterbury declined drastically in the pre-Reformation generations, from a spectacular £370 in 1390–1439 to only £27 in 1440–89 and £14 in 1490–1539. The average annual offerings to St Cuthbert's shrine at Durham also fell, from £31 in 1370–1419 to £20 in 1420–69 and £9 in 1470–1519. These figures, together with the evidence of verbal opposition, suggest that support for at least some of the traditional cults may already have been in significant decline.[37]

Could they withstand the Henrician Reformation? Some well-rites were apparently suppressed. In c.1540 Leland noted that the inhabitants of Droitwich in Worcestershire had 'used, of late times', to decorate a well associated with a local saint, and to organise drinking, games, and revels around it on his day. More extensive, however, was the devastation of relics and their shrines. In as early as 1536 the northern rebels objected to 'the violating of relics by the [monastic] suppressors, with the unreverent demeanour of the doers thereof'. Popularly venerated shrines were subsequently demolished in monasteries at Canterbury, Durham, and elsewhere, as well as in secular cathedrals such as Exeter, Lincoln, and York. At Lincoln, offerings to the shrine of St Hugh slumped to £18 in 1537, £5 in 1538, and nil thereafter. In 1540 this cathedral was despoiled of 2621 ounces of gold, 4285 ounces of silver, and a great number of pearls and precious stones, all associated with the recently demolished shrines of St Hugh and St John of Dalderby. The pillage was officially justified on the ground that 'the simple people' had been lured by the shrines into 'great superstition and idolatry'.[38]

Parish churches suffered similar loss. Of the sampled English parishes with extant accounts, all that had possessed relics appear to have obeyed the 1538 injunction by delivering them to the bishop for destruction. Long Melford's portion of Christ's pillar had been delivered to William Mayor by 1541, and by 1547 had disappeared. At North Elmham in Norfolk, in 1542, the church-wardens sold 'silver that was upon the cross that the relics were in'. A similar fate met the shrine of Endelient, an early-medieval female hermit, at St Endellion in Cornwall. 'Her tomb', reports Nicholas Roscarrock, 'was defaced in King Henry VIII's time'.[39]

The destruction was not always immediate. Leland, in about 1540, discovered that at Bodmin 'the shrine and tomb of St Petrock yet standeth in the east part of the [priory] church', while at Hereford St Thomas de Cantelupe 'lieth at this time in the [cathedral] church, richly shrined'. In 1541, however, on the ground that shrines or their accoutrements 'do yet remain in sundry places of our realm', the king ordered his bishops to ensure their immediate eradication, '[so] as there remain no memory of it'. By 1547 such cult-objects seem almost everywhere to have been suppressed. Despite some exceptions – as at Perranzabuloe, where relics of St Piran appear to have been hidden – evidence of the survival of pre-Reformation relics into Mary's reign is strikingly rare. Equally rare, except in the north in 1536, was significant local resistance to the destruction of objects that had until recently attracted an extensive veneration.[40]

Patterns

The evidence surveyed would suggest that on the eve of the Henrician Reformation, traditional religion continued to attract a substantial and often impressive degree of popular support. This support, however, was markedly higher for some components (like parish churches) than for others (like monasteries). In general, and with innumerable local variations, it seems also to have been higher in the north and west than in the south-east. The evidence further suggests that the impact of the Henrician Reformation upon this traditional religion was both more extensive and more destructive than has often been depicted. Resistance to the official assaults was markedly less common than acquiescence or cooperation, and levels of support for the traditional practices and institutions began to wane. Though strongest in the south-east, these trends were evident also in most other regions of the realm.

These conclusions would seem to be largely verified by several other types of evidence. One such is an analysis of the 200 extant or recorded sepulchral brasses in Cornwall, Devon, Gloucestershire, Somerset, Surrey and Wiltshire. This reveals that the percentage of new brasses bearing a traditionalist inscription (like 'Pray for the soul of') or a traditionalist depiction (such as the Virgin Mary) fell from 95 in 1490–1509, and 95 in 1510–29, to 74 in 1530–49.[41]

Similarly suggestive of local responses to the Henrician Reformation is an examination of the rebellions allegedly raised against it. Major insurrections occurred only in 1536, when they gained extensive support in Lincolnshire and further north. Even these were by no means wholly aimed against the Reformation. Rebel grievances included not only religious changes but also taxes, enclosures, entry-fines, the Statute of Uses, and parliamentary representation. A further secular incentive to rebellion was the prospect of plunder. The rebels, moreover, were opposed by local loyalists such as the townsmen of Hull, as well as by the substantial forces raised outside the region. It would be unwise to accept at face value the duke of Norfolk's claim that these forces were sympathetic to the rebel cause: Norfolk was in fact seeking excuses for his own failure to fight the rebels. What is certain is that the risings were never emulated in the south-east, the Midlands, or even the south-west. In Cornwall a government agent reported 'as much conformity amongst men, and as ready to obey the king's authority, injunctions, and other orders declared to them, as ever I saw any men obey the same'.[42]

In addition to the rebellions, some 197 cases of treason were reported from the north and west in 1532–40, and 224 from the (much more densely populated) south and east. After rising steadily from 4 in 1532 to 128 in 1537, the number of such cases declined to 30 in 1540, and to an annual average of 15 for the rest of the reign. If the rise reflects an increasing opposition to official religious policies as these grew more destructive, the fall most probably indicates a declining willingness to risk overt resistance.[43]

Other types of evidence appear to confirm the existence of regional variations. An examination of seven counties suggests that in 1480–1540, the percentage value of charitable bequests directed to traditional religion was generally higher in the north and west than in the south and east. Percentages of 70 for both Lancashire and Yorkshire, and 68 for Somerset, compare with 60–61 for Buckinghamshire, Kent, and Norfolk, and only 45 for Middlesex. The churchbuilding statistics point in the same direction. In four counties of the north and west, namely Cheshire, Devon, Lancashire, and Yorkshire, the number of parish churches and chapels with evidence of major construction rose from 48 in 1490–1509 to 58 in 1510–29; then it fell to 36 in 1530–49. In four counties of the south and east, namely Kent, Middlesex, Norfolk, and Suffolk, the initial figure was markedly higher – primarily because of this region's greater wealth – but the subsequent decline was markedly more steep. A total of 84 in 1490–1509 fell to 71 in 1510–29, and to only 29 in 1530–49.[44]

Some evidence, finally, suggests the existence of social and occupational variations. As a group, the clergy seems usually to have proved more conservative than the laity. Although priests, monks, and friars together constituted less than 5 per cent of the English population, they provided 55 per cent of the individuals reported for ordinary treason in 1532–40. In the dioceses of Durham and York, moreover, the percentage of testators arranging intercessions was consistently higher among clerics than among laypeople. There may also have been an overall distinction between rural communities and major towns. An analysis of ten counties in 1480–1540 suggests that the percentage value of charitable bequests directed to religion was significantly higher among predominantly rural groups than among their urban counterparts. Percentages of 91 for husbandmen, 81 for yeomen, and 70 for the lower gentry, compare with 64 for artisans, 57 for tradesmen, and only 48 for merchants. The pattern of chantry foundation is similarly suggestive. In the rural areas of six counties, the number of new foundations fell from 98 in 1350–99 to 56 in 1400–49, but recovered to 72 in 1450–99 and 83 in 1500–48. In the corresponding urban communities, however, namely Boston, Canterbury, Colchester, Coventry, Hull, Lincoln, Salisbury and York, the decline was continuous – from 31 to 27, 21, and 8. The apparent existence of such variations does not of course mean that particular social groups or local communities were necessarily homogeneous in their religion. At Exeter, for example, in 1531–2, most of the cathedral clergy and many of the townspeople were virulently hostile to a local heretic, but the mayor and a number of his fellow-citizens were manifestly less antagonistic.[45]

Spiritual motivations

The decline of local support for traditional religion appears to have commenced to a limited extent before 1529, but to have accelerated markedly in the succeeding years. How is this decline to be explained? Was it motivated primarily by a spiritual conversion to alternative forms of Christianity? Or were the impelling forces in fact more often secular?

The frequent importance of essentially spiritual motivations can scarcely be denied. Native Lollardy, stemming largely from the fourteenth-century teaching of John Wycliffe, emphasised person-

al piety and scripture-reading but opposed the sacramental, sacer-
dotal, and cultic elements of traditional religion. Its survival on
the eve of the Reformation was noted by the Italian visitor, who
observed in c.1500 that 'many' of the English people held 'various
opinions concerning religion', and by the dean of St Paul's, who
lamented in 1511 that 'we are ... nowadays grieved of heretics,
men mad with marvellous foolishness'. In 1515 the bishop of
London complained that Londoners were 'maliciously set in
favour of heretical wickedness'. All these observations were based
on the south-east, where diocesan records confirm that Lollards
were relatively numerous. Of 461 suspected heretics in
1480–1522, 64 per cent originated in the south or east, primarily
in Buckinghamshire, Essex, Kent, and Middlesex. Their main
centres were usually towns, including Bristol and Coventry as well
as Colchester, Maidstone, and London itself. Though including
merchants, they were most often artisans.[46]

Protestantism, originating in Germany and Switzerland from
about 1517, stressed not only personal devotion and Bible-study
but also the psychologically potent doctrine of justification by
faith alone. By 1547 it appears to have become a significant force
in south-east England, particularly in Kent, Middlesex, the
Thames Valley, and East Anglia. Its progress was attested by traditionalists like the bishop of Norwich, who in 1530 noted the conversion of 'merchants, and such that hath their abiding not far
from the sea', as well as by displays of local support for its persecuted adherents, as at Ipswich in 1546. It began also to win converts in other regions, particularly in towns and ports like Bristol
and Exeter. Though doubtless aided by the survival of Lollardy in
the south-east and in towns, its advance probably owed more to
the relatively high literacy of these places, and to their commercial links with Protestant-influenced north-west Europe. The
former factor favoured a scripturally focused faith; the latter
facilitated the influx of Protestant literature and ideas.[47]

On the other hand, both Lollards and Protestants appear to
have remained rare in the north and west, in non-industrial areas,
and in the lowest social strata. Of the 461 suspected heretics in
1480–1522, only 166 originated in the north and west. Of these
the great majority came from the dioceses of Salisbury and
Coventry and Lichfield, and a smaller number from Bath and
Wells. In most dioceses of the far north and west, namely Carlisle,
Durham, Exeter, Hereford, Worcester, and York, heresy was
minimal or unknown. Nor does the subsequent progress of heresy

in these regions appear to have been rapid. Of 80 supposed Lollards or Protestants in York diocese in 1510–58, only 2 were recorded in 1510–19, 6 in 1520–9, 9 in 1530–9, and 16 in 1540–6. Heretics were similarly uncommon in the south-west. By 1531, apart from 'a shearman or two' and some other 'favourers of the gospel', even Exeter contained 'few or none ... that knew anything of God's matters'.[48]

The slowness of Protestant advance in the north and west is attributable to their relative freedom from Lollardy; to their comparatively low level of literacy; and, along the western coast, to their commercial links with predominantly Catholic countries like Ireland, France, Portugal, and Spain. It may also be that the greater precariousness of existence in impoverished highland communities rendered them less willing than the prosperous south-eastern lowlands to risk experiment in either social behaviour or religious thought.[49]

Yet even in the south-east the extent of heresy should not be overestimated. In 1511 the dean of St Paul's asserted that Lollardy was 'pestilent and pernicious unto ... the people', while in 1530 the bishop of Norwich reported the rarity of Protestantism among gentlemen and the 'commonalty'. Bequests to Protestant causes such as reformed preaching appeared in no more than a tiny proportion of wills from 1520–47 – in less than 1 per cent from Sussex, for example. In most dioceses, moreover, the supposedly 'Protestant' form of preamble – which asserted the testator's confidence in his salvation through God or Christ alone – was wholly absent from wills before the 1530s. It appeared in 6 per cent of London wills for 1530–9, and 13 per cent for 1539–47. In the diocese of Canterbury, however, it was found in only 1 per cent for 1535–40, and 4 per cent for 1541–6, while it appeared in only 1 per cent of wills from the dioceses of Durham and York for 1534–46. Although traditional preambles were beginning to decline, the forms which replaced them were much less often 'Protestant' than neutral or non-committal.[50]

Similarly revealing were attitudes towards the English Bible. It was read diligently by groups like the cloth-workers of Hadleigh and the townsmen of Chelmsford. At Chelmsford, where it was recited by literates in the parish church, 'many would flock about them to hear their reading'. Yet local responses to the injunction ordering its purchase in 1538 were rarely as enthusiastic. A survey of churchwardens' accounts throughout England shows that although virtually all parishes had acquired their copy by the end of the reign, only 45 per cent had done so by the end of 1540. In the south-west, only 50 per cent record a purchase before 1541. Eventual compliance was due mainly to a proclamation of 1541, which imposed fines for further delay.[51]

Secular motivations

Although anti-Catholic behaviour was sometimes motivated by spiritual convictions of a Lollard or Protestant type, these were never sufficiently widespread to explain why the great majority of English people either acquiesced in or cooperated with the Henrician assaults upon traditional religion. Alternative motivations for acquiescence and cooperation must therefore also be reviewed.

One such complex of motivations was to be found in the loyalty, respect, and even reverence that the dynasty inspired. Acquiescence in the religious policies of the Tudor regime was powerfully induced by its habitual representation as a protector against foreign invasion, as a bulwark against internal disorder, and, above all, as an institution appointed and approved by heaven itself. Resistance was widely perceived to be a sin, which might even imperil one's salvation. This explains (for example) why even the chronicler of the London Franciscans, a religious conservative, acknowledged that the rebellious northern 'pilgrims' of 1536 deserved to die.[52]

A second possible inducement to acquiescence was material interest. Cooperation with the monastic dissolutions, for example, was patently motivated in many cases by a desire to acquire the confiscated properties. This, rather than any conversion to Protestant doctrines, usually explains the purchase of monastic land by gentlemen or wealthy merchants, and the plunder of dissolved houses by local populations. Again, the decline of investment in ritual apparatus owed less to Protestant belief than to an expectation – voiced as early as 1536 in counties as far apart as Lincolnshire and Cornwall – that it was about to suffer official confiscation. At Davidstow in Cornwall, for instance, the parishioners' sale of a chalice in c.1545 was impelled by a rumour that such treasures were about to be seized by royal commissioners. They were also persuaded to sell oxen, the hire of which had maintained a chantry priest, 'lest they be taken in like manner for the king'.[53]

A third possible explanation for acquiescence in the Henrician Reformation was physical fear. Punishments for overt opposition ranged from whipping or imprisonment to hanging, beheading, drawing, quartering, and the public display of bodily parts. After the northern rebellion, Henry VIII ordered the duke of Norfolk to cause 'dreadful execution upon a good number of the inhabitants, hanging them on trees, quartering them, and setting their heads and quarters in every town'. The avowed purpose of such punishment was 'the terrible example of others'. It proved effective. 'The counties in the north was never in a more dreadful and true obeisance', reported Sir Arthur Darcy in 1537. Even in remote Cornwall, by 1537, papist sympathisers had been compelled to 'do show outward, for avoiding of danger of the law'.[54]

It was therefore a combination of factors that induced the predominantly acquiescent and cooperative responses of the English people to the Henrician Reformation, and thus ensured that its anti-traditionalist policies were to a remarkable degree effectively implemented at the level of the local community. The damage thus inflicted upon the traditional religion was unmistakably evident not only to its supporters – like the conservatives of Axminster, who despairingly concluded that the king and his council must be dangerous heretics – but also to its opponents, who proclaimed that a new era of religious enlightenment had been inaugurated by Henry VIII. The pope's power, rejoiced the Protestant Philip Nichols in the following reign, 'is taken from him; his bulls be not regarded; his superstitious sects of religion be gone; and a great many of his Mohametry and other baggage did the worthy King Henry destroy.'[55]

Appendix I: New Nominations as JPs 1536–9

The nominations (see chapter 2, p. 56) were as follows: Aclone, John; Acton, Sir Robert; Alne, John; Amadas, John; Andrews, Thomas; Arundell, Sir Thomas; Ashley, Henry; Aske, John; Assheton, Christopher; Awmond, Anthony; Babington, John; Babington, Roland; Bainham, George; Barlowe, John, clk; Barton, Andrew; Barton, John; Bassett, John; Bere, John; Berners, John; Billington, Thomas; Blake, John; Boswell, John; Boyse, John; Boyse, William; Brayne, Richard; Britt, Robert; Broke, Robert; Bromley, Thomas; Browne, Robert; Bury, Anthony; Button, William; Carew, Wymond; Catesby, Sir Richard; Cave, Thomas; Chaworth, Sir John; Chidley, Robert; Clerkson, Michael; Clifton, Sir Gervase; Clinton, Edward, lord; Cokayne, Francis; Cokesey, William; Colchester, John, abbot of St Osyth's; Colt, George; Constable, John; Constable, William; Conyers, Sir George; Corbet, Roger; Coryton, Peter; Cotton, Richard; Cranmer, Thomas, archbishop of Canterbury 1532–53; Crayford, Guy; Croke, John; Cromwell, Thomas; Daniell, Thomas; Darrell, Thomas; Digges, Thomas; Dingley, John; Dormer, Sir Robert; Downes, Robert; Doyle, Henry; Drury, Robert; Dunnolde, Thomas; Eggecombe, Sir Richard; Everard, William; Everyingham, Sir Henry; Fitzalan, Henry, lord Mautravers, earl of Arundel; Foljambe, Sir James; Fortescue, Lewis; Fox, James; Frobisher, Francis; Fuller, Robert, abbot of Waltham Holy Cross; Gatacre, William; Gery, William; Goodrich, Henry; Goodrich, Thomas, bishop of Ely 1534–54; Goodyear, Francis; Greneway, Thomas; Grenville, John; Greville, Sir Fulke; Griffith, Edward; Guildford, Sir John; Gyes, John; Hales, James; Hall, Thomas; Hamlin, John; Harcourt, Sir John; Hardys, Thomas; Harlakenden, Thomas; Harman, John, jun; Harris, John; Hasilwood, John, sen; Hasilwood, Sir John, jun; Hassell, Richard; Hatcliffe, Thomas; Hill, Robert; Holland, Blaise; Hungate, William, sen; Huntley, John; Hyde, George; Kingston, Sir Anthony; Kirkham, Sir Robert; Lane, John; Lane, Ralph, jun; Latimer, Hugh, bishop of Worcester 1535–9; Leder, Oliver; Lee, Roland, bishop of Coventry and Lichfield 1534–43; Lee, Thomas; Leke, Jasper; Leke, John; Leveson, James; Ligin, Sir Richard; Limsey, John; Lowe, Thomas; Lynde, George; Mainwaring, Sir Richard; Malet, Roger; Mallory, Sir William; More, Roger; Moyle, Sir Thomas; Newdigate, John; Newport, John; North, Edward; Norton, John; Paget, Sir William; Parker, Sir Henry; Pawtrell, Thomas; Pollard, John; Pollard, Richard; Porter, Arthur; Poyntz, John; Poyntz, John, of Huckington, Essex; Poyntz, Sir Nicholas; Prideaux, Humphrey; Pulleyn, Ralph; Radcliffe, Henry, lord Fitzwater, earl of

Sussex; Rede, John; Rede, Richard; Rede, William; Roberts, Thomas; Rookwood, Robert; Ryse, Robert; Sandys, Anthony; Savile, Thomas; Scrope, John; Seckford, Thomas; Sewster, John; Shaxton, Nicholas, bishop of Salisbury 1535–9; Siddenham, Thomas; Somerset, Sir George; Southwell, John; Stafford, Henry lord; Stanhope, Michael; Stourton, Roger; Sulyard, Eustace; Sulyard, Sir William; Sutton, Sir Henry; Tawe, John; Tracy, Richard; Tubbe, John; Tyrell, Sir John; Tyrwhitt, Sir Robert, jun; Wadland, Walter; Wakefield, John; Wastnesse, George; Wentworth, Thomas; Wharton, Richard; Williams, John; Winterson, Henry; Wombwell, Thomas; Wood, Alexander; Wriley, William, jun; Wyvill, Marmaduke. (This tabulation is derived from current research by John Guy.)

List of Abbreviations

BIHR	*Bulletin of the Institute of Historical Research*
BL	British Library
BL Add. MS	British Library, Additional Manuscript
BL Cott. MS	British Library, Cottonian Manuscript
BL Harley MS	British Library, Harleian Manuscript
BL Lansd. MS	British Library, Lansdowne Manuscript
BL Royal MS	British Library, Royal Manuscript
BN	Bibliothèque Nationale, Paris
Bod. Lib.	Bodleian Library, Oxford
CUL	Cambridge University Library
CRO	County Record Office
CS	Camden Society publications
CSPD	*Calendar of State Papers, Domestic*
CSPF	*Calendar of State Papers, Foreign*
CSPSp	*Calendar of State Papers, Spanish*
CSPV	*Calendar of State Papers, Venetian*
EcHR	*Economic History Review*
EHR	*English Historical Review*
Foxe	*The Acts and monuments of John Foxe,* ed. G. Townshend and S.R. Cattley, 8 vols (London, 1837–41)
Hall (Whibley)	*The Lives of the Kings: the Triumphant Reign of Henry VIII by Edward Hall,* ed. C. Whibley, 2 vols (London: T.C. and E.C. Jack, 1904)
HJ	*Historical Journal* (formerly *Cambridge Historical Journal*)
HR	*Historical Research*
HMC	Historical Manuscripts Commission
H of C, 1509–58	*The History of Parliament: the House of Commons, 1509–58,* ed. S.T. Bindoff, 3 vols (London: Secker & Warburg, 1982)
JEH	*Journal of Ecclesiastical History*
Kaulek	*Correspondance Politique de Mm. de Castillon et de Marillac ...,* ed. J. Kaulek (Paris, 1885)
Lisle Letters	*The Lisle Letters,* ed. M. St Clare Byrne, 6 vols (Chicago and London: Chicago UP 1981)
LJ	*Journals of the House of Lords*
LP	*Letters and Papers, Foreign and Domestic, of the Reign of Henry VIII,* ed. J.S. Brewer, J. Gairdner and R.H. Brodie, 21 vols in 33 parts (1862–1910 and

	revision of vol. I, and II part addenda, by Brodie, 1920–32)
More Correspondence	*The Correspondence of Sir Thomas More*, ed. E.F. Rogers (Princeton: Princeton UP, 1947)
NQ	*Notes and Queries*
Orig. Let.	*Original Letters relative to the English Reformation ...*, ed. H. Robinson (2 vols, PS, 1846–7)
PP	*Past and Present*
PRO	Public Record Office
PS	Parker Society publications
RO	Record Office
RSTC	*A Short Title Catalogue of Books printed in England, Scotland, and Ireland and of English Books Printed Abroad*, ed. A.W. Pollard and G.R. Redgrave, rev. W.A. Jackson and F.S. Ferguson and completed by K.F. Pantzer, 3 vols (London: Bibliographical Society, 1976–91)
Rymer, *Foedera*	*Foedera ...* ed. T. Rymer and R. Sanderson, 20 vols (London, 1704–32)
SCJ	*Sixteenth Century Journal*
StP	*State Papers published under the authority of His Majesty's Commission, King Henry VIII*, 11 vols (London, 1830–52)
Surtz and Murphy	*The Divorce Tracts of Henry VIII*, ed. E. Surtz and V. Murphy (Angers: Moreana, 1988)
TRHS	*Transactions of the Royal Historical Society*
TRP	*Tudor Royal Proclamations*, ed. P. Hughes and J. Larkin, 3 vols (New Haven and London: Yale UP, 1964–9)
UP	University Press

Bibliography

1. HENRY VIII: THE POLITICAL PERSPECTIVE *Eric Ives*

Contemporary works which give the flavour of politics and court life
are George Cavendish's *The Life and Death of Cardinal Wolsey*, best ed.
R.S. Sylvester (Early English Text Society, 243, 1959), and Thomas
Wyatt's poems, notably his three Satires and his comments on life at
court and on various political crises: *Collected Poems*, ed. J. Daalder
(Oxford: OUP, 1975) items vii, lix, cv, cvi, cvii, cxliii, cxlix, clx, clxiii,
clxxxi. There is no modern edition of the Eltham Ordinances.

For the royal court see S. Thurley, *The Royal Palaces of Tudor England*
(New Haven, CT: Yale UP, 1993); D.R. Starkey, 'Intimacy and Innovation:
the Rise of the Privy Chamber', in *The English Court from the Wars of the
Roses to the Civil War*, ed. D.R. Starkey (London: Longman, 1987)
pp. 71–118, and 'Court and Government', in *Revolution Reassessed*, ed.
C. Coleman and D.R. Starkey (Oxford: Clarendon, 1986) pp. 30–58.

The nature of Henrician politics is discussed in: G.R. Elton, 'Tudor
Government: the Points of Contact; III the Court', in *TRHS*, 5, ser. 26
(1976) 211–28, also in G.R. Elton (ed.), *Studies in Tudor and Stuart Politics
and Government* (Cambridge: CUP, 1974–92) III, 38–57; E.W. Ives,
'Faction at the Court of Henry VIII: the Fall of Anne Boleyn', *History*, 57
(1972) 169–88, and *Faction in Tudor England*, 2nd edn (Historical Assoc.:
London, 1986); D.R. Starkey, 'From Feud to Faction', and 'Privy Secrets:
Henry VIII and the Lords of the Council', in *History Today*, 32 (November
1982) 16–22 and 37 (August 1987) 23–9. For the local dimension of
faction see: E.W. Ives (ed.), *The Letters and Accounts of William Brereton*
(Record Society of Lancashire and Cheshire, 116, 1976), and 'Court and
County Palatine in the Reign of Henry VIII: the Career of William
Brereton', *Trans. Historic Society of Lancashire and Cheshire*, 123 (1972);
W.R. Robinson, 'Patronage and Hospitality in early-Tudor Wales', *BIHR*,
51 (1978) 20–36.

For attempts to undermine the factional interpretation of Henrician
politics see G.W. Bernard, 'Politics and Government in Tudor England',
HJ, 31 (1988) 159–67, 'The Fall of Anne Boleyn', *EHR*, 106 (1991)
584–610 and *EHR*, 107 (1992) 665–74; also G. Walker (below). At the
opposite pole, J.S. Block seeks to argue in *Factional Politics and the English
Reformation, 1520–40* (Woodbridge: Royal Historical Soc., 1993) that
faction was 'driven by religious ideology'.

Accounts of the politics of the reign or parts of it include: J.A. Guy, *The Public Career of Sir Thomas More* (Brighton: Harvester, 1980), and 'Wolsey and the Tudor Polity', in S.J. Gunn and P.G. Lindley (eds), *Cardinal Wolsey, Church, State and Art* (Cambridge: CUP, 1991) pp. 54–75; E.W. Ives, *Anne Boleyn* (Oxford: Blackwell, 1986); L.B. Smith, *Henry VIII: the Mask of Royalty* (London: Cape, 1971); D.R. Starkey, *The Reign of Henry VIII* (London: George Philip, 1985).

See also for the accession of Henry VIII: S.J. Gunn, 'The Accession of Henry VIII', *HR*, 64 (1991) 278–88; the crisis of 1519: G. Walker, 'The Expulsion of the Minions Reconsidered', *HJ*, 32 (1989) 1–16; the fall of Wolsey and 1529–32: G.R. Elton, 'Sir Thomas More and the Opposition to Henry VIII', *BIHR*, 41 (1968) 19–34, also in Elton, *Studies*, I, 155–72; E.W. Ives. 'The Fall of Wolsey', in *Wolsey, Church, State and Art*, pp. 286–315; the fall of Anne Boleyn: E.W. Ives, 'The Fall of Anne Boleyn Reconsidered', *EHR*, 107 (1992) 651–64 and 'Anne Boleyn and the early Reformation in England', *HJ*, 37 (1994) 389–400; the Pilgrimage of Grace and the emergence of the privy council: J.A. Guy, 'Privy Council: Revolution or Evolution', in Coleman and Starkey (eds), *Revolution Reassessed*, pp. 59–85 and above pp. 48–53 and G.R. Elton, 'Politics and the Pilgrimage of Grace', in B. Malament (ed.), *After the Reformation* (Pittsburgh: University of Pennsylvania, 1980) pp. 25–56, also in Elton, *Studies*, III, 183–215; the fall of Cromwell: G.R. Elton, 'Thomas Cromwell's Decline and Fall', in *HJ*, 10 (1951) 150–85, also in Elton, *Studies*, I, 189–230; S. Brigden, 'Popular Disturbance and the Fall of Thomas Cromwell and the Reformers, 1539–40', in *HJ*, 24 (1981) 257–78; the last months: R.A. Houlbrooke, 'Henry VIII's Wills: a Comment', *HJ*, 37 (1994) 891–9; E.W. Ives, Henry VIII's Will: a Forensic Conundrum', *HJ*, 35 (1992) 779–804 and the 'The Protectorate Provisions of 1546–7', *HJ*, 37 (1994) 901–14; H. Miller, 'Henry VIII's Unwritten Will', in E.W. Ives et al (eds), *Wealth and Power in Tudor England* (London, Athlone Press, 1978) pp. 87–105.

2. THOMAS WOLSEY, THOMAS CROMWELL AND THE REFORM OF
   HENRICIAN GOVERNMENT *John Guy*

The following works are essential: *LP*; *StP*; *Lisle Letters; Acts of the Privy Council of England*, ed. J.R. Dasent (46 vols; London, 1890–1964); *Proceedings and Ordinances of the Privy Council of England*, ed. N.H. Nicolas (7 vols; London, 1834–7); *Calendar of Letters, Despatches, and State Papers Relating to the Negotiations between England and Spain* (13 vols; London, 1862–1954); G. Mattingly (ed.), *Further Supplement to Letters, Despatches and State Papers Relating to the Negotiations between England and Spain* (London, 1940); R.B. Merriman (ed.), *Life and Letters of Thomas Cromwell* (2 vols; Oxford: Clarendon Press, 1902); G.R. Elton, *The Tudor Constitution* (2nd edn; Cambridge UP, 1982); Elton, *The Tudor Revolution in Government* (Cambridge UP, 1953); Elton, *Policy and Police: The Enforcement of the*

Reformation in the Age of Thomas Cromwell (Cambridge UP, 1972); Elton, *Reform and Reformation: England, 1509–1558* (London: Edward Arnold 1977); Elton, *Reform and Renewal: Thomas Cromwell and the Common Weal* (Cambridge UP, 1973); Elton, *Studies in Tudor and Stuart Politics and Government* (4 vols, Cambridge UP, 1974, 1983, 1992); Alistair Fox and John Guy, *Reassessing the Henrician Age: Humanism, Politics and Reform* (Oxford: Clarendon Press, 1986); John Guy, *Tudor England* (Oxford: Clarendon Press, 1988); Guy, 'Thomas More as Successor to Wolsey', *Thought: Fordham University Quarterly*, 52 (1977) 275–92; Guy, *Christopher St. German on Chancery and Statute* (Selden Society, London, 1985); Guy, *The Cardinal's Court: The Impact of Thomas Wolsey in Star Chamber* (Hassocks: Harvester, 1977); Guy, *The Court of Star Chamber and its Records to the Reign of Elizabeth I* (London: HMSO, 1985); Guy, *The Public Career of Sir Thomas More* (Brighton and New Haven: Harvester, 1980); Guy 'Reassessing Thomas Cromwell', *History Sixth*, 6 (1990) 2–6; Guy, 'Wolsey and the Tudor Polity', in *Cardinal Wolsey: Church, State and Art*, ed. S.J. Gunn and P. Lindley (Cambridge UP, 1991) pp. 54–75; Guy, 'The "Imperial Crown" and the Liberty of the Subject: the English Constitution from Magna Carta to the Bill of Rights', in *Court, Country and Culture: Essays on Early Modern British History in Honor of Perez Zagorin*, ed. B. Kunze and D. Brautigam (Rochester UP, 1992) 65–87; Guy, 'The Tudor Theory of "Imperial" Kingship', *History Review*, 17 (1993) 12–16; Guy, 'The Tudor Commonwealth: Revising Thomas Cromwell', *HJ*, 23 (1980) 681–7; Guy, 'The Henrician Age', in *The Varieties of British Political Thought, 1500–1800*, ed. J.G.A. Pocock (Cambridge UP, 1993) 13–46; Guy, 'The Rhetoric of Counsel in Early Modern England', in *Tudor Political Culture*, ed. D. Hoak (Cambridge UP, 1995) 292–310; J.J. Scarisbrick, *Henry VIII* (London: Eyre & Spottiswoode, 1968); Scarisbrick, 'Clerical Taxation in England, 1485 to 1547', *JEH*, 11 (1960) 41–54; Scarisbrick, 'The Pardon of the Clergy, 1531', *HJ*, 12 (1956) 22–39; Roger S. Schofield, 'Parliamentary Lay Taxation, 1485–1547', unpublished Cambridge PhD dissertation (1963); Schofield, 'Taxation and the Political Limits of the Tudor State', in C. Cross, D. Loades, and J.J. Scarisbrick (eds), *Law and Government under the Tudors* (Cambridge UP, 1988) 227–55; D.R. Starkey (ed.), *The English Court from the Wars of the Roses to the Civil War* (London: Longman, 1987); Starkey, 'The King's Privy Chamber, 1485–1547', unpublished Cambridge PhD dissertation (1973); C. Coleman and David R. Starkey (eds), *Revolution Reassessed: Revisions in the History of Tudor Government and Administration* (Oxford: Clarendon Press, 1986); Starkey, *The Reign of Henry VIII: Personalities and Politics* (London: George Philip, 1985); Starkey, 'A Reply: Tudor Government: the Facts?', *HJ*, 31 (1988) 921–31; Starkey, 'Court, Council and Nobility in Tudor England', in *Princes, Patronage and the Nobility*, ed. R.G. Asch and A.M. Birke (Oxford: Clarendon Press, 1991) pp. 175–203; Starkey, 'From Feud to Faction: English Politics c. 1450–1550', *History Today*, 32 (Nov. 1982) 16–22; Starkey, 'Representation through Intimacy: A Study in the Symbolism of Monarchy and Court Office in Early-Modern England', in I. Lewis (ed.), *Symbols and Sentiments: Cross-cultural*

Studies in Symbolism (London: Academic Press, 1977) pp. 187–224; P. Williams, *The Tudor Regime* (Oxford: Clarendon Press, 1979); P. Williams and G.L. Harriss, 'A Revolution in Tudor History?', *PP*, no. 25 (1963) 3–58; Williams and Harriss, 'A Revolution in Tudor History?' *PP*, no. 31 (1965) 87–96; J.D. Alsop, 'Innovation in Tudor Taxation', *EHR*, 99 (1984) 83–93; Alsop, 'The Theory and Practice of Tudor Taxation', *EHR*, 97 (1982) 1–30; J.J. Goring, 'Social Change and Military Decline in Mid-Tudor England', *History*, 60 (1975) 185–97; J.J. Goring, 'The General Proscription of 1522', *EHR*, 86 (1971) 681–705; S.J. Gunn, *Charles Brandon, Duke of Suffolk, 1484–1545* (Oxford: Blackwell, 1988); Gunn, 'Introduction', in *Cardinal Wolsey: Church, State and Art*, ed. Gunn and Lindley, pp. 1–53; G.W. Bernard, *War, Taxation and Rebellion in Early Tudor England: Wolsey and the Amicable Grant of 1525* (Brighton: Harvester, 1985); A.G. Dickens, *Thomas Cromwell and the English Reformation* (London: English Universities Press, 1959); Peter Gwyn, *The King's Cardinal: the Rise and Fall of Thomas Wolsey* (London: Barrie & Jenkins, 1990); A.F. Pollard, *Wolsey* (London: Longman, 1929); Glyn Redworth, *In Defence of the Church Catholic: the Life of Stephen Gardiner* (Oxford: Blackwell, 1990); Arthur J. Slavin, 'Lord Chancellor Wriothesley and Reform of Augmentations: New Light on an Old Court', in Slavin (ed.), *Tudor Men and Institutions* (Baton Rouge, LA: Louisiana State UP, pp. 49–69; R.S. Sylvester and D.P. Harding (eds), *Two Early Tudor Lives: The Life and Death of Cardinal Wolsey by George Cavendish; The Life of Sir Thomas More by William Roper* (New Haven, CT: Yale UP, 1962); Simon Thurley, *The Royal Palaces of Tudor England* (New Haven and London: Yale UP, 1993); G. Walker, *John Skelton and the Politics of the 1520s* (Cambridge, 1988); S.G. Ellis, 'Crown, Community and Government in the English Territories, 1450–1575', *History*, 71 (1986) 187–204; Ellis, 'England in the Tudor State', *HJ*, 26 (1983) 201–12; Ellis, 'Tudor Policy and the Kildare Ascendancy in the Lordship of Ireland, 1496–1534', *Irish Historical Studies*, 20 (1977) 235–71; Ellis, *Reform and Revival: English Government in Ireland, 1470–1534* (Woodbridge: Boydell, 1986); Ellis, *Tudor Ireland: Crown, Community and the Conflict of Cultures, 1470–1603* (London: Longman, 1985); J. Gwynfor Jones, *Early Modern Wales c. 1525–1640* (London, Macmillan, 1994); W.E. Wilkie, *The Cardinal Protectors of England: Rome and the Tudors before the Reformation* (Cambridge UP, 1974); E.W. Ives, *Anne Boleyn* (Oxford: Clarendon Press, 1986); Ives, 'Faction at the Court of Henry VIII: The Fall of Anne Boleyn', *History*, 57 (1972) 169–88; S.E. Lehmberg, *The Reformation Parliament, 1529–1536* (Cambridge UP, 1970); Lehmberg, *The Later Parliaments of Henry VIII, 1536–1547* (Cambridge UP, 1977); H. Miller, *Henry VIII and the English Nobility* (Oxford: Blackwell, 1986); Rachel R. Reid, *The King's Council in the North* (London: Longmans, 1921); W.C. Richardson, *The History of the Court of Augmentations, 1536–1554* (Baton Rouge, LA: Louisiana State UP, 1961); Richardson, *Tudor Chamber Administration, 1485–1547* (Baton Rouge, LA: Louisiana State UP, 1952); B.P. Wolffe, 'Henry VII's Land Revenues and Chamber Finance', *EHR*, 79 (1964) 225–54; Wolffe, *The Crown Lands, 1461–1536* (London: George Allen & Unwin, 1970); Wolffe,

Royal Demesne in English History: The Crown Estate in the Governance of the Realm from the Conquest to 1509 (London: George Allen & Unwin, 1971); M.L. Zell, 'Early Tudor JPs at Work', *Archaeologia Cantiana*, 93 (1977) 125–43. All documents cited in this paper are located at the PRO unless otherwise stated. Crown copyright documents are quoted with the permission of the Comptroller of HM Stationery Office.

3.   THE PROGRESSES OF HENRY VIII 1509–1529   *Neil Samman*

There has been relatively little published on the progresses of Henry VIII, particularly for the first half of his reign. The most useful work has been provided by architectural historians researching Tudor royal palaces, particularly H.M. Colvin, *The History of the King's Works*, vol. IV (London: HMSO, 1982) and most recently by S.J. Thurley, *The Royal Palaces of Tudor England. Architecture and Court Life 1460–1547* (New Haven, CT and London: Yale UP, 1993) and 'Palaces for a nouveau riche King', *History Today*, 41 (1991). Dr Thurley has used the architectural plans of royal palaces to good effect and this has furthered our understanding of how the itinerant court operated. Likewise, M. Howard, *The Early Tudor Country House. Architecture and Politics 1490–1550* (London: George Philip, 1987) discusses some of the houses which Henry VIII visited on his progresses.

More work has been completed on royal progresses outside this period: itineraries have been published for Henry VI in B.P. Wolffe, *Henry VI* (London: Eyre Methuen, 1981) and for Henry VII in G. Temperley, *Henry VII* (London: Constable, 1917). See also J.G. Meagher, 'The First Progress of Henry VII', *Renaissance Drama*, 7 (1968). Elizabeth's progresses are discussed in E.K. Chambers, *The Elizabethan Stage*, I (Oxford: Clarendon Press, 1923) and very extensively in J. Nichols, *The Progresses and Public Processions of Queen Elizabeth*, 3 vols (London, 1823).

P. Olver, 'The Tudor Royal Progress', Swansea MA dissertation, 1985, provides an introduction to the court on progress but does not use the evidence provided by the cofferer's and comptroller's accounts and therefore provides an incomplete itinerary for Henry VIII. For further information on the nature of the royal progress and the itinerant court, Cardinal Wolsey's itinerary and its political significance see N. Samman, 'The Henrician Court during Cardinal Wolsey's Ascendancy *c.* 1514–1529', University of Wales PhD thesis, 1989. Appendix I gives a full itinerary for Henry VIII and Cardinal Wolsey for the years 1514–30.

For the political significance of court spectacle reference should be made to S. Anglo, *Spectacle, Pageantry and Early Tudor Policy* (Oxford: Clarendon Press, 1968) which gives a very detailed description of Charles V's entry into London in 1522 and the Field of Cloth of Gold in 1520. See also J.G. Russell, *The Field of Cloth of Gold: Men and Manners in 1520* (London: Routledge & Kegan Paul, 1969). C.W. Holt, 'The Royal Entry in Medieval and Early Tudor England', Manchester University PhD thesis, 1969, is very useful in this context.

The role of Cardinal Wolsey has been revised by P. Gywn in *The King's Cardinal. The Rise and Fall of Thomas Wolsey* (London: Barrie & Jenkins, 1990) and in a collection of essays edited by S.J. Gunn and P.G. Lindley, *Cardinal Wolsey* (Cambridge: Cambridge UP, 1991) which re-examines Wolsey's artistic patronage and his role in government.

There has been more work completed on court politics. Dr Starkey's pioneering work on the privy chamber, developed in D.R. Starkey, 'The Development of the Privy Chamber, 1485–1547', Cambridge University PhD thesis, 1974, D.R. Starkey, *The Reign of Henry VIII: Personalities and Politics* (London: George Philip, 1985) and D.R. Starkey, 'From Feud to Faction: English Politics c.1450–1550', *History Today*, 32 (November 1982), 16–22. A number of biographies of noblemen at the court of Henry VIII have been published, including S.J. Gunn, *Charles Brandon, Duke of Suffolk* (Oxford: Blackwell, 1988); G.W. Bernard, *The Power of the Early Tudor Nobility: A Study of the Fourth and Fifth Earls of Shrewesbury* (Brighton: Harvester 1985); B.J. Harris, *Edward Stafford, Third Duke of Buckingham 1478–1521* (Stanford, CA: Stanford UP, 1986) and S. Vokes, 'The Early Career of Thomas, Lord Howard, Earl of Surrey and Third Duke of Norfolk 1474–c.1525', Hull University PhD thesis, 1989. A general survey is provided by H. Miller, *Henry VIII and the English Nobility* (Oxford: Blackwell, 1986).

4.　WAR AND PUBLIC FINANCE　*Richard Hoyle*

A short bibliographical essay on this subject is, of necessity, short. As has already been said, the ur-source upon which historians have relied is F.C. Dietz, *English Government Finance 1485–1547* (University of Illinois, 1921), repr. as vol. 1 of *English Public Finance 1485–1641* (1964). The task for the next generation of historians is to replace this. P. Williams, *The Tudor Regime* (Oxford: Clarendon Press, 1978) ch. 2 ('The Financial Resources of Government') is an excellent introduction in a wonderful book. A quite different work is P.K. O'Brien and P.A Hunt, 'The Rise of a Fiscal State in England, 1485–1815', *HR*, 66 (1993) which puts a 38-year period firmly in context.

Most of the work which has been published since the Second World War has been essentially institutional, that is concerned with the development of accounting institutions, their staff, procedures and their relationship with the monarch and household. Sir Geoffrey Elton, *The Tudor Revolution in Government* (Cambridge UP, 1953) has had a quite remarkable run and wears well: but see now C. Coleman and D. Starkey (eds), *Revolution Reassessed. Revisions in the History of Tudor Government and Administration* (Oxford: Clarendon Press, 1986) in which the 'younger' generation with differing degrees of success try to challenge the master on his own turf. But one reads all this material with a sense that financial considerations are at best secondary to other arguments.

The other institutional historian whose work has not always worn well is W.C. Richardson. Richardson produced two valuable works on the chamber and the Court of Augmentations: *Tudor Chamber Administration 1485–1547* (Baton Rouge, LA: Louisiana State UP, 1952) and *History of the Court of Augmentations* (Baton Rouge, LA: Louisiana State UP, 1961). Both are marked by a strange allergy to figures: neither contains the analyses of the accounts which one would expect to find there.

The various financial reserves are discussed by Starkey in his contribution to *Revolution Reassessed* and D. Hoak, 'The Secret History of the Tudor Court: the King's Coffers and the King's Purse, 1542–1553', *Journal of British Studies*, 26 (1987).

Other areas of public finance are very poorly covered. There is no financial or economic account of the crown lands before 1558 comparable with R.W. Hoyle (ed.), *The Estates of the English Crown, 1558–1640*, (Cambridge, 1992), although I hope in time to go some distance towards supplying this deficiency. B.P. Wolffe, *The Crown Lands, 1461–1536. An Aspect of Yorkist and early Tudor government* (London: George Allen & Unwin, 1970) is essentially an institutional study and not at all of the crown as landowner. A great deal of work was done in the 1950s on the sale of crown lands as an aspect of the gentry controversy, for instance J. Youings, 'The Terms of Disposal of the Devon Monastic Lands, 1536–58', *EHR*, 69 (1954) and Sir John Habbakuk, 'The Market for Monastic Property, 1539–1603', *EcHR*, 10 (1958). For the Wards after 1540 see J. Hurstfield, 'The Profits of Fiscal Feudalism', *EcHR*, 8 (1955). For the Wards before that date, there are some useful comments in H.E. Bell, *An Introduction to the History and Records of the Court of Wards and Liveries* (Cambridge UP, 1953) and in Richardson, *Tudor Chamber Administration*. For the administration of taxation the classic account is R.S. Schofield, 'Parliamentary Lay Taxation, 1485–1547', Cambridge PhD thesis, 1963. (Schofield's thesis is now [1994] in course of publication.) Much of the recent work on taxation is quasi-constitutional in approach and elementary questions about the role of taxation in public finance have not been asked. The debate prompted by Elton's 1976 'Taxation for War and Peace in early Tudor England', most conveniently in his *Studies in Tudor and Stuart Politics and Government* (4 vols, Cambridge UP, 1974–93) III, 216–33, continued in G.L. Harriss, 'Thomas Cromwell's "new principle of taxation"', *EHR*, 93 (1978); J.D. Alsop, 'The Theory and Practice of Tudor Taxation' and Harriss, 'Theory and Practice in Royal Taxation: Some Observations', both *EHR*, 97 (1982); Alsop, 'Innovation in Tudor Taxation', *EHR*, 99 (1984). I will not be universally thanked for reviving this debate; R.W. Hoyle, 'Crown, Parliament and Taxation in Sixteenth Century England', *EHR*, 109 (1994). M.L. Bush in his 'Tax Reform and Rebellion in early modern England', *History*, 76 (1991) is one of the few historians to appreciate that people may not have warmed to paying taxes and behaved accordingly. For clerical taxation we have J.J. Scarisbrick,

'Clerical Taxation in England, 1485–1547', *JEH*, 11 (1960) until the work of Patrick Carter becomes available.

All discussions of the mint and the currency in general defer to C.E. Challis, *The Tudor Coinage* (Manchester UP, 1978).

There is little on the spending departments which is helpful here. D. Loades, *The Tudor Navy* (Aldershot: Scolar Press, 1992) maintains the Eltonian tradition of indifference to figures. We still lack a full study of the financing of the household.

The best account drawing together war, politics and finance is G.W. Bernard, *War, Taxation and Rebellion in early Tudor England. Henry VIII, Wolsey and the Amicable Grant of 1525* (Brighton: Harvester, 1525) which is chronologically wider in scope than its title suggests. There is nothing equivalent for the 1540s. Two pieces by W.C. Richardson, 'Some Financial Expedients of Henry VIII', *EcHR*, 7 (1954) and his *Stephen Vaughan, Financial Agent of Henry VIII* (Baton Rouge, LA: Louisiana State UP, 1953) are narrowly conceived but for the moment indispensable.

5. FOREIGN POLICY   *David Potter*

The most essential sources for Henrician foreign policy in the state papers at the PRO, BL and other collections are to be found variably summarised in *LP*, though these must sometimes be treated with caution over dating. Many, though not all, of the most important documents were published in extenso in a slightly earlier compilation, *StP*. In particular, some of the important exchanges between the king and his chief ministers, notably Cardinal Wolsey, are to be found in vol. I of *StP* and the correspondence with ambassadors in part V (vols VI–XII), foreign correspondence. *LP* also calendars a wide variety of correspondence between foreign ambassadors in England and their home governments from the early 1520s onwards. Much of this material was published separately as *CSPSp* (dealing with Habsburg documents from a number of different archives). French ambassadors' reports are calendared for the most part in *LP* but three main French publications are important: *Ambassades en Angleterre de Jean du Bellay*, ed. V.L. Bourrilly and P. de Vaissière (Paris: Picard, 1905) followed by *La correspondance du cardinal Jean du Bellay*, ed. R. Scheurer, Société de l'Histoire de France, 2 vols so far (Paris: Klincksieck, 1969–74) and the *Correspondance politique de MM. de Castillon et de Marillac*, ed. J. Kaulek (Paris, 1885).

It was Sir John Seeley in *The Growth of British Policy* (2 vols, Cambridge UP, 1897) who emphasised the importance of what he called the 'British problem' in English diplomacy of the sixteenth century, the idea that England should 'close the back door' to foreign powers by assuring its dominance of Scotland. Both A.F. Pollard in *Henry VIII* (London: Longmans, 1902, 1925) and R.B. Wernham in *Before the Armada: The Growth of English Policy, 1485–1588* (London, 1961) pursued this idea that

Henry VIII consciously, especially in his later years, sought in this policy
the counterpart to internal consolidation. Wernham went on to argue
that the reign of Henry VIII, in showing the final failure of English territorial ambitions in Europe, opened a new era of 'oceanic strategies' for
England in the Elizabethan era. This was the same tradition in which P.S.
Crowson produced the disappointing *Tudor Foreign Policy* (London: Black,
1973) a book too overshadowed by English experiences in the twentieth
century and containing maps of a remarkable inexactitude. More recent
historians of the Henrician period, led by Sir Geoffrey Elton in his incisive critique of Wernham's book, have been increasingly reluctant to
accept the reality of such grand strategies. Old nostrums, however, linger
on.

Much recent interest has concentrated on the shaping of foreign
policy by the king and his councillors. For foreign policy, the wider
debate initiated in the different interpretations of the king's role in G.R.
Elton, *Henry VIII* (London: Routledge, 1962) and J.J. Scarisbrick, *Henry
VIII* (London: Eyre & Spottiswoode, 1968) and reviewed by Elton in 'King
of Hearts', *Studies in Tudor and Stuart Politics and Government* (4 vols,
Cambridge UP, 1974–92) pp. 100–8 is important. It is continued by D.
Starkey, *The Reign of Henry VIII: Politics and Personalities* (London: George
Philip, 1985). All these are of importance for the near-impossible task of
assessing the degree to which Henry VIII shaped policy. A.F. Pollard,
Cardinal Wolsey (London: Longmans, 1929) advanced the theory that
Wolsey's personal ambition shackled English policy to the Papal See, a
view effectively demolished in D.S. Chambers, 'Cardinal Wolsey and the
Papal Tiara', *BIHR*, 28 (1965). More recently P. Gwyn, *The King's
Cardinal. The Rise and Fall of Thomas Wolsey* (London: Barrie & Jenkins,
1990) has provided a sustained argument for the view that Wolsey's chief
preoccupation was to serve the king and maintain his honour. Ultimately,
the strings lay in the king's hands.

Gwyn's views are largely shared by G. Bernard, *War, Taxation and
Rebellion in Early Tudor England: Henry VIII, Wolsey and the Amicable Grant of
1525* (Brighton: Harvester, 1986), one of the best recent studies of
English foreign policy in the early 1520s. The importance of the king's
honour in Wolsey's calculations is also stressed by the work of S.J. Gunn
on the subject, notably his 'Wolsey's foreign policy and the Domestic
Crisis of 1527–8' in S.J. Gunn and P. Lindley (eds), *Cardinal Wolsey,
Church, State and Art* (Cambridge: CUP, 1991) one of the most richly documented and incisive studies of policy in the late 1520s. In comparison,
the 1530s and the policies of Thomas Cromwell in foreign affairs have
not attracted much attention despite the great work of Sir Geoffrey
Elton, although there is now R. McEntegart, 'England and the League of
Schmalkalden 1531–1547: faction, foreign policy and the English
Reformation', London School of Economics PhD thesis, 1992. On the
1540s, there is as yet only D. Potter, 'Diplomacy in the Mid-Sixteenth
Century: England and France 1536–1550', Cambridge PhD thesis, 1973.

On warfare in the period, S.J. Gunn, 'The French Wars of Henry VIII'
in J. Black (ed.), *The Origins of War in Early Modern Europe* (Edinburgh:

John Donald, 1987) provides a useful overview and the campaigns of the early years are covered in G. Cruickshank, *Army Royal. Henry VIII's Invasion of France in 1513* (Oxford: Clarendon Press, 1969) and *The English Occupation of Tournai, 1513–19* (Oxford: Clarendon Press, 1971). Military organisation is covered by two important theses: C.S.L. Davies, 'Supply Services of the English Armed Forces, 1509–50' (Oxford: OUP, 1963) and J. Goring, 'The Military Obligations of the English People, 1511–58' (London, 1955). Some aspects of dealings with mercenaries are covered in J.G. Millar, *Tudor Mercenaries and Auxiliaries, 1485–1547* (Charlottesville: Virginia UP, 1980). The 1523 campaign is meticulously handled in S.J. Gunn, 'The Duke of Suffolk's March on Paris', *EHR*, 101 (1986) 496–558 and the 1544 campaign newly discussed by L. Macmahon, 'The English Invasion of France, 1544', MA thesis, Warwick, 1992. Calais and its problems are examined in P. Morgan, 'The Government of Calais, 1485–1558', Oxford, DPhil thesis, 1966. On the navy, D. Loades, *The Tudor Navy. An Administrative, Political and Military History* (Aldershot: Scolar, 1992), while pointing out the continuities with Henry VII's navy, brings out the remarkable expansion in the first half of the reign of Henry VIII.

Studies of a more specialist kind that throw light on particular periods may be found in J. Russell, *The Field of the Cloth of Gold. Men and Manners in 1520* (London: Routledge, 1969) and Russell, 'The Search for Universal Peace: the Conferences of Calais and Bruges in 1521', *BIHR*, 44 (1971); P. Gwyn, 'Wolsey's Foreign Policy: the Conferences of Calais and Bruges Reconsidered', *HJ*, 23 (1980) 755–72. G. Jacqueton, *La politique extérieure de Louise de Savoie. Relations diplomatiques de la France et de l'Angleterre pendant la captivité de François Ier (1525–6)* (Paris: Boullon, 1892) remains essential for the mid-1520s. R. Scheurer, 'Les relations franco-anglaises pendant la négociation de la paix des Dames (1528–9)', in P.M. Smith and I.D. McFarlane (eds), *Literature and the Arts in the Reign of Francis I* (Lexington, 1985) exploits the du Bellay correspondence of which he is the editor. The role of Anglo-French relations in the divorce problems of Henry VIII was explored by V.-L. Bourrilly, 'François Ier et Henry VIII: l'intervention de la France dans l'affaire du divorce', *Rev. d'hist. moderne et contemporaine*, 1 (1889) 271–84. Involvement in the Baltic region has been explored by K.J.V. Jespersen, 'Henry VIII of England, Lubeck and the Count's War, 1533–35', *Scandinavian Journal of History*, 8 (1981).

There are many biographies of English courtiers and diplomats that shed light on the foreign policy of the period, including: S.J. Gunn, *Charles Brandon, Duke of Suffolk* (Oxford: Blackwell, 1988); W.S. Richardson, *Stephen Vaughan, Financial Agent of Henry VIII* (Baton Rouge, LA: Louisiana State UP, 1953); E.F. Rogers (ed.), *The Letters of Sir John Hackett, 1526–34* (Morgantown, 1971); G. Redworth, *In Defence of the Church Catholic. The Life of Stephen Gardiner* (Oxford: Blackwell, 1990); S.R. Gammon, *Statesman and Schemer: William, first Lord Paget* (London: David & Charles, 1973); A.J. Slavin, *Politics and Profit. A Study of Sir Ralph*

Sadler, 1507–47 (Cambridge: CUP, 1966); B. Ficaro, 'Nicholas Wotton, Dean and Diplomat', University of Kent, Canterbury, PhD thesis, 1981.

On the practice of diplomacy, the classic interpretation is G. Mattingly, *Renaissance Diplomacy* (London: Cape, 1955); J. Russell, *Peacemaking in the Renaissance* (London: Duckworth, 1976). These need to be supplemented by C. Giry Deloison, 'La naissance de la diplomatie moderne en France et en Angleterre au debut du XVIe siècle (1475–1520)', *Nouvelle Revue du seizième siècle* (1987) and Deloison, 'Le personnel diplomatique au début du XVIe siècle', *Journal des Savants* (1987). See also, D. Potter, 'Diplomacy in the Mid-sixteenth Century' (above) ch. 6; C.B.A. Behrens, 'The Origins of the Office of English Resident Ambassador at Rome', *EHR*, 49 (1934) 640–58.

On England and Scotland there is an overview in D.M. Head, 'Henry VIII's Scottish Policy: a Reassessment', *Scottish Historical Review*, 61 (1982) 1–24; on the earlier part of the reign, see R.G. Eaves, *Henry VIII's Scottish Diplomacy, 1513–24; English Relations with the Regency Government of James V* (New York: Exposition, 1971); Eaves, *Henry VIII and James V's Regency Government, 1524–28* (London, Lanham: UP of America, 1987). On the 1540s, M. Merriman, 'The Assured Scots', *Scottish Historical Review*, 47 (1968) 10–34; Merriman, 'War Propaganda during the Rough Wooing', *Scottish Tradition*, IX–X (1979–80); E. Bonner, 'The First Phase of the *Politique* of Henri II in Scotland, its Genesis and the Nature of the "Auld Alliance", 1547–54', University of Sydney PhD thesis, 1993.

6. THE LITERATURE AND PROPAGANDA OF HENRY VIII'S FIRST DIVORCE
    Virginia Murphy

The starting point for any modern study of the divorce still remains J.J. Scarisbrick's biography of Henry VIII (London: Eyre & Spottiswoode, 1968; Berkeley, CA: California UP, 1968) especially his ground-breaking account of the canon law of the divorce. Scarisbrick's interpretation has in part been superseded by H.A. Kelly's *The Matrimonial Trials of Henry VIII* (Stanford, CA: Stanford UP, 1976); while focusing on the court records of the three trials which considered the validity of Henry's various marriages, it also analyses a number of the divorce treatises. It is particularly good on the canonical and theological issues raised by the king's marital complications. An older but still useful chronological history of the divorce is Geoffrey de C. Parmiter, *The King's Great Matter: A Study of Anglo-Papal Relations 1527–1534* (London: Longman, Green, 1967). The introduction to Edward Surtz and Virginia Murphy (eds), *The Divorce Tracts of Henry VIII* (Angers: Moreana, 1988), an edition of the Latin and English texts of *Censurae*, provides a concise guide to recent thinking on the King's first divorce. Complementary to Surtz and Murphy, there is Guy Bedouelle and Patrick Le Gal (eds), *Le 'Divorce' du Roi Henry VIII* (Geneva: Librarie Droz, 1987) on the continental side of the debate; valuable in many respects, it should be treated cautiously for it is regrettably marred by a number of factual errors. A number of biographies or studies of the principal characters have also recently appeared, among them Richard Rex, *The Theology of John Fisher* (Cambridge and New York: Cambridge UP, 1991), E.W. Ives, *Anne Boleyn* (Oxford and New York: Blackwell, 1986) and Peter Gwyn, *The King's Cardinal: The Rise and Fall of Thomas Wolsey* (London: Barrie & Jenkins, 1990). The first two are of an especially high order. The results of Graham Nicholson's important research on the background to Henrician propaganda and legislation are now more widely available in 'The Act of Appeals and the English Reformation' in Claire Cross, David Loades and J.J. Scarisbrick (eds), *Law and Government under the Tudors* (Cambridge and New York: Cambridge UP, 1988) ch. 2. Most of the tracts on the divorce remain in manuscript but modern printed texts of *Censurae* and *Determinations* can be consulted in Surtz and Murphy above, and of the *Glass of the Truth* in Nicholas Pocock, *Records of the Reformation: the Divorce 1527–1535* (2 vols, Oxford: Clarendon Press, 1870) II, 385–421.

7. HENRY VIII AND THE REFORM OF THE CHURCH
   Diarmaid MacCulloch

The standard biography of Henry VIII, J.J. Scarisbrick, *Henry VIII* (London: Eyre & Spottiswoode, 1968), contains much of value on Henry VIII's religious evolution, and further context can be gained from M.K. Jones and M.G. Underwood, *The King's Mother: Lady Margaret Beaufort, Countess of Richmond and Derby* (Cambridge UP, 1992). A lively account is D. Starkey, *Henry VIII: Personalities and Politics* (London: George Philip, 1985). An English translation of 1688 of the *Assertio Septem Sacramentorum* is reprinted with introduction by F. Macnamara in *Miscellaneous Writings of Henry the Eighth* ... (London: Golden Cockerel, 1924). An excellent survey of the whole reign is R. Rex, *Henry VIII and the English Reformation* (Basingstoke: Macmillan, 1993), and for a survey of the church's development before the Henrician changes, J.C. Dickinson, *An Ecclesiastical History of English: the Later Middle Ages from the Norman Conquest to the Eve of the Reformation* (London: A & C. Black, 1979).

Among the key people close to Henry, Anne Boleyn remains capable of arousing controversy. The biography by E.W. Ives, *Anne Boleyn* (Oxford: Blackwell, 1986), especially pp. 160–3 and chs 13–14, presents the view of Anne as evangelical patron, as does M. Dowling, 'Anne Boleyn and Reform', *JEH*, 35 (1984) 30–45; G.W. Bernard criticises them in 'Anne Boleyn's Religion', *HJ*, 36 (1993) 1–20, to which Ives has replied: 'Anne Boleyn and the early Reformation in England: the Contemporary Evidence', *HJ*, 37 (1994) 389–400. Important new comparative evidence on Anne and French reformism is to be found M.D. Orth, 'Radical Beauty: Marguerite de Navarre's Illuminated Protestant Catechism and Confession', *SCJ*, 24 (1993) 383–427. Thomas Cromwell still awaits a modern biographer. On his religious beliefs, see S. Brigden, 'Thomas Cromwell and the "brethren"', in C. Cross, D. Loades and J.J. Scarisbrick (eds), *Law and Government under the Tudors* (Cambridge UP, 1988) pp. 31–49, and G.R. Elton, *Reform and Renewal: Thomas Cromwell and the Common Weal* (Cambridge UP, 1973). J. Guy, *The Public Career of Sir Thomas More* (Brighton: Harvester, 1980) examines the interaction between More's religion and politics in the crucial years 1529–32, while R. Marius, *Thomas More* (London: Collins, 1984) provides a full biography.

Of Henry's leading clergy during the Reformation, one cannot ignore the information provided in P. Gwyn, *The King's Cardinal: the Rise and Fall of Thomas Wolsey* (London: Barrie & Jenkins, 1990), but a good starting point is S.J. Gunn and P.G. Lindley (eds), *Cardinal Wolsey: Church, State and Art* (Cambridge UP, 1991). John Fisher is illuminated by B. Bradshaw and E. Duffy (eds), *Humanism, Reform and the Reformation: the Career of Bishop John Fisher* (Cambridge UP, 1989) and R. Rex, *The Theology of John Fisher* (Cambridge: Cambridge UP, 1991). J. Ridley, *Thomas Cranmer* (Oxford: Clarendon UP, 1962) has long been a reliable biography; see also D. MacCulloch, *Thomas Cranmer: a Life* (New Haven, CT: Yale UP, forthcoming in 1996). P. Ayris and D. Selwyn (eds), *Thomas Cranmer: Churchman and Scholar* (Woodbridge: Boydell, 1993) have gathered a valuable set of essays. G. Redworth, *In Defence of the Church Catholic: the Life of Stephen Gardiner* (Oxford: Blackwell, 1990) is useful, but inclined to take Gardiner at his own assessment. J.F. Mozley, *William Tyndale* (London: SPCK, 1937) is still a good beginning for study, although see now also D. Daniell, *William Tyndale: a Biography* (New Haven, CT: Yale UP, 1994).

Of the vast literature on the Henrician dissolutions, starting points are J. Youings, *The Dissolution of the Monasteries* (London: George Allen & Unwin, 1971) and C. Kitching, 'The Disposal of Monastic and Chantry Lands', in F. Heal and R. O'Day (eds), *Church and Society in England: Henry VIII to James I* (Basingstoke: Macmillan, 1977) ch. 6. Magisterial treatments are D. Knowles, *The Religious Orders in England*, vols II and III (Cambridge UP, 1955, 1959) (note shortened version, *Bare Ruin'd Choirs: the Dissolution of the English Monasteries*, Cambridge UP, 1976), and A. Kreider, *English Chantries: the Road to Dissolution* (Cambridge, MA: Harvard UP, 1979). See also J.J. Scarisbrick, 'Henry VIII and the Dissolution of the Secular Colleges', in Cross, Loades and Scarisbrick (eds), *Law and Government under the Tudors*; E.M. Hallam, 'Henry VIII's Monastic Refoundations of 1536–7 and the Course of the Dissolution', *BIHR*, 51 (1978) 124–31; S.E. Lehmberg, *The Reformation of Cathedrals: Cathedrals in the Tudor Age* (Cambridge UP, 1989). On the Pilgrimage of Grace, the standard discussion is still M.H. and R. Dodds, *The Pilgrimage of Grace and the Exeter Conspiracy* (Cambridge UP, 1915), although a useful modern introduction is A. Fletcher, *Tudor Rebellions* (London: Longman, 3rd edn 1983) ch. 4. Monographs on aspects of the Pilgrimage include C. Haigh, *The Last Days of the Lancashire Monasteries and the Pilgrimage of Grace* (Chetham Society, 3rd series 17, 1969) and S.M. Harrison, *The Pilgrimage of Grace in the Lake Counties 1536–7* (London: Royal Historical Society, 1981). Much recent discussion weighing up religious and political versus economic and social motivations remains in the form of articles, e.g. M.L. Bush, ' "Up for the Commonweal": the Significance of Tax Grievances in the English Rebellions of 1536', *EHR*, 106 (1991) 299–318; C.S.L. Davies, 'Popular Religion and the Pilgrimage of Grace', in A. Fletcher and J. Stevenson (eds), *Order and Disorder in early Modern England* (1985) pp. 58–91; G.R. Elton, 'Politics and the Pilgrimage of Grace', in B. Malament (ed.), *After the Reformation*, and repr. in *Studies in Tudor and Stuart Politics and Government* (Cambridge UP, 4 vols, 1974–92) III, 183–215; S.J. Gunn, 'Peers, Commons and Gentry in the Lincolnshire Revolt of 1536', *PP*, 123 (May 1989) 52–79 (a reassessment of M.E. James, 'Obedience and Dissent in Henrician England: the Lincolnshire Rebellion, 1536', in James, *Society, Politics and Culture: Studies in early modern England* (Cambridge UP, 1986) pp. 188–269, repr. from *PP*, 48 (August 1970) 3–78.

Much remains controversial in the standard literature about the nature of Reformation under Henry VIII; for instance, on the Ten Articles of 1536, see the contrasting views presented in Rex, *Henry VIII and the English Reformation*, pp. 145–7 and B. Hall in Ayris and Selwyn, *Cranmer*, pp. 21–3. On the *Bishops' Book* of 1537, see E.G. Rupp, *Studies in the Making of the English Protestant Tradition* (Cambridge UP, 1947) pp. 134–47. On the *King's Book* (1543): Rupp, *Studies*, pp. 149–54; B. Reardon, *Religious Thought in the Reformation* (London: Longman, 1981) pp. 244–5. On the Supremacy, despite what is probably a misjudgement of Henry VIII's redrafting of the Coronation oath, see W. Ullmann, ' "This realm of England is an Empire" ', *JEH*, 30 (1979) 175–203. On Cranmer's 1534 visitation and the setting up of the vicegerency, see F.D. Logan, 'Thomas Cromwell and the Vicegerency in Spirituals: a Revisitation', *EHR*, 103 (1988) 658–67, and P. Ayris in Ayris and Selwyn (eds), *Thomas Cranmer: Churchman and Scholar*, pp. 122–9.

On the evangelicals, besides the biographies and Rupp's *Studies* cited above, W.A. Clebsch, *England's Earliest Protestants 1520–1535* (New Haven, CT: Yale UP, 1964) is showing its age, and is usefully criticised in C. Trueman, *Luther's Legacy: Salvation and English Reformers 1525–1556* (Oxford: Clarendon Press, 1994). On Lollardy, standard treatments are A. Hudson, *Lollards and their Books* (London: Hambledon, 1985); M. Aston, *Lollards and Reformers: Images and Literacy in late Medieval Religion* (London: Hambledon, 1984); J.A.F. Thomson, *The Later Lollards, 1414–1520* (Oxford: Clarendon Press, 1965). Recent discussions about the importance of the movement in the prehistory of the Reformation and its social composition are A. Hope, 'Lollardy: the Stone and Builders Rejected?', in P. Lake and M. Dowling (eds), *Protestantism and the National Church in Sixteenth Century England* (London: Croom Helm, 1988); D. Plumb, 'The Social and Economic Spread of Rural Lollardy: a Reappraisal', in W.J. Sheils and D. Wood (eds), *Voluntary Religion* (*Studies in Church History*, 23, 1986); R.G. Davies, 'Lollardy and Locality', *TRHS*, 6th ser. 1 (1991) 191–212. On humanism, J.K. McConica, *English Humanists and Reformation Politics under Henry VIII and Edward VI* (Oxford: Clarendon Press, 1965), is still valuable, though now much supplemented by M. Dowling, *Humanism in the Age of Henry VIII* (London, Croom Helm,

1986), and A. Fox and J. Guy, *Reassessing the Henrician Age: Humanism, Politics and Reform 1500–1550* (Oxford: Blackwell, 1986). For a useful warning that the phrase 'New Learning' was then used to describe evangelical views and not humanism in general, see R. Rex, 'The New Learning', *JEH*, 44 (1993) 26–44.

8. LITERATURE, DRAMA AND POLITICS   *Seymour House*

The historical context and conditions of drama and literature is an expanding field with wide scope for further development. New studies have been published focusing on print culture which will have a tremendous impact on the way in which we approach this interdisciplinary field. Essential methodological concerns are discussed in Louis Montrose's 'Renaissance Literary Studies and the Subject of History' and Jean Howard's 'The New Historicism in Renaissance Studies', both found in *English Literary Renaissance*, 16 (1986) 5–43. Also important are Robert Hume's 'Texts within Contexts: Notes Toward a Historical Method', *Philological Quarterly*, 71 (1992) 69–100, and Linda Woodbridge's 'Patchwork: Piecing the Early Modern Mind in England's First Century of Print Culture', *English Literary Renaissance*, 23 (1993) 5–45.

At present, scholarly literature on the early Tudor press and stage is generally divided along two lines: sources and analyses. The sources are clearly crucial, and having critically reliable texts is essential when facsimiles or filmed originals are unavailable. Chief among the collections of dramatic sources for this period is the ongoing *Records of Early English Drama* series from Toronto University Press, which publishes archival records dealing with drama and performance. Also important is Ian Lancashire, *Dramatic Texts and Records: A Chronological Topography to 1558* (Toronto: Toronto UP, 1984) which includes a comprehensive bibliography. The best editions of the works of individual authors are found in the 'Tudor Interludes' series published by Brewer. Volumes to date include *Three Rastell Plays*, ed. R. Axton; *The Plays of Henry Medwall*, ed. A. Nelson; *Three Tudor Classical Interludes*, ed. M. Axton; *The Complete Plays of John Bale*, ed. P. Happé; and *The Plays of John Heywood*, ed. R. Axton and P. Happé.

For dramatic analysis of the period as a whole, see Glynne Wickham, *Early English Stages 1300–1660* (London: Routledge & Kegan Paul; New York: Columbia UP; 3 vols, 1959–81: vol. 1, 2nd edn, 1980). Sydney Anglo's essential *Spectacle, Pageantry and Early Tudor Politics* (Oxford: Clarendon Press, 1969) documents the political use of Tudor display, while Gail Gibson, *The Theatre of Devotion: East Anglian Drama and Society in the Later Middle Ages* (Chicago and London: Chicago UP, 1989) and Marianne Briscoe and John Coldeway (eds), *Contents for Early English Drama* (Bloomington: Indiana UP, 1989) offer illuminating background material on specific aspects of late-medieval popular drama. The political uses of the stage during Henry VIII's reign have been recently addressed by Paul White's *Theatre and Reformation: Protestantism, Patronage and Playing in Tudor England* (Cambridge: Cambridge UP, 1993) and Greg Walker, *Plays of Persuasion: Drama and Politics at the Court of Henry VIII* (Cambridge: Cambridge UP, 1991).

Sources for literary texts of the period are too numerous to mention individually. Major authors like More, Wyatt and Skelton have their modern editors while the Early English Text Society and the Medieval and Renaissance Texts and Studies series issue editions of important early English printed or MS texts. The vast majority of popular titles during the period remain unedited.

For analytical studies of individual authors or themes, the student is more amply provided for. Useful introductions to the humanist literature in the reign of Henry VIII are David Carlson, *English Humanist Books: Writers and Patrons, Manuscript and Print, 1475–1525* (Toronto and London: Toronto UP, 1993) and Alistair Fox, *Politics and Literature in the Reigns of Henry VII and Henry VIII* (Oxford: Blackwell, 1989) and Alistair Fox and John Guy, *Reassessing the Henrican Age: Humanism, Politics and Reform 1500–1550* (Oxford: Blackwell, 1986). Protestant literature is treated in John King's *English Reformation Literature: The Tudor Origins of the Protestant Tradition* (Princeton, NJ: Princeton UP, 1982). For traditional pious literature, see Eamon Duffy, *The Stripping of the Altars: Traditional Religion in England 1400–1580* (New Haven and London: Yale UP, 1992) chs 2, 6, 7 and Helen White, *The Tudor Books of Private Devotion* (Madison, WI: Wisconsin UP, 1951). For More's polemical works, see the indispensable introductions to the individual volumes in the Yale series, *The Complete Works of St. Thomas More* (New Haven and London: Yale UP, 1964–). Increasing attention is being paid to so-called popular culture and its role in the politics of Henry VIII's reign. For the prophecies, see Sharon Jansen, *Political Protest and Prophecy under Henry VIII* (Woodbridge: Boydell, 1991). The standard summary of Cromwell's efforts as censor and propagandist is still G.R. Elton, *Policy and Police: The Enforcement of the Reformation in the Age of Thomas Cromwell* (Cambridge: Cambridge UP, 1972; paperback, 1985) but Elton's forté was political rather than literary analysis. For Cromwell's stable of writers, see Edward Riegler, 'Printing, Protestantism and Politics; Thomas Cromwell and Religious Reform', unpublished PhD dissertation, UCLA, 1978.

The most important new area to open in the study of literature in the early modern period concerns what is being called print culture. Essential general reading in this field is Lucien Febvre and Henri-Jean Martin, *The Coming of the Book: The Impact of Printing, 1450–1800* (trans. D. Gerard, London: Verso, 1984) and Elizabeth Eisenstein, *The Printing Press as an Agent of Change* (Cambridge: Cambridge UP, 2 vols, 1979; reissued in one volume paperback, 1980). That such concerns are profoundly political has been amply demonstrated by recent studies; Tessa Watt's *Cheap Print and Popular Piety, 1550–1640* (Cambridge: Cambridge UP, 1991) and R.W. Scribner's *For the Sake of Simple Folk* (Cambridge: Cambridge UP, 1981).

9. LOCAL RESPONSES TO THE HENRICIAN REFORMATION
Robert Whiting

An overview of the Henrician Reformation is provided by R. Rex, *Henry VIII and the English Reformation* (London: Macmillan, 1992). There exists no full-scale examination of its local impact, but relevant material is to be found in general surveys of the English Reformation, in analyses of specific elements, and in local studies.

A. *General surveys*. The most vigorous advocacy of the 'revisionist' interpretation is C. Haigh, *English Reformations: Religion, Politics, and Society under the Tudors* (Oxford: Clarendon Press, 1993). Similar emphasis upon religious conservatism is found in J.J. Scarisbrick, *The Reformation and the English People* (Oxford: Blackwell, 1984) and E. Duffy, *The Stripping of the Altars: Traditional Religion in England, c.1400–c.1580* (New Haven and London: Yale UP, 1992). The opposite interpretation, stressing the role of Lollardy, Protestantism, and anticlericalism in preparing English society for religious change, is still best represented by A.G. Dickens, *The English Reformation* (London: Fontana, 1964; 2nd edn Batsford, 1989).

B. *Analyses of specific elements*. The foundation and dissolution of chantries are carefully examined by A. Kreider, *English Chantries: the Road to Dissolution* (Cambridge, MA: Harvard UP, 1979). Resistance to the Henrician changes, and its suppression, are analysed by G.R. Elton, *Policy and Police: The Enforcement of the Reformation in the Age of Thomas Cromwell* (Cambridge: Cambridge UP, 1972). M.H. and R. Dodds, *The Pilgrimage of Grace and the Exeter Conspiracy* (2 vols, Cambridge: Cambridge UP, 1915) remains useful for the risings of 1536–7. On Lollardy, see especially A. Hudson, *The Premature Reformation: Wycliffite Texts and Lollard History* (Oxford: Oxford UP, 1988).

C. *Local studies*. A number may be selected as particularly valuable for the local history of the Henrician Reformation. M. Bowker, *The Henrician Reformation: The Diocese of Lincoln under John Longland, 1521–47* (Cambridge: Cambridge UP, 1981) contains useful information on England's largest diocese. S. Brigden, *London and the Reformation* (Oxford: Clarendon Press, 1989) follows in detail the progress of religious change in the capital. A county relatively open to religious change is examined in P. Clark, *English Provincial Society from the Reformation to the Revolution: Religion, Politics, and Society in Kent, 1500–1640* (Hassocks: Harvester, 1977). A.G. Dickens, *Lollards and Protestants in the Diocese of York, 1509–1558* (new edn London: Hambledon, 1982) pioneered the regional approach to English Reformation history. C. Haigh, *Reformation and Resistance in Tudor Lancashire* (Cambridge: Cambridge UP, 1975) is a well-written examination of a particularly conservative county. A particularly conservative city is examined by D. Palliser, *Tudor York* (Oxford: Clarendon Press, 1979). R. Whiting, *The Blind Devotion of the People: Popular Religion and the English Reformation* (Cambridge: Cambridge UP, 1989) investigates the south-west, using church art as well as documentary sources such as churchwardens' accounts.

Notes and References

INTRODUCTION   *Diarmaid MacCulloch*

1. D. MacCulloch, *Suffolk and the Tudors: Politics and Religion in an English County 1500–1600* (Oxford, 1986) pp. 226–7.
2. See now the important thesis on this by R. McEntegart: 'England and the League of Schmalkalden 1531–1547: faction, foreign policy and the English Reformation', London School of Economics PhD, 1992.
3. R.W. Hoyle, 'Crown, Parliament and taxation in the 16th century', *EHR*, 109 (1994).
4. J. Strype, ed. P.E. Barnes, *Memorials ... of ... Thomas Cranmer ...* (2 vols, London, 1853) I, 63.
5. R. O'Day, *The Debate on the English Reformation* (London, 1986) p. 28, and cf. W. Haller, *Foxe's Book of Martyrs and the Elect Nation* (London, 1963) pp. 121–2.
6. J.J. Scarisbrick, 'Henry VIII and the dissolution of the secular colleges', in C. Cross, D. Loades and J.J. Scarisbrick (eds), *Law and Government under the Tudors* (Cambridge, 1988) p. 61.
7. See below, p. 187.

1.   HENRY VIII: THE POLITICAL PERSPECTIVE   *Eric Ives*

1. Thomas Smith, *De Republica Anglorum*, ed. M. Dewar (Cambridge, 1982) p. 88.
2. Thomas Starkey, *A Dialogue between Pole and Lupset*, ed. T.F. Mayer (CS, 4th ser., 37, 1989) p. 33: 'from the princes and rulers of the state cometh all laws order and policy, all justice, virtue and honesty to the rest of this politic body'.
3. Smith, *De Republica*, p. 88.
4. Edmund Plowden, *Commentaries and Reports* (London, 1779) p. 213 [re *The Duchy of Lancaster Case*].
5. PRO, E36/143 fos 29, 40 [*LP*, VI, nos 1370–1].
6. PRO, SP1/80 fo. 94r [*LP*, VI, no. 1417].
7. S. Thurley, *The Royal Palaces of Tudor England* (New Haven, CT, 1993) p. 70.
8. *English Historical Documents, IV, 1327–1485*, ed. A.R. Myers (London, 1969) p. 432.
9. *LP*, VI & VII passim.
10. *Letters and Accounts of William Brereton of Malpas*, ed. E.W. Ives (Record Soc. of Lanc. and Ches. 116, 1976) pp. 22–4.

11. PRO, E163/12/25/5.

12. *LP*, VII no. 587 (1, 2, 3, 6, 7, 8, 14, 19, 23, 24, 25, 27); 589 (1, 4, 14, 18, 19); 1601 (24).

13. D.R. Starkey: 'Representation through intimacy', in *Symbols and Sentiments*, ed. Ioan Lewis (London, 1977) pp. 187–224, 'Court and Government', in *Revolution Reassessed*, ed. C. Coleman and D.R. Starkey (Oxford, 1986) pp. 30–6, and 'Intimacy and Innovation: the Rise of the Privy Chamber', in *The English Court from the Wars of the Roses to the Civil War*, ed. D.R. Starkey (London, 1987) pp. 71–118; Thurley, *Royal Palaces* pp. 120–28, 135–43.

14. *Collection of Ordinances and Regulations for the Royal Household*, ed. Lort, Gough et al. (London Society of Antiquaries, 1790) pp. 154–5, 169 [*LP*, XX (2), App. 2.2. vi].

15. E.W. Ives, *Anne Boleyn* (Oxford, 1986) pp. 347–9, 356–7, 371.

16. Ibid., pp. 146–7; E.W. Ives, 'The Fall of Wolsey', in S.J. Gunn and P.G. Lindley (eds), *Cardinal Wolsey, Church, State and Art* (Cambridge, 1991) pp. 300–1.

17. Ives, 'The Fall of Wolsey', p. 301   n. 69; Ives, *Anne Boleyn*, pp. 147–50.

18. PRO, SP1/81 fo. 89 [*LP*, VI, no. 1634].

19. *Letters and Accounts of William Brereton*, pp. 53–5.

20. Ibid, pp. 27–8.

21. Starkey, 'Court and Government', p. 55; E.W. Ives, 'Henry VIII's Will – a Forensic Conundrum', *HJ*, 35 (1992) 782–7.

22. E.W. Ives, 'Court and County Palatine in the Reign of Henry VIII: the Career of William Brereton of Malpas', *Trans. Historic Soc. Lancs. and Ches.*, 123 (1972) 7–8.

23. G. Cavendish, *Life and Death of Cardinal Wolsey* (EETS, 1959) pp. 101–4, 110–12.

24. Ibid, p. 156.

25. Exeter, Rochford, Browne, Bryan, Carew, Cheney, Russell, Wellisbourne: BL Add.MS 9835 fos 24r, 26r; G.R. Elton, *The Tudor Revolution in Government* (Cambridge, 1959) pp. 379–80. cf. the Eltham Ordinance: 'of the ... gentlemen [of the privy chamber] divers be well languaged, expert in outward parts, and meet and able to be sent on familiar messages or otherwise, to outward princes'. *Household Ordinances*, p. 155.

26. William Fitzwilliam, treasurer 1525–39, admiral 1536–40, earl of Southampton 1537. For the military equivalent cf. Starkey, 'Intimacy and Innovation', pp. 86–90.

27. *Household Ordinances*, p. 156.

28. *LP*, XIII (2) no. 1120.

29. Starkey, 'Intimacy and Innovation', pp. 94–6.

30. Ibid, pp. 96–8 and R.W. Hoyle, below, p. 86.

31. H.M. Colvin (ed), *The History of the King's Works* (London, 1982) IV (2) pp. 2–5; Thurley, *Royal Palaces*, pp. 49–50, 69.

32. Thurley, *Royal Palaces*, p. 73.

33. For details of this and other royal movements, see PRO OBS 1419.

34. Thurley, *Royal Palaces*, pp. 68–70; Colvin, *King's Works*, IV (2) p. 5.

35. Thurley, *Royal Palaces*, pp. 69–70. For discussion of progresses particularly of the first half of the reign, see N. Samman below, ch. 3. For the progress of 1535 see Ives, *Anne Boleyn*, pp. 335–9 and D.R. Starkey (ed.), *Henry VIII: a European Court in England* (London, 1991) pp. 118–25.

36. The exception outside the Thames Valley was Beaulieu *al.* New Hall nr. Chelmsford in Essex.

37. Elton, *Tudor Revolution in Government*, pp. 66–71. For a more favourable view of Henry's involvement in affairs, especially in his later years, see L.B. Smith, *Henry VIII: the Mask of Royalty* (London, 1971) pp. 38–49.

38. Arthur Lord Grey, *Commentary on the Services of William Lord Grey of Wilton* (CS, 40, 1847) pp. 3–9.

39. Cavendish, *Life of Wolsey*, p. 12.

40. For the following see J.A. Guy, 'Privy Council: Revolution or Evolution' in *Revolution Reassessed*, pp. 62–3; 'Wolsey and the Tudor Polity', in *Wolsey: Church, State and Art*, pp. 60–1; S.J. Gunn, 'The Act of Resumption of 1515', in D. Williams (ed.) *Early Tudor England* (Woodbridge, 1989) pp. 91, 94.

41. H. Ellis (ed.), *Original Letters Illustrative of English History*, 3rd. ser. (1846) III, 370.

42. For the following see S.J. Gunn, 'The Accession of Henry VIII', *HR*, 64 (1991) 278–88; J.A. Guy, *The Cardinal's Court* (Hassocks, 1977) pp. 23–6, and *Tudor England* (Oxford, 1988) pp. 80–1.

43. *TRP*, I, 81–3.

44. J.J. Scarisbrick, *Henry VIII* (London, 1968) pp. 24–9; D.R. Starkey, *The Reign of Henry VIII* (London, 1985) pp. 48–9.

45. Cavendish, *Life of Wolsey*, pp. 11–12.

46. Ibid., p. 12

47. Guy, 'Wolsey and the Tudor Polity', pp. 62–3; Gunn, 'Act of Resumption', pp. 91–4.

48. Cavendish, *Life of Wolsey*, p. 24; Guy, 'Wolsey and the Tudor Polity', p. 57. Other evidence suggests that Wolsey spent Monday nights at court: *StP* I, p. 289 [*LP*, IV no. 4335].

49. Guy, 'Privy Council: Revolution or Evolution', pp. 67–8 and 'Wolsey and the Tudor Polity', pp. 58–9.

50. Ives, 'Fall of Wolsey', pp. 289–90.

51. Starkey, *Henry VIII*, pp. 73–80 and 'Intimacy and Innovation', pp. 79–80, 103–4. Cf. G. Walker, 'The Expulsion of the Minions Reconsidered', *HJ*, 32 (1989) 1–16.

52. *LP*, II, no. 4355; III, no. 2317; IV, no. 1329.

53. Starkey, 'Intimacy and Innovation', pp. 105–7; Guy, 'Wolsey and the Tudor Polity', pp. 63–4.

54. Guy, *Cardinal's Court*, pp. 23–40.

55. G. Nicholson, 'The Act of Appeals and the English Reformation', in C. Cross, D. Loades and J.J. Scarisbrick (eds), *Law and Government under the Tudors* (Cambridge, 1988) pp. 25–8.

56. Ives, *Anne Boleyn*, pp. 353–7, 413–15.

57. Susan Brigden, 'Popular Disturbance and the Fall of Thomas Cromwell and the Reformers, 1539–40', *HJ*, 24 (1981) 257–78; and 'Thomas Cromwell and the Brethren', in *Law and Government under the Tudors*, pp. 31–49.

58. For the following see J.A. Guy below , pp. 50–3.

59. See above, pp. 22–3.

60. Ives, 'Henry VIII's Will', *HJ*, 35, 781–4.

61. See the correspondence between the councillors in London and those at court, e.g. *StP*, I. pp. nos. 851–5, 858–62, 872–6, 879–80, 882 [*LP*, XXI (2), nos. 19, 34, 58, 134, 172, 273].

62. Cf. Paget's own comments on his relationship with Henry: Germain Lefevre-Pontalis (ed.), *Correspondence Politique de Odet de Selve* (Paris, 1888) p. 216; *CSPSp 1547–1549*, pp. 30–1.

63. G.R. Elton, *Studies in Tudor and Stuart Politics and Government* (Cambridge, 1974–92) III, 55.

64. Quoted in Smith, *Henry VIII*, p. 243.

65. E.W. Ives, 'Faction at the Court of Henry VIII: the Fall of Anne Boleyn', *History*, 57 (1972) 179–81, *Letters and Accounts of William Brereton*, pp. 31–3, *Faction in Tudor England*, 2nd edn (London, 1986) pp. 16–18, *Anne Boleyn*, pp. 347–57, 414–18, 'Fall of Wolsey', pp. 302–5, 311–12, and 'The Fall of Anne Boleyn Reconsidered', *EHR*, 107 (1992) 659–62.

66. Ives, 'Faction at the Court of Henry VIII', 180–1.

67. Ives, 'Henry VIII's will', 783–4, 800.

68. Ives, *Anne Boleyn*, p. 122; G.R. Elton, 'Politics and the Pilgrimage of Grace', in *Studies*, III, 207–15.

69. See above, n. 57.

70. Thomas More, *Utopia*, ed. G.M. Logan & R.M. Adams (Cambridge, 1989) pp. 13–38.

71. PRO, SP6/1 fo. 9.

72. C.H. Williams (ed), *English Historical Documents, V, 1485–1558* (London, 1967) pp. 393–4.

73. D.M. Loades, *Mary Tudor* (Oxford, 1989) pp. 100–3.

74. Edward Herbert, Lord Herbert of Chirbury, *The History of England under Henry VIII* (London, 1870) p. 745.

75. Shakespeare, *Henry VIII*; Samuel Rowley, *When You See Me You Know Me*.

76. Nicholson, 'Act of Appeals', in *Law and Government under the Tudors*, pp. 25–6; Ives, *Anne Boleyn*, pp. 117–18, 186–7, 212–13.

77. Smith, *Henry VIII* is the principal exposition of this view. Cf. G. Redworth, *In Defence of the Church Catholic* (Oxford, 1990) pp. 116–18, 183–4, 200–2, 242–7.

78. G.W. Bernard, 'Politics and Government in Tudor England', *HJ*, 31 (1988) 159–67; 'The Fall of Anne Boleyn', *EHR*, 106 (1991) 591–5, 609–10, and 'The Fall of Anne Boleyn – a rejoinder', EHR, 107 (1992) 671–4; P. Gwyn, *The King's Cardinal* (London, 1990) pp. 4–5, 8–19, 23, and passim.

79. *CSPV*, no. 1527–33, no. 637; Ives, *Anne Boleyn*, pp. 358–9; *LP*, XVI, no. 590; Ralph Morice, 'Anecdotes of Archbishop Cranmer', in

J.G. Nichols (ed.), *Narratives of the Days of the Reformation* (CS, 77, 1859) p. 255; Ives, *Anne Boleyn*, pp. 189–93, 212–13, 361–70.

80. Known by the copies made by Remigius van Leemput in 1667 and 1669: Royal Collection (HM the Queen), Petworth House (Lord Egremont), and by the cartoon for the figures of Henry VII and VIII, formerly at Chatsworth: National Portrait Gallery no. 4027.

81. Trs. E.W. & C.R. Ives. For the Latin text see R. Strong, *Holbein and Henry VIII* (London, 1967) p. 57.

2. THOMAS WOLSEY, THOMAS CROMWELL AND THE REFORM OF HENRICIAN GOVERNMENT *John Guy*

1. See especially G.R. Elton, *The Tudor Revolution in Government* (Cambridge, 1953); Elton, *Reform and Reformation: England, 1509–1558* (London, 1977); Elton, 'The Tudor Revolution: A Reply', *PP*, no. 29 (1964) 26–49; Elton, 'A New Age of Reform?', *HJ*, 30 (1987) 709–16; C. Coleman and David R. Starkey (eds), *Revolution Reassessed: Revisions in the History of Tudor Government and Administration* (Oxford, 1986); John Guy, *Tudor England* (Oxford, 1988); David R. Starkey (ed.), *The English Court from the Wars of the Roses to the Civil War* (London, 1987); Starkey, *The Reign of Henry VIII: Personalities and Politics* (London, 1983); Starkey, 'A Reply: Tudor Government: the Facts?' *HJ*, 31 (1988) 921–31; P. Williams and G.L. Harriss, 'A Revolution in Tudor History?', *PP*, no. 25 (1963) 3–58; Williams and Harriss, 'A Revolution in Tudor History?', *PP*, no. 31 (1965) 87–96.

2. For a recent discussion with specific reference to Tudor England, see Arthur J. Slavin, 'The Tudor State, Reformation and Understanding Change: Through the Looking Glass', in Paul A. Fideler and T.F. Mayer, *Political Thought and the Tudor Commonwealth* (London, 1992) pp. 223–53.

3. Roy Porter and M. Teich, *The Renaissance in National Context* (Cambridge, 1992); Roger Doucet, *Les Institutions de la France au XVIᵉ siècle* (2 vols; Paris, 1948); Doucet, *Etude sur le gouvernement de François Ier dans ses rapports avec le Parlement de Paris* (2 vols; Paris, 1921–6); R.J. Knecht, *Renaissance Warrior and Patron: the Reign of Francis I* (Cambridge, 1994); Knecht, 'The Court of Francis I', *European Studies Review*, 8 (1978) 1–22; John Guy, 'The French King's Council, 1483–1526', in *Kings and Nobles in the Middle Ages. A Tribute to Charles Ross*, ed. R.A. Griffiths and J.W. Sherborne (Gloucester, 1986) pp. 274–94; G. Jacqueton, 'Le Trésor de l'Epargne sous François I, 1523–47', *Revue Historique*, 55 (1894) 1–43, and 56 (1894) 1–38; J. Russell Major, 'The Crown and the Aristocracy in Renaissance France', *American Historical Review*, 69 (1964) 631–45; Russell Major, *Representative Institutions in Renaissance France, 1421–1559* (Madison, WI, 1960) pp. 126–47; Russell Major, *Representative Government in Early Modern France* (New Haven, CT, 1980) pp. 1–204; John Headley, *The Emperor and his Chancellor: A Study of the Imperial Chancellery of Gattinara* (Cambridge, 1983); D.M. Loades,

The Tudor Court (London, 1986); D.R. Starkey, 'Representation through Intimacy: A Study in the Symbolism of Monarchy and Court Office in Early-Modern England', in I. Lewis (ed.), *Symbols and Sentiments: Cross-cultural Studies in Symbolism* (London, 1977); Starkey (ed.), *The English Court from the Wars of the Roses to the Civil War* (London, 1987); S. Thurley, *The Royal Palaces of Tudor England* (New Haven, CT, 1993); S. Anglo, *Images of Tudor Kingship* (London, 1992); M. Aston, *The King's Bedpost* (Cambridge, 1994); F.A. Yates, *Astraea: The Imperial Theme in the Sixteenth Century* (London, 1975).

4. *Disputatio inter clericum et militem super potestate prelatis ecclesiae atque principibus terrarum commissa sub forma dialogi* (London, ?1531); *A Dialogue between a Knight and a Clerk, Concerning the Power Spiritual and Temporal; RSTC*, nos 12510–12511a; Knecht, *Renaissance Warrior and Patron*, pp. 519–40; S.W. Haas, 'Henry VIII's *Glasse of Truthe*', *History*, 64 (1980) 353–62; Graham Nicholson, 'The Act of Appeals and the English Reformation', in C. Cross, D. Loades and J.J. Scarisbrick (eds), *Law and Government under the Tudors* (Cambridge, 1988) pp. 19–30; Nicholson, 'The Nature and Function of Historical Argument in the Henrician Reformation', unpublished Cambridge PhD dissertation (1977).

5. Robert R. Harding, *Anatomy of a Power Elite: the Provincial Governors of Early Modern France* (New Haven, CT, 1978), pp. 1–168; Knecht, *Renaissance Warrior and Patron*, pp. 54–8.

6. Jacqueton, 'Le Trésor de l'Epargne sous François I, 1523–47'; M. Wolfe, *The Fiscal System of Renaissance France* (New Haven, CT, 1972); Knecht, *Renaissance Warrior and Patron*, pp. 58, 60–1, 197–9, 345–9, 506–7, 559.

7. Guy, 'The French King's Council, 1483–1526'; Knecht, *Renaissance Warrior and Patron*, pp. 49–52; François Decrue, *De consilio regis Francisci I* (Paris, 1885), Roland Mousnier, *Le Conseil du roi de Louis XII à la révolution* (Paris, 1970); Noël Valois, 'Etude historique sur le conseil du roi', in introduction to N. Valois, *Inventaire des arrêts du conseil d'état, règne de Henri IV* (Inventaires et Documents publiés par la Direction Générale des Archives Nationales, 2 vols; Paris, 1886).

8. Virginia Murphy discusses this in detail below in ch. 6.

9. Quentin Skinner, 'The State', in T. Ball, James Farr, and R.L. Hanson (eds), *Political Innovation and Conceptual Change* (Cambridge, 1989), pp. 90–131; G.R. Elton, *The Parliament of England, 1558–1581* (Cambridge, 1986); D.M. Dean and N.L. Jones (eds), *The Parliaments of Elizabethan England* (Oxford, 1990).

10. For this interpretation, see especially J.J. Scarisbrick, *Henry VIII* (London 1968) pp. 43–6; G.W. Bernard, *War, Taxation and Rebellion in Early Tudor England: Wolsey and the Amicable Grant of 1525* (Brighton, 1985) pp. 3–45; J. Guy, 'Wolsey and the Tudor Polity', in *Cardinal Wolsey: Church, State and Art*, ed. S.J. Gunn and P. Lindley (Cambridge, 1991) 61–3; Peter Gwyn, *The King's Cardinal: the Rise and Fall of Thomas Wolsey* (London, 1990) passim.

11. See the essay by Neil Samman below, ch. 3, which explores the way in which Wolsey kept in touch with the king.

12. Guy, *Tudor England*, pp. 80–115; Guy, *The Cardinal's Court: The Impact of Thomas Wolsey in Star Chamber* (Hassocks, 1977) passim; Gwyn, *The King's Cardinal*, passim; J.J. Scarisbrick, 'Cardinal Wolsey and the Common Weal', in E.W. Ives, R.J. Knecht, and J.J. Scarisbrick (eds), *Wealth and Power in Tudor England* (London, 1978), pp. 45–67.

13. R.S. Sylvester and P.P. Harding (eds), *Two Early Tudor Lives: The Life and Death of Cardinal Wolsey by George Cavendish; The Life of Sir Thomas More by William Roper* (New Haven, CT, 1962) p. 12; Starkey, 'Court, Council and Nobility in Tudor England', in *Princes, Patronage and the Nobility*, ed. R.G. Asch and A.M. Birke (Oxford, 1991) pp. 175–203.

14. R.B. Merriman (ed.) *Life and Letters of Thomas Cromwell* (2 vols; Oxford, 1902) I, 1–55; G. Elton, *Studies in Tudor and Stuart Politics and Government* (4 vols; Cambridge, 1974, 1983, 1992) II, 215–35, III, 373–90; A.J. Slavin, 'The Gutenberg Galaxy and the Tudor Revolution', in G.P. Tyson and S.S. Wagonheim (eds), *Print and Culture in the Renaissance: Essays on the Advent of Printing in Europe* (Newark, NJ, 1986) pp. 90–109; J. Guy, *The Public Career of Sir Thomas More* (Brighton and New Haven, 1980) pp. 113–40. See also discussion by Richard Hoyle, below, ch. 4.

15. For this interpretation, see especially Guy, *The Public Career of Sir Thomas More*, pp. 128–201; Alistair Fox and John Guy, *Reassessing the Henrician Age: Humanism, Politics and Reform* (Oxford, 1986) passim; Guy, *Tudor England*, pp. 116–89; Guy 'Reassessing Thomas Cromwell', *History Sixth*, 6 (1990) 2–6; Guy, 'The Tudor Commonwealth: Revising Thomas Cromwell', *HJ*, 23 (1980) 681–7.

16. Surtz and Murphy, 'Introduction', pp. i–xxxvi; Virginia Murphy, 'The Debate over Henry VIII's First Divorce: An Analysis of the Contemporary Treatises', unpublished Cambridge PhD dissertation (1984); Fox and Guy, *Reassessing the Henrician Age*, pp. 151–78; Nicholson, 'The Act of Appeals and the English Reformation', pp. 19–30.

17. In ch. 8 below, Seymour House shows how much energy Cromwell devoted to influencing literature and drama in the royal interest.

18. Guy, *The Public Career of Sir Thomas More*, pp. 175–201; G.R. Elton, *Policy and Police: The Enforcement of the Reformation in the Age of Thomas Cromwell* (Cambridge, 1972) passim.

19. E.W. Ives, *Anne Boleyn* (Oxford, 1986) passim; Ives, 'Faction at the Court of Henry VIII: The Fall of Anne Boleyn', *History*, 57 (1972) 169–88.

20. Coleman and Starkey (eds), *Revolution Reassessed*, pp. 76–80; Fox and Guy, *Reassessing the Henrician Age*, pp. 121–47; M.H. Dodds and R. Dodds, *The Pilgrimage of Grace, 1536–1537, and the Exeter Conspiracy, 1538* (2 vols; Cambridge, 1915).

21. F. Donald Logan, 'Thomas Cromwell and the Vicegerency in Spirituals: a Revisitation', *EHR*, 103 (1988) 658–67.

22. *English Historical Documents*, V: *1485–1558*, ed. C.H. Williams (London, 1967), nos 113, 115; Guy, *Tudor England*, pp. 178–84.

23. *StP*, VIII, pp. 349–59; *LP*, XV, no. 765; Susan Brigden, 'Thomas Cromwell and the "Brethren" ', in Cross, Loades, and Scarisbrick (eds),

Law and Government under the Tudors, pp. 31–49; A.G. Dickens, *Thomas Cromwell and the English Reformation* (London, 1959) passim.

24. Roger S. Schofield, 'Taxation and the Political Limits of the Tudor State', in Cross, Loades, and Scarisbrick (eds), *Law and Government under the Tudors*, p. 255.

25. Ibid., pp. 231–3.

26. Ibid., pp. 233–6; Schofield, 'Parliamentary Lay Taxation, 1485–1547', unpublished Cambridge PhD dissertation (1963) passim.

27. Schofield, 'Taxation and the Political Limits of the Tudor State', pp. 234–5.

28. Ibid., p. 232; Schofield, 'Parliamentary Lay Taxation, 1485–1547', table 40 (facing p. 416); M.J. Kelly, 'Canterbury Jurisdiction and Influence during the Episcopate of William Warham, 1503–1532', unpublished Cambridge PhD dissertation (1963), pp. 301, 316–17.

29. John Guy, 'Wolsey and the Parliament of 1523', in Cross, Loades, and Scarisbrick (eds), *Law and Government under the Tudors*, pp. 1–18.

30. Ibid., p. 18.

31. Bernard, *War, Taxation and Rebellion*, pp. 53–72.

32. Ibid., pp. 136–48; D. MacCulloch, *Suffolk and the Tudors: Politics and Religion in an English County, 1500–1600* (Oxford, 1986), pp. 290–3.

33. The 'loans' were deemed retrospectively to have been taxation. S.E. Lehmberg, *The Reformation Parliament, 1529–1536* (Cambridge, 1970) pp. 89–91; Guy, *The Public Career of Sir Thomas More*, p. 119.

34. The French pensions are discussed further by David Potter, ch. 5 below.

35. A precedent for this existed in Wolsey's act of 1515 granting a fifteenth and tenth; some limitation should be placed on the idea that the grant of 1534 announced a revolutionary new principle. J.D. Alsop, 'The Theory and Practice of Tudor Taxation', *EHR*, 97 (1982) 1–30; Alsop, 'Innovation in Tudor Taxation', *EHR*, 99 (1984) 83–93; G.L. Harriss, 'Thomas Cromwell's "New Principle" of Taxation', *EHR*, 93 (1978) 721–38; G.R. Elton, *Studies in Tudor and Stuart Politics and Government*, III, 216–33. For an alternative view, see Richard Hoyle, below, pp. 83, 264 n. 28.

36. Schofield, 'Taxation and the Political Limits of the Tudor State', p. 232; Schofield, 'Parliamentary Lay Taxation, 1485–1547', table 40; Kelly, 'Canterbury Jurisdiction and Influence during the Episcopate of William Warham, 1503–1532', pp. 312–13.

37. F.C. Dietz, *English Public Finance, 1485–1641* (2 vols; Urbana, IL, 1921; 2nd edn, London, 1964) I, 137–49; D. Knowles, *The Religious Orders in England*, vol. III, *The Tudor Age* (Cambridge, 1959; repr. 1971) pp. 393–401; J. Youings, *The Dissolution of the Monasteries* (London, 1971) pp. 117–31.

38. H.M. Colvin (ed.), *The History of the King's Works*, vol. IV (London, 1982) pp. 6–7, 369–401.

39. D.R. Starkey, 'Court and Government', in Coleman and Starkey, *Revolution Reassessed*, pp. 42–6; Starkey, 'After the Revolution', in ibid., pp. 199–208.

40. See especially *The Governance of England*, ed. C. Plummer (Oxford, 1885; 2nd edn, 1926) passim; Guy, *Tudor England*, pp. 4–10.

41. B.P. Wolffe, *The Crown Lands, 1461–1536* (London, 1970) passim; Wolffe, 'Henry VII's Land Revenues and Chamber Finance', *EHR*, 79 (1964) 225–54; M.M. Condon, 'Ruling Elites in the Reign of Henry VII', in C. Ross (ed.), *Patronage, Pedigree and Power* (Gloucester, 1979) pp. 109–42.

42. *CSPSp*, IV, ii. p. 623.

43. *LP*, VII, no. 1355; Youings, *Dissolution of the Monasteries*, p. 145.

44. *StP*, I, 646–760.

45. Ibid., 763–5, 767–70.

46. The main (and conflicting!) authorities are: Elton, *The Tudor Revolution in Government*, passim; Elton, 'A New Age of Reform?'; John Guy, 'The Privy Council: Revolution or Evolution?', in Coleman and Starkey (eds), *Revolution Reassessed*, pp. 59–85; Starkey (ed.), *The English Court from the Wars of the Roses to the Civil War*, passim; Starkey, 'A Reply: Tudor Government: the Facts?'; Starkey, 'Court, Council and Nobility in Tudor England', pp. 175–203. See also Thurley, *Royal Palaces of Tudor England*, pp. 137–9.

47. S.G. Ellis, *Reform and Revival: English Government in Ireland, 1470–1534* (Woodbridge, 1986) pp. 31–48.

48. *A Collection of Ordinances and Regulations for the Government of the Royal Household* (London, 1790) pp. 159–60; Guy, 'The Privy Council: Revolution or Evolution?', pp. 67–8; Fox and Guy, *Reassessing the Henrician Age*, pp. 135–6.

49. 27 Henry VIII, c. 63. Sir William Fitzwilliam (later earl of Southampton) was the inspiration behind the act. D.R. Starkey, 'Privy Secrets: Henry VIII and the Lords of the Council', *History Today*, 37 (Aug. 1987) 31.

50. *LP, Addenda*, I, no. 944.

51. Cf. Starkey, 'Court, Council, and Nobility', p. 192.

52. *LP*, VI, no. 551.

53. Cromwell's mind was simultaneously thinking on a completely different track. He wrote in his memoranda: 'to appoint the most assured and most substantial of all gentlemen within every shire of this realm to be sworn of the King's Council, and they to have commandment to explore and ensearch to know who shall preach, teach and speak anything to the advancement of the pope's authority'. BL Cott. MS. Titus B. I, fo. 466 (*LP*, VII, no. 420).

54. *LP*, VI, no. 1071.

55. *StP*, I, pp. 646–7.

56. *LP*, XIII, i, no. 1 (wrongly dated by *LP* to 1538); from internal evidence it appears that the document was compiled shortly after the Pilgrimage was suppressed. Guy, 'Privy Council: Revolution or Evolution', pp. 74–85; J. Guy, *The Court of Star Chamber and its Records to the Reign of Elizabeth I* (London, 1985) pp. 6–8; Guy, *Tudor England*, pp. 161–3, 475 nn. 27, 30.

57. An attempt to date the reconstruction of the privy council to 'the middle of 1536' on the grounds of the alleged exclusion of the lord mayor of London at this date is inconclusive and irrelevant. See Guy, *Tudor England*, p. 161. For a different interpretation which argues that the privy council was not institutionally established before 1540, see Starkey, 'Court, Council and Nobility in Tudor England', pp. 175–203.

58. Guy, ' Privy Council: Revolution or Evolution?', pp. 76–80.

59. Ibid., pp. 78–9; Starkey, 'Privy Secrets', pp. 29–31; the ideological input is stressed more strongly still by Starkey, 'Court, Council and Nobility in Tudor England', pp. 175–203.

60. Elton, *Tudor Revolution in Government*, p. 337; Guy, 'Privy Council: Revolution or Evolution?', pp. 77–80.

61. *LP*, XI, nos 701, 753, 799, 885, 1040, 1228, 1237; *LP*, XII, i, nos 291, 332–3, 505, 558, 636, 667, 846, 864. In addition, *LP*, XI, nos 817, 823, 836; *LP*, XII, i, no. 125 represent drafts or copies of letters written in the collective name of the council. See also Elton, *Tudor Revolution in Government*, p. 338.

62. For the practice between 1509 and 1513 and its significance, see Guy, 'Wolsey and the Tudor Polity', pp. 60–1.

63. *LP*, XI, nos 738, 775, 800–1, 803, 825, 837, 844, 852, 909, 921, 1242; *LP*, XII, i, nos. 319, 321, 373, 382, 398, 444, 468, 594, 651, 916, 993, App. 2. An illustration of the insistence of the privy council that despatches be addressed to it collectively, and not to individuals, is *StP*, VIII, pp. 443–6; *LP*, XVI, no. 122. See also Scarisbrick, *Henry VIII*, p. 426.

64. PRO, SP 1/106, fos 217–18; *StP*, I, 459–61.

65. PRO, SP 1/107, fo. 46 (*LP*, XI, no. 580 [3]). The memorandum was written immediately after the outbreak of the Pilgrimage.

66. Starkey, 'Court, Council, and Nobility', pp. 191–2. What the memorandum actually proves is that at this date the term 'Privy Council' was still a turn of speech and not the name of a settled institution, and this is what Starkey finally concludes on p. 192.

67. PRO, SP 1/107, fo. 46.

68. Chris Given-Wilson, *The Royal Household and the King's Affinity: Service, Politics and Finance in England, 1360–1413* (New Haven, CT, 1986) pp. 203–57.

69. D.A.L. Morgan, 'The House of Policy: the Political Role of the late Plantagenet Household, 1422–1485', in Starkey (ed.), *The English Court from the Wars of the Roses to the Civil War*, pp. 64–7.

70. The breakdown is 50 knights for the body, 70 esquires for the body, 69 gentlemen ushers, 65 yeomen ushers, 82 sewers of the chamber, 39 yeomen of the chamber, 68 grooms of the chamber, and 50 pages of the chamber.

71. In other words, free food and accommodation.

72. BL Cott. MS., Titus B. I, fo. 192 (formerly fo. 184) *LP*, III, i, no. 576 [3]).

73. E 36/130, fos 165–231 (*LP*, III, i, no. 578). This document can be read only under ultraviolet light.

74. The book concludes with a consolidated list of 74 grooms. My figures exclude chaplains and a handful of foreigners.

75. *LP*, IV, i, no. 1939 (8).

76. *LP*, II, i, no. 2735 (wrongly dated to 1516).

77. Guy, 'Wolsey and the Tudor Polity', pp. 68–70.

78. M.L. Zell, 'Early Tudor JPs at work', *Archaeologia Cantiana*, 93 (1977) 126–7.

79. In Yorkshire the number of local gentry in the commissions was significantly reduced during the 1520s, and the number of 'outsiders' correspondingly increased. Six clerical JPs with close ties to Wolsey (of whom five were appointed to the duke of Richmond's Council in the North) were placed on the commissions for Cumberland, Westmorland, Northumberland and Yorkshire. The nominations were as follows: Thomas Dalby (archdeacon of Richmond); William Franklin (chancellor of Durham); Brian Higdon (archdeacon and dean of York); William Holgill (Wolsey's steward as archbishop of York); Thomas Magnus (archdeacon of East Riding, Wolsey's secretary as archbishop of York); William Tate (almoner to the duke of Richmond). All except Holgill were members of the northern Council appointed in 1525. Rachel R. Reid, *The King's Council in the North* (London, 1921) pp. 103–4. For further discussion, see R.B. Smith, *Land and Politics in the England of Henry VIII: The West Riding of Yorkshire, 1530–46* (Oxford, 1970), pp. 153–5, and table 15.

80. See Appendix 1.

81. *StP*, I, pp. 411–15, 545–7; Elton, *Policy and Police*, pp. 217–62; A.S. Bevan, 'The Role of the Judiciary in Tudor Government,1509–1547', unpublished Cambridge PhD dissertation (1985) chs 7–8.

82. Guy, 'Wolsey and the Tudor Polity', p. 70.

83. Mary L. Robertson, 'Thomas Cromwell's Servants: the Ministerial Household in Early Tudor Government and Society', unpublished UCLA PhD dissertation (1975), pp. 314–48, 438–595.

84. *OED*, s.v. 'manred'.

85. *LP*, XIV, i, no. 643.

3. THE PROGRESSES OF HENRY VIII 1509–1529   *Neil Samman*

1. A.H. Thomas and I.D. Thornley, *The Great Chronicle of London* (London, 1938) p. 215.

2. J.G. Meagher, 'The first progress of Henry VII', *Renaissance Drama*, 1 (1968). Henry VII's itinerary has been published in G. Temperley, *Henry VII* (London, 1917). Miss M. Condon is currently researching a more reliable itinerary.

3. B.P. Wolffe, *Henry VI* (London, 1981) p. 94. Itinerary of Henry VI, pp. 361–71.

4. C. Ross, *Edward IV* (London, 1974) p. 273 H.M. Colvin, *The History of the King's Woks* (London, 1982) IV, ii, p. 78.

5. H.M. Baillie, 'Etiquette and the Planning of the State Apartments in Baroque Palaces', *Archaeologia*, 101 (1967). S. Thurley, *The Royal Palaces of Tudor England, Architecture and Court Life 1460–1547* (New Haven and London, 1993).

6. PRO E101 416/15 fos 27v–32v. E36 215 p. 70 (*LP*, II, ii, p. 1447). Hall (Whibley), p. 515.

7. Thomas and Thornley, *Great Chronicle*, p. 342. This is confirmed by Edward Hall.

8. For Henry VIII's itinerary see N. Samman, 'The Henrician Court during Cardinal Wolsey's ascendancy *c*. 1514–1529', University of Wales PhD 1989, Appendix I.

9. C. Rawcliffe, *The Staffords, Earls of Stafford and Dukes of Buckingham 1394–1521* (Cambridge, 1978) p. 138. However, on p. 134 Rawcliffe estimates that an 'extra £1000 was spent on hospitality for the Court'. B.J. Harris, *Edward Stafford, Third Duke of Buckingham, 1478–1521* (Stanford, CA, 1986) p. 101 Hall (Whibley) p. 597. When Pace arrived at Penshurst, he found the king 'playing with the hostages', PRO SP1/18 fo. 276 (*LP*, III, i, no. 412).

10. Hall (Whibley) p. 599.

11. J.J. Scarisbrick, 'Thomas More: The King's Good Servant', *Thought: Fordham University Quarterly*, 52 (1977) 251.

12. The three surviving contemporary lists for the period 1509–30 are: (a) 18 July 1518, 'giests' prepared for Princess Mary, PRO SP1/17 fo. 4 (*LP*, II, ii, no. 4326[2]; (b) 18 August 1526, 'giests' for the second half of the king's summer progress from Winchester to Ampthill, PRO SP1/39 fo. 46 (*LP*, IV, ii, no. 2407[2]; (c) 13 June 1528, 'giests' for the king's proposed summer progress, PRO SP1/235 fo. 266 (*LP Addenda*, I, no. 589). These 'giests' are undated but they are in Fitzwilliam's hand and begin three days after his letter written in June 1528. PRO SP1/48 fo. 181 (*LP*, IV ii, no. 4367) 'Giestes' appears to be an archaic form of 'joists', possibly in the sense of 'supports'.

13. PRO E101 465/16.

14. PRO SP1/235 fo. 174–174v (*LP Addenda* I, no. 538).

15. PRO E101 419/9 fo. 15v–16. *LP*, III, ii nos 3495[9], 2992[3].

16. PRO SP1/39 fo. 31 (*LP*, IV ii no. 2368).

17. *LP* IV, iii, no. 5774. PRO SP/1 37 fo. 64 (*LP*, IV, i no. 1939[8]. LS 13/278 fo. 153.

18. PRO E36 130 fo. 196. BL Add. MS 21, 116 fo. 1 (*LP*, III, ii, no. 1899).

19. PRO E101 419/13 fos. 25–25v. Calvin, *King's Works*, IV, ii, p. 220.

20. PRO SP1/39 fo. 31 (*LP*, IV, ii no. 2368).

21. R.J. Knecht, *Francis I* (Cambridge, 1982) pp. 85, 93.

22. PRO E36 215 fo. 219 (*LP*, II, ii, p. 1451).

23. Longleat House, Seymour Papers, XVII, fo. 31.

24. PRO SP1/39 fo. 31v (*LP*, IV, ii, no. 2768); *LP*, II, ii, no. 3311.

25. PRO SP1/39 fo. 1 (*LP*, IV, ii, no. 2343). E101 419/13 fo. 26. SP1/39 fo. 75 (*LP*, IV, ii, no. 2407).

26. PRO E101 419/13 fos 27–27v, 28v–29.

27. PRO SP1/23 fo. 29 (*LP*, III, ii, no. 1516). Lambeth Palace, Shrewsbury MS 3192, fo. 32v.E. Lodge, *Illustrations of British History* (3 vols, London, 1838) I, 11 (*LP*, II, i, no. 1861).

28. PRO PROB/199.

29. *The Victoria County History of the Counties of England, Essex*, IV, 191. See Samman, 'Henrician Court', PhD, 1989, Appendix IV.

30. PRO SP1/21 fo. 34 (*LP*, III, i, no. 950).

31. *H of C. 1509–58*, II, pp. 18–19. PRO E36 130 fo. 171. *A Collection of Ordinances and Regulations for the Government of the Royal Household* (1790) p. 154. L.T. Smith, *The Itinerary of John Leland in or about the years 1535–1543* (5 vols, London, 1964) I, 127. E36 130 fo. 203. *VCH, Gloucestershire*, VII, 74–5. E36 216 p. 203 (*LP*, III, ii, p. 1542).

32. PRO C82 450 (*LP*, II, ii no. 3474). E101 419/13 fos 27–27v. Edward Hall, *Chronicle*, ed. Ellis (1809) p. 690.

33. BL Add. MS 21, 116, fo. 1 (*LP*, III, ii, no. 1899).

34. In 1519 the cofferer's and comptroller's accounts are imprecise and only specify that the king stayed with Lord Bergavenny. PRO E101 418/15 fo. 26v.

35. PRO SP1/19 fos 85–7. (*LP*, III, i, no. 491). SP1/22 fo. 154 (*LP*, III, i, no. 1290). The marquis of Exeter, as keeper of the manor, prepared Birling for the king's visit. PRO E101 631/25 fo. 6: these accounts were calendared incorrectly as Lord Bergavenny's in *Letters and Papers*, *LP*, IV, ii, no. 3734[4].

36. M. Howard argues that the sale was cancelled in 1522 ('Courtier Houses in the reign of Henry VIII', London PhD, 1985, p. 526) but in fact Bergavenny was not allowed to buy Birling back until 1530. PRO C82/626 (*LP*, IV, iii, no. 6363[1]).

37. Colvin, *King's Works*, IV, p. 3.

38. Wolffe, *Henry VI*, pp. 74–5.

39. BL Cott, MS Vit. B III fo. 245 (*LP*, II, ii, no. 4034).

40. *Rutland Papers*, ed. William Jerdan, Camden Society, Old Series, 21 (1842) p. 91, PRO E101 420/11 fo. 15v.

41. Colvin, *King's Works*, IV, ii, pp. 25–6.

42. PRO E101 419/1 fos 4v, 6v, 7v–8v. Henry E. Huntington Library, San Marino, California, Ellesmere MS 2655 fo. 354, 355.

43. HMC 14th Report, Appendix Part VIII, p. 36. A.F. Johnston and M. Rogerson, *Records of Early English Drama: York* (Toronto, 1979) I, 272–5. See C.W. Holt, 'The Royal Entry in Medieval and Tudor England', Manchester PhD, 1969.

44. *Records of Early English Drama: Coventry*, ed. R.W. Ingram (Toronto, 1981) p. 107.

45. HMC 14th Report, Appendix, Part VIII, p. 36.

46. HMC 9th Report, Appendix, Part I, pp. 150, 152.

47. BL Add. MS 27,449 fo. 10. The king was entertained by Sir Roger Townsend at Raynham.

48. *CPSSp Further Supplement*, p. 164.

49. PRO SP1/16 fo. 317 (*LP*, II, ii, no. 4276). HMC Tenth Report, Appendix, Part IV, p. 448. SP1/16 fo. 318 (*LP*, II, ii, no. 4288).

50. The only possible exception is 1526. Samman, 'Henrician Court', pp. 219–20.

51. PRO SP/1 48 fo. 181 (*LP*, IV, ii, no. 4367).

52. *LP*, II, i, no. 2222. BL Cott. MS Calig. B VI fo. 119 (*LP*, II, i, no. 2347). PRO C82 438 (*LP*, II, i, no. 2370).

53. PRO E101 418/15 fo. 26v. E36 216 fo. 112 (*LP*, III, ii, p. 1537).

54. Samman, 'Henrician Court', Appendix I.

4.   WAR AND PUBLIC FINANCE   *Richard Hoyle*

I am indebted to Dr G.W. Bernard and the editor for reading a draft of this essay. It claims to be no more than a preliminary account of a little traversed region: readers unsympathetic to back-of-an-envelope calculations should turn elsewhere. All MS cited are in the Public Record Office.

1. *English Government Finance, 1485–1558* (Illinois, 1921), repr. as *English Public Finance 1485–1641*, I (2 vols, 1964) without the statistical appendices contained in the first edition. For pointed criticisms of Dietz, see, for instance, J.D. Alsop, 'The Exchequer of Receipt in the reign of Edward VI', Cambridge PhD, 1978, pp. 198–204.

2. The debate over whether the 1530s saw a 'revolution' in taxation was begun by G.R. Elton in 1978; for a full list of the contributions to the debate see below, note 28. For the most recent discussion, which denies that there was any revolution, see R.W. Hoyle, 'Crown, Parliament and Taxation in the Sixteenth Century', *EHR*, 109 (1994).

3. As is illustrated by the figures provided by P.K. O'Brien and P.A. Hunt, 'The Rise of a Fiscal State in England, 1485–1815', *HR*, 66 (1993) 153.

4. B.P. Wolffe, *The Royal Demesne in English History. The Crown Estate in the Government of the Realm from the Conquest to 1509* (London, 1971) p. 219.

5. B.P. Wolffe, *The Crown Lands, 1461–1536. An Aspect of Yorkist and early Tudor Government* (London, 1970) p. 84; for the queens' jointures, pp. 45–6.

6. *Dictionary of National Biography* sub nomine: I cannot immediately confirm the accuracy of this figure.

7. E.W. Ives, *Anne Boleyn* (Oxford, 1986) see pp. 256–8.

8. On the dispersal of Buckingham's lands, see C. Rawcliffe, *The Staffords, Earls of Stafford and Dukes of Buckingham, 1394–1521* (Cambridge, 1978) pp. 182–4.

9. For customs see the figures (based on G. von Schanz, *Englishe Handelspolitik gegen Ende des Mittelalters*, Leipzig, 1881) given by W.G. Hoskins, *The Age of Plunder. The England of Henry VIII, 1500–1547* (London, 1976) pp. 177–85.

10. Wolffe, *Royal Demesne*, pp. 217, 223.

11. S.J. Gunn, 'The Act of Resumption of 1515', in D. Williams (ed.), *Early Tudor England* (Woodbridge, 1989).

12. On 1525 see A.P. Newton, 'Tudor Reforms in the Royal Household', in R.W. Seton-Watson (ed.), *Tudor Studies* (London, 1924) pp. 238–46. David Starkey's concentration on the political aspects of household reform has tended to overshadow the cost-cutting aspect; for instance see D. Starkey, *The Reign of Henry VIII. Personalities and Politics* (London, 1985) pp. 86–9.

Steven Gunn has shown that the reforms effected alterations in the management of the crown's estates in North Wales which increased revenues but also speeded their receipt (S.J. Gunn, 'The Regime of Charles, duke of Suffolk, in North Wales and the Reform of Welsh Government, 1509–25', *Welsh History Review*, 12 (1985) 486–7), but it has not been established how general these reforms were.

13. J. Guy, 'Henry VIII and the praemunire manoeuvres of 1530–1', *EHR*, 97 (1982), 491–2.

14. *LP*, VI, no. 1381 (3).

15. D. Starkey, 'Court and Government', in C. Coleman and D. Starkey (eds), *Revolution Reassessed. Revisions in the History of Tudor Government and Administration* (Oxford, 1986) p. 44.

16. D. Potter, 'Foreign Policy', below, ch. 6.

17. Northamptonshire Record Office, F(M) C. 13.

18. About £20,000: a crown of the sun (or *écu d'or soleil*) was conventionally worth 4s. 6d. sterling, other crowns 4s.

19. Guy, 'Praemunire manoeuvres'; G.W. Bernard, 'The Pardon of the Clergy Reconsidered', *JEH*, 37 (1986).

20. For debt settlements, see the references in R.W. Hoyle, 'Henry Percy, sixth earl of Northumberland and the Fall of the House of Percy', in G.W. Bernard (ed.), *The Tudor Nobility* (Manchester, 1992) pp. 193–4, 207 n. 69.

21. S.E. Lehmberg, *The Reformation Parliament, 1529–1536* (Cambridge, 1970) p. 147.

22. R.W. Hoyle, 'Thomas Master's Narrative of the Pilgrimage of Grace', *Northern History*, 21 (1985) 75.

23. On the income drawn from the church and clerical taxation generally, see J.J. Scarisbrick, 'Clerical Taxation in England, 1485–1547', *JEH*, 11 (1960) and F.M. Heal, 'Clerical Tax Collection under the Tudors: the Influence of the Reformation', in R. O'Day and F. Heal (eds), *Continuity and Change. Personnel and Administration of the Church in England, 1500–1640* (Leicester, 1976).

24. The following section is based on R.W. Hoyle, 'The Origins of the Dissolution of the Monasteries', forthcoming in *HJ*.

25. Printed in full in L. Stone, 'The Political Programme of Thomas Cromwell', *BIHR*, 24 (1951) 11–17 and more conveniently in J. Youings, *The Dissolution of the Monasteries* (London, 1971) pp. 145–7.

26. The following account is based on E.W. Ives, 'The Genesis of the Statute of Uses', *EHR*, 82 (1967).

27. *LP*, XVI, no. 352 although we know nothing of where this money was expended: I am grateful to Patrick Carter of Selwyn College, Cambridge, for confirming this.

28. The literature which sees something new happening to taxation in the 1530s begins with Sir Geoffrey Elton, 'Taxation for War and Peace in early Tudor England', in his *Studies in Tudor and Stuart Politics and Government* (4 vols, Cambridge, 1974–93) III, 216–33. For the debate which ensued, see G.L. Harriss, 'Thomas Cromwell's "new principle of taxation', *EHR*, 93 (1978); J.D. Alsop, 'The Theory and Practice of Tudor Taxation', *EHR*, 97 (1982); Harriss, 'Theory and Practice in Royal Taxation: Some observations', *EHR*, 97 (1982) 811–19; Alsop, 'Innovation in Tudor Taxation', *EHR*, 99 (1984). The views offered here, which will no doubt be found contentious (cf. John Guy above, p. 46) may be found stated at greater length in Hoyle, 'Crown, Parliament and Taxation'.

29. *LP*, XVI, no. 352.

30. J. Hurstfield, 'The Profits of Fiscal Feudalism', *EcHR*, 8 (1955) table 4.

31. A. Savine, *English Monasteries on the Eve of the Dissolution* (Oxford, 1909) p. 100.

32. W.C. Richardson (ed.), *The Report of the Royal Commission of 1552* (Morgantown, VA, 1974) p. 100.

33. In 1544 receipts from lands in the charge of Augmentations came to £44,945. *LP*, XIX (ii) no. 328 (p. 170).

34. Figures taken from the Augmentations Treasurer's accounts *LP*, XIII (ii) no. 457; XIV (ii) no. 236; XVIII (ii) no. 231. These are the sums yielded by sale: the rental value of the land is about a twentieth of this.

35. £27,411 was spent on the purchase of lands and others exchanged; but not all of this was rent-yielding. The whole question deserves examination. The figures are taken from the Augmentations Treasurer's accounts cited before.

36. For transfers to the privy coffers, Starkey, 'Court and Government', p. 45.

37. *LP*, XVI, no. 352; XVIII, no. 231, p. 1343.

38. The surviving materials are described by D. Hoak, 'The Secret History of the Tudor Court: the King's Purse 1542–1550', *Journal of British Studies*, 26 (1987).

39. Figures from Dietz, *English Public Finance*, p. 91 (based on the king's book of payments, *LP*, II (ii), pp. 1441–66).

40. *LP*, I (i) no. 1463.

41. *LP*, I (ii) no. 2479.

42. On one occasion, however, we can. Heron's accounts show Sir William Sandys having £80,858 from John Heron: but Sandys' own accounts show that he returned a balance of £33,500 on 28 December 1512. *LP*, I (i) nos 1463, sect. ix; 1495.

43. R.S. Schofield, 'Parliamentary Lay Taxation', Cambridge PhD thesis, 1963), table 40, pt B.

44. Dietz, *English Public Finance* (first edn) p. 227.

45. *LP*, II (ii) p. 1461.

46. Wolffe, *Crown Lands*, pp. 86–7.

47. Reported by G.R. Elton, *Reform and Reformation. England,1509–1558* (Cambridge, 1977) pp. 30–1.

48. This treasury may be the Chamber or a separate treasury akin to that employed for the 1522–3 loans: for present purposes it barely matters. Taxation revenue was paid into the Exchequer of Receipt and then almost entirely paid over into Wyatt's hands as may be seen from the Teller's roll, e.g. E405/93, mm. 4, 5, 10, 14, 17; /94, mm. 13–14, 15, 17, 22–23; /95, mm. 6, 9, 18, etc. The anticipation of the first payment of the subsidy was to be paid directly to Wyatt: J.P. Collier (ed.), *The Egerton Papers* (CS, 12, 1841), p. 6.

49. J.J. Goring, 'The general proscription of 1522', *EHR*, 76 (1971). R.W. Hoyle, *Tudor Taxation Records. A Guide for Users* (London, 1994) ch. 4 discusses and lists the surviving records.

50. G.W. Bernard, *War,Taxation and Rebellion in early Tudor England* (Brighton, 1986) supplemented by G.W. Bernard and R.W. Hoyle, 'The instructions for the Levying of the Amicable Grant, March 1525', *HR* 77 (1994).

51. *LP*, III (ii) no. 2750 is a summary of the payments made by the Chamber 1 June 1521–1 Jan. 1523, of which £47,000 is broadly military expenditure. *LP*, IV (i) no. 417 is a summary declaration by Edmund Peckham giving (1) the balance inherited from John Mucklow, treasurer of the Chamber, who died in May 1521; (2) sums received in lay and clerical loans and the clerical subsidy totalling £130,792 and giving a gross figure for military expenditure, sanctioned on the king's and Wolsey's warrants, of £123,325. This latter document appears to relate to a treasury stocked with extraordinary income and to be distinct from the Chamber proper.

52. Payments for war before the autumn of 1522 must have come from the reserves via the Chamber as may be seen from *LP*, III (ii) no. 2750; the payment of cash from the 'loan treasury' to the reserves may perhaps be seen as reimbursement of money 'lent' to the war effort.

53. *LP*, IV (ii) no. 2751, printed in full from another copy by C.T. Martin, 'Sir John Daunce's Account of Money Received from the Treasurer of the King's Chamber, *temp.* Henry VIII', *Archaeologia*, 47 (1882), 326–36.

54. J. Guy, 'Wolsey and the parliament of 1523', in C. Cross, D. Loades and J.J. Scarisbrick (eds), *Law and Government under the Tudors* (Cambridge, 1988) p. 4.

55. Bernard, *War, Taxation and Rebellion*, pp. 53–4; instructions for the anticipation, Collier, *Egerton Papers*, pp. 3–5, *LP*, IV (ii) no. 3866 (2) (misdated).

56. It is quite possible that it was used to finance the French in Italy in 1527–8. Certainly in the latter part of 1527 Henry found £47,500 from somewhere. S.J. Gunn, 'Wolsey's Foreign Policy and the Domestic Crisis of 1527–8', in Gunn and P.G. Lindley (eds), *Cardinal Wolsey. Church, State and Art* (London, 1991) p. 163.

57. *LP*, III (ii) no. 2745; yields from Table 4.2.

58. The means whereby war was funded in the 1540s were first established by C.E. Challis, 'The Debasement of the Coinage, 1542–1551', *EcHR*, 20 (1967) 454. The figures offered here for taxation and landsales are based on a new computation: Challis' figures for landsales appear to include rental income as well as the sale of land.

We lack a full description of the war finance of the 1540s. W.C. Richardson, 'Some Financial Expedients of Henry VIII', *EcHR*, 7 (1954–5) is invaluable, but concentrates on some of the more desperate measures resorted to (lead sales, alum trading) rather than the overall picture.

59. SP10/15 no. 11, printed in abstract in C.S. Knighton (ed.), *Calendar of State Papers,Domestic Series, of the Reign of Edward VI, 1547–1553* (London, 1992) pp. 258–63.

60. The figures which follow make no allowance for contributions out of the privy coffers, now replenished: Starkey, 'Court and Government', p. 45.

61. *LP*, XIX, no. 272 (2).

62. *LP*, XX (i) no. 324.

63. *LP*, XX (ii), no. 366, printed Dietz, *English Public Finance*, p. 157.

64. J.D. Alsop, 'Exchequer of Receipt', pp. 227–8. Alsop gives the total taxation revenue over Edward VI's reign at £335,988: most of the balance between the Reliefs and the total came from the second subsidy granted in 1545 but collected after Henry's death. See his thesis, Table 12 on p. 225 and pp. 228–9, and Table 4.4, below.

65. No exact figures for the yield of these clerical subsidies can be found in the secondary literature, but the yield of the Marian subsidies shows that a payment of 2*s.* in the pound was worth about £13–14,000. Dietz, *English Public Finance*, p. 227. The clergy were harassed to pay their tax in advance of the dates stipulated by the act: see Heal, 'Clerical Tax Collection under the Tudors', pp. 106–7.

66. If the subsidy of 1540 is counted in on the grounds that it was granted to aid the building of the domestic fortifications included in Table 4.3, then the proportion rises to about a third, say £1.185m out of £3.5m. These figures may seem quite at variance with Alsop, 'The Theory and Practice of Tudor Taxation', pp. 22–3; but the figures given there are not for *government* income and expenditure but for income and expenditure channelled through the Exchequer of Receipt, quite a different matter.

67. Calculated from the figures provided by Dietz, *English Public Finance* (1st edn) p. 217. For helpful comments, see W.C. Richardson, *The History of the Court of Augmentations* (Baton Rouge, LA, 1961) p. 235.

68. J. Hurstfield, 'The Greenwich Tenures of the Reign of Edward VI', *Law Quarterly Review*, 65 (1949) 75–7.

69. *Statutes of the Realm*, III, p. 988; *Acts of the Privy Council 1547–50*, p. 185, both cited in A. Kreider, *English Chantries. The Road to Dissolution* (Cambridge, MA, 1979) pp. 171–2.

70. Challis, 'Debasement of the Coinage', p. 454.

71. Dietz, *English Public Finance*, p. 191 fn. 9: for additional estimates, some slightly lower, Richardson (ed.), *Royal Commission of 1552*, p. xxv.

72. As Table 4.3 shows, the siege and fortification of the town cost about £1 million over three years, but by the treaty of the Camp (June 1546) the French agreed to buy it back in 1554 for £600,000. By the Treaty of Boulogne (1550) they secured it for £133,333.

73. Foodstuffs 1535–9 compared with 1551–5, calculated from the average price of the Phelps Brown – Hopkins basket of consumables, in E.H. Phelps Brown and S.V. Hopkins, 'Seven Centuries of Consumables Compared with Builder's Wage Rates', in P.H. Ramsey (ed.), *The Price Revolution in Sixteenth-Century England* (London, 1971) p. 39; labour from J. Thirsk (ed.), *The Agrarian History of England and Wales* IV (London 1967), Table 15 (p. 864), 'Agricultural day wage-rates in southern England', comparing 1530–9 with 1550–9.

74. Pensions cost £42,877 in 1551. Richardson (ed.), *Royal Commission of 1552*, p. 100.

75. O'Brien and Hunt, 'Rise of a Fiscal State', p. 153.

76. *LP*, XIX (ii) no. 689.

77. The case for taxation prompting rebellion is made by M.L. Bush, 'Tax Reform and Rebellion in early modern England', *History*, 76 (1991).

78. C.E. Challis, *The Tudor Coinage* (Manchester, 1978) p. 238.

79. Cited Bernard, *War, Taxation and Rebellion*, p. 117. There are reports of taxpayers offering the tax collectors cattle or plate. The commissioners for the anticipation of the subsidy of 1523 in Gloucestershire reported that some persons had told them they were unable to pay so quickly and others 'have offered us cattle and other stuff'. PRO E179/113/215B fo. 7v. In 1542 Peckham was authorised to accept plate for the loan; *LP*, XVII no. 189.

80. *LP*, IV (ii) no.4772; Bernard, *War, Taxation and Rebellion*, p. 115.

81. Ibid., pp. 141–2.

82. D. Loades, *The Mid-Tudor Crisis, 1545–1565* (Basingstoke, 1993) p. 3.

83. I hope to discuss this further in the future.

5.   FOREIGN POLICY   *David Potter*

1. J. Scarisbrick, *Henry VIII* (London 1968) esp. pp. 67–95, 125–34; P. Gwyn, *The King's Cardinal. The Rise and Fall of Thomas Wolsey* (London, 1990) esp. pp. 5–27 contains an extended commentary on the centrality of Henry to Wolsey's policy formulations. See also G.W. Bernard, *War, Taxation and Rebellion in early Tudor England. Henry VIII, Wolsey and the Amicable Grant of 1525* (Brighton, 1986) pp. 40–5. For examples of the king's working methods with ministers, see *StP*, I, passim and examples at pp. 96, 125, 129, 131, 137, 151.

2. On the audiences of ambassadors, examples: V.-L. Bourrilly and P. de Vaissière, *Ambassades en Angleterre de Jean du Bellay* (Paris, 1905) pp. 77–526 passim; *LP*, X, passim; XI, nos 7–479 passim. BL Calig. B VI fo. 321 (*LP*, III, ii, no. 3421): Wolsey to Surrey, 12 Oct. 1525, PS by Tuke. Bourrilly, *Ambassades*, p. 539: du Bellay, 25 Jan. 1529. On English agents at the French court, D. Potter, 'Diplomacy in the mid-16th Century: England and France, 1536–1559', Cambridge PhD thesis, 1973, pp. 312–17.

3. *LP*, X, no. 699; XI, no. 479 (PRO 31/18/2, ii fo. 202r). Kaulek, p. 24.

4. This analysis of English envoys is drawn partly from G.M. Bell, *A Handlist of British Diplomatic Representatives, 1509–1688* (London, 1990), passim.

5. Académie des Sciences Morales et Politiques, *Catalogue des actes de François Ier* (10 vols, Paris 1887–1908) IX, 1–87.

6. C. Giry-Deloison, 'Le personnel diplomatique au début du XVIe siècle. L'exemple des relations franco-anglaises de l'avènement de Henry VII au camp du drap d'or (1485–1520)', *Journal des Savants* (July–Dec. 1987) 207–53.

7. On the terminology and status of ambassadors in this period, cf. Potter, 'Diplomacy in the mid-16th Century', pp. 273–343 and the lucid analysis of terminology in Giry-Deloison, 'Le personnel diplomatique', 207–9 and Giry-Deloison, 'La naissance de la diplomatie moderne en France et en Angleterre au début du XVIe siècle (1475–1520)', *Nouvelle revue du seizième siècle* (1987) 41–58.

8. Norfolk: *StP*, VIII, p. 260, 'Bishops be no mete men for ambassadors here'; Wallop: *LP*, XV, no. 343.

9. *Catalogue des actes de François Ier*, IX, 1–87 passim; on the necessity of clerical appointments at Rome, cf. Grignan to Montmorency, G. Ribier, *Lettres et mémoires d'estat* (Paris, 1666) I, 443: 'Il est mieux de tenir (ici) un evesque qu'un homme de robe courte.'

10. Middle Temple, Petyt MSS 538/47 fos 7–8.

11. Pierre de Bourdeille de Brantôme, *Oeuvres complètes*, ed. J. Buchon (2 vols, Paris, 1838) I, 247: as for du Mortier, 'cela n'estoit son gibier'.

12. Giry-Deloison, 'Le personnel diplomatique', 240–6; Wriothesley was sent on three special embassies, cf. Bell, *A Handlist*, pp. 72, 175–6, Petre only on one in 1545, ibid., p. 51.

13. W. Paravicini, 'The Court of the Dukes of Burgundy', in R.E. Asche and A.M. Birke (eds), *Princes, Patronage and the Nobility* (Oxford, 1991) p. 75.

14. *StP*, VIII, p. 73 on the poor treatment of Browne.

15. Potter, 'Diplomacy', pp. 274–300.

16. J.A. Muller, *The Letters of Stephen Gardiner* (Cambridge, 1933, repr. Westport, CT, 1970) pp. 81–91 (*LP*, XIII, ii, no. 143.1). *StP*, IX, p. 176: Paget, 24 Sept. 1542. BL Harley MS, 282 fo. 119 (*LP*, XIII, i, no. 671): Cromwell to Wyatt, 4 April 1538.

17. Gwyn, *The King's Cardinal*, pp. 385, 407–8, where he argues that Wolsey had to resist this tendency. E.g. PRO 31/18/2, ii fo. 264r (*LP*, XI,

no. 359): Chapuys on bishops Richard Sampson and Edward Foxe 'qui ont jusques à cest heure fait profession de bons imperialz'.

18. Muller, *Letters of Gardiner*, p. 267.

19. For classical interpretation, J. Seeley in *The Growth of British Policy* (2 vols, Cambridge, 1897), on 1558–1688; in the same mould, R.B. Wernham, *Before the Armada: the Growth of English Policy, 1485–1588* (London, 1961); P.S. Crowson, *Tudor Foreign Policy* (London, 1973), heavily influenced by twentieth-century experience, argued that the main aim of Tudor policy after 1529 was defence of the realm and maintenance of the dynasty.

20. G.V. Scammell, 'Shipowning in England, *c.* 1450–1550', *TRHS*, 5th ser, 12 (1962) 105–22, drew attention to the range of investment in shipping under Henry VIII. In 1535, Norfolk and Fitzwilliam took Chapuys to Greenwich to view the king's new ships, boasting that with the ships then in the Thames they could fight the whole world. cf. *LP*, VIII, no. 48. See most recently, D.M. Loades, *The Tudor Navy* (Aldershot, 1992) pp. 74–138 on the insitutionalisation of the navy under Henry VIII.

21. A.F. Pollard, *Henry VIII* (1st pub. London 1902, 1925 edn) pp. 362–4, 405–7.

22. R.G. Eaves, *Henry VIII's Scottish Diplomacy, 1513–1524; English Relations with the Regency Government of James V* (New York, 1971) p. 11; Eves, *Henry VIII and James V's Regency, 1524–28* (London, Lunham, 1987).

23. M. Merriman, 'James Henrisoun and "Great Britain": British Union and the Scottish Commonweal' in R. Mason (ed.), *Scotland and England, 1280–1815* (Edinburgh, 1987) pp. 85–112, esp.p.89. See also William Thomas, *Works*, ed. A. d'Aubant (1774) p. 107: 'one self devyded nacion and realme, one self perpetuall united people' (refo. in P. Laven, 'The Life and Writings of William Thomas', MA thesis, London, 1954, p. 108; A.J. Slavin, *Politics and Profit. A Study of Sir Ralph Sadler, 1507–47* (Cambridge, 1966) p. 82. J. Bain, *Letters and Papers Illustrating the Political Relations between England and Scotland in the XVIth Century Formerly in the Possession of the Dukes of Hamilton* (2 vols, Edinburgh, 1890–2) I, no. 13: report on the treaty of Perpetual Peace with Scotland, 9 July 1534. Rymer, *Foedera*, XII, 368, 480–81.

24. Bain, *Hamilton Papers*, I, xiii–xiv.

25. D.M. Head, 'Henry VIII's Scottish Policy: a Reassessment', *Scottish Historical Review*, 61 (1982) 1–24.

26. Kaulek, p. 290.

27. G. Bers, *Die Allianz Frankreich-Kleve während des geldrischen Kriegs (Julich'sche Fehde) 1539–43* (Cologne, 1969); J.-D. Pariset, *Les relations entre la France et l'Allemagne au milieu du XVIe siècle* (Strasbourg, 1981) p. 32.

28. Bain, *Hamilton Papers*, I, no. 85, pp. 99–100: Wharton to the Council, 25 Sept. 1541. E. Bonner, 'The First Phase of the *Politique* of Henri II in Scotland, its Genesis and the Nature of the "Auld Alliance", 1547–1554', University of Sydney PhD, 1993; Bonner, 'The Genesis of Henry VIII's "Rough Wooing" of the Scots' (unpub. paper) pp. 13, 16. M.H. Merriman, 'War Propaganda during the Rough Wooing', *Scottish Tradition*, IX-X (1979–80).

29. BL Cott. MS, Vesp. C II, fos 263r–64 (*LP*, IV, i, no. 30): Sampson and Jerningham, 14 Jan. 1524.

30. Bonner, 'The First Phase of the Politique', pp. 51–135; Bonner, 'The Genesis of Henry VIII's "Rough Wooing", passim; Thomas More, *Utopia* (trans. Turner), p. 58.

31. M.H. Merriman, 'The Assured Scots', *Scottish Historical Review*, 47 (1968) 10–34.

32. Hall (Whibley) I, 228; cf. also *The First English Life of King Henry the Fifth*, ed. C.L. Kingsford (Oxford, 1911) pub. in English in 1513, p. 93: 'the desire of justice and his right, which every man is bounden to his power to demand and seek'.

33. S.J. Gunn, 'The French Wars of Henry VIII' in J. Black (ed.), *The Origins of War in early Modern Europe* (Edinburgh, 1987) pp. 28–51, at p. 38.

34. Treaty of Peace and Alliance, Westminster, 30 April 1527, *Ordonnances, Frncois Ier*, V, no. 452, pp. 41–56; Treaty of Perpetual Peace, Amiens, 18 Aug. 1527, Rymer, *Foedera*, XIV, 218–27, art. IV/V: 'neque ... inquietabunt, turbarunt, molestabunt, infestabunt ... sed sinent & permittent *Christianissimum regem* modernum ...suos dictis Possessionibus quiete, tranquile & pacifice frui uti gaudere...'

35. Kaulek, no. 375, p. 359: Marillac, 13 Nov. 1541. PRO 31/18/2, ii, fos 202r–203 (*LP*, XI, no. 479, p. 195): Chapuys to Charles V, 22 Sept. 1536.

36. R.B. Merriman, *The Life and Letters of Thomas Cromwell* (2 vols, Oxford, 1902, repr., 1968) I, 30–44, esp.p. 39, 43; the phrase was common currency, cf. Shakespeare, *Henry V*, Act I, sc.ii, 11.166–8.

37. Bernard, *War, Taxation and Rebellion*, pp. 3–7.

38. Hall (Whibley) II, 123–5. Bourrilly and Vaissière, *Ambassades de Jean du Bellay*, p. 482 (*LP*, IV, ii, no. 5016): Du Bellay, 9 Dec. 1528. S.J. Gunn, 'Wolsey's Foreign Policy and the Domestic Crisis of 1527–8' in S.J. Gunn and P. Lindley (eds), *Cardinal Wolsey, Church, State and Art* (Cambridge, 1991) pp. 149–77.

39. G. Walker, *John Skelton and the Politics of the 1520s* (Cambridge, 1988), pp. 80–9 argues that Skelton, in criticising Wolsey's handling of the 1521 talks, was deliberately trying to echo what he thought were Henry's wishes for a general alliance against the Turk.

40. *StP*, I, p. 33; Hall (Whibley) I, 231.

41. C. Kitching, 'Broken Angels: the Response of English parishes to the Turkish Threat to Christendom, 1543', W.J. Sheils and D. Wood (eds), *The Church and Wealth* (Oxford, 1987) pp. 209–17. Scarisbrick, *Henry VIII*, pp. 69–74.

42. Walker, *John Skelton*, pp. 81–3. Hall (Whibley) I, 226.

43. D. Potter, *A History of France 1460–1560: The Emergence of a Nation State* (London, 1995) ch. 8 passim and pp. 255–6.

44. BL Add. MS 28173 fos 125–6 (*LP*, IV, iii, app. no. 15): De Praet to Lannoy, 20 Dec. 1524, 'puisque Dieu ne veult que ung seul soit le monarque de la Chrestienté, que du moins eulx deux par ensemble la gouvernent.'

45. Stephen Gardiner, Advice to Bonner, Muller, *Letters of Gardiner*, p. 90.

46. F.C. Dietz, *English Government Finance, 1485–1558* (Illinois, 1920); R. Doucet, *L'état de finances de 1523* (Paris, 1923); K. Brandi, *The Emperor Charles V* (London, 1965) pp. 463–5.

47. C. Gaier, 'L'invincibilité anglaise et le grand arc après la guerre de cent ans: un mythe tenace', *Tijdschrift voor Geschiedenis*, 91 (1978) 379–85; *LP*, I, no. 1656. BL Egerton 22 fo. 125: La Trémoïlle to Montmorency, 8 Nov. (1523). J. Goring, 'Social Change and Military Decline in mid-Tudor England', *History*, 60 (1975) 185–97, esp. 185–7.

48. J. Goring, 'The General Proscription of 1523', *EHR*, 341 (1971) 681–705. S.J. Gunn, 'The Duke of Suffolk's March on Paris in 1523', *EHR*, 101 (1986) 496–558; Gunn, 'The French Wars'. On 1544: L. MacMahon, 'The English Invasion of France, 1544', MA thesis, Warwick, 1992; L.R. Shelby, *John Rogers, Tudor Military Engineer* (Oxford, 1967).

49. R.H. Tawney (ed.), *Tudor Economic Documents* (3 vols, London, 1924) III, 329.

50. J. Goring, 'The Military Obligations of the English People, 1511–58', London, PhD Thesis, 1955, pp. 112–37; Goring, 'Social Change', pp. 187–9.

51. Potter, 'Diplomacy in the mid-16th Century', pp. 83–115; Potter, 'Les Allemands et les armées françaises au XVIe siècle', *Francia*, 22, ii (1993) 1–20; 21/2 (1994) 1–62, esp. 1–29; J.G. Millar, *Tudor Mercenaries and Auxiliaries, 1485–1547* (Virginia, 1980).

52. BL Cott. MS, Vesp. C II fos 263r–264 (*LP*, IV, i, no. 30): Sampson and Jerningham, 15 Jan. 1524.

53. G. Jacqueton, *La politique extérieure de Louise de Savoie* (Paris, 1892) p. 61.

54. BL Cott. MS, Galba B VIII fos 109–10 (*LP*, IV, i no. 24): W. Knight, 13 Jan. 1524.

55. *StP* VI, no. 58, pp. 159–60.

56. *StP* I, no. 75, pp. 135–40; Gunn, 'The Duke of Suffolk's March on Paris'; Gunn, 'The French Wars of Henry VIII'. Bernard, *War, Taxation and Rebellion*, pp. 13ff.

57. BL Cott. MS, Vesp. C II fo. 263r (*LP*, IV, i, no. 24): Sampson and Jerningham, 15 Jan. 1524.

58. BL Add. MS, 28173, fos 125–6, copy (*LP*, IV, iii, app. no. 15): De Praet to Lannoy, 20 Dec. 1524, 'ces Seigneurs icy, lesquelz se plaindent d'avoir despendu de grosses sommes de deniers sans avoir rien acquiz.'

59. C.S.L. Davies, 'Supply Services of English Armed Forces, 1509–50', Oxford DPhil, 1963, ch. 8.

60. W. Busch, *Drei Jahre englischer Vermittlungspolitik, 1518–21* (Bonn, 1884); Scarisbrick, *Henry VIII*, p. 95.

61. Gwyn, *The King's Cardinal*, p. 358; Guy, *The Public Career of Sir Thomas More*, p. 23 on Wolsey's outline to More of the need for involvement. For Scarisbrick, the pulling apart of king and cardinal is most apparent in March 1524 (*Henry VIII*, p. 132), while Gwyn denies any serious rift over policy (*The King's Cardinal*, pp. 387–8).

62. R. Scheurer (ed.), *La correspondance du cardinal Jean du Bellay* (2 vols, so far, Paris, 1969–73) p. 59: Du Bellay to Montmorency, 30 June 1530. On French involvement in Henry's case, see A. Hamy, *Entrevue de François Ier avec Henry VIII à Boulogne-sur-Mer en 1532* (Paris, 1898); V.-L. Bourrilly, 'François Ier et Henry VIII: l'intervention de la France dans l'affaire du divorce', *Revue d'histoire moderne et contemporaine*, 1 (1889) 271–84.

63. Muller, *Letters of Stephen Gardiner*, p. 99.

64. Jacqueton, *La politique extérieure*, p. 32.

65. P. Gwyn, 'Wolsey's Foreign Policy: the Conferences of Calais and Bruges Reconsidered', *HJ*, 23 (1980) 755–72, esp. 772; Muller, *Letters of Stephen Gardiner*, pp. 94, 98: 12, 17 May 1542; pp. 79–80: 23 Jan. (1538).

66. R. Scheurer, 'Les relations franco-anglaises pendant la négociation de la paix des Dames (juillet 1528–août 1529)' in P.M.Smith and I.D. McFarlane (eds), *Literature and the Arts in the Reign of Francis I. Essays presented to C.A. Mayer* (Lexington, 1985) pp. 142–62, esp. p. 143; Gunn, 'Wolsey's Foreign Policy', 161–2. *LP*, Add. 1524, 1524.2. E. Ives, 'The Fall of Wolsey' in Gunn and Lindley (eds), *Cardinal Wolsey*, p. 292.

67. P. Friedemann, *Anne Boleyn* (2 vols, London, 1884) II, 91 ff.

68. *LP*, XIII, i, no. 279. BL Add. MS, 25114 fo. 282. *LP*, XIII, i, no. 900.

69. H. Keniston, 'Peace Negotiations between Charles V and Francis I (1537–8)', *Proceedings of the American Philosophical Society*, 102 (1958) 142–7.

70. BL Harley MS, 282 fo. 255 (*LP*, XII, ii, no. 1053.2): Wyatt's memorandum for Dudley, *c.* 10 Nov. 1537.

71. BL Add. MS, 25114 fo. 282 (*LP*, XIII, i, no. 279): Henry VIII to Gardiner, 15 Feb. 1538.

72. Treaty of Peace with Louis XII, London, 7 Aug. 1514, Rymer, *Foedera*, XIII, 413–23; Treaty of Calais, 14 July 1520, *LP*, III, i, no. 914, groundwork for the treaty of Windsor, 19 June 1522 with the emperor, *LP*, III, ii, no. 2333. For the five interconnected treaties of The More with France, 30 Aug. 1525, Rymer, *Foedera*, XIV, 48–75. For the treaties with France of 1527, see above, note 34. For the Treaty of Closer Amity with France, 23 June 1532, Rymer, *Foedera*, XIV, 434–8. For the Treaty of Mutual Aid with the emperor, 11 Feb. 1543, Rymer, *Foedera*, XIV, 768–76 (*LP*, XVIII, i, no. 144).

73. 29 July 1521: commissions to conclude immediate alliance with the emperor, an alliance with Francis I and a league with pope, emperor and France, *LP*, III, i, nos 1443.10; 1443.3 (Rymer, *Foedera*, XIII, 749–50); 1443.5 (Rymer, XIII, 750–52). Gwyn, 'Wolsey's Foreign Policy'.

74. Jacqueton, *La politique extérieure*, p. 60; Gwyn, *The King's Cardinal*, pp. 394–7; Bernard, *War, Taxation and Rebellion*, pp. 34–45.

75. BL Cott. MS, Vesp. C II, fo. 207v (*LP*, III, ii, no. 3532): Sampson and Jerningham, 12 Nov. 1524; Vesp. C II, fo. 264, cipher (*LP*, IV, i, no. 30): same, 15 Jan. 1525. See also *LP*, III, ii, nos 3462, 3532, 3533. Jacqueton, *La politique extérieure*, pp. 66–7.

76. BL Arundel MS, 151 fos 390–1, a well-informed treatise arguing that France was under obligation to England for its support in these

years. E.F. Rogers (ed.), *The Letters of Sir John Hacket, 1526–1534* (Morgantown, 1971) p. 98: on the undesirability that the emperor 'should have all his will and mind of the king of France ... for he should wax too great a lord'. On accusations of hegemonism against the Habsburgs raised in Henry's presence, 1536, cf. *LP*, XI, no. 7, pp. 4, 7. See also PRO 31/18/2, ii fo. 184v (*LP*, XI, no. 147): Chapuys to Charles V, 23 July 1536, 'led. sr. roy me obiecta, que Vre. Maté. tendoit à ceste monarchie, mais je le ramenay par tout raisons au logis qu'il ne me sçeut responder parolle du monde.'

77. Gunn, 'Wolsey's Foreign Policy', 163–75.

78. W.C. Richardson, *Stephen Vaughan, Financial Agent of Henry VIII* (Baton Rouge, LA, 1953) pp. 1–12.

79. Francis in 1533 advised Henry first to assemble noble opinion behind him and then to go ahead with the divorce (*LP*, VI, no. 954, *StP*, VII, 493). Henry countered with the suggestion that Francis too break with Rome. Francis thanked him but predictably said no (Paris, Bibliothèque Nationale [hereafter BN] fr. 3005 fo. 129). By 1534–5, it was tacitly agreed to let the question of Henry's anti-papal legislation sleep (*LP*, VII, no. 784.2; VIII, no. 174).

80. PRO 31/18/2, ii fos 201v–202r (*LP*, XI, no. 479): Chapuys, 22 Sept. 1536, Henry did not wish to quit 'le certain pour l'incertain'.

81. Vienna, Haus, Hof und Staatsarchiv (hereafter HHuSA), Frankreich, Varia 4, fos 83–97 (letters of Hannart to Chapuys); fos 98–156 (letters of Chapuys to Hannart, Feb. 1535–April 1536); fos 115–16 (John Wallop to Hannart, 22 May 1535); fo. 138v (Chapuys to Hannart, 24 Dec. 1535).

82. BL Harley MS, 282 fos 7–14 (*LP*, X, no. 726): Henry VIII to Pate, 25 April 1536.

83. PRO 31/18/2, ii fos 186–7 (*LP*, XI, no. 219): Chapuys to Charles V, 5 Aug. 1536. On Cromwell's fall, G.R. Elton, 'Thomas Cromwell's Decline and Fall', in Elton, *Studies in Tudor and Stuart Politics and Government* (4 vols, Cambridge, 1974–92) I, 173–230, repr. from *HJ*, 10 (1951) 150–85; more recently G. Redworth, *In Defence of the Church Catholic: The Life of Stephen Gardiner* (Oxford 1990) pp. 105–29.

84. Middle Temple, Petyt MSS 538/47 fo.10v. BL Harley 282 fos 155–7 (*LP*, XIV, ii no. 766): Wyatt, 30 Dec. 1539.

85. Potter, 'Diplomacy in the Mid-16th Century', pp. 51ff.

86. BL Harley MS, 282, fo. 121 (*LP*, XV, no. 320): Wyatt to Henry, 9 March 1540.

87. *StP*, VIII, p. 261, 21 Feb. 1540.; PRO SP1/157 fos 186–7 (*LP*, XV, no. 224); *StP*, VIII, pp. 265, 268.

88. *StP*, VIII, p. 243.

89. *StP*, VIII, pp. 247, 249–50. *LP*, XV, no. 223.

90. H.M. Vose, 'Marguerite of Navarre: "that Right English Woman"', *SCJ*, 16 (1985) 315–33, esp. 328. *StP*, VIII, no. 582, pp. 327–30.

91. *LP* XV, no. 374. *StP*, VIII, p. 327.

92. PRO SP1/161 fos. 65–6 (*LP*, XV, no. 864): 9 July 1540. An imperial official, van Dyke, came to Pate to open very tentative talks in October 1540, cf. *StP*, VIII, pp. 455, 477–8.

93. *LP* XVI, no. 548 (p. 260), 676, 711, 733, 870, 910. *CSPV*, V, pp. 257–8; Redworth, *In Defence of the Church Catholic*, pp. 141–55, gives a detailed and lucid analysis of this crucial embassy.

94. *Henry VIII and his Ambassadors at the Diet of Ratisbon, 17 June 1541*, ed. C.J. Black and C.E. Challis (York, 1968).

95. Potter, 'Diplomacy in the Mid-16th Century', pp. 61–6.

96. *State Papers*, IX, pp. 1–16. Muller, *Letters of Stephen Gardiner*, pp. 94–100.

97. *CSPSp*, VI, no. 13, Kaulek, no. 444. *StP*, XI, no. 1344.

98. Gwyn, *The King's Cardinal*, p. 22. On the rhetoric of honour in public life as a positive quality to be striven for, cf. M. Greaves, *The Blazon of Honour* (London, 1964); C.B. Watson, *Shakespeare and the Renaissance Concept of Honor* (Princeton, NJ, 1960); G. Kipling, *The Triumph of Honour* (Leiden, 1977) pp. 94–5, 157–68.

99. Edward Hall, *Chronicle*, ed. Ellis (1809) p. 635; *Ordonnances des rois de France, règne de Francois Ier*, IV, no. 359, pp. 299–300: Ord. of 25 Sept. 1523. Vienna, HHuSA, Frankreich, Varia 4 fos 200–1: Francis I to the Archbishop of Lyon, 12 Lyon 1536.

100. Gwyn, 'Wolsey's Foreign Policy', passim; Walker, *John Skelton*, ch. 5 passim.

101. BL Cott. MS Calig. E II fos 246: minute for dealing with the French ambassador.

102. Gwyn, *The King's Cardinal*, pp. 535–6, 546.

103. *LP*, I, no. 490, p. 67; Bourrilly, *Ambassades de Jean du Bellay*, pp. 360, 365.

104. Middle Temple, Petyt MSS 538/47 fo. 358r (Muller, *Letters of Stephen Gardiner*, p. 86).

105. *LP*, XIV, i, no. 451; *StP*, VIII, p. 170.

106. Muller, *Letters of Stephen Gardiner*, pp. 98–9.

107. C. Giry-Deloison, 'La politique étrangère d'Henry VIII. L'exemple des relations avec la France' (forthcoming, Acts of the Conference on Henry VIII and Francis I, Two Princes of the Renaissance, French Institute 1991). Hall (Whibley) II, 131. Rawdon Brown, *Four Years at the Court of Henry VIII* (2 vols, 1854) I, 237; *LP*, I, no. 5820.

108. There were many different kinds of pensions paid by the French crown. The most common were the supplements to royal officers' emoluments paid on a virtually automatic basis, or the subventions to lesser members of the royal affinity. The sums paid out at the end of Louis XI's reign amounted to 950,000 *lt*. This was retrenched in the subsequent period but stood at about 570,000 *lt*. in 1525 (cf. Potter, *France, 1460–1560*, pp. 199–202, 266–8). For purposes of comparison, in the *état par estimation* of the Epargne of 1532 (1st quarter), with a receipt of 1,234,548 *lt*., 254,000 went to the Swiss cantons and 259, 594 to the English. The royal household received 203,777 *lt*. (BN fr. 20502 fos 108–10).

109. Guillart's 1525 speech, printed in A. Pommier, *Chroniques de Souligné-sous-Vallon et Flacé* (Angers, 1889) pp. 140–2. Hall (Whibley) II, 133. Kaulek, pp. 11, 15, 54.

110. With the *écu d'or soleil* then worth 4s.6d. Accounts of Passano, Paris, BN fr. 12158; Archives Nationales (hereafter AN), J 923. The sum was equivalent to 189,472 *lt.* There were about 8.8 *livres* to the £ sterling (remarkably close to the modern £-franc parity). Hall (Whibley) II, 105–6.

111. Giry-Deloison, 'La politique étrangère d'Henry VIII'. On Wolsey in Star Chamber, Oct. 1527: Hall (Whibley) II, 105–6, ed. H. Ellis (1809), p. 733.

112. *LP*, VII, no. 1554.

113. J. Le Laboureur (ed.), *Memoires de M. de Castelnau* (1731) I, 405 (*LP*, VIII, no. 174): Palamède Gontier to Chabot, 5 Feb. 1535. Brussels, Archives du Royaume, Négociations de France, II, fo. 18: Hannart to Mary of Hungary, 5 June 1535.

114. BL Add. MS, 25114 fo. 282 (*LP*, XIII, i no. 379): Henry VIII to Gardiner, 15 Feb. 1538. BN Dupuy fo. 200: Memorandum of Morette, Castelnau and d'Inteville, 1535.

115. Muller, *Letters of Stephen Gardiner*, pp. 82–3, 98.

116. At the rate of 4s.8d: cf. Council to Paget, 29 Jan. 1543, *StP*, IX, pp. 277–83; arrears account, 1 May 1542, ibid., VIII, p. 717. *LP*, XVII, no. 288. Kaulek, no. 375: memorandum of French case, 1541.

117. Potter, 'Diplomacy in the Mid-16th Century', pp. 142–61. BN fr. 10375 fos 35–6. The rate of the *écu sol.* was now 46s. to the *livre tournois*, ibid., fos 30–2; commission to Bonacorsi, 31 June 1546, to pay pensions 'que pourrions accorder et faire payer cy après tant aud. roy d'Angleterre que à aucuns seigneurs particliers de son royaulme'.

118. D. Potter, 'The Treaty of Boulogne and European Diplomacy, 1549–50', *BIHR*, 55 (1982) 63; Pottes, 'Diplomacy in the Mid-16th Century', pp. 151–7.

119. *StP*, I, p. 111 (*LP*, III, ii, no. 2555): More to Wolsey, 21 Sept. 1522.

120. C. Giry-Deloison, 'Money and Early Tudor Diplomacy. The English Pensioners of the French King (1475–1547)', forthcoming in *Medieval History*.

121. Wolsey's and other pensions, listed in BN fr. 12158. PRO, SP1/158 fo. 32 (*LP*, XV, no. 329): Norfolk to Cromwell, 11 March 1540.

122. *Ordonnances, François Ier*, VII, 115 (18 March 1534). BL Cott. MS, Calig. E II fo. 199.

123. *Ordonnances, François Ier*, VII, 115.

124. S.J. Gunn, *Charles Brandon, Duke of Suffolk* (Oxford, 1988) p. 138, no. 187.

125. Hall (Whibley) II, 126.

126. For Wolsey and Spanish pensions, Gwyn, *The King's Cardinal*, p. 95; unpaid in 1524, see *CSPSp*, Further Supplement, II, p. 407: de Praet, 10 Nov. 1524. On Charles V's offers in 1536, PRO 31/18/2, ii fo. 191r (*LP*, XI, no. 285): Chapuys to Charles V, 12 Aug. 1536. PRO

31/18/2, ii fo. 349v (*LP*, XI, no. 441): emperor to Chapuys, 11 Sept. 1536.

127. Scheurer, *Correspondance de Jean du Bellay*, II, no. 396, pp. 409–11 (*LP*, XI, no. 228): Bishop of Tarbes to du Bellay, 4 Aug. 1536.

128. Giry-Deloison, 'Money and early Tudor Diplomacy', p. 28.

129. Bourrilly, *Ambassades de Jean du Bellay*, pp. 379, 387, 472, 510–11.

130. Redworth, *In Defence of the Church Catholic*, p. 108.

131. Giry-Deloison, 'Money and early Tudor Diplomacy', p. 29; Gunn, *Suffolk*, pp. 14–41; Gwyn, *The King's Cardinal*, pp. 570–1.

132. For Norfolk's views in the 1520s: Gunn, 'Wolsey's foreign policy', 170. Gwyn, *The King's Cardinal*, pp. 566–8 argues that Norfolk was virtually bound to be regarded as a rival to Wolsey by foreign observers. In any case, the evidence that he had a consistent 'line' in foreign policy is thin. For his role in the 1530s and 1540s, cf. Potter, 'Diplomacy in the Mid-16th Century', pp. 6–7, 34–5 and above n. 126. Cromwell told Chapuys, who noted that the duke no longer received his pension from Charles V, that Norfolk did not bear the emperor ill-will but was a little variable and greedy and liked to make it known that he did not have a French pension for nothing (*LP* XI, no. 40, pp. 21–2: Chapuys, 8 July 1536). BN fr. 2997 fo. 42 (*LP*, XI, no. 146): Castelnau to La Rochepot, 22 July (1536).

133. Scheurer, 'Les relations franco-anglaises', 143.

134. Ives, 'The Fall of Cardinal Wolsey', 302. On the question of faction in 1509–11, see Gwyn, *The King's Cardinal*, pp. 6–14; Gunn, 'The French Wars', p. 43. Guillart's speech: Pommier, *Chroniques de Souligné*, p. 141.

135. D. Starkey, *The Reign of Henry VIII, Personalities and Politics* (London, 1985) pp. 48–59; M.J. Tucker, *The Life of Thomas Howard, Earl of Surrey and Second Duke of Norfolk, 1443–1524* (The Hague, 1964).

136. Gwyn, *The King's Cardinal*, pp. 571–81; Bourrilly, *Ambassades de Jean du Bellay*, pp. 64–5. BN Clairambault MS, 329 fo. 292: Guillaume du Bellay to Montmorency, 23 Aug. 1529, on the hostility between Suffolk and Wolsey. Bourrilly, *Ambassades*, p. 482: Jean du Bellay, 9 Dec. 1528, on Wolsey isolated in the 'plus estroict Conseil'.

137. On the 1528 declaration, PRO 31/18/2, ii fo. 203 (*LP*, XI, no. 479, p. 195): Chapuys, 22 Sept. 1536. On 1519, the reports of the Venetian and French envoys in Rawdon Brown, *Four Years at the Court of Henry VIII*, II, 271. *LP*, III, no. 235. The French minimised the pro-French qualities of those dismissed and preferred to emphasise Wolsey's hostility to them. cf. also G. Walker, 'The Expulsion of the Minions Reconsidered', *HJ*, 32 (1989) 1–16.

138. L.R. Gardiner, 'Further news of Cardinal Wolsey's End, November–December 1530', *BIHR* (1984) 99–107. *StP*, VIII, p. 349.

139. Gwyn, *The King's Cardinal*, pp. 20–4; Walker, 'The Expulsion of the Minions'; G. Bernard, 'Politics and Government in Tudor England', *HJ*, 31 (1988) 159–82; Ives, 'The Fall of Wolsey', 310–15; Ives, *Anne Boleyn* (Oxford, 1986).

140. On this period, see Potter, 'Diplomacy', pp. 136–61 and for the quotation, pp. 138, 148–9.

6. THE LITERATURE AND PROPAGANDA OF HENRY VIII'S FIRST DIVORCE
Virginia Murphy

1. I am grateful to the late Professor Sir Geoffrey Elton, Professor John Guy, Dr Richard Rex and the editor for their comments on an earlier draft of this chapter.
2. This chronology follows E.W. Ives, *Anne Boleyn* (Oxford, 1986) pp. 99–109.
3. PRO SP 1 42, fo. 160v (*LP*, IV, no. 3231).
4. G.R. Elton, 'The King of Hearts' in *Studies in Tudor and Stuart Politics and Government*, I (Cambridge, 1974) and *Reform and Reformation: England, 1509–1558* (London, 1977) p. 116; see also his '*Lex Terrae Victrix*: The Triumph of Parliamentary Law in the Sixteenth Century' in D.M. Dean and N.L. Jones, *The Parliaments of Elizabethan England* (Oxford, 1990) pp. 15–36. For a recent presentation of the opposing viewpoint, see P. Gwyn, *The King's Cardinal: The Rise and Fall of Thomas Wolsey* (London, 1990).
5. The central document here is BL Cott. MS Otho C x, fos 184–98 (*LP*, IV, nos 5730 and 6201). This exchange and Fisher's subsequent contributions to the debate are discussed in R. Rex, *The Theology of John Fisher* (Cambridge and New York, 1991) pp. 162–83.
6. BL Cott. MS Otho C x, fo. 184 (translated from Latin).
7. Cambridge Corpus Christi MS 418, fo. 175, printed in *Martini Buceri Opera Latina*, III (1988) pp. 74–5 (translated from Latin).
8. Ibid., fos 175–8. The address is found in BL Cott. MS Otho C x, fos 184–5v.
9. Ives, *Anne Boleyn*, p. 101. For a contrasting view, see Gwyn, *The King's Cardinal*, pp. 512–13.
10. BL Cott. MS Otho C x, fos 186–97.
11. Ibid., fo. 185v (translated from Latin).
12. Ibid., fos 186, 192rv, 195, 196v.
13. G. de C. Parmiter, *The King's Great Matter: A Study of Anglo-Papal Relations 1527–34* (London, 1967) pp. 125–6, H.A. Kelly, *The Matrimonial Trials of Henry VIII* (Stanford, CA, 1976) pp. 66–7 and G. Bedouelle, 'Le deroulement historique' in G. Bedouelle and P. Le Gal (eds), *Le 'Divorce' du Roi Henry VIII* (Geneva, 1987) p. 30.
14. R. Wakefield, *Kotser codicis* (c.1534), RSTC 24943, sig. Pivd (*LP*, IV, no. 3234).
15. R. Wakefield, *On the Three Languages*, ed. G. Lloyd Jones (Medieval and Renaissance Texts and Studies, 1989) p. 64.
16. *Kotser*, sigg. Piiid–Piv.
17. BL Cott. MS Cleopatra E vi, fos 145v–6v (*LP*, VII, no. 289).
18. For a full discussion of this work, see V.M. Murphy, 'The Debate over Henry VIII's First Divorce: an Analysis of the Contemporary Treatises', unpublished doctoral dissertation, Cambridge, 1984, pp. 40–55.
19. Rymer, *Foedera*, VI, p. 119 (translated from Latin), PRO SP 1 52, fo. 112v (*LP*, IV, no. 5156).
20. BL Microfilm, M 485/52, Hatfield MS 198, fo. 31v (*LP*, IV, no. 3913). See also *LP*, IV, no. 4120.

21. *LP*, IV, no. 4942.

22. J.J. Scarisbrick, *Henry VIII* (London, 1968) p. 231 and Gwyn, *The King's Cardinal*, p. 522.

23. W. Roper, *The Lyfe of Sir Thomas Moore, knighte* (Early English Texts Society, 1935) p. 67. See also R. Rex, 'The English Campaign against Luther in the 1520s', *TRHS*, 39 (1989) 85–9. A recent critical edition of the *Assertio* is available in P. Fraenkel (ed), *Assertio septem sacramentorum adversum Martinum Lutherum/Henry VIII* (1992). I owe this reference to Dr Richard Rex.

24. PRO SP 1 63, fos 244–407v (*LP*, V, no. 5 (8)). For a detailed analysis of these drafts and their relationship to the king's legatine tract and other works, see Surtz and Murphy, pp. v–xxiv.

25. Graham Nicholson, 'The Act of Appeals and the English Reformation' in C. Cross, D. Loades and J.J. Scarisbrick (eds), *Law and Government under the Tudors* (Cambridge and New York, 1988), pp. 20–6.

26. A. Moss, 'Printed Commonplace-Books in the Renaissance', *J. Institute of Romance Studies*, 2 (1993) 203–13.

27. Cambridge Trinity MS B.15.19. For a detailed discussion of this work, see Surtz and Murphy, pp. viii–xix.

28. PRO SP 1 94, fo. 98 (*LP*, VIII, no. 1054).

29. *LP*, V, no. 623.

30. M. St Clare Byrne, *The Letters of Henry VIII* (London, 1936) p. 82 (*LP*, IV, no. 4597).

31. BL Cott. MS Titus B I, fo. 306 (*LP*, IV, no. 4409).

32. Trinity MS B.15.19, fo. 2v (translated from Latin).

33. Ibid., fos 15rv.

34. CUL MS ff.5.25 (*LP*, IV, no. 5728); this is the document discussed by Richard Rex as 'Licitum fuisse' – see Rex, *Theology*, p. 171.

35. PRO SP 1 54, fos 130–64 (Gardiner's section) and fos 166–217v (Henry's section) (*LP*, IV, no. 5729). The address appears on fos 166–9 and is printed in P. Janelle, *Obedience in Church and State: Three Political Tracts by Stephen Gardiner* (Cambridge, 1930) pp. 2–9.

36. SP 1 54, fo. 130 (translated from Latin).

37. Ibid., fo. 166 (translated from Latin).

38. Cleopatra E vi fo. 147v.

39. *CSPSp*, IV, 547.

40. G.B. Skelly, 'Henry VIII consults the Universities of Oxford and Cambridge' in Bedouelle and Le Gal, *Le 'Divorce'*, pp. 59–75.

41. Nicholson, 'The Act of Appeals', pp. 25–6, 28.

42. *LP*, V, p. 313.

43. Surtz and Murphy, pp. 1–273.

44. PRO SP 1 94, fo. 98.

45. Surtz and Murphy, pp. xxv–xxxii; the text of the presentation copy is printed in pp. 274–7.

46. Surtz and Murphy, pp. 261–71.

47. For the *Glass of the Truth* (*c*.1531), *RSTC* 11918–19, see N. Pocock (ed.), *Records of the Reformation: the Divorce 1527–35* (2 vols, Oxford, 1870)

II, 387. For a discussion of the dating of the *Glass*, see S.W. Haas, 'Henry VIII's *'Glasse of Truthe'*, *History*, 64 (1979) 355–7: on St Albans, PRO, SP 67 no. 2 (*LP*, VIII, no. 589: I owe this reference to Diarmaid Mac-Culloch).

7. HENRY VIII AND THE REFORM OF THE CHURCH
Diarmaid MacCulloch

1. J.C. Dickinson, *An Ecclesiastical History of England: the Later Middle Ages from the Norman Conquest to the Eve of the Reformation* (London, 1979) pp. 66–8.

2. B. Bradshaw, *The Dissolution of the Religious Orders in Ireland under Henry VIII* (Cambridge, 1974) ch. 1; I.B. Cowan, *The Scottish Reformation: Church and Society in sixteenth century Scotland* (London, 1982) chs 1–3.

3. On Lollardy, see bibliographical note.

4. R.L. Storey, *Diocesan Administration in Fifteenth Century England* (York, 1972) pp. 29–30.

5. [Anon., possibly F.E. Brightman], 'Cranmer's Liturgical Projects', *Church Quarterly Review*, 31 (1891) 459. cf. R. O'Day, *The Debate on the English Reformation* (London, 1986) ch. 4.

6. The 'Walsingham Hymn' was written by Sir William Milner (8th baronet, 1893–1960).

7. On Grynaeus and his mission, see my *Thomas Cranmer: a Life* (New Haven, CT, 1996) ch. 3. The second major Reformer to meet the king was Friedrich Myconius, Superintendent of Gotha, member of the Lutheran delegation to England in 1538.

8. For Henry's friendly response in August/September 1538 to a gift from Zwingli's successor at Zürich, Johann Heinrich Bullinger, see *Orig. Let.* 610, 617, but for his negative response to the book's contents, J.J. Scarisbrick, *Henry VIII* (London, 1968) p. 418.

9. On Cuddington Church and Rewley Abbey, see H.M. Colvin et al. (eds), *The History of the King's Works* (6 vols, plus plans, London, 1963–82) IV, 179, 132.

10. Act, from *Rotuli Parliamentorum*, VI, p. 270, conveniently presented in G.R. Elton, *The Tudor Constitution* (2nd edn, Cambridge, 1982) p. 4.

11. W. Ullmann, 'This Realm of England is an Empire', *JEH*, 30 (1979) 182–4. I agree with Pamela Tudor-Craig against Ullman that it is most unlikely that Henry drafted this oath in 1509 or then used it; nor was it subsequently used. P. Tudor-Craig, 'Henry VIII and King David', in D. Williams (ed.), *Early Tudor England* (Woodbridge, 1989) pp. 187–9, 199.

12. J.E. Cox (ed.), *Works of Archbishop Cranmer* (2 vols, PS, 1844 [vol. I in two paginations], 1846) II, 100, 106.

13. cf. discussion of the manuscripts in Tudor-Craig, 'Henry VIII and King David', 193–7. For a late draft of a revision for the *King's Book* by Henry, see PRO, SP 1/178 fos 107–9 (*LP*, XVIII, i no. 609.2).

14. M.K. Jones and M.G. Underwood, *The King's Mother: Lady Margaret Beaufort, Countess of Richmond and Derby* (Cambridge, 1992) especially pp. 208–10.

15. Colvin, *History of the King's Works*, III, 195–6, IV, 105, 227–8.

16. J.K. McConica, *English Humanists and Reformation Politics under Henry VIII and Edward VI* (Oxford, 1965) p. 63. W.D. Hamilton (ed.), *A Chronicle of England ... by Charles Wriothesley, Windsor Herald* (2 vols, CS 2nd ser. 11, 20, 1875, 1877) p. 109.

17. H. Walter (ed.), *Expositions and Notes on sundry portions of the Holy Scriptures together with the Practice of Prelates. By William Tyndale ...* (PS, 1849) p. 81. 'Friars' in this instance is a loose usage for 'brothers'.

18. Scarisbrick, *Henry VIII*, p. 29.

19. A. Fox and J. Guy, *Reassessing the Henrician Age: Humanism, Politics and Reform 1500–1550* (Oxford, 1986) p. 167.

20. T.F. Mayer, 'Tournai and Tyranny: Imperial Kingship and Critical Humanism', *HJ*, 34 (1991) esp. 263–8.

21. Scarisbrick, *Henry VIII*, pp. 110–17, 270–1. See bibliographical note for the edition in translation of the *Assertio* cited in the notes.

22. On Suffolk's religious outlook, see S.J. Gunn, *Charles Brandon, Duke of Suffolk c.1484–1545* (Oxford, 1988) esp. pp. 103–7, 159–64, 199–201.

23. J. Guy, 'Thomas More and Christopher St. German', in Fox and Guy, *Reassessing the Henrician Age*, ch. 5.

24. *CSPSs*, IV, pt. i, no. 224, pp. 349–50. On the aristocratic programme, see J. Guy, *The Public Career of Sir Thomas More* (Brighton, 1980) pp. 106–7 and Appendix 2 (cf. *LP*, IV, iii, no. 5749).

25. For discussion of the debate around Anne Boleyn, see bibliographical note.

26. For pioneering uses of the word 'Protestant' by Edward Underhill in 1553, see J.G. Nichols (ed.), *Narratives of the Reformation*, (CS, 1st ser. 77, 1859) pp. 141, 148, 163, and for gingerly use of it by Marian martyrs, J. Ayre (ed.), *The Works of Thomas Becon* (3 vols, PS, 1843–4) III, 211; A. Townsend (ed.), *The Writings of John Bradford ...* (2 vols, PS, 1848, 1853) I, 452; H. Christmas (ed.), *The Works of Nicholas Ridley, ...* (PS, 1843) p. 14.

27 D. MacCulloch, 'England', in A. Pettegree (ed.), *The Early Reformation in Europe* (Cambridge, 1992) esp. pp. 169–74. cf. also C. Trueman, *Luther's Legacy* (Oxford, 1994) passim.

28. On Stokesley, *Narratives of the Reformation*, pp. 277–8. Gardiner claimed to have cooperated on Bible translation in 1535 (*StP*, I, p. 430), but in the 1540s he would lead the conservative bishops' hostility to the officially issued Great Bible: G. Redworth, *In Defence of the Church Catholic: the Life of Stephen Gardiner* (Oxford, 1990) pp. 159–64. On Fisher, R. Rex, *The Theology of John Fisher* (Cambridge, 1991) pp. 149, 158–9.

29. For arguments against Skip's evangelicalism, G.W. Bernard, 'Anne Boleyn's Religion', *HJ*, 36 (1993) 15–16. Bernard's apparent strong point, the argument that Skip in a crucial sermon of 2 April 1536 defended the use of traditional ceremonies, is in fact a pointer to Skip's evangelical

credentials: to defend ceremonies by explaining their educational purpose was an evangelical strategy under Henry VIII.

30. On Wilkinson's Boleyn connection, see M. Dowling (ed.), 'William Latymer's Chronickille of Anne Bulleyne', *Camden Miscellany*, 30 (CS 4th ser. 39, 1990) 28. Astonishingly, Christina Garrett did not think that Wilkinson or indeed any other woman merited a separate entry in Garrett's *The Marian Exiles: a Study in the Origins of Elizabethan Puritanism* (Cambridge, 1938): cf. ibid., p. 334. Wilkinson's will of 1556 (PRO, Prerogative Court of Canterbury 29 Chayney, PROB 11/42B fos. 233–234v), is ample proof of her importance.

31. This letter-book is now BL MS Harley 6148. It contains letters to other key political figures, such as the king himselfo.

32. The best treatments of this episode and its relation to the vicegerency are in F.D. Logan, 'Thomas Cromwell and the Vicegerency in Spirituals: a Revisitation', *EHR*, 103 (1988) 658–67, and P. Ayris in P. Ayris and D. Selwyn (eds), *Thomas Cranmer: Churchman and Scholar* (Woodbridge, 1993) pp. 122–9. See also John Guy, above, pp. 42–3.

33. Bod. Lib. MS Jesus 74, fo. 299v.

34. For Cranmer's involvement in 1535, see *LP*, VIII, no. 846; he also seems obliquely to be describing his interrogation of Anabaptists in a letter of 25 May 1535, *Works of Archbishop Cranmer*, II, 306. See also D. Mac-Culloch, 'Archbishop Cranmer: Tolerance and Concord in a Changing Church', forthcoming in O. Grell and R. Scribner (eds), *Tolerance and Intolerance in the European Reformation* (Cambridge, 1996).

35. R. Rex, 'The New Learning', *JEH*, 44 (1993) 26–44.

36. For Robert Wakefield as an example of this breach, see Rex, *Theology of John Fisher*, p. 168; another case was Richard Croke, although his quarrel with Fisher predated the annulment controversy: ibid., p. 56.

37. D. MacCulloch, *Suffolk and the Tudors: Politics and Religion in an English County* (Oxford, 1986) pp. 151–3.

38. For reading on the Pilgrimage, see bibliographical note.

39. R.W. Hoyle, 'The Origins of the Dissolution of the Monasteries', *HJ* (forthcoming).

40. For suggestions about approachable discussions of the doctrinal statements, see bibliographical note. Six Articles text: Elton, *Tudor Constitution*, pp. 399–401; cf. P. Avis, *The Church in the Theology of the Reformers* (London, 1981) esp. p. 25. I am indebted to Sir Geoffrey Elton for reminding me of the presence of 'congregation' in the Articles.

41. Hall (Whibley) II, 356; S.E. Lehmberg, *The Later Parliaments of Henry VIII 1536–1547* (Cambridge, 1977) pp. 229–31.

42. cf. Hall (Whibley) II, 357 and *Works of Archbishop Cranmer*, II, 118–25, esp. p. 122.

43. *LP*, XVIII, ii, p. 353, qu. Corpus Christi College Cambridge MS 128, p. 245.

44. G.E. Corrie (ed.), *Sermons and Remains of Hugh Latimer ...* (PS, 1845) pp. 379–80.

45. Lambeth Palace MS 1107 fos 125–32. Discussion of these documents has been unnecessarily complicated by their modern editor, who

for no strong reason printed them as if they were associated with a later document of 1540, and also failed to notice that they comprised two different drafts: C.S. Cobb (ed.), *The Rationale of Ceremonial 1540–1543 with Notes and Appendices and an essay on the Regulation of Ceremonial during the Reign of Henry VIII (Alcuin Club Collections*, 18, 1910) pp. 44–52. For the text of the Ten Articles, see C.H. Williams (ed.), *English Historical Documents 1485–1558* (London, 1967) pp. 795–805.

46. Latimer, *Sermons and Remains*, p. 247.

47. A. Kreider, *English Chantries: the Road to Dissolution* (Cambridge, MA, 1979) p. 152, and cf. ibid., pp. 127, 134–8.

48. Scarisbrick, *Henry VIII*, pp. 412–18.

49. Redworth, *In Defence of the Church Catholic*, pp. 98–9. cf. *Assertio*, pp. 97–9.

50. The annotations are printed in Tudor-Craig, 'Henry VIII and King David', pp. 200–2: NB Henry's comments on Psalms 53(54), 96(97), 105(106).

51. See the debate between Henry and Cranmer, *Works of Archbishop Cranmer*, II, 83–114.

52. G. Rupp, *Studies in the Making of the English Protestant Tradition* (Cambridge, 1947) pp. 140–1.

53. Scarisbrick, *Henry VIII*, pp. 419.

54. M. St. Clare Byrne, *The Letters of King Henry VIII ...* (London, 1936), p. 86.

55. January: *Works of Archbishop Cranmer*, II, 414–17. August: Foxe, V, pp. 561–4. For a good introduction to Henry's last year, see D. Starkey, *Henry VIII: Personalities and Politics* (London, 1985) pp. 140–67.

56. C. Haigh, *English Reformations: Religion, Politics and Society under the Tudors* (Oxford, 1993) p. 162 and R. Rex, *Henry VIII and the Reformation* (Basingstoke, 1993) pp. 169–70, are both sceptical that Henry VIII consciously chose evangelicals as tutors. McConica, *English Humanists*, pp. 213–18, presents a still convincing case to the contrary, except that he probably overstresses the role of Catherine Parr.

57. *The Gratulation of the most famous Clerk M. Martin Bucer ...*, tr. and with preface by T. Hoby (1548, *RSTC* 3963) sigs. Biv–Bv.

58. Here, see the excellent discussion in P. Tudor-Craig, 'Henry VIII and King David', passim.

8. LITERATURE, DRAMA AND POLITICS *Seymour House*

1. Gardiner to Paget, 9 February 1547, PRO SP 10/1 fos 8–8v (*CSPD*, I, no. 5).

2. For the players of the earls of Oxford, see I. Lancashire, *Dramatic Texts and Records: a Chronological Topography to 1558* (Toronto, 1984) p. 406. The 1541–2 performance attributed to the players of the 15th earl (d. 1540) may in fact belong to those of his son, the 16th earl. Gardiner's suspicions regarding the status of these players illustrate the polemical

heritage of drama in Henry VIII's reign – the 15th earl was an early patron of Protestant playwright John Bale, whom Cromwell later deployed against religious conservatives until his fall in 1540. For players claiming dubious patronage, see Lancashire, *Dramatic Texts and Records*, p. 402, no. 304.

3. J. Guy, *Tudor England* (Oxford, 1988) p. 198.

4. J. Wasson (ed.), *Records of Early English Drama: Devon* (Toronto, 1986) p. 223; Lancashire, *Dramatic Texts and Records*, p. 198; S. Brigden, *London and the Reformation* (Oxford, 1989) p. 186; the earl was, of course, Anne Boleyn's father, publicising his 'triumph' over Wolsey whom he blamed for obstructing Anne's rise to the throne.

5. Lancashire, *Dramatic Texts and Records*, pp. 194–5; *LP*, III, ii, pp. 1558–9.

6. S. Anglo, *Spectacle, Pageantry and Early Tudor Policy* (Oxford, 1969) pp. 186–202.

7. P. Gwyn, *The King's Cardinal: The Rise and Fall of Thomas Wolsey* (London, 1990) p. 136; Lancashire, *Dramatic Texts and Records*, p. 196.

8. For his plays, see P. Happé and R. Axton (eds), *The Plays of John Heywood*, (Cambridge, 1991) passim, and Appendix 1. For the commissioning of a play about the 'Parts of Man' by Archbishop Cranmer, see James M. Osborn (ed.), *The Autobiography of Thomas Whythorne* (London and New York, 1962) pp. 6, 60.

9. Lancashire, *Dramatic Texts and Records*, p. 199; *LP*, VII, no. 24; *Lisle Letters*, no. 108 (7 January 1534).

10. *LP*, VIII, no. 949.

11. For More's refusal, see R.W. Chambers, *Thomas More* (London, 1945) pp. 292–4; for the fear of a Catholic invasion, see Guy, *Tudor England*, p. 184; for Marillac's descriptions, see *LP*, XIV, i, nos 1137, 1261.

12. In addition to public sermons denouncing fraudulent relics, Cromwell seems to have authorised the publication of a book of the enormities, which is now lost. John Bale refers to it in 1553: 'I have the Register of the Visitation of the Cloisters of England ...' P. Happé and J. King (eds), *The Vocacyon of Johan Bale* (Binghampton, 1990) p. 48. Again in 1558 when he refers to the 'breviary of the things found out in abbeys, assemblies, colleges, etc.' J. Bale, *The Pageant of Popes*, trans. J. Studley (London, 1574; *RSTC*, 1303) fo. cii verso.

13. Lancashire, *Dramatic Texts and Records*, p. 65; G.R. Elton, *Policy and Police: The Enforcement of the Reformation in the Age of Thomas Cromwell* (Cambridge, 1972; pbk edn, 1985) p. 186.

14. See e.g. J. Taylor, 'The Dramatic Structure of the Middle English Corpus Christi, or Cycle, Plays', in J. Taylor and A. Nelson (eds), *Medieval English Drama* (Chicago and London, 1972) pp. 148–56.

15. For Cromwell's use of drama in the suppression of the monasteries, see S. House, 'Cromwell's Message to the Regulars: The Biblical Trilogy of John Bale, 1537', *Renaissance and Reformation*, ns, 15 (1991) 123–37.

16. Wylley wrote to Cromwell apparently in 1537, offering several plays and in indicating his stance against the pope anticipated the passage of

anti-papal legislation. In April 1538 he is listed as 'Mr. Hopton's priest', which suggests that his ecclesiastical patron Sir Arthur Hopton of Yoxford, an MP and Cromwell supporter, was influential in gaining him an audience. See *LP*, XII, i, no. 529; *LP*, XIV, ii, p. 335; For Hopton, see S.T. Bindoff, *H of C, 1509–58*, ii, pp. 387–9; P. White, *Theatre and Reformation: Protestantism, Patronage and Playing in Tudor England* (Cambridge, 1993) pp. 69, 215 n. 10. White gives no reasons for his redatings, and his stipulation that the payment was for April 1537 is clearly in error – the entry states that the payment was for 2 April, 29 Henry VIII, that is, 1538.

17. Knight to Cromwell, 5 October 1538, PRO SP 1/137 fos 112–13 (*LP*, XIII, ii, no. 542; my italics); For the performance, iconoclasm, and court at Canterbury, see *LP*, XIV, ii, p. 337; *LP*, XIII, ii, nos 296, 302, 303, and 317. See also *LP*, XIII, ii, no. 995; *LP*, XIV, i, no. 371; *LP*, XIV, ii, no. 206.

18. *LP*, XIII, ii, no. 401; J.A. Muller, *Stephen Gardiner and the Tudor Reaction* (New York, 1926) p. 77.

19. White, *Theatre and Reformation*, p. 29.

20. Some records detailing the payment of players were based on a fiscal year that went from Michaelmas to Michaelmas, while others were dated according to the regnal or even Gregorian year. For a rough chronology of patronised performances during the early Tudors, see Lancashire, *Dramatic Texts and Records*, App. 1.

21. *Lisle Letters*, nos 1241, 1242. If *Rex Diabole* was not a scriptural interlude – perhaps it was a morality play? Lord Lisle lodged with Cromwell during their Canterbury sojourn, *Lisle Letters*, no. 1218; *LP*, XIII, ii, no. 317.

22. Lancashire, *Dramatic Texts and Records*, pp. xxviii–xxix.

23. *LP*, XIV, i, no. 1261.

24. *LP*, XII, i, nos 1212, 1284.

25. *LP*, XVII, no. 176; see Lancashire, *Dramatic Texts and Records*, pp. 202–3.

26. *TRP*, i, pp. 341–2; Brigden, *London and the Reformation*, pp. 344 ff.

27. Lancashire, *Dramatic Texts and Records*, p. 205.

28. J. Bale, *Epistle Exhortatorye* ([Antwerp: 1544?]; *RSTC*, 1291) fos xvi–xvi (verso).

29. The flyting, centring on Cromwell, his supporter William Grey and the conservative Thomas Smith (and unknown others) is revealing. The format of several pieces – a single sheet folio – is typical of the popular and ad hoc nature of such controversies. See E. Dormer, *Gray of Reading: a Sixteenth-century Ballad Writer* (Reading, 1923); Brigden, *London and the Reformation*, pp. 322 ff; S. House, 'An Unknown Tudor Propaganda Poem c. 1540', *NQ*, 237 (1992) 282–5.

30. *TRP*, i, no. 186.

31. *TRP*, i, no. 272.

32. D. Loades, 'The Theory and Practice of Censorship in Sixteenth-century England', *TRHS*, 5th ser., 24 (1974) 141–57.

33. For humanist dialogue as a genre, see R. Deakins, 'The Tudor Prose Dialogue: Genre and Anti-genre', *Studies in English Literature*, 20 (1980) 5–23.

34. See A. Edwards and C. Meale, 'The Marketing of Printed Books in Late Medieval England', *The Library*, 6th ser. 15 (1993) 95–124.

35. See L. Febvre and H.-J. Martin, *The Coming of the Book: the Impact of Printing, 1450–1800*, trans. D. Gerard, ed. G. Nowell-Smith and D. Wootton (London, 1976) ch. 8.

36. T. Watt, *Cheap Print and Popular Piety*, 1550–1640 (Cambridge and New York, 1991) p. 11.

37. Ibid., p. 40.

38. See e.g. Bishop Longland's efforts in 1521, M. Bowker, *The Henrician Reformation: the Diocese of Lincoln under John Longland, 1521–1547* (Cambridge, 1981) pp. 57 ff.

39. For the text of this commission, see *More Correspondence*, no. 160.

40. LP, X, p. 446. For the role of prophecies in creating what Alistair Fox has called 'a myth of destiny', see A. Fox, 'Prophecies and Politics in the Reign of Henry VIII', in A. Fox and J. Guy, *Reassessing the Henrician Age* (Oxford, 1986) pp. 77–94; Anglo, *Spectacle, Pageantry and Early Tudor Policy*, pp. 263–5.

41. E. Eisenstein, *The Printing Press as an Agent of Change* (2 vols, Cambridge, 1979; combined pbk edn, 1980) p. 342, quoting E.H. Harbison, *The Christian Scholar in the Age of the Reformation* (New York, 1956) p. 101; for the text of Erasmus's *Paracelsis*, see J. Leclerc (ed.), *Desiderii Erasmi Roterodami Opera Omnia* (10 vols, Leiden, 1703–6) vol. 5.

42. M. Spufford, *Small Books and Pleasant Histories* (Athens, GA, 1981) p. 14.

43. For Coverdale's songs, see R.A. Leaver, *'Goostly psalms and spirituall songes': English and Dutch Metrical Psalms from Coverdale to Utenhove, 1535–1566* (Oxford, 1991).

44. LP, XIV, i, p. 154. Ironically, just at this time the king was entertaining the court with a masque, written by Heywood, on King Arthur's knights. LP, XIV, i, no. 402.

45. E. Riegler, 'Printing, Protestantism and Politics; Thomas Cromwell and Religious Reform', unpublished PhD dissertation, UCLA, 1978, p. 287.

46. *TRP*, i, p. 297.

47. S. Lehmberg, *The Later Parliaments of Henry VIII, 1536–1547* (Cambridge, 1977) pp. 186–7 and see discussion by D. MacCulloch, ch. 7 above; A.G. Dickens, *The English Reformation* (London, 1964; rev. ed, 1967) p. 264.

48. E. Duffy, *The Stripping of the Altars: Traditional Religion in England 1400–1580* (New Haven and London, 1992) pp. 84–5; see P.L. Heyworth, 'The Earliest Black-letter Editions of *Jack Upland*', *Huntington Library Quarterly*, 30 (1967) 307–14; A. Hudson, '"No newe thyng": The Printing of Medieval Texts in the Early Reformation Period', in D. Gray and

E. Stanley (eds) *Middle English Studies Presented to Norman Davis in Honour of his Seventieth Birthday* (Oxford, 1983) pp. 153–74; J. King, *English Reformation Literature: The Tudor Origins of the Protestant Tradition* (Princeton, NJ, 1982) pp. 323–39.

49. See e.g. *RSTC*, 19903, 19904, 19905, 19906, 19907 etc. For Piers and the Marprelate tracts, see the [1589?] quarto *O read me, for I am of greate antiquitie* (*RSTC*, 19903a.5); Brigden, *London and the Reformation*, p. 438.

50. See e.g. M. Sargent, 'The Transmission by the Carthusians of some Late Medieval Spiritual Writings', *JEH*, 27 (1976) 225–40; J.T. Rhodes, 'Syon Abbey and its Religious Publications in the Sixteenth Century', *JEH*, 44 (1993) 11–25.

51. For primers, see C. Butterworth, *The English Primers* (1529–1545) (Philadelphia, 1953; repr. New York, 1971); for psalms, see R. Zim, *English Metrical Psalms: Poetry as Praise and Prayer, 1535–1601* (Cambridge, 1987) app. I.

52. See J. Yost, 'Taverner's Use of Erasmus and the Protestantization of English Humanism', *Renaissance Quarterly*, 23 (1970) 266–76. For Taverner, see also Duffy, *The Stripping of the Altars*, pp. 425–7.

53. D. Bailey, *Thomas Becon and the Reformation of the Church in England* (Edinburgh, 1952) p. 18.

54. J. Ayre (ed.), *The Works of Thomas Becon* (3 vols, Cambridge:, PS, 1843–4) i, p. 29.

9. LOCAL RESPONSES TO THE HENRICIAN REFORMATION
   Robert Whiting

1. For the conflicting views of historians, and for the differing types of evidence, see the bibliographical note. For a detailed examination of the advantages and limitations of wills, and of the queries raised by e.g. E. Duffy, *The Stripping of the Altars: Traditional Religion in England, c. 1400–c. 1580* (New Haven and London, 1992) esp. pp. 504–19, see R. Whiting, *Communities in Conflict: Local Responses to the English Reformation* (Basingstoke, forthcoming).

2. R. Whiting, *The Blind Devotion of the People: Popular Religion and the English Reformation* (Cambridge, 1989) pp. 113–14; Foxe, IV, 177, 205.

3. *LP*, XI, no. 1246; M.H. and R. Dodds, *The Pilgrimage of Grace and the Exeter Conspiracy* (2 vols, Cambridge, 1915); Whiting, *Blind Devotion*, pp. 114–18; G.R. Elton, *Policy and Police: The Enforcement of the Reformation in the Age of Thomas Cromwell* (Cambridge, 1972); R. Hutton, 'The Local Impact of the Tudor Reformations', in C. Haigh (ed.), *The English Reformation Revised* (Cambridge, 1987) p. 116.

4. Whiting, *Blind Devotion*, pp. 118–22; C. St German, 'A Treatise concerning the Division between the Spiritualty and Temporalty', in

C.J. Barry (ed.), *Readings in Church History* (Westminster, MD, 1985) pp. 659–63.

5. D. Knowles and R.N. Hadcock, *Medieval Religious Houses: England and Wales* (London, 1971), analysis by R. Whiting; G. Turnpenney, 'Wills as a Source for the Reformation Historian', University College of Ripon and York St John (hereinafter UCRYSJ) Special Study (1992) tables; Whiting, *Blind Devotion*, p. 277; M. Bowker, *The Henrician Reformation: the Diocese of Lincoln under John Longland, 1521–47* (Cambridge, 1981) p. 177; S. Pettit, 'The Reformation in the Diocese of Norwich, 1520–1559', UCRYSJ Special Study (1990) tables; N.P. Tanner, *The Church in Late-Medieval Norwich, 1370–1532* (Toronto, 1984) pp. 222–3.

6. Whiting, *Blind Devotion*, p. 277; J.A.F. Thomson, 'Piety and Charity in Late-Medieval London', *JEH*, 16 (1965) 178–95; Bowker, *Henrician Reformation*, p. 177.

7. *LP*, XI, no. 1246; M. Bateson, 'The Examination of Robert Aske', *EHR*, 5 (1890) 550–73; A. Fletcher, *Tudor Rebellions* (2nd edn, London, 1973) pp. 21–47; Whiting, *Blind Devotion*, pp. 122–5; G.H. Cook, *Letters to Cromwell and others on the Suppression of the Monasteries* (London, 1965) pp. 246–7; L.T. Smith (ed.), *The Itinerary of John Leland in or about the Years 1535–1543* (5 vols, London, 1964) I, 37–8, 132; II, 58; V, 104.

8. Cook, *Letters*, pp. 211–12; A.G. Dickens, 'Tudor Treatises', *Yorkshire Archaeological Society Record Series*, 125 (1959) 123–6.

9. Haigh, *Reformation Revised*, pp. 70–1; Bowker, *Henrician Reformation*, pp. 40,125,177; Turnpenney, 'Wills', tables; Whiting, *Blind Devotion*, p. 277; J.W. Clay (ed.), *Testamenta Eboracensia*, 6 (Surtees Society, 106, 1902) 10–11; J. Bruton, 'The Reformation in Bristol and Somerset: The Evidence of Wills', UCRYSJ Special Study (1987) tables.

10. Knowles and Hadcock, *Medieval Religious Houses*, analysis by R. Whiting; Haigh, *Reformation Revised*, pp. 69–70; C.H. Williams (ed.), *English Historical Documents, 1485–1558* (London, 1967) pp. 652–60; St German, 'Treatise', pp. 659–63; Foxe, IV, 177, 205; D. MacCulloch, *The Later Reformation in England, 1547–1603* (London, 1990) p. 140; S. Lander, 'Church Courts and the Reformation in the Diocese of Chichester, 1500–58', in Haigh, *Reformation Revised*, p. 42; A.G. Dickens, *The English Reformation* (London, 1964) pp. 90–102.

11. Sir T. More, 'Apology', in Barry, *Readings*, p. 665; Haigh, *Reformation Revised*, pp. 67–9; Lander, 'Church Courts', pp. 34–55; Whiting, *Blind Devotion*, pp. 125–44.

12. Whiting, *Blind Devotion*, pp. 125–44; Haigh, *Reformation Revised*, pp. 61,72; A.G. Dickens and D. Carr (eds), *The Reformation in England* (London, 1967) pp. 118–19.

13. *LP*, XI, no. 1246; Lander, 'Church Courts', pp. 34–55; Whiting, *Blind Devotion*, pp. 140–1.

14. Bowker, *Henrician Reformation*, pp. 40, 125, 177; P. Hughes, *The Reformation in England* (3 vols, London, 1950–4) III, 53; Haigh, *Reformation Revised*, p. 71; Bruton, 'Bristol and Somerset', tables; Turnpenney, 'Wills', tables; Whiting, *Blind Devotion*, p. 277; I. Darlington

(ed.), *London Consistory Court Wills, 1492–1547* (London Record Society, 3, 1967) pp. 56–150, analysis by R. Whiting.

15. Whiting, *Blind Devotion*, pp. 83–105; Smith, *Leland*, I, 127. I intend to extend and document my survey of the eight counties in my forthcoming book.

16. Whiting, *Blind Devotion*, pp. 90–1.

17. Whiting, *Blind Devotion*, pp. 91–2, 220, 276; Tanner, *Norwich*, pp. 222–3; Pettit, 'Diocese of Norwich', tables; Bowker, *Henrician Reformation*, p. 177; Bruton, 'Bristol and Somerset', tables; Turnpenney, 'Wills', tables; Lander, 'Church Courts', p. 42.

18. Whiting, *Blind Devotion*, pp. 93–5, 276; Pettit, 'Diocese of Norwich', tables; Bowker, *Henrician Reformation*, p. 177; Turnpenney, 'Wills', tables; Bruton, 'Bristol and Somerset', tables; Darlington, *London Wills*, pp. 56–150.

19. Whiting, *Blind Devotion*, pp. 95–105; Smith, *Leland*, I, 169; II, 38; D. Dymond and C. Paine, *The Spoil of Melford Church: The Reformation in a Suffolk Parish* (Ipswich, 1989) pp. 12, 34. I intend to extend and document my analysis of accounts in my forthcoming book.

20. Whiting, *Blind Devotion*, pp. 105–8, 277; Bruton, 'Bristol and Somerset', tables; Turnpenney, 'Wills', tables; Bowker, *Henrician Reformation*, p. 177; Pettit, 'Diocese of Norwich', tables.

21. Whiting, *Blind Devotion*, pp. 108–10, 277; J.J. Scarisbrick, *The Reformation and the English People* (Oxford, 1984) pp. 19–39; Bruton, 'Bristol and Somerset', tables; Bowker, *Henrician Reformation*, p. 177; Turnpenney, 'Wills', tables; Darlington, *London Wills*, pp. 56–150; Pettit, 'Diocese of Norwich', tables.

22. Whiting, *Blind Devotion*, pp. 17–23; Williams, *Documents*, pp. 192–201; Dymond and Paine, *Melford Church*, pp. 5–25.

23. Foxe, IV, 177, 205, 584; Whiting, *Blind Devotion*, p. 23.

24. Whiting, *Blind Devotion*, pp. 23–34; A.G. Dickens, *Lollards and Protestants in the Diocese of York, 1509–1558* (new edn, London, 1982) pp. 18–52; K. Thomas, *Religion and the Decline of Magic* (Harmondsworth, 1973) pp. 190–1; Dymond and Paine, *Melford Church*, pp. 26–35.

25. W. Page (ed.), *The Certificates of the Commissioners ... in the County of York* (Surtees Society, 91–2, 1894–5) especially p. 166; Whiting, *Blind Devotion*, pp. 18–20; A. Kreider, *English Chantries: The Road to Dissolution* (Cambridge, MA, 1979) especially pp. 78,87, and additional information from Dr Kreider.

26. Kreider, *English Chantries*, pp. 78, 87, and additional information; C. Haigh, *Reformation and Resistance in Tudor Lancashire* (Cambridge, 1975) pp. 69–70, 194; Turnpenney, 'Wills', tables; Whiting, *Blind Devotion*, p. 30; Bowker, *Henrician Reformation*, p. 177; Pettit, 'Diocese of Norwich', tables; Bruton, 'Bristol and Somerset', tables; Thomson, 'Piety and Charity', 178–95; Foxe, IV, 584.

27. Kreider, *English Chantries*, pp. 78, 86–92, 154–60, and additional information; Haigh, *Reformation and Resistance*, pp. 71–2, 147; Whiting, *Blind Devotion*, pp. 30–2; Page, *Certificates*, pp. 168, 296.

28. Haigh, *Reformation and Resistance*, pp. 69–70, 194; Turnpenney, 'Wills', tables; Whiting, *Blind Devotion*, p. 30; Pettit, 'Diocese of Norwich', tables; Bowker, *Henrician Reformation*, p. 177; Bruton, 'Bristol and Somerset', tables; G.J. Mayhew, 'The Progress of the Reformation in East Sussex, 1530–1559: The Evidence from Wills', *Southern History*, 5 (1983) 38–67; Darlington, *London Wills*, pp. 56–150.

29. Williams, *Documents*, pp. 652–60; D. Palliser, *Tudor York* (Oxford, 1979) pp. 250–1; Turnpenney, 'Wills', tables; Pettit, 'Diocese of Norwich', tables.

30. Foxe, IV, pp. 177, 205; Whiting, *Blind Devotion*, p. 62; Palliser, *Tudor York*, pp. 250–1; Turnpenney, 'Wills', tables; P. Clark, *English Provincial Society from the Reformation to the Revolution: Religion, Politics, and Society in Kent, 1500–1640* (Hassocks, 1977) p. 58; S. Brigden, *London and the Reformation* (Oxford, 1989) pp. 381–4; Pettit, 'Diocese of Norwich', tables.

31. Whiting, *Blind Devotion*, pp. 48–55; Clay, *Testamenta*, 6, pp. 10–11; Williams, *Documents*, pp. 835–7; Dymond and Paine, *Melford Church*, pp. 1–2,10–25.

32. Foxe, IV, p. 177; J. Nichols (ed.), *Narratives of the Days of the Reformation* (CS, 77, 1859) pp. 348–51.

33. Hutton, 'Local Impact', pp. 116–17; Dymond and Paine, *Melford Church*, pp. 10–35; Whiting, *Blind Devotion*, pp. 65–7; Smith, *Leland*, I, 165, 208; III, 91–2; V, 47.

34. Whiting, *Blind Devotion*, pp. 67–8, 75–6; G. Gorham, *Gleanings ... A.D. 1533–88* (London, 1857) pp. 17–19.

35. Whiting, *Blind Devotion*, pp. 64–5; Turnpenney, 'Wills', tables.

36. Whiting, *Blind Devotion*, pp. 55–61; Dymond and Paine, *Melford Church*, p. 11; J. Raine, *St Cuthbert* (London, 1828) pp. 111–12.

37. Bowker, *Henrician Reformation*, p. 93; F. Woodman, *The Architectural History of Canterbury Cathedral* (London, 1981) p. 221; Raine, *St Cuthbert*, pp. 115–17.

38. Smith, *Leland*, II, 93; Bateson, 'Examination', 550–73; Raine, *St Cuthbert*, p. 176; Whiting, *Blind Devotion*, pp. 72–3; Bowker, *Henrician Reformation*, pp. 93–5.

39. Whiting, *Blind Devotion*, p. 73; Hutton, 'Local Impact', p. 116; Dymond and Paine, *Melford Church*, pp. 26, 44–7; J.C. Cox, *Churchwardens' Accounts* (London, 1913) pp. 139–40.

40. Smith, *Leland*, I, 180; III, 48; Bowker, *Henrician Reformation*, p. 95; Whiting, *Blind Devotion*, pp. 73–4.

41. I intend to extend and document my analysis of brasses in my forthcoming book. See also R. Rex, 'Monumental Brasses and the Reformation', *Transactions of the Monumental Brass Society*, 14 (1990) 376–95.

42. *LP*, XI, nos 909, 1246; Dodds and Dodds, *Pilgrimage of Grace*, I, II; A.G. Dickens, 'Secular and Religious Motivation in the Pilgrimage of Grace', in G.J. Cuming (ed.), *Studies in Church History*, 4 (Leiden, 1967) pp. 39–64; C.S.L. Davies, 'The Pilgrimage of Grace Reconsidered', *PP*, 41 (1968) 54–76; M.E. James, 'Obedience and Dissent in Henrician England', *PP*, 48 (1970) 3–78; Whiting, *Blind Devotion*, p. 117.

43. Elton, *Policy and Police*, especially pp. 383–400.

44. W.K. Jordan, *The Charities of London, 1480–1660* (London, 1960) p. 423; *The Forming of the Charitable Institutions of the West of England* (American Philosophical Society, NS 50, 1960) p. 92; *Social Institutions in Kent, 1480–1660* (*Archaeologia Cantiana*, 75, 1961) p. 158; *The Charities of Rural England, 1480–1660* (London, 1961) pp. 438–40; *The Social Institutions of Lancashire* (Chetham Society, 1962) p. 117.

45. Elton, *Policy and Police*, pp. 383–400; Turnpenney, 'Wills', tables; W.K. Jordan, *Philanthropy in England, 1480–1660* (London, 1959) pp. 385–7; Kreider, *English Chantries*, pp. 78,87; Whiting, *Blind Devotion*, pp. 114, 116.

46. J.A.F. Thomson, *The Later Lollards, 1414–1520* (Oxford, 1965) analysis by R. Whiting; Dickens, *English Reformation*, pp. 41–62; J.F. Davis, *Heresy and Reformation in the South-East of England, 1520–1559* (Royal Historical Society Studies in History, 34, 1983); A. Hudson, *The Premature Reformation: Wycliffite Texts and Lollard History* (Oxford, 1988); Williams, *Documents*, pp. 195, 656, 663.

47. Dickens, *English Reformation*, pp. 91–121; Foxe, V, 530–2.

48. Thomson, *Later Lollards*; Dickens, *Lollards and Protestants*, especially pp. 18–52; Whiting, *Blind Devotion*, pp. 161, 170.

49. Whiting, *Blind Devotion*, pp. 197–9, 218–19; D. Palliser, 'Popular Reactions to the Reformation during the Years of Uncertainty, 1530–70', in Haigh, *Reformation Revised*, p. 104.

50. Williams, *Documents*, p. 656; Dickens, *English Reformation*, p. 104; Mayhew, 'East Sussex', p. 52; Brigden, *London*, pp. 381–4; Clark, *Provincial Society*, p. 58; Turnpenney, 'Wills', tables.

51. Dickens, *English Reformation*, p. 369; Nichols, *Narratives*, pp. 348–51; Hutton, 'Local Impact', pp. 116,118; Whiting, *Blind Devotion*, pp. 190–1.

52. Fletcher, *Tudor Rebellions*, pp. 3–7; Whiting, *Blind Devotion*, pp. 172–3; J. Nichols (ed.), *The Chronicle of the Grey Friars of London* (CS, 53, 1852) pp. 40–1.

53. Whiting, *Blind Devotion*, pp. 175–6,178–80; Fletcher, *Tudor Rebellions*, p. 21.

54. Whiting, *Blind Devotion*, pp. 184–5; *LP*, XII (1), no. 479; Williams, *Documents*, p. 784.

55. Whiting, *Blind Devotion*, pp. 115–16, 178.

Notes on Contributors

JOHN GUY is Provost of St Leonard's College and Professor of Modern History at the University of St Andrews. He teaches early modern British and French history, and has published extensively. His books include *Tudor England* (Oxford, 1988), *The Public Career of Sir Thomas More* (Brighton and New Haven, 1980), and most recently the edited collection *The Reign of Elizabeth I: Court and Culture in the Last Decade* (Cambridge). He is a co-editor of *Cambridge Studies in Early Modern British History*, and is currently writing the *New Oxford History of England, 1461–1547*.

SEYMOUR BAKER HOUSE is Lecturer in Literature at Mount Angel Seminary, Oregon. He studied at Oregon and Concordia University in Montreal, and received his PhD in Ecclesiastical History from the University of St Andrews. From 1990 to 1992 he was a Research Fellow at the University of Otago's Early Modern English Textbase and Lexicon Project, and later lecturer in History and Literature there. He has published several articles on Tudor history and literature, and is on the editorial board of *Moreana*.

RICHARD HOYLE was a research fellow of Magdalen College, Oxford, and a lecturer at the University of Bristol before taking up his present post at the University of Central Lancashire, where he teaches economic history. His interests lie in the rural history of the sixteenth and seventeenth centuries, public finance and the regional history of Northern England. His work includes his contributions to *The Estates of the English Crown, 1558–1640* (Cambridge, 1992) which he edited, and a forthcoming study of the Pilgrimage of Grace.

ERIC IVES is Professor in the School of History and Head of Department in Modern History at the University of Birmingham. His books include *The Common Lawyers of Pre-Reformation England. Thomas Kebell: a case study* (Cambridge, 1983) and *Anne Boleyn* (Oxford, 1986), and besides numerous articles, he has written on *Faction in Tudor England* for the Historical Association (1979).

DIARMAID MacCULLOCH has held Research Fellowships from Churchill College, Cambridge, and the Leverhulme and Wingate Trusts. He lectures in the Department of Theology and Religious Studies in Bristol University and also writes and lectures independently. His writings include *Suffolk and the Tutors: Politics and Religion in an English County 1500–1600* (Oxford, 1986), *The Later Reformation in England 1547–1603*

(London, 1990), and *Building a Godly Realm: the Establishment of English Protestantism 1558–1603* (for the Historical Association, 1992). His biography of Archbishop Thomas Cranmer is due to be published by Yale University Press in 1996.

VIRGINIA MURPHY is an Honorary Fellow of the Department of History, University of Durham. She was educated at Smith College and at Clare College, Cambridge, where she completed her PhD under the supervision of Professor Sir Geoffrey Elton. Until 1989 she was a commissioning editor in history for an academic publisher in Oxford. She is the editor (with Edward Surtz) of *The Divorce Tracts of Henry VIII* (Angers, 1988).

DAVID POTTER graduated from the University of Durham and was a research fellow at Emmanuel College, Cambridge, where he wrote his PhD dissertation on Anglo-French diplomacy in the sixteenth century. He is now a senior lecturer in History at the University of Kent, Canterbury, and his most recent work includes *War and Government in the French Provinces: Picardy, 1470–1560* (Cambridge, 1993) and *A History of France, 1456–1560: the Emergence of a Nation State* (London, 1995).

NEIL SAMMAN is Senior Administrative Assistant at the University of Reading. He completed his postgraduate study under the supervision of Professor D.M. Loades at UCNW, Bangor, and was awarded his PhD from the University of Wales in 1989.

ROBERT WHITING is Principal Lecturer in History at the University College of Ripon and York St John. He was awarded double first class honours in the History tripos at Cambridge University, where he was elected to a senior scholarship of Trinity College. He gained his PhD (for research into the Reformation in the south-west) at Exeter University. His publications include articles on the local impact of the Reformation, and the full-length study *The Blind Devotion of the People: Popular Religion and the English Reformation* (Cambridge, UP, 1989). He is completing for publication a study of local responses to the English Reformation.

Index

The list of justices of the peace in Appendix 1 (pp. 227–8) has not been indexed.

293

DATE DUE			
			Printed In USA